Computing Skills and the User Interface

Computers and People Series

Edited by

B.R. GAINES

The series is concerned with all aspects of man-computer relationships, including interaction, interfacing, modelling and artificial intelligence. Books are inter-disciplinary, communicating results derived in one area of study to workers in another. Applied, experimental, theoretical and tutorial studies are included.

Computing Skills and the User Interface

Edited by

M.J. COOMBS and J.L. ALTY
Computer Laboratory, University of Liverpool, Liverpool, England

1981

ACADEMIC PRESS

A Subsidiary of Harcourt Brace Jovanovich, Publishers
London · New York · Toronto · Sydney · San Francisco

ACADEMIC PRESS INC. (LONDON) LTD
24–28 Oval Road,
London NW1

U.S. Edition published by
ACADEMIC PRESS INC.
111 Fifth Avenue,
New York, New York 10003

British Library Cataloguing in Publication Data

Computing skills and the user interface.
(Computers and people series)
1. Data processing
2. Man–machine systems
I. Coombs, M.J.   II. Alty, J.L.   III. Series
001.64   QA76   80-42082

ISBN 0-12-186520-7

Typeset by Gilbert Composing Services, Leighton Buzzard, Bedfordshire
Printed and bound by T.J. Press (Padstow) Ltd, Padstow, Cornwall

List of Contributors

J.L. ALTY *Computer Laboratory, University of Liverpool, Brownlow Hill, Liverpool L69 3BX*

R. AULD *Computer Centre, University of Birmingham, Birmingham B15 2TT*

C. BOLDYREFF *South-West Regional Computer Centre, University of Bath, Claverton Down, Bath BA2 7AY*

M.J. COOMBS *Computer Laboratory, University of Liverpool, Brownlow Hill, Liverpool L69 3BX*

L. DAMODARAN *Department of Human Sciences, University of Technology, Loughborough, Leicestershire LE11 3TU*

B. DU BOULAY *Department of Computer Science, University of Aberdeen, Old Aberdeen AB9 2HB*

K.D. EASON *Department of Human Sciences, University of Technology, Loughborough, Leicestershire LE11 3TU*

E.A. EDMONDS *School of Mathematics, Computing and Statistics, Leicester Polytechnic, Leicester LE1 9BH*

D.W. EMBLEY *Department of Computer Science, University of Nebraska-Lincoln, Lincoln, Nebraska 68588, USA*

M.J. FITTER *MRC/SSRC Social and Applied Psychology Unit, Department of Psychology, University of Sheffield, Sheffield S10 2TN*

R. GIBSON *Computer Laboratory, University of Liverpool, Brownlow Hill, Liverpool L69 3BX*

T.R.G. GREEN *MRC/SSRC Social and Applied Psychology Unit, Department of Psychology, University of Sheffield, Sheffield S10 2TN*

E.B. JAMES *Computer Centre, Imperial College, University of London, London SW7*

K. LANG *Computer Centre, University of Birmingham, Birmingham B15 2TT*

T. LANG *Computer Centre, The Polytechnic, Wolverhampton WV1 1LY*

F.J. LUKEY *Logica Ltd., 64 Newman Street, London W1A 4SE*

G. NAGY *Department of Computer Science, University of Nebraska–Lincoln, Lincoln, Nebraska 68588 USA*

T. O'SHEA *Institute of Educational Technology, Open University, Walton Hall, Milton Keynes MK7 6AA*

M.E. SIME *MRC/SSRC Social and Applied Psychology Unit, Department of Psychology, University of Sheffield, Sheffield S10 2TN*

R.C. THOMAS *Department of Computer Studies, University of Leeds, Leeds LS2 9JT*

Preface

Many occupations now require the use of computer systems as routine. However, the majority of people using such systems are not computer professionals, but view the computer as one of many tools available to them in the furtherance of their employment. It is important that they should be able to utilize computers with the minimum of technical knowledge and a minimum of training. This change in the computing environment has created a demand for a new type of computer professional who is sensitive to the difficulties users find with computer systems *in addition* to the problems of machine efficiency. In many applications a knowledge of both areas will be necessary because the hardware places a significant constraint on the designs possible with a given budget, although with the advent of relatively cheap hardware the needs of the user interface will tend to predominate. We therefore propose that there is an urgent need for a new enterprise concerned with the design of effective user interfaces. This will require an interdisciplinary approach involving computer science and the human behavioural sciences in the study of such topics as the assessment of user interests and capabilities, the writing of "sympathetic" software, and the design of instructional and guidance systems.

Whilst the software industry is beginning to change its priorities in systems design, it is ill-prepared. For example, there are as yet no well-established principles for designing and testing man–machine dialogues, no empirically sound theories of program comprehension, and few interface languages which will permit a system to evolve to match its users' preferred styles of interaction. However, it is not true that there has been no research in these areas. A substantial body of work already exists on many aspects of *computing skills and the user interface* but much of it is difficult to access because it is either unpublished or scattered across the journals of many disciplines. This book arose out of a recognition of this fact.

This need first became evident to us at a Workshop on "Computing Skills and Adaptive Systems" which we held at the Computer Laboratory, University of Liverpool in order to promote communication in the area. The Workshop drew together people with a common interest in computer training and interface design and from a range of academic and commercial backgrounds. During the proceedings it became clear that much research was only well known within the disciplines in which it was carried out. There was thus a need for a publication to review relevant research over the whole area and to present some as yet unpublished work which we expect will open up new areas of interest. These requirements formed the objectives of the present volume.

Contributions to the book have been grouped into three sections. The first selection of papers discusses the main issues involved in providing computer facilities for two classes of new user: university researchers who want specialized packages which are easy to use yet are both flexible and adaptive, and commercial users who want a simple, supportive system which will cause minimum disruption to their normal work practices. The second group of papers are mainly concerned with research on the nature of computing skills and techniques of instruction, although the section also includes brief reports of recent work on both program comprehension and the influence of differences in cognitive style on learning a first computer language. Papers in the final section are divided between those focusing on the formulation of a philosophy for interface design and those reporting practical attempts to design improved user interfaces.

Although many of the papers in this book have originated from a number of different disciplines they actually reflect several common themes. We have therefore used our editorial position to influence contributors in order to produce a reasonably integrated volume. We are indebted to all our authors for the patience and forbearing they have shown in willingly revising their material in order to meet this editorial objective. In line with this objective we have attempted to rationalize the notations used throughout the book. Although total consistency has not always been possible, we have sought to abide by the following rules.

— With ALGOL-like code everything has been printed in lower-case

italics except procedure names and keywords, which appear in lower-case bold type.
- FORTRAN-like code is printed in upper-case roman type.
- Experimental languages are printed with procedure names and keywords in bold upper-case type and everything else in roman.

Conventions used for the description of interface and editing languages discussed in Part III of the book differ between chapters and are therefore defined as they are introduced.

We would like to take this opportunity of thanking Alan Dawson for many important discussions on issues raised in the papers, for liaising with authors on matters of detail and for ensuring that they adhered, as far as possible, to a common set of conventions. Olive Williamson deserves our thanks for a substantial contribution to the editing of Part III. We also wish to thank Maureen Stanton for re-typing several manuscripts and showing fortitude during the evolution of our own contributions.

Finally, we hope that the work reported in the book will stimulate research and discussion in an area which we believe will increasingly influence software developments.

Liverpool, 1980   M.J. Coombs
                                                             J.L. Alty

Contents

Part III. The Design of the User Interface

Part I
The Needs of Computer Users

Introduction

Many people now use computers as part of their daily work, having little or no training in the technicalities of computing. This development is important for the continued growth of the industry but will necessitate a new philosophy towards the user. Whereas in the past systems have been designed with a central objective of obtaining maximum processing out of scarce and expensive hardware, the user being expected to adapt to the demands of machine-oriented software, future systems will have to take more account of users' current work practices and expertise. It is unlikely that the majority of users will wish to be extensively trained in computing, and commercial employers will certainly wish to minimize user training costs. Furthermore, inadequate user interfaces cost real money.

The three chapters in this first section are intended to provide a background to the specific topics concerned with computing skills and the user interface discussed in Parts II and III. It may thus come as a surprise that, given the predominance of the commercial market for computer systems, two of the chapters are concerned with university users and only one with commercial applications. While it is clear that commercial users form, and will continue to form, the largest body of "new" users (or "naive users", as they are termed by Eason and Damodaran) computer centres within universities have gained substantial experience in supporting a large and diverse population of such people and provide an ideal situation for carrying out research which would be very difficult in a production environment. Much of this experience is certainly relevant to the commercial world, along with solutions to additional user difficulties which have arisen from the rapid introduction of microprocessors to university research.

The two chapters concerned with the problems and guidance of university users report research carried out as part of a project on "The Provision of Guidance to University Computer Users", funded from 1976 by the Social Science Research Council at the Universities of Liverpool and Birmingham. The Liverpool work (Alty and Coombs, p. 7) concentrates upon problems of communication between computer professionals working in university computer centres and university users, which were studied by recording interactions in the computing advisory service. This research clearly identifies the difficulties which non-computer professionals find in using systems with a traditional machine-oriented interface, and the difficulties which professionals find in adapting to users whose understanding of computing is approached from application knowledge. The chapter provides some useful guidelines for improving communication between computer professionals and users.

The Birmingham research (Auld, et al. p. 73) is aimed both at producing a global description of the use of university guidance services—documentation, advisory services, machine-based "help" systems, etc.—and identifying some characteristics of users which are critical in determining their success at computing. With respect to the first objective, the paper confirms the importance of face-to-face communication between users and computer professionals which had been studied in detail at Liverpool. Work directed towards the second objective identifies six important user characteristics. These broadly indicate that successful users of traditional applications software need a scientific or technical background combined with intensive use of a particular computer system. It is interesting to note that casual or infrequent users have almost as many difficulties as users from non-technical backgrounds. This should have relevance to the design of computer-based information systems for occasional use by management.

The chapter by Eason and Damodaran (p. 115) seeks first to classify commercial users in a manner which will be useful to the software designer by permitting him to predict interface and training requirements. The authors base their classification on a description of the user's work task and on his role within the organization. The effect of these two groups of variables will, however, be modified by individual psychological characteristics such as personality and intelligence. Eason and Damodaran emphasize that if a system is to succeed, there must be a close fit both between the user's task and the processing functions offered by the computer, and between the user's expectations of the system and its actual performance. A user will judge a system by the extent to which it enables him to better perform his job. Users will not be tolerant towards the machine or explore its capabilities for their own sake. While this will not be true of all commercial users, it will apply to the majority. The user-friendliness of a system is thus a matter of considerable concern to designers and will influence its marketability.

The chapters in this section emphasize that the design of an effective computer system is as much a matter of behavioural science as of computer science, requiring careful study of such factors as the work environment in which it will be used, its frequency of use and the motivation of users. However, this information is not only important at the design stage. Users will need effective advice and guidance via courses, documentation and machine-based facilities, all of which must be closely matched to user knowledge and needs.

1. Communicating with University Computer Users: A Case Study

J.L. ALTY and M.J. COOMBS

Computer Laboratory, University of Liverpool, Liverpool, England

I. INTRODUCTION

In order to conduct research in most academic disciplines, it is necessary to be able to make effective use of a computer. However, in common with other "background" skills, computing is rarely taught in depth outside its specialist department. Students and researchers are expected to acquire competence via a short introductory course. For scientists and engineers this is usually in a high-level language such as FORTRAN, while social scientists and arts users usually learn to use a relevant applications package. Such courses avoid any detailed discussion of the fundamental principles of computing, limiting themselves to syntactic details and simple job-submission procedures. After an introductory course, the research workers' main official sources of support are the information and guidance services provided by their university computer centre.

Professional guidance in computing is given by all university computer centres. In addition to face-to-face guidance, this usually includes formal lecture courses on the main languages and packages, a full range of professional documentation, and machine-based sources of information. However, there is evidence that the range of resources normally available for these additional services do not adequately provide for all sections of a university population, particularly for novice users and those from academic disciplines new to computing, such as medicine or social science (see Chapter 2 in this volume). This is because most sources of information and guidance function as one-way communication systems and therefore do not adapt to the needs of individual users. Their effectiveness is thus critically dependent upon the user's knowledge of computing and upon the designer's ability to assess such knowledge. Novices

7

from all disciplines often lack appropriate knowledge to find the information they require, and those from the disciplines new to computing suffer the additional problem of using a system which has evolved to meet the needs of engineers and scientists.

The advisory service is an exception among the official sources of information. At the advisory service a user can, without appointment, consult a computer professional on any aspect of the computer or information system, as well as on problems with his own programs. The advice may therefore be adapted to the needs of individual users, which potentially makes the service an invaluable source of information for novices and the new groups of users.

It was this characteristic of adaptability which first identified the advisory service as a focus for research into the provision of guidance to university computer users. From a study of the service we expected to obtain information on:

(i)   the effectiveness of present advisory services;
(ii) principles for maximizing effectiveness;
(iii) common sources of user difficulty;
(iv) the general problems of designing other guidance materials (including documentation and machine-based sources).

This chapter reports findings relating to (i) and (ii); the findings concerning objectives (iii) and (iv) are being reported elsewhere (Alty and Coombs, 1980).

A search through the literature was first undertaken to seek a well-supported theory of the nature and acquisition of computing information which would allow for the statement of pertinent hypotheses concerning methods of face-to-face advice-giving. However, having failed to find such a theory, we decided that the initial work should be descriptive and should aim to provide a thorough and systematic characterization of interactions between advisors and users. From this descriptive work, we expected variables to emerge which could be subjected to controlled experiments in order to formulate principles for improving communication. The present chapter reports the descriptive stage of our work and makes some critical proposals for improvement.

The study was centred on the advisory service of the Computer Laboratory, University of Liverpool, although findings were followed up at four other university sites: Imperial College, University of London; University College of Swansea; the University of Birmingham; and the University of Surrey. Because of the importance to the study of the work conducted at Liverpool and of the similarity of findings between sites, the research will be primarily presented as a case study of the Liverpool Advisory Service. However, we will present findings from other universities where they provide an interesting contrast or where they significantly support a principle of advice-giving.

In most computer centres two modes of service have evolved for the provision of face-to-face guidance. These may be termed "advisory services" and "consultancy services". The advisory service provides instant guidance on programming errors and acts as an index to other official sources of information, while the consultancy service is intended to guide users in the design stage of a program and help them solve more complex problems. Consultation is by appointment with a computer professional who specializes in a given area. The present study concerns itself only with the advisory service, although many of the findings would apply equally to interactions with consultants.

II. THE STAFFING AND ORGANIZATION OF THE LIVERPOOL ADVISORY SERVICE

The staffing of the advisory service is the responsibility of the computer professionals in the Laboratory. This includes all programming staff but excludes engineers, operators and managers. The service is manned in rotation. Each week is covered by two people, although only one person is on duty at any time. Throughout the present study there has been an eligible staff of around sixteen, each person thus being required to do 2½ days duty about every 8 weeks.

The Liverpool service operates for three sessions a day from Monday to Friday, an advisor being in attendance from 0915–1045, 1100–1215, and 1400–1615. Users attend during these hours whenever they require assistance. If advisors find they are unable to answer a query, they can call on other members of staff. This tends to blur the distinction between the advisory and consultancy services. For example, a specialist called in to solve an immediate query may offer to extend his assistance throughout the user's programming project.

Advisory sessions are conducted in an office shared with the Information Service. Interactions are conducted across a desk and are close to the main thoroughfare of the office. Behind the adviser is a video display unit which is used for accessing users' computer files as an aid in diagnosing errors. A number of predictions can be made about the likely effects of this physical advisory environment, which is fairly common at other centres. First, the placing of the advisor and user on either side of the table will increase the probability either of confrontation or of the domination of the interaction by one participant. This contrasts with the increased likelihood of co-operation when participants sit beside each other (Sommer, 1965). Secondly, the advisory location is open to interference from the noise of people in transit through the information room and from other users waiting for advice. It may be expected that each of these factors, and particularly the social pressure from a queue of users, would reduce the efficiency of interactions.

The academic background of advisers at Liverpool is typical of those at other sites. During the two years of the study the maximum number of staff eligible for advisory duties was eighteen, and of these only three had been trained as computer scientists. All the others had first degrees either in mathematics or in the physical sciences, the most common degree being chemistry. Many had formerly been users of university computer services who had become sufficiently interested in computing to adopt it as a career. They were therefore largely self-taught, their only formal training having been received from user courses. None had been trained in techniques of answering computer queries.

III. THE RESEARCH PHILOSOPHY

From the outset of the investigations it was necessary to adopt some research strategy which would enable us to analyse individual advisory interactions in some depth, while at the same time enabling us to assess the generality of results. A pilot study of advisory conversations recorded at Liverpool revealed the time-consuming nature of such research. For example, a detailed analysis of a conversation required transcription of the recorded dialogue, debriefing sessions with the advisor and user, and the painstaking assessment of utterances, so that a typical session of ten minutes might well involve more than one hour of analysis. It was therefore evident that it would be impossible to analyse in depth a statistically representative number of university sites. In this event two courses of action were open to us. We could either focus on a small number of variables over many sites, or conduct an investigation as a series of detailed small-scale studies, with the reliability of results being assessed by running a series of replications under varying conditions. In the absence of a suitable theory that would enable us to select variables for special attention, it was decided to adopt the latter strategy. The research would therefore use procedures similar to those recommended for single case studies (see Hersen and Barlow, 1976).

Two complementary forms of investigation were used at all university sites. An external view of guidance services was obtained by using small-scale surveys, structured interviews and attitude questionnaires. These gave global information on such topics as the reasons for users' attendance at the advisory service, their expectations of it and their satisfaction with the advice. An internal view of the service was given by a detailed study of individual sessions. These studies focused on the dynamics of interactions, providing information on both the effectiveness of advice and on communication problems experienced by specific groups of users. This information was later to be used to provide the substance of an advisor training course.

In the following section those survey findings relating to users' attitudes towards the advisory service will be reported. A full report of the survey is given in Coombs (1979a). Although the survey was initially considered a minor part of the investigation, the information about users' attitudes proved to be very valuable. This was because it firmly directed attention towards certain user characteristics at an early stage of the research, so narrowing the field of critical dimensions to be considered in the study of individual advisory sessions. This considerably eased the problems of sampling combinations of advisors, users and interactions.

IV. USERS' EVALUATIONS OF THE ADVISORY SERVICE

A. A User Survey

The main objectives of the survey were (i) to assess the relative importance to users of the various sources of advice and guidance available in a computer centre, and (ii) to investigate user activity prior to and following advisory visits. These objectives were achieved by using a multiple-choice questionnaire combined with an interview which employed non-directive questioning techniques (Rogers, 1951). The questionnaire was administered verbally by the investigator. Users were read one question at a time and were asked to choose from a number of prepared responses. After each response the answer was "reflected back" to the user, indicating that the investigator expected either more information or an explanation of the response. For example, the investigator might first ask a question such as "How many jobs do you run on average per week?" to which the user might respond "25". The investigator would then repeat this answer back to him, saying "You run about 25 jobs a week?", and so obtain a new response such as "Well, sometimes 30, although I haven't used the computer at all for the last six months." In this way a more complete and accurate picture of the user's activity would develop.

The survey was run on a quota sample of 45 Liverpool users selected from the user work area of the Computer Laboratory (15 from each of the three main faculties: Science (S), Engineering (E), and Social and Environmental Studies (S&ES)). These three faculties accounted for almost all of the user population at Liverpool, (Coombs, 1979b). The same basic survey materials were incorporated into studies of advisory services at the four additional university sites, although users at the other sites, with the exception of Birmingham, completed the questionnaire without an accompanying interview.

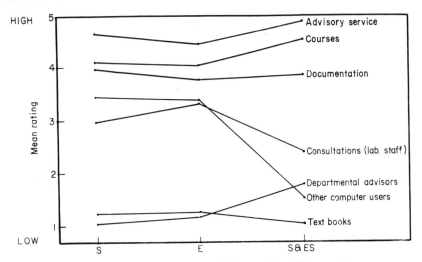

Fig. 1. Rated importance of sources of information—Liverpool survey (*N*=45, *n*=15).

An examination of the log of advisory interactions kept by advisors at Liverpool indicates that 65-70% of active users (those running 6+ jobs per year) visited the advisory service at least once during the year. There was thus evidence that the advisory service did make a significant contribution to user guidance. This finding was supported by our survey. Not only did all of the sample of 45 users attend the advisory service, but almost all of them rated the service as their most valued source of information. Moreover, the high evaluation was independent of faculty: the service was valued equally highly by scientists, engineers and social scientists. The importance of the various information sources, as rated by users from each of the three faculties, is shown in Fig. 1. The results from the four other universities are remarkably similar, with the advisory service consistently rated more highly than any other source of information.

The reasons for this high evaluation clearly emerged from users' answers to subsequent survey questions. It was found, for example, that the majority of queries (78%) arose from failed programs. However, instead of users going to advisory as soon as they had discovered that their program had failed (as we had expected), many of them made a realistic attempt at a solution. By the time a visit to the advisory service was considered, most users had reached the limits of their own knowledge and that of any colleagues they may have consulted. The advisory service was thus regarded as the final opportunity for finding a solution. A user's evaluation of an advisory consultation should thus be seen in the context of the often considerable effort he has invested in solving his own problem. The majority of users who were interviewed expected the first solution they received from the advisor to be correct (given that he was a computer professional), and they usually found that it was.

Four additional reasons were frequently given for valuing the advisory service, all of which appeared significant with reference to the effort users invested in solving their own queries. First, users valued the immediate availability of advice from the advisory service. It is interesting that this feature was regarded as particularly important by those users who claimed to work hard at solving their own problems. These users appeared to attend advisory when they were not only frustrated with debugging but also close to project deadlines. Secondly, users valued the service as a source of references to alternative sources of information (often documentation). Again, this feature was particularly valued by those who made a serious attempt at their own solutions; in this case because it was felt that the alternative source would help them gain greater independence. Thirdly, some users valued advisory because it provided for them the only easily available source of information on some aspects of the system, for example, the handling of magnetic tapes. Fourthly, the service was often valued by new users as the first, and often only, contact with the staff of the Computer Laboratory after an introductory course. This feature appeared to be particularly important for new social science users because of their unfamiliarity with the structure and organization of a computer centre. The advisory service thus functioned for these people as a general guide to the use of the Computer Laboratory as well as a source of information for solving specific problems.

From the above results it may seem reasonable to conclude that users were highly satisfied with the advisory service. However, subsequent questions indicated that this was not the case. Although the advisory service was highly valued for correct and immediate advice, users also claimed that on a significant percentage of occasions (40%) they did not fully understand the advice (and felt it would have been an advantage for them to have done so). Users also claimed that many interactions were "painful", or at best only moderately pleasurable, events. The apparent contradiction seemed to us to be sufficiently fundamental to warrant detailed investigation, it being recognized from the literature (Sharrock and Turner, 1978) as a source of dissonant attitudes which could inhibit effective and efficient advisory communication. Highly similar results were obtained from a similar survey conducted at the Computer Centre, University of Birmingham.

B. An Anatomy of User Attitudes

A clue to the nature of the contradiction identified above was first noted in the comments on the advisory service which users at Liverpool and Birmingham made in the follow-up to their evaluation of the various information sources. Three independent observers from outside the Liverpool Computer Laboratory inspected the comments and agreed with the investigators that many users did hold contradictory attitudes. However, the precise form of the contradiction was difficult to characterize from the comments alone.

The observers agreed that many users discussed the advisory service with reference to not more than four criteria. The first and most frequently quoted of these was the correctness of advice. Although users applied this criterion to all sources of face-to-face guidance, they appeared to be less strict in their judgement of information from colleagues. Official sources of guidance were expected to provide correct information most of the time, whereas unofficial sources were allowed to be wrong. The second criterion identified by observers was the extent to which advice was given in a form that was meaningful to users, although it appeared that most users found it difficult to elaborate their principles for assessing meaningfulness. Only two principles were clearly stated, these being related to the user's ability to appreciate the evolution of the solution and to relate the advice to the context of the query. The context could be stated in either applications or computing terms. It was again found that users gave greater licence to colleagues to be unclear than to official sources of face-to-face advice. The last two criteria concerned users' emotional, or affective, responses to guidance sessions. The third criterion of assessment was the degree to which an advisor was perceived as being friendly or sympathetic towards a query. This was mediated by a fourth factor, which was the extent to which a user felt he had made a useful contribution to the advisory discourse.

Although the three independent observers agreed with the investigators that the above four criteria could be found in users' comments, their relative importance to the assessment of the service was not clear. It was therefore decided to undertake a separate investigation of users' attitudes to the advisory service. The method of evaluation adopted was to use a set of standard seven-point semantic differential scales (Osgood *et al.,* 1957). This tool for assessing attitudes was chosen because the above four criteria could be easily expressed as five pairs of polar adjectives, all of which had been classified by Osgood *et al.* as evaluative. The method also avoided the lengthy piloting of questionnaires which would be necessary with other forms of study. The five pairs of polar adjectives were:

Meaningful — Meaningless
Intelligent — Unintelligent
Successful — Unsuccessful
Pleasurable — Painful
Friendly — Unfriendly

Two pairs of concepts, each representing a vital component of an advisory interaction, were rated on each of the five scales shown above. The pairs of concepts were: "*the user* as a participant in the interaction" / "*the advisor* as a participant in the interaction", and "*the query*" / "*the advice*", all of which, of course, were judged by users.

Attitudes to the advisory service were assessed from a sample of 26 users, who were selected at random over a period of four days as they entered the information office of the Liverpool Computer Laboratory. A summary of the results is given in Fig. 2. These are expressed as mean scores and 95% parametric confidence intervals. Comparisons between concepts were made using *t*-tests. Although the meaning of some of the scale/concept combinations was rather ambiguous, this did not appear to give too much difficulty to

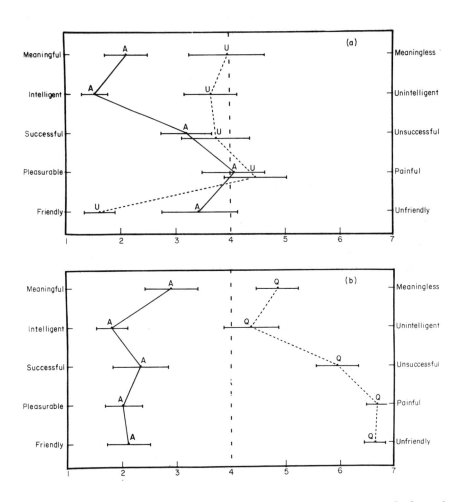

Fig. 2. User attitude survey (*N*=26). (A=Advisor/Advice; U=User; Q=Query.)

respondents. As is usual with semantic differential scales, individuals found their own interpretations. These were noted by the investigator when questioning users at the end of the formal interviewing session.

It can be seen from Fig. 2 that on all scales "advice" was rated more positively than "query". Differences were significant well above the 0·01 level in all cases. However, the positioning of the means for the two concepts requires comment. First, it should be noted that the query was not rated as entirely meaningless or unintelligent but was placed near the centre line. When questioned about this, users maintained that in most cases they had done some work to solve their own query and therefore often attended advisory feeling they had made some progress towards a solution. This supported our earlier finding from the user survey. Secondly, the advice was not rated as totally meaningful and intelligent. Users maintained that this was because they often felt they did not completely understand the advice even though they could recall it and apply it.

The interpretation of the concepts "advisor . . ." and "user . . ." in the context of the scales "meaningful" and "intelligent" was anticipated to present problems. This was because in both cases the scales could be applied either to the concepts themselves (e.g. was the advisor intelligent?) or to the role of the concept in an advisory interaction (e.g. did the advisor play an intelligent role?). This ambiguity first became apparent during some pilot tests. Care was therefore taken to ensure that the two concepts were interpreted as:

— the user/advisor was more or less intelligent in his contribution to the interaction; and

— the interaction was more or less meaningful to the user/advisor.

Using these interpretations, it was found that there were significant differences between the two concepts at above the 1% level in both cases. It thus appeared that users perceived their own contributions as less intelligent than those of advisors and that the interaction was less meaningful to users. However, it should be noted that users rated themselves on the positive side of the scale in both instances.

There proved to be no significant difference between the ratings of the concepts "advisor . . ." and "user . . ." on the successfulness scale. In both cases the ratings were at the moderately successful level (3–4). These ratings were lower than expected and so it was decided to further investigate the results by interviewing the respondents. Users claimed that they thought advisors were successful at solving their queries but that they were not so good at explaining the solutions. Indeed, 13 out of 26 users claimed that there was usually at least one aspect of the answer which they did not understand. However, in contrast, advisors claimed that users did not want explanations but simply wanted to know "what to do". This contradiction appeared to be so fundamental, and potentially disruptive to good communication, that it was noted for detailed exploration in our study of actual face-to-face interactions.

There was no significant difference between users' ratings of themselves and of advisors with respect to the pleasure of engaging in advisory interactions. In each case the ratings fell just to the negative side of the scale. The reasons behind users' assessment of the pleasure gained by advisors in interactions appeared to be twofold: a number of users were aware that manning advisory was for most advisors a least-favoured activity, and some users reasoned that the types of problem they were taking to advisory were not of great interest. These points were used further to explain some unfriendliness or rigidity in advisors' responses, whereas users usually saw themselves as being friendly.

The results of the attitude survey can be summarized as follows. On all scales the advice was rated significantly more positively than the query, but users were less happy with the interaction itself. They maintained that the interaction was significantly less meaningful for themselves than for advisors and that their contribution was significantly less intelligent. It also appeared that many users realized that the manning of advisory was not a favoured activity, and thought that this was the main reason why they did not always receive a friendly response.

C. Expertise and User Attitudes

While interviewing the respondents, it was noted that a number of users were very understanding of the advisors' point of view. It was typically reported by this group that the advisors' task was a difficult one. Moreover, they often claimed to have no real difficulty in communicating with advisors, and thought that any misunderstandings were usually due to their own lack of knowledge. The two users who expressed these views most strongly were considered by advisors to be highly expert in their use of the Liverpool computing system. Furthermore, advisors reported that user expertise contributed greatly to the interest of an advisory interaction, and that they would be prepared to become more involved with an expert user's problem. It therefore seemed appropriate to re-analyse the attitude scales on the basis of expertise, since this would possibly provide one material basis for characterizing advisory interactions.

The 26 respondents were accordingly split into two groups on the basis of ratings for expertise made by advisors on a five-point scale. Research reported by Alty and Coombs (1980) has indicated that such ratings are reliable measures of the effectiveness with which

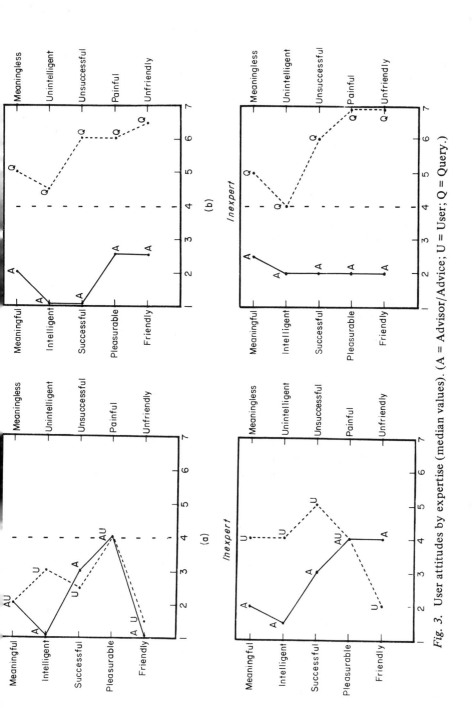

Fig. 3. User attitudes by expertise (median values). (A = Advisor/Advice; U = User; Q = Query.)

users employ the computer systems. The mean value of three advisor ratings for each user was computed and users were allocated to expert or inexpert groups accordingly. An inter-rater reliability measure was computed by analysis of variance (Burroughs, 1971, pp. 70–77) and was found to be high at above 0·95. The results of the re-analysis according to expertise are given in Fig. 3. Statistical tests were conducted using the Wilcoxon matched-pairs signed-ranks test, as the small size of the groups and the skewed distributions made t-tests inappropriate.

It can be seen from Fig. 3 that for both experts and inexperts there were significant differences on all scales between the concepts "query" and "advice". However, there were discrepancies between the evaluations of the advisors' and the users' behaviour as participants in the interaction. With the inexpert users the pattern of response was very much as previously described with reference to the whole sample. There were significant differences at above the 1% level on all scales except for the pleasurable/painful scale. Interactions were seen to be more meaningful and successful for the advisor, and the advisor's behaviour was seen as more intelligent, but advisors were judged to be not as friendly as users. However, the pattern for expert users was found to be very different. Expert users made no distinction between their own responses to interactions and those of the advisor on any of the scales except that of intelligence. Both experts and inexperts rated advisors' behaviour to be more intelligent than their own. However, the expert user saw himself and the advisor as being equally friendly and the interaction as being equally meaningful and successful for both sides. Communication during the interaction therefore appeared to be more equally balanced with the expert users.

It may be concluded from our survey that each of the five scales was meaningfully employed by users for assessment of advisory interactions, but that users' evaluations were moderated to some extent by their expertise. The more expert users generally found both the advice and the interaction itself to be meaningful and successful. They also felt that they interacted smoothly with the advisor during the solving of their problem. Inexperienced users, on the other hand, were usually satisfied with the advice but found it less meaningful. In contrast to the views of expert users, they felt that advisors were often not sympathetic or sensitive to their needs.

D. Conclusions on User Attitudes

The findings reported above gave us confidence to continue our study with a close analysis of the Liverpool Advisory Service. Not only did the Liverpool service, in its staffing and general organization, appear typical of many other university sites, but it held a similar status among the various information and guidance systems, and so it was reasonable to expect that many of the Liverpool findings would generalize to other universities. The study would therefore continue as planned with a detailed analysis of interactions in the Liverpool Advisory Service, the results from which would be used to generate hypotheses for testing at other centres.

The two surveys gave us some factual information on the activities that typically surround an advisory consultation. Before bringing a query to the advisory service, most users make some effort to solve their own problem and feel that they have progressed some way towards a solution. While working on their problem they are likely to have consulted either some form of document or a computing colleague. The query itself is likely to have resulted from the failure of a program or other piece of software. A user is unlikely to understand all of the advice but can usually follow any concrete instructions.

The two surveys also helped to focus our attention on potential independent variables. From the contact with other university computer centres it was found that practically all advisors were former users of the computer services, and had backgrounds in the physical sciences rather than formal training in computer science. Much of their computing knowledge had been acquired through experience rather than training, and their interest was essentially practical, not theoretical. Furthermore, few advisors had any significant experience in academic teaching and none had been trained in advisory techniques. All these factors may be expected to be of importance when advising novice users, particularly when the novices do not share a common physical science background with advisors.

It is clear from the initial survey that the advisory service is a very highly valued source of information and guidance at all five of the university sites we studied. To a considerable extent its value arises from its availability and from the measure of adaptation it offers to the needs of individuals (although such adaptation is in practice far from optimal). There is, however, a contradiction between this high evaluation and the negative affective response to interactions declared by many users. A study has been made of this contradiction and it has been found to arise mainly from the use of mixed criteria by users for evaluating advisory interactions. The advisory service is highly valued as an instant source of guidance on any computing topic, the information in most cases being pertinent and correct. On the other hand, it was claimed that the information was not always completely meaningful and that advisors were not aware of the user's level of knowledge. Advisors, however, claimed that users did not want explanations of advice but simply wanted to know what to do to achieve a given result. The origin of these contrary points of view and their effects on the course of advisory conversation will be studied in depth in the following section, as they represent the type of misunderstanding likely to result in frustration for both parties.

One of the most interesting findings from this study is the influence of a user's expertise on his evaluation of advisory interactions. The finding that the inexpert user perceives an interaction quite differently from the expert user ought to have an important bearing on future advisory service provision. It seems that present advisory services cater better for the expert, whereas it is the needs of the inexpert user which perhaps ought to provide the principal guiding factors in advisory provision.

V. ANALYSIS OF FACE-TO-FACE INTERACTIONS

A. An Approach to the Analysis of Conversation

The objective of the second part of the investigation was to ascertain how far advisory interactions between different advisors and users, and concerning different computing problems, were sufficiently similar to be regarded as an identifiable category of face-to-face encounter. To do this we examined samples of interactions in detail and assessed the effects of such independent variables as user expertise and academic background.

A system for formally describing face-to-face interactions was a prerequisite for any systematic study, and the literature offered a wide range of approaches, but no one system was sufficiently mature to make it an obvious choice. Indeed, the area of discourse analysis is currently in dispute between scholars from a wide range of disciplines, each with their characteristic objectives. For example, linguists are engaged in exploring the proposition that language can be analysed in terms of grammatical rules which extend outside the sentence to longer units of text (e.g. Halliday, 1973); philosophers are concerned with formally exploring the concept of meaning in terms of the sense, reference and implications of sentences (Austin, 1962) and of sentence contexts (Grice, 1975); psychologists have used passages of text to study more general problems of cognition, including the role of context in comprehension (e.g. Garrod and Sanford, 1977); and ethnographers (e.g. Hymes, 1974) have sought to account for given conversational structures with reference to proposed goals or purposes behind a given interaction. There are also a considerable number of applied studies looking at discourse in specific and complex situations (e.g. teaching: Sinclair *et al.*, 1972; therapy: Labov and Fanshel, 1978). Such studies often have the dual functions of exploring the dynamics of a given conversational situation and developing some system for describing it.

A researcher is faced with a fundamental decision when using conversational material as data. It is necessary to decide whether to first concentrate upon the verbal text itself, and seek to isolate linguistic structure with reference to a general description of the purpose of the interaction, or whether to first obtain a detailed account of these goals, concentrating on the meaning rather than the structure of the text. The two approaches are, of course, far from independent. A linguistic structure (e.g. question and statement) implies some cognitive or behavioural outcome within a particular social context, and similarly a given behavioural objective implies the use of particular linguistic structures.

The final aim of the analysis of advisory conversations was to determine the extent to which they fulfilled users' needs. It was therefore necessary that at some stage we should identify the interactive goals of participants, in order to evaluate the effectiveness of the methods used by participants to reach them. The nature of the research therefore pointed to a description of goals as the obvious starting point. In this respect the work followed the method proposed by Mathiot and Garvin (1975), and more recently Mathiot (1978).

Mathiot (1978) views conversations as cultural events. As such it may be assumed that a conversation is governed by given social objectives and that it can be validly analysed only in terms of those objectives. A list of the various goals maintained by participants is thus necessary in order to provide a "frame of reference" to enable the researcher to differentiate relevant from accidental structure. The analysis must first ascertain the various functions of communicative behaviour during an occasion of face-to-face interaction. From these functions it becomes possible to ascertain the related structures, which may be units of language or of action. Finally, having isolated the significant structures, it is possible to identify more specific, low-level functions behind each communicative act.

B. The Sampling and Analysis of Liverpool Advisory Interactions

In order to achieve our objective of determining whether advisory interactions were sufficiently uniform, at least at the functional level, to be considered as a separate class of interactions, it was necessary to decide on a manageable sample size that would adequately represent Liverpool advisory interactions. An arbitrary sample size of 14 interactions was judged to be reasonable, this being later upheld by a statistical check. It was also noted that for a study of the depth we envisaged, 14 conversations was above the size used by other authors (e.g. Sinclair *et al.*, 1972;. Labov and Fanshel, 1978).

The conversations were selected from the queries answered by two duty advisors in the Liverpool Advisory Service over one week. (Out of an estimated 30 queries answered by each advisor in a week, a sequence of 7 sessions was randomly pre-selected for analysis.) Although it was not possible to conveniently obtain a random sample of advisors, the two advisors were selected to differ in ways that were thought to have some influence on advisory style: one advisor was male and one was female; the male advisor specialized in numerical analysis while the female was a specialist in handling survey data and had special responsibility for SPSS (Statistical Package for the Social Sciences). However, both advisors were very experienced and both had backgrounds in the physical sciences.

The investigator attended the advisory service for the entire week, and as users filling the pre-selected slots entered the information office they were asked if they would agree to participate. After a user had agreed to help, he was requested to continue presenting his query in the normal way. All conversations were recorded, the tape-recorder and microphone being on view on the advisory desk throughout. At the close of each conversation, the user was taken to another part of the information office for a first debriefing, where he was asked to repeat his query and to recall the answer he had been given. He was also asked to complete a short questionnaire designed to assess the extent of his use of the computing system and his general attitude towards the advisory service. The advisor was asked to comment on the interaction and to rate the user for expertise on a five-point scale.

Some days later a session was held separately with each of the participants (advisor and user) for a second, detailed debriefing. In preparation for these sessions the 14 sample conversations had been transcribed verbatim and the text divided into utterances. The criteria used for this division were simple but had the advantage of being easily achieved and of making the minimum number of structural assumptions. An utterance was defined as a string of text bounded by one of the following:

(a) text uttered by another participant;
(b) an implied utterance (e.g. a silence following the question "O.K.?");
(c) a period of silence lasting two or more seconds.

At the start of the debriefing the participant was asked some general questions concerning his expectations and attitudes at the start of the advisory session and his initial understanding of the nature of the query. The participant was then taken through the text of the interaction, and after each of his utterances was asked to declare his reason for making it. By this method it was planned to gather information from the user on the origin of his query, his comprehension of the advice, and his attitude towards the advisor at each stage. From the advisor it was planned to find out about his understanding of the query, the reasoning behind the solution, and his assessment of the user's understanding of the solution. At the end of the session each participant was taken quickly through and text and asked to group it into episodes. The complete debriefing session was tape-recorded for later analysis.

The cycle of data collection, transcription, debriefing and analysis which was adopted for the initial sample of 14 conversations proved very time-consuming. It was therefore decided that the research would have to continue to use small samples for detailed analysis, although this information would be supplemented with further observations to provide specific additional data as required.

The reliability of findings from the detailed analysis of the first sample of interactions was tested on a second sample of 14 conversations involving two different advisors. These were selected to include one advisor with computer science training and one advisor with a reputation amongst users for being very sympathetic and knowledgeable. A change was made in the procedure for recording conversations to counter the criticism that the interactions would be affected by users' knowledge that they were being recorded. Users were accordingly informed that they could be tape-recorded at any time during the following weeks. However, they were always recorded immediately after being contacted, although care was taken to ensure that both the recorder and microphone were hidden from view. Successive users were selected as they attended advisory rather than being pre-selected at random over a sampling period.

Debriefing appointments were made on the initial contact.

Sessions were run on similar lines to those of the first sample, except that the texts of interactions were presented auditorily. Information arising from the interviews was recorded manually by the investigator. Users were also asked to complete a questionnaire similar to that completed by the first sample. The final corpus of advisory conversations recorded at Liverpool thus consisted of 28 interactions with four advisors (seven interactions each). No user contributed more than one conversation.

Four groups of chi-square tests (Siegel, 1956)[1] were conducted on the complete sample and on the two sub-samples of conversations to assess the extent to which they were representative of the distribution of users and types of query, for the academic year of the study, with respect to four important variables:

- the three major faculties of Science, Engineering, and Social and Environmental Studies;
- the four ranges of Jobs-per-Query (JPQ) ratio which had been found to denote ranges of user expertise (Alty and Coombs, 1980);
- the classification of queries into those arising directly from the failure of an item of software and those being simply a request for advice;
- the classification of queries, by computing facility employed, in the survey of "User Computing Experience and the Use of the Advisory Service" (Coombs, 1979b).

These variables were selected because they represented factors which were judged by advisors to influence their style of interaction with a user. The analysis indicated that both the full sample and the sub-samples of users were representative of the total user population in terms of the distribution of users between faculties and user expertise (as measured by the JPQ ratio). The analysis also showed no significant difference between the samples and the total number of queries in a year with regard to the proportion of queries arising from program failure. While the second sub-sample of conversations appeared to be less representative of the total in terms of the classification of queries by computing facility, representativeness was restored by considering the total sample.

The sample of 28 advisory interactions was the main source of data for the Liverpool analysis, and it was found that they included

---

[1] Although the size of expected frequencies was often critically small in the assessment of sub-samples, this yielded a conservative test of the hypothesis that there were no significant differences between the user population and the samples.

examples of most of the independent variables we wished to consider. When examples could not be found or were insufficient in number, the sample was supplemented either by selected interactions or by event counts taken over several interactions.

C. The Structure of Liverpool Advisory Interactions

The analysis of the transcribed advisory interactions and of the list of goals obtained from users and advisors during debriefing was initially restricted to the first sample of 14 conversations. It was later extended to include the further 14 conversations in order to check the validity of findings from the first sample. The analysis was carried out informally by two independent observers—the second author and an advisor from the Liverpool Computer Laboratory.

The observers first considered the divisions identified by advisors and users in their own conversations. To the surprise of both observers the interactions were found to be very stereotyped. All conversations could be easily divided into three logical episodes: Definition of Query; Formulation of Answer; Communication of Solution. There was also found to be little iteration between episodes, with most users only asking a single query and many queries being answered in a single pass through the three episodes. There was considerable agreement between observers on all counts, the same two conversations being recognized as containing an additional episode (concerned with the retrospective checking of the solution of the query) and the same conversations being identified as containing more frequent iterations than normal.

In the analysis of the individual statements of goals given by users there was, as may be expected, more variation, but the goals also appeared somewhat stereotyped. The lists of goals were used to confirm the division of conversations into episodes and stages. A summary of these divisions is given in Fig. 4. Categories in parentheses were present in only 35% or less of interactions. In all 28 conversations the advisor was able to conclude the conversation in a manner which was generally acceptable to the user. In 79% of cases (22) the advisor produced a correct solution to the user's query. In two cases the advisor gave an incorrect solution and four queries were referred for additional information, following some action by the user in one instance and by the advisor in the others.

The final breakdown of utterances offered by the eight stages given in Fig. 4 enabled us to make a finer test of the apparent simplicity of interactions. The recorded objectives of the 28 users and

Episode 1.   *DEFINITION OF QUERY*
    a. Presentation of query
    (b. Clarification of query)

Episode 2.   *FORMULATION OF ANSWER*
    (c. Identification of sources of information
    concerning query)
    d. Collection of background facts
          or
    e. Formulation and testing of hypotheses
    towards a solution

Episode 3.   *COMMUNICATION OF SOLUTION*
    f. Statement of solution
    (g. Justification of solution)
    h. Closure

Fig. 4. A summary of interactive episodes.

four advisors were thus coded in terms of the eight categories. A count was then taken of the occasions in which there was a backward transition to an earlier stage of an interaction. Separate counts were taken for advisors and users. It was found that on 36% of occasions there were no backward transitions, on 14% of occasions there was one backward transition initiated by the advisor, and on 50% of occasions there were one or more backward transitions initiated by each participant. In all cases backward transitions were between Episodes 2 and 3 and were the result of second thoughts on a solution to a query by the advisor. Users only initiated a backward transition if the advisor had already done so in the conversation. It was interesting to note that there were no instances of a return to Episode 1.

At the start of the study it had been anticipated that there would be great difficulty in classifying participants' statements of goals. However, this was far from the case. The motivations behind advisory interactions appeared to be both very clear and very straightforward. There was thus no problem in identifying significant structure at the global level. Each of these global classes of advisor/ user activity will now be discussed in turn with the purpose of identifying the lower level structural units and the typical content of conversations.

1. *Definition of Query*

(a) Presentation of Query

The query was usually presented by the user in a single utterance which was rarely questioned by the advisor. Typical examples were:

1. I don't understand why I haven't got any output; there aren't any error messages.
2. I put this format statement in and the computer said that it was inadmissible.
3. I checked in here a short time ago about how to get some output from certain files and they said put it out to "MULTIPLE". Now I've done this and they have given me the output but it was cut.

If advisor and user know each other well there may be a quick word of recognition but otherwise the query is introduced in the same brief and business-like manner. It is very rare for an advisor to start an interaction: no instances were observed in our sample of 28 recorded interactions and only one example was found in a further 23 interactions observed for other purposes.

Most users presented their query with a statement of fact relating to their computing needs or to some action taken by the computer. On 11 occasions the critical information for defining the query was contained within the first complete sentence. On those occasions when it came later, the initial material usually gave a short history of the events leading up to the query (see Example 3). These comments usually contained little computing information but were a record of previous action taken to get a program to run, reiteration of previous advice, or comments on the research work that gave rise to the need to use a computer. If the advisor thought that any of the information he had been given was incorrect, he did not usually remark upon this but simply ignored the information in his consideration of the query. Example 4 below illustrates an occasion where the user tried to express his problem and then suggested a possible solution to it, or at least a possible cause of it.

4. All I want to do is to input this bunch of data. Now you can see what it's doing [*user points*]. The things may . . . the very first card which . . . . I don't know what's happening here . . . will have an *A* in column 10, you see, and maybe this is what it doesn't like?

It was not unusual for users to suggest a tentative solution to their query, but advisors rarely responded to this. They often ignored it completely or dismissed it quickly in order to concentrate on finding their own (correct) solution to the problem.

It was found during debriefing sessions that most of the 28 users regarded their queries on presentation as relatively trivial, as scored on a five-point scale from trivial (1) to complex (5), and did not change this view significantly during the course of the interaction.

(Rating on presentation: $\bar{x} = 2 \cdot 07$, $s = 1 \cdot 25$; at the end of interaction $\bar{x} = 2 \cdot 12$, $s = 1 \cdot 40$.) When asked at the end of interactions, advisors usually agreed with users' ratings of the triviality of queries (advisor rating: $\bar{x} = 1 \cdot 82$, $s = 1 \cdot 02$; Pearson correlation with final user rating: $r = 0 \cdot 98$, $p < 0 \cdot 01$).

Following the analysis of query types made by Alty and Coombs (1980), it was found that 20 out of the sample of 28 queries (71%) were in some way related to the failure of a piece of software, while the remaining 29% were requests for general advice or specific items of information. Ten per cent of queries arising from failure of software appeared to result, in part at least, from previous advice which was either incorrect or incomplete.

No marked differences were found at the query presentation stage between users with different levels of expertise. However, it was noted that several very inexperienced users gave an over-concrete and restricted description of their query. These users later claimed that they had had difficulty in expressing their real query and had hoped that it might become clear to the advisor during consideration of the more restricted case. It was also noted that the more inexpert users tended to give longer and less precise comments in support of their queries, although this was not uniformly the case. At this stage of the interaction, no variations were found to be dependent on any other relevant variables, such as the user's faculty and the origin of the query (failure of software or general advice).

(b) Clarification of Query

The objective of this stage was to establish a consensus definition of a query when the initial statement was regarded as ambiguous by the advisor. This stage was not present in most conversations, but this does not mean that users' presentations were usually unambiguous. In cases where the query resulted from the failure of an item of software, users were strongly encouraged to bring along the evidence; at the very least they were expected to bring a monitoring file and a listing of their program. These documents usually contained sufficient information for the advisor to define the problem for himself. It was sometimes difficult to distinguish this stage from the beginning of the problem solution in Episode 2. We had three clear instances of clarification of a query, and there were other suggestions of its presence in the goals given by advisors at around the junction of Episodes 1 and 2 in some conversations. Users, however, did not usually recognize the presence of the stage.

Advisors claimed that the query as presented was ambiguous in 12 out of 28 conversations (43%) but the meaning of 11 of these queries was clear in the context of the monitoring file or program listing.

2. Formulation of Solution

This episode was made up from a series of stages which we have defined in relatively general terms. This is because the micro-structure varied greatly according to such factors as the topic of the query and the experience of the advisor. Indeed, the conversational activity within the episode was often very complex. For example, it was noted that comments made by advisors while working through a problem were made for the benefit of both parties. They helped the advisor to clarify ˙his thoughts, and at the same time were intended to enable the user to judge their relevance. An attempt to analyse the episode at the finer level of detail was abandoned as it would have required a far more formal system for describing conversations. This episode will therefore be described in terms of the stages given in Fig. 4.

(a) Identification of Sources of Information Concerning Query

Given that the majority of queries arise from the failure of a user's program, the information relevant to the solution of a query can usually be found in the job-monitoring file and in the listing of the program. In this case the "Identification of Sources" stage is not invoked. In other instances, however, sources of relevant information may not be obvious to either advisor or user, and only become clear in the course of interaction. Relevant information was usually collected by advisors by asking a series of questions. For example:

5. *A.* Have you got your monitoring file?
U. My what?
A. I want your monitoring file, where it's . . . .

The reasons for requesting a particular source of information were not usually made explicit to the user.

(b)   Collection of Background Facts and Formulation and Testing of Hypotheses Towards a Solution

These two stages tended to occur together in the Liverpool advisory conversations, but because there was evidence from the participants' goals that this was not necessarily the case, they have been separately defined.

Information was usually collected by the advisor via a sequence of closed questions. It was noted that some users consistently treated such questions as open and therefore as having a wide range of possible answers. This lack of understanding between user and advisor appeared to occur most frequently when the user was inexperienced and had little knowledge of the relevant computing area.

In many cases the questioning of a user involved the collection of a wide range of information from which the solution to the query emerged, without any obvious formulation and testing of hypotheses by the advisor. The transition between information-collection and hypothesis-testing was not obvious in such cases, often the only indication of a change of stage being the increasing statement of part-solutions.

During these stages advisors were almost completely occupied with finding a solution to the query. They were not concerned with the communication of their reasoning to the user. However, while advisors primarily regarded the user as a source of information, they all claimed to be sensitive to the general response of the user to their line of argument. This is interesting in view of users' claims that they frequently did not understand the advisor but responded positively to him in order to keep him working at their problem. Such lack of understanding may be reflected in the frequency with which some users (usually novices) followed their answer to a question with a lengthy elaboration. Again no differences were found between the responses of users from different faculties.

3. *Communication of Solution*

This episode was not always clearly divisible from the process of finding a solution to a query. The solution itself usually evolved slowly and was expressed as the advisor's final statement in Episode 2.

(a) Statement of Solution

The solution to a query usually consisted of a set of operations to be performed by the user. These were rarely supported either by a review of the reasoning which had led to the solution or by a conceptual explanation of the solution. The user did not always understand the advice but in most cases did not ask for further explanation. There was also no evidence of explicit checking by advisors to ensure that the user was able to carry out the advice. The closest to a real check that advisors performed was the placing of the tag-question "O.K.?" after each instruction. For example:

6. . . . no this should be "DATA" . . . instead of "SF" you should have "DATA=", O.K.?

Users often responded positively to such tag-questions even though they did not necessarily appreciate the relevance of the instruction.

(b) Justification of Solution

A separate stage for justifying the solution to a query was not a necessary component of an advisory interaction. Indeed, it was only clearly present in nine conversations (32%), and in all but one of these the stage was very brief. The object of the justification stage was either for the advisor to clarify the advice in his own mind or to ensure that the user knew the correct actions to take. In seven out of the nine cases of justification we identified, the primary objective appeared to be reinforcement for the advisor rather than instruction for the user.

(c) Closure

Closure was usually brief, the user simply thanking the advisor and giving his user number to be recorded in the advisory log. There was rarely any friendly, informal comment made by the advisor to close the interaction. In seven instances there was a brief restatement of the advise as the user left the advisory desk.

4. *Summary of Findings*

All the interactions observed at Liverpool had a comparatively simple and uniform structure, falling into the three episodes which would usually be expected of an interaction concerned with problem-solving. Throughout the interactions the flow of information appeared to be controlled by the advisor, although there were some notable exceptions. These were all conversations involving expert users. Extended period of two-way communication between advisors and users tended to occur only at the start of Episode 2, when the advisor was trying to gather sufficient information to enable him to define the query accurately and to establish the basic information which might assist in a solution. It was also noted that there were few iterations between episodes during the course of conversations, the final response being generated by a single pass through the three episodes.

The 28 advisory conversations in the sample were stereotyped not only in terms of their general structure but also in terms of the types of utterances spoken. Most utterances were concerned with the task of eliciting or conveying factual information. Indeed, this factual information was usually of an operational nature and concerned the actions to be performed either by a program or by the user. The final advice was also usually given in operational terms and was only rarely supported by explanation. Only occasionally did advisors ask users to copy down the instructions given, or explicitly attempt to test if the user understood them.

We may therefore make the following two generalizations about the Liverpool advisory conversations:

(i) The flow of information was primarily one-way from advisor to user, except when the advisor required information to help him understand the problem. Control of the interaction seemed, therefore, to be clearly invested in the advisor.

(ii) The information communicated from advisor to user usually took the form of operational details, which were rarely supported by an explanation. Users were rarely helped to remember these operations and were infrequently tested for their understanding of them.

D. A Quantitative Analysis of Conversations

The findings (i) and (ii) outlined above were converted into hypotheses which were tested in the next stage of the study. In order to do this it was necessary to quantify both the control exercised over a conversation by its participants and the type of information communicated.

1. Control of Conversations

It is commonly observed that utterances in a conversation are usually balanced between participants; an interrogative utterance made by participant A is followed by an indicative utterance made as a response by B; an indicative utterance made by A may be acknowledged by B with a second indicative utterance. Such balanced sets of utterances are known as "adjacency pairs" (Schegloff and Sacks, 1973) and occurred frequently in the sample conversations. Moreover, in most adjacency pairs the first part of the pair either served to elicit the information given in the second part of the pair or was countered by the second part. It was proposed that these were instances of control by one participant over the other. In the first case the first speaker is seeking to control the information uttered by the respondent, and in the second case the second speaker is influencing the status of a previous utterance.

The direction of control is most clearly visible when information is being elicited; i.e. in "question/answer" (Q/A) adjacency pairs. A question can be seen as a declaration that the speaker has recognized a gap in his knowledge which he wishes to be filled. The question thus serves to constrain the partner to respond with information to fill that gap. Examples of question/answer pairs taken from the sample conversations are given below.

7. *A.* Are you inputting your data from cards?
   U. Yes.
8. *A.* Have you got your monitoring file?
      U. My what?
      A. I want your monitoring file, where it's . . . .
   U. Well, I've got that. These are the only two things that came out.

It will be noted from Example 8 that adjacency pairs do not necessarily consist of adjacent utterances. Indeed, nested pairs occurred fairly frequently in our sample interactions.

A second type of adjacency pair which occurred with some frequency consists of two statements, the second statement being a contradiction or amendment to the first. Thus the second utterance can be seen as a control on the validity of the information presented in the initial utterance. We termed this a "statement/statement" (S/S) adjacency pair, examples of which are given below.

9. *U.* This data should be input from cards.
   A. It would be better to first put the data into a file and input from that.
10. *U.* The computer has ignored the terminator—four dollars.
   A. There is no reason I can see why it wouldn't like dollars. I wouldn't mind them.

The numbers of Q/A and S/S pairs occurring in the 28 conversations were counted, with a note taken of whether the controlling utterance was made by the advisor or the user. For each conversation the scores for the advisor and the user were then expressed as a percentage of the total number of relevant pairs for that conversation. The reliability of the scoring of Q/A and S/S pairs was tested by having a second observer (an advisor who had not been recorded) score a random selection of 14 conversations. It was found that the correlation between the two scorings was very high in both cases (Q/A adjacency pairs: Pearson $r = 0.95, p < 0.01$; S/S adjacency pairs: Pearson $r = 0.91, p < 0.01$). The initial scoring of the full 28 conversations was then used to test the hypothesis that conversations are significantly controlled by advisors.

Figure 5 gives the mean percentage of Q/A and S/S adjacency pairs controlled by advisors and by users. Differences between the percentage of pairs controlled by the advisor and by the user were tested using the Wilcoxon matched-pairs signed-ranks test (Siegel,

1956). This test discounted conversations in which no instances of an index occurred.

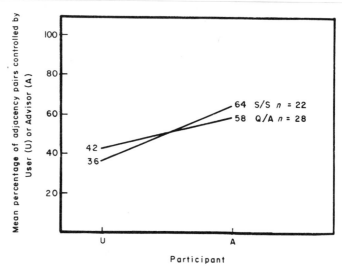

Fig. 5. Analysis by adjacency pairs. (S/S = Statement/Statement; Q/A = Question/Answer.)

It can be seen from Fig. 5 that mean percentages were in the expected direction, with advisors exercising more control than users. However, whilst with the S/S index the difference was significant at above the 1% level (T = 32·5, N = 19) on a two-tailed test, the difference with the Q/A index was not significant (T = 101·3, N = 24).[2]

2. The Explanation of Instructions

Finding a means of testing our second hypothesis by assessing the degree to which operational information was supported by explanation was problematic. The initial requirement was to identify operational instructions, which proved very straightforward. Examples are given below.

11. You should terminate with four *A*s.

12. Don't use a SAVE FILE. Use a normal scratch file.

It was also reasonably easy to identify those utterances which contained some sort of explanation, and it was observed that

[2]   In the Wilcoxon matched-pairs tests, equal pairs of values are discarded from the analysis, hence N is less than n in some cases.

explanations could be purely operational in nature (Example 13) or, more rarely, could involve some conceptual or metaphorical element (Example 14).

13. The fault is not necessarily at that point. You see the computer only checks at certain points in the program.
14. Computer languages are wrapped around each other like the layers of an onion.

It proved very difficult, however, to identify a one-to-one correspondence between an instructional utterance and an explanatory one. Also, there were difficult questions about the acceptable "psychological distance" between two utterances. In order to avoid such complexity, which could have taken years of research to unravel, we decided to classify as "supported" only those operational instructions which were unmistakably related to an explicit explanation in close proximity (up to five advisor/user utterances away). The mean percentage of instructional utterances either supported (IE) or unsupported (I) by explanation is given in Fig. 6.

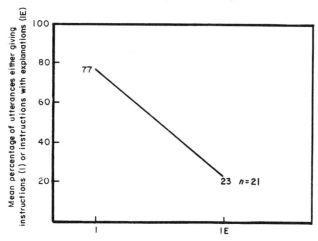

Fig. 6. Analysis of computing advice.

Comparisons between the two classes of instructional utterance were again made using the Wilcoxon test (Siegel, 1956), and there was found to be a difference between instructions given with and without explanatory support which was significant beyond the 1% level ($T = 31{\cdot}4$, $N = 20$).

A final analysis was made of the Q/A, S/S and I/IE data to determine whether there were differences between the four advisors in the control they exercised over conversations or in the degree to which they gave explanatory support to their instructional statements. Comparisons between advisors were made using the Kruskal-Wallis non-parametric analysis of variance (Siegel, 1956), and no significant differences were found (Q/A: $H = 2\cdot57$, 3df, ns; S/S: $H = 2\cdot65$, 3df, ns; I/IE: $H = 0\cdot68$, 3df, ns).

3. Characterizing Users

The above analysis confirmed our observation that the advice given face-to-face in the advisory service usually consists of unsupported

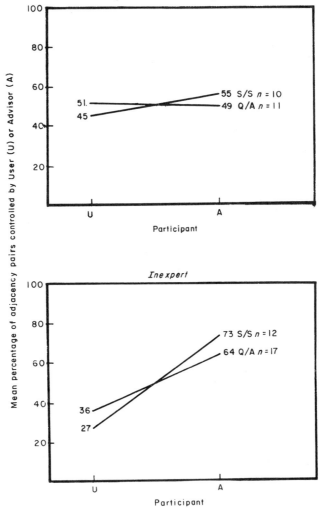

Fig. 7. Adjacency pair analysis of users at different levels of expertise.

instructions, but there was conflicting statistical support for the proposition that advisors dominated interactions. The latter result was surprising given that in 13 of the 28 conversations over 80% of questions were asked by the advisor, which supported the general impression of many users that they had been given few opportunities to actively contribute to the conversation. Of the two indices of control, the Q/A measure ought to have confirmed this impression. This contradiction was taken as sufficient ground to suspect that the sample contained different types of conversation, with differing degrees of advisor control. The most likely candidate for an independent variable for classifying conversations was that of user expertise, given its effects on user attitudes reported in Section IV. It was accordingly decided to re-analyse the quantitative data on control and content of conversations on the basis of user expertise.

All 28 users were rated for expertise on a five-point scale by three advisors who were familiar with the users but had not taken part in recordings. A high level of agreement was found between the advisors' ratings, a coefficient of reliability derived from analysis of variance being above 0·95 (Burroughs, 1971, p. 77). The users were then divided at the mode into two groups, with all users falling on the mode, or to the inexpert side of it, being counted as inexpert, and the remaining users being counted as expert. This gave a conservative measure of expertise. The resulting mean percentages for Q/A and S/S adjacency pairs after this division of users are given in Fig. 7. A similar division was carried out on the supported/unsupported instructions data (Fig. 8).

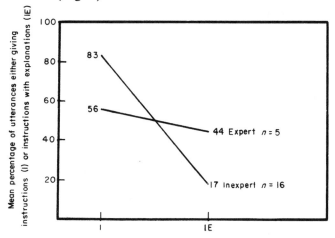

Fig. 8. Analysis of computing advice by expertise.

Comparisons within the groups were again made using the Wilcoxon matched-pairs signed-ranks test. A direct comparison using parametric statistics was contemplated but rejected on the grounds that the expertise measure gave poor discrimination around the modal value. The analysis should thus be regarded as a test of effects with a group of very expert users and a test of effects with the remainder of the sample. Using the non-parametric methods it was concluded that advisors exercised more control over conversations with inexpert users (Q/A index: $T = 18.0$, $N = 14$, $p < 0.05$; S/S index: $T = 3.5$, $N = 10$, $p < 0.01$), while control of information flow was fairly well balanced in conversations with expert users (Q/A index: $T = 23.5$, $N = 10$, ns; S/S index: $T = 14.0$, $N = 9$, ns). It was also found that advisors' instructions to inexpert users were rarely supported by explanations ($T = 15.0$, $N = 16$, $p < 0.01$), whereas expert users were given explanations with almost half of their instructions.

E. Validation Studies

Following the foregoing investigations, similar studies were carried out at four additional universities to test the generality of the results. These were selected to include representations of the main differences in organization and staffing found between university computer centres. Recordings were made at:
- Computer Centre, University of Birmingham (15 conversations);
- Computer Centre, Imperial College, University of London (28 conversations);
- Computing Unit, University of Surrey (19 conversations);
- Computer Centre, University College of Swansea (28 conversations).

1. Sampling of Conversations for Validation Studies

(a) Computer Centre, University of Birmingham

The Birmingham site was of particular interest because of its similarity to Liverpool. The Computer Centre has a computer in the same series (an ICL 1906A), with a similar operating system, and is used by people from a similar mix of disciplines.

Fifteen conversations with two advisors were recorded at the Birmingham Advisory Service. Seven conversations were recorded with the first advisor and eight were recorded with the second. Successive users were asked to participate as they entered the advisory office. Immediately after the recording both the user and advisor were individually debriefed and the user was asked to complete the standard questionnaire that had been used at Liverpool. There were no follow-up debriefing sessions.

(b) Computer Centre, Imperial College, University of London

Imperial College was selected because it differed in four important respects from both the Universities of Liverpool and Birmingham:

- The institution has a very strong scientific and technological bias and a strong tradition of computing. Both individual departments and the Computer Centre run intensive courses which have been designed for specific groups of students and have been refined over a number of years. This contrasts with the less intensive courses which are run at Liverpool and Birmingham for users from more varied backgrounds.
- The advisory service is manned by a core of specialist advisors and is open all working hours. These staff divide their week between attending advisory (2½ days), running courses and maintaining applications software. They are supported by three part-time advisors who serve on one day per week. At Liverpool and Birmingham the advisory service is manned by all programming staff for approximately 2½ days each, every 8 weeks.
- Imperial College is unusual in having a well-established computer education section which has over a long period of time produced a number of well-tried documents to meet the needs of specific groups of users.
- The computing system at Imperial College is complex, consisting of two programmable machines—a CDC Cyber 174 and a CDC 6/500—which are run as a dual configuration.

Twenty-eight conversations were recorded: eight with each of two full-time advisors, five with another full-time advisor, and seven with one of the part-time advisors. The recording procedure was identical with that used at Birmingham, but in addition the participants in a random sample of five interactions were subjected to a thorough follow-up debriefing. Users were also given a more comprehensive questionnaire than had been used at other sites, and certain standard information about each interaction was collected from the advisor via a brief questionnaire rather than verbally.

(c) Computing Unit, University of Surrey

The University of Surrey was selected for the third validation because, although the user population is in many respects similar to

Imperial College, it is a newer university, the computer centre staff work part-time on the advisory service and offer a lower level of educational support. At the time of the study the machines were an ICL 1905F and an ICL 1905E, so that the operating system was similar to that at Liverpool and Birmingham.

Nineteen interactions were recorded with three advisors—seven with each of two advisers and five with one advisor. Sampling and recording procedures were the same as at Imperial College, but there was no follow-up debriefing with a sub-sample of users.

(d) Computer Centre, University College of Swansea

University College of Swansea was of special interest because the advisory service is staffed entirely by four part-time employees, all of them female, who spend all their working time on the advisory service.

Twenty-eight conversations were recorded, with the four advisors contributing seven each. Debriefing sessions with both advisor and user were conducted at the end of an interaction whenever there was time available.

2. Validation Results

(a) Qualitative analysis

Interactions at all four sites bore a close structural similarity to those that had been observed at Liverpool. Almost all of the conversations could be divided into the same three logical episodes: Definition of Query, Formulation of Solution, and Communication of Solution. However, some differences within these episodes were observed and will now be considered.

(i) *Episode 1: Definition of Query.* It may be recalled that at Liverpool the query was almost always presented by the user in a single brief, business-like, unquestioned utterance. There was rarely any informal comment or word of recognition and the interaction was never initiated by the advisor. This pattern was followed very closely at Surrey, but it was noticeable that informal opening remarks were more common in conversations at Birmingham, Imperial College and Swansea. At these three centres irrelevant comments and asides were also more common throughout the conversation. In general though, the user began the interaction and presented his query in a similar way at all sites. This usually involved giving a factual statement about a computing failure or requirement, and on some occasions the user also gave a brief summary of his previous actions or suggested a possible reason or solution for the problem. Any questions asked by the advisor at this stage were almost always designed to identify and define a specific problem.

(ii) *Episode 2: Formulation of Solution.* In the Liverpool conversations it was observed that for most of this episode the advisor was working towards a solution by either collecting background facts or formulating and testing hypotheses. In some conversations there was also a preliminary stage involving identification of sources of information concerning the query. At Birmingham, Surrey and Imperial College the pattern of conduct and interaction was similar to this, with the main activity being the advisor questioning the user, but it was usually impossible to be certain whether the advisor was testing a hypothesis or collecting background facts. However, it was observed that some advisors seemed particularly quick to grasp the precise nature of a problem and to judge the likely cause of it.

The pattern at Swansea was rather different. All advisors appeared to take more care than at other computer centres to ensure that users understood their questions and the purpose behind them. They also made more attempt to ensure that users understood their reasoning when solving a programming problem.

(iii) *Episode 3: Communication of Solution.* The similarity between advisory conversations at different universities was closest in this episode of the interactions. The following findings were found to apply to four of the five centres that have been studied, the exception again being Swansea.

- The advisor usually found and communicated a solution to a user's query. If he did not, he was able to offer recommendations which were almost always regarded as satisfactory by the user.
- The solution to a query usually consisted of a set of operations to be performed by the user. Advisors rarely gave either a conceptual explanation of the solution or an account of how the solution was reached.
- Advisors only infrequently made an explicit check on a user's understanding of the solution or on his ability to carry out the advice.
- Most of the user's questions occurred in this episode of the interaction. Users rarely indicated that they did not understand the advisor's instructions, yet they often returned with the same or very similar problems.

In contrast, advisors at Swansea more often made explicit checks on a user's understanding of a solution. Where failure to understand was detected, the advisors sometimes engaged in lengthy explanations, drawing concepts from the user's application area when this was known. Some noticeable variation in advising style was also detected at Birmingham. For example, on a high proportion of occasions the advisor referred the user to an alternative source of information. This was sometimes for help in solving the immediate problem but more often for future reference and general information. At the other centres it was much less common for users to be referred elsewhere.

Despite the differences which have been briefly outlined above, the advisory conversations recorded at all centres showed remarkably similar characteristics. All of them were strongly goal-directed, their main purpose being to find a definite answer to a definite problem. This functional similarity determined the structural similarity, with most of the interactions being limited to a single pass through the three episodes without iteration. From this evidence it is reasonable to assume that both advisors and users at all centres hold a similar view of the role of the advisory service.

(b)   Quantitative analysis

The pattern of quantitative results also displayed considerable similarity between centres. The Q/A measure again indicated that advisors exercised significantly more control over conversations than inexpert users, and that the flow of control was by contrast fairly well balanced in interactions involving expert users. However, the measure using the S/S adjacency pairs strongly indicated advisor control over conversations at Liverpool but not at any other centres. Indeed, the S/S pairs were found to be much less frequent at other centres, and this often invalidated statistical comparison between advisors and users. It must be concluded that the advisors' tendency to dominate interactions by modifying or contradicting users' statements is only noticeable at Liverpool, whereas at all centres advisors exercise control by asking most of the questions. These findings only apply to interactions involving expert users.

F. Summary and Initial Conclusions

Our first objective in this study was to discover whether advisory interactions between different advisors and users, concerning different computing problems, were sufficiently similar to be regarded as an identifiable category of face-to-face encounter.

The study of conversations between advisors and users at five university sites has indicated that the "advisory interaction" is indeed a clearly identifiable form of exchange. Moreover, it is identifiable both in terms of the goals or objectives of the participants and also the general structure of the interaction. The only major differences identified were related to the expertise of the user, but even in this case the resulting conversations may be seen as variations upon a single theme rather than separate types of interaction. Differences were only clearly discernible at the lowest level of structure, as the higher level goals were found to be uniform.

The analysis of participant goals revealed that the conversations were structured as a simple form of face-to-face problem-solving session. This structure usually consisted of a single pass through three episodes, which exhibited the following characteristics:

(i)   *Definition of Query* – the query was usually presented as a statement of fact with limited evidence. This query definition by the user was rarely explicitly questioned by the advisor.

(ii) *Formulation of Solution* – this involved a detailed search for additional information by the advisor in a manner which often left the user confused.

(iii) *Communication of Solution* – this was often a very brief stage in which the user was told how to solve the query. Little attempt was made by the advisor either to check the user's understanding or to explain how the particular solution was derived.

We found that there was moderate advisor control over the whole sample of conversations and that the advice given was largely operational in nature. However, some conversations showed marked differences from these conclusions. Investigations revealed that the users associated with these conversations were generally regarded as expert by all advisors, and we hypothesized that user expertise was significantly affecting the nature of the advisory interaction.

A re-analysis of the conversations grouped by a conservative measure of expertise showed that:

– there was far more advisor control with inexpert users;

– the information communicated to inexpert users was highly operational in nature;

– conversations between advisors and expert users were more balanced, with control being shared between participants;

– advisors gave more explanations to expert users than to inexperts.

These results lead to a number of interesting conclusions about the nature and function of the advisory service. The service appears to function rather narrowly as a problem-solving institution, and as such works well for both expert and inexpert users. However, there is considerable room for advisors to develop greater flexibility of response, particularly when dealing with less experienced users. These users often failed to appreciate the reasoning behind problem solutions and were thus unable to generalize the advice to other problems. Advisors usually omitted to check effectively for user understanding or to give useful explanations in support of their advice to inexpert users. It therefore seems that the very people who would most benefit from explanation and sensitive guidance do not receive it, and that a real improvement in the efficiency of the advisory service might result from training advisors to recognize common comprehension difficulties and to supply appropriate explanations. Such training should in addition serve to raise the status of the advisory function and improve advisor motivation.

VI. IMPROVING COMMUNICATION BETWEEN ADVISORS AND USERS

From the research reported in the previous sections it was concluded that problems of advisory services were primarily concerned with communication rather than with advisors' ability to solve problems. In this section we aim to identify a number of significant communication difficulties between advisors and novice users and to suggest some possible causes and solutions.

All face-to-face interactions can be seen as being partially controlled by sets of social and institutional rules. In the case of advisory services these are largely implicit and have evolved over a number of years. They serve to define such factors as the limits of an advisor's responsibility (the advisor's role) and the behaviour to be expected from a user (the user's role).

Until recently most university computer users possessed a first degree in a science subject, were concerned with numerical applications, and wrote their own programs. Moreover, many of them were interested in computing for its own sake and were therefore prepared to invest considerable effort in becoming familiar with their local system. This is no longer the case. A significant and growing proportion of users now come from the social sciences, medicine, and the arts (and the proportion of social science users with arts backgrounds is increasing). Such users typically have a low level of computing knowledge, want to use the computer as a tool with as little groundwork as possible, and do not share the advisors' "scientific" culture. The assumptions traditionally made by advisors, that users have a sound basic knowledge of computing and that their problems are ones of fact rather than a lack of basic skills and concepts, are no longer valid.

The style of advisory interaction that has followed from these assumptions has several undesirable features for the inexpert user which are particularly serious when he is also a social scientist. These include:

— limited personal contact with advisors;
— little attempt to ensure that the user understands the cause of his problem or the derivation of the solution;
— little attempt to ensure that the user can recall or follow the operational details of the advice;
— little attempt to extend the user's knowledge.

Although our research has been able to identify these difficulties, the solutions are not necessarily easy to find. The problems listed imply that a solution would involve the advisor taking on the role of a teacher to a certain extent. However, there are important differences between teaching and advising. A teacher's primary goal is usually student understanding rather than simply ensuring that students can successfully perform a fixed set of actions. Teaching is thus organized, notionally at least, to allow plenty of time for explanation. Advisors, on the other hand, are often pressed for time. Extended explanations at "teaching" sessions would not be well received by other users queueing for solutions. Furthermore, a teacher usually knows in advance the answers to problems set for students, whereas an advisor has to discover the answer, or an answer, before he can communicate it to the user. Thus the advisor cannot plan any specific educational objectives in advance.

If we accept the limitations on the advisors' time, and the importance of some teaching element in the advice given, advisors will have to be able to rapidly identify deficiences in users' knowledge and where possible supply succinct explanations. They need to be familiar with a range of expressions, metaphors and analogies which can quickly communicate simple points or complex concepts to the user. During our studies of advisory interactions there were many occasions when a brief explanation would, we feel, have transformed a user's understanding. It was therefore decided to make a detailed analysis of a sample of our recorded advisory conversations, to isolate some common causes of communication failure and suggest possible techniques for avoiding such failure. This information could then be incorporated into a training course for advisors.

A. An Analysis of Common Communication Problems

The following sections illustrate and summarize some common communication problems experienced at all five university sites. These problems are discussed with reference to both the recorded conversations and the questionnaire data, and lead to a number of recommendations for improving advisory services.

1. *Emotional Tone of Interactions*

The overriding objective of advisory conversations is, of course, the solving of queries, and most mental activity is directed towards this end. It is therefore not surprising that interactions are mainly concerned with the exchange of factual information, with "personal" contact between advisors and users being limited to a mutual nod of the head as the user approaches or leaves the advisory desk. However, this style of interaction does not solely result by default from advisors' concern with problem-solving, but appears to be positively encouraged—users at Liverpool who attempted to develop closer relationships often claimed that they failed to obtain any positive response.

From our interviews with users at all stages of the study, it was clear that an impersonal style of interaction was appreciated by expert users. Expert users usually attended the service knowing what they wanted from the advisor. Moreover, they could usually communicate their needs effectively and did not expect the advisor to guide them closely while they applied the solution. The needs of inexpert users, however, were very different. They were often not sure what information they wanted, yet attached considerable importance to presenting their query in a form which would sound reasonable to the computer professional. Many inexperienced users also wanted the advisor to supervise their application of the advice in order to ensure success.

The present style of advisory interaction has the effect of maintaining, or even increasing, anxiety in novice users. This appears to have three unfortunate effects upon their ability to benefit from an interaction. First, anxiety will reinforce the common tendency for an inexperienced user to aim at short-term solutions to his programming problems, rather than aiming at long-term improvements in programming effectiveness. On several occasions it was observed that inexperienced users failed to take full advantage of the opportunity to follow up their doubts about the basic design of a program, the interaction with the advisor being limited to discussing the details of a given failure. Secondly, it was noted that the most anxious users were slow to learn the "rules of the house". These implicit rules governed such factors as the time advisors expected users to work on a problem before attending advisory, the type of query which was acceptable at advisory and the extent of advisor involvement in user education. Thirdly, the anxious users were less open during the information-gathering phase of an interaction. This meant that advisors sometimes obtained inaccurate or restricted information, which could be misleading during the problem-solving stage.

From the above, it may be concluded that a significant group of users would benefit from a more positive emotional atmosphere in the advisory service. We have considered a variety of ways of achieving this, bearing in mind lack of expense, ease of implementation and expected effectiveness. The following suggestions meet these three criteria in full:

— The link between advisor and user could be made more personal by providing users with useful details about advisory staff. Relevant information would include advisors' names, professional responsibilities, areas of expertise and timetable of advisory duty. These details could be published in the computer centre newsletter and a user handout. Users could also be helped to identify individual advisors by the placing of photographs on the computer centre notice-board and nameplates on the advisory desk.

— The quality of interactions could be improved by seating the advisor and user next to each other rather than either side of the advisory desk. This would discourage confrontation—many advisors have complained of the aggressiveness of certain users—and aid user involvement in problem-solving by making it easy for both participants to view print-out or documentation. Further improvement could be obtained by having a glass partition around the advisory area. This is now the case at the University of Birmingham, where it has significantly improved the quality of interaction by increasing participants' sense of involvement and reducing pressure from other users waiting for a consultation. (At both the Universities of Surrey and Swansea the advisory service has its own room, with side-by-side seating for advisors and users, and at these centres the atmosphere was noticeably more relaxed and friendly than at Liverpool or Imperial College).

— At the start of an interaction it is important that the advisor should give the user his whole attention. Lack of attention is usually interpreted (quite reasonably) by the user as showing a lack of interest in the interaction. Full attention will help the user to relax and follow the advisor's reasoning, and so help him to retain information from the session.

— There are several actions an advisor could take which would improve the affective quality of interactions as well as providing him with detailed background knowledge about the user and his problems. These include: (i) ensuring the user knows how to prepare for a consultation, e.g. what documents to bring; (ii) asking for feedback on the advice (and positively following up a query which has been referred); and (iii) allowing time towards the end of an advisory session to "talk around" the problem. The latter activity could give valuable information on the limits of a user's knowledge and his reasons for adopting a particular computing method, as well as making him feel more at ease with the advisor.

In contrast to the impersonal and business-like exchanges usually observed in advisory services, the following recorded excerpt displays a refreshing friendliness between participants. The conversation concerns a user's difficulty in accessing a file. It is hoped that this style of interaction would become more common with the implementation of the above proposals.

15. *U*: You misled me on Thursday Steve.
 A: Ha ha, that's a good start.
 U: Yes, you er . . . you told me it was PTR "O", in fact it's PTR zero.
 A: Ah.
 U: (*Indistinctly*.) Papertape reader zero so er . . . .
 A: O.K., fair enough. I'm glad we've settled that one once and for all. (*Pause*.) Did you get it working after the second time?
 U: Well you can see what happened yourself from the day file which I've just collected.

. . . .

 U: Is that output normally picked up by Reception?
 A: Er . . . it should be, but sometimes . . . .
 U: There's nothing in the er . . . pigeon hole.

A: If you go down and see Reception, er . . . see Peter Ball, or Heather. I'm not sure whether she's still here, yes Heather's still here, or Maureen, you know Maureen?

U: No.

A: Maureen is the forty-year-old one who works part-time. Now those three know what's going on, we've got a lot of new staff down there and it's possible that they don't understand, that they've got to look for output from the TASK, O.K., so in which case the cleaners probably get it.

U: Ah well that's probably not the case because this was on the floor since Thursday.

A: Mmm, quite amazing.

....

A: Hang on I'll just get er . . . . (*Pause.*) Yes P86 is one of the directories which have been tampered with.

U: Not my copy of STARTREK?

A: Er . . . what's the password on it?

U: There isn't a password on it.

A: Ah hard luck! Well somebody's had that by now. Yeah, somebody's got into your number. Please, I'm telling you as a friend not to advertise the fact, don't tell anyone I've told you. Change your password, don't tell anyone why you're doing it.

2. *Identifying the Real Query*

Queries were usually presented to the advisor either in terms of an operational failure or in terms of a request for an operational item of information. This applied to all users, irrespective of their level of expertise. However, while expert users were usually able to correctly identify their "real" problem and to frame an appropriate question, inexpert users often found it difficult to express themselves. Rather than presenting their query in an ambiguous manner, they preferred to present a particular portion of their problem that could be expressed in fairly concrete, operational terms, so failing to convey their real problem, which was often conceptual in nature.

Example 16a illustrates a typical programming query presented by an inexperienced user

16a. *U*: What I wanted to do now was changing noughts to ones and ones to noughts, and then do something with them. Now one way I could . . . I thought of was stating IF "X1" . . . suppose this is "X1", that's "X1 + 1" and if it is "1" then "X1-1".

      A: Why don't you say "X1 = 0" or "X1 = 1"?

Here the user presented his query as a request for advice on techniques for changing "noughts to ones and ones to noughts". His query appeared to concern logical programming method. The advisor therefore proceeded to answer the problem as such, indicating that it could be done either by using IF statements or integer division. However, it was later revealed that the user already knew of both these methods. His "real" concern was to find out which method was more efficient, as he was planning to make a very large number of conversions in his program. The advisor eventually discovered this concern with machine efficiency, but only after he had expended considerable time and effort in telling the user what he already knew.

How may this situation be avoided? Perhaps the clearest clue to the "real" query in such cases is a discourse structure which is frequently present but usually ignored. Many inexperienced users followed the operational description of their problem with a "comment"; this gave general information on either the context of the problem or the user's assessment of the validity of his query. Example 16b below illustrates this; it follows the previous passage and contains the user's "comment" that he was interested in finding a method of swopping 0s and 1s which would "save time".

16b. *U*: Yes "X1 = 0" or "1", and changing it over to the other one and that involves a lot of IF statements that I reckon will take a lot of time. . . . I want to save that time. Can you suggest any other way?

It is difficult to see how the user could have been more explicit about his real needs, and yet at a detailed debriefing the advisor stated that he "didn't really notice that saving time was that important".

On occasions when a user finds it difficult to formulate his general problem, the meaning of an error message often provides a concrete question to present at advisory. In example 17a the user's FORTRAN program has failed with a "Run Time Fault":

17a. *U*: I've tried it several times, it er . . . it gives a Run Fault Time, what is that? A Run Time Fault.

A: Yes.

U: It says the expression is out of range.

A: Yes, but what happens is that it only checks these things at certain points in the program. It does not necessarily imply that it happened exactly on that line. So . . . what could it be? (*Pause.*) It could be that it's undefined. Yes . . . mm . . . .

U: I was thinking probably the Cafeteria system was unable to handle the calculations.

After delivering his problem the user's "comment" concerned the possible limitations of the Cafeteria system (the fast turnround system at Liverpool intended for short jobs and the development of programs). The advisor's reply totally dismissed the user's suspicions, and he began to look for an error in the program:

17b. *A*: I doubt it, actually. It is probably checking something that you would get away with on the batch system but would be wrong in fact and you might not know about it. (*Pause.*) I think what's probably happened is that one of the elements of this array has not been allocated a value. Now just how that's happened could take some time to figure out. (*Pause.*) That seems O.K. actually. A possibility is, you see, that "M" is 16 here when the program fails, and that statement says that if "M" is greater than 15 go to "26". Now, could that statement have been obeyed before these elements were assigned values? Here . . . this loop . . . .

U: Oh.

During debriefing it was revealed that the user was a complete beginner and had modified his program on three occasions to allow for imagined limitations of the Cafeteria system—the advisor could have discovered this and adjusted his advice accordingly if he had followed up the user's doubts about the Cafeteria system. The user had in fact begun to suspect that the faults were in his programming rather than with the system, but he had not known how to formulate this into a specific question. By omitting to follow up the user's comment the advisor missed two significant educational opportunities: (i) to explain about the use and meaning of job control parameters and the Liverpool macro for controlling input/ output; (ii) to suggest useful techniques for debugging FORTRAN programs.

In conversations recorded at all centres, several other instances were noticed where the advisor missed opportunities to follow up the user's comments and so failed to get closer to the real query. More education and less misunderstanding could well result if advisors were more sensitive to such comments and doubts—however unfounded they seem—and if they concentrated less on problem-solving until they were certain they were attacking the "real" problem. Such strategies would not necessarily take more time, as much work involved in solving superficial or "wrong" problems would be saved, and in the long term of course, advisors would be less troubled by sequences of "trivial" queries resulting from users' misconceptions.

3. Checking for Understanding

The communication problems which often arose from over-concrete presentation of queries by novice users were compounded by:
- the tendency of advisors to avoid conceptual explanations of their advice;
- the failure of advisors to effectively check for understanding.

Both these characteristics were observed at all stages of interactions but their effect was most serious when the advisor's conclusions were being given to the user. The results of failure to give any conceptual explanation or to check for understanding are illustrated in Example 18.

The user in this case was a psychologist who was using SPSS (Statistical Package for the Social Sciences) to analyse experimental data. She had no experience of computing beyond an introductory SPSS course run by the computer centre and had only run two jobs prior to her attendance at advisory.

18a. *U*: I don't understand why I haven't got any output, there aren't any error messages.

A: Have you got your monitoring file?

U: My what?

A: I want your monitoring file, where it's . . . .

U: Well, I've got that. These are the only two things that came out.

A: (*Pause.*) Is this the first time you've run it?

U: I don't know. What I wanted . . . .

A: You've input your data into that?

U: Mmm.

A: So you've no data in your job?

U: So what should I have done?

It was clear to the advisor at the start of the conversation that the user was very inexperienced (from her not knowing about monitoring files and her blank responses to questions). As the conversation continued it became evident that the job had been run from cards and had failed because the program had not been able to access the data. This had happened because the user had not known the difference between saving the data by putting it into her filestore (a GEORGE file) and saving it along with the program by putting it into an SPSS file. The advisor informed her that the job had failed because it had tried to access a GEORGE file with an SPSS file-handling command. However, there was no explanation of the difference between these two types of file, nor any explicit check of the user's understanding of the difference (Example 18b).

18b. *U*: What I wanted was to make a file of the data so that I could use it again.

   A: That's fine. This parameter "SF" is for saving a file. O.K.?

   U: Yes.

   A: Which isn't where your data is, so this should actually be "DATA=". Instead of "SF" you should have "DATA=".

   U: What, "SPSS DATA="?

   A: Yes, "SPSS DATA=ATTITUDE1". Were you actually planning to save the file?

   U: Yes, I thought so, so that I wouldn't need to use the cards over and over again.

   A: Oh! No, there's two ways of saving a file. I mean, you're putting this into a GEORGE file and that will be there, O.K.? Just from having input that once, that will now be there. In fact, you won't have to input it again.

   U: What, you mean that will be there anyway, despite the fact I've got this?

   A: Yes, because you've input. O.K.? And the second thing is that you can save all this information, descriptions of the variables and the data in an SPSS "SAVE FILE", and that's why you need to save that.

   U: I don't think I'm necessarily bothered about that.

   A: No. Then as long as you want to define these every time you don't need the "SAVE FILE", and you don't need the "SF" parameter.

   U: Hmm.

The only check on understanding made in this passage was the tag-question "O.K.?", which occurred three times. Our research has shown that users habitually answer "Yes" to this, even if they do not understand. In the present case, the user's lack of understanding became evident later in the conversation when she declared that she would access data stored in the GEORGE file "ATTITUDE1" with the SPSS "GET FILE" command (Example 18c).

18c. *U*: Yes, you do that "GF" thing. Get file.

   A: No. That's only if you save a file, there are two different ways of saving it. You can just save your data, put it in a GEORGE file, then it's more or less equivalent to reading it from the deck, except instead of reading it from a card reader it then goes to the file and reads it. O.K.? But within SPSS, you can also save all this information plus your data and produce a file.

   U: So it's not appropriate, that "SF"?

> *A*: Well if you do that, you put an "SF=" parameter on it, and put all
> that information into a file, O.K.? And then you'd use a "GF" to
> get that file back again. O.K.?
> *U*: I was getting confused. Does this contain all I need apart from the
> SPSS things that need changing?

There are many techniques that an advisor could use for verbally checking understanding. The weakest of these is "O.K.?", but more explicit phrases such as "Do you understand?" and "Is that all right?" are not much more effective and fail for a number of reasons. First, we found that users would often answer "Yes", knowing that they did not understand but hoping that the positive response would keep the advisor talking or working on the problem and that the meaning would eventually become clear. Secondly, it is often not clear to an inexperienced user what would constitute understanding. In such cases the user may honestly answer "Yes", although his "comprehension" is in fact slight or even non-existent. Thirdly, we found occasions where a user knew that he did not understand, but believed he had gained sufficient information to be able to solve the problem for himself.

These simple methods of checking for understanding thus fail because they make it unlikely that the advisor will discover the user's actual level of understanding. They thereby encourage a common reluctance among users to express their own lack of knowledge and understanding. This reticence is increased by users' perception of advisors as being reluctant to spend time giving tutorial explanations, and compounded by the high intellectual esteem with which advisors are held. Few people are happy to explicitly reveal their ignorance to an acknowledged expert.

From observations made at one particular university computer centre, where the advisors adopted a more tutorial role towards novice users, we have evidence that other forms of comprehension checking can be much more effective. These techniques involve the use of questions which directly query the user's understanding by making an explicit reference to the operation or concept under consideration. The simple act of referring to a particular part of the advice or instruction appears to have the desired effect of forcing a user to examine his understanding. It also gives the impression that the advisor really is interested in whether the user understands, and is not just expressing a conversational formality. An illustration of this type of checking is given below:

> 19a. *A*: Well have you . . . have you followed the way I've done the program
> now?

U: Ye-ah.

A: That you start off with your job card as you've been told there, and your Cafe FORTRAN card, and then this program section, which is really only used for telling the READs and WRITEs . . . .

U: Yeah . . . do I have to write this pro . . . this . . . ?

A: No, it will put it in by default so you can . . . you needn't bother to put that in.

Here the advisor responds to a note of doubt in the user's reply ("Ye-ah") to the first general question by enumerating the individual items of procedural advice previously given. This method of checking can be extended by including a question which explicitly requests factual information from the user. In Example 19b for instance, the advisor asks the user to explain the difference between real numbers and integers. The user's misconception is thus forced into the open, so giving the advisor an opportunity to define the difference and avoiding confusion at a later stage.

19b. *A*; You've been told about integers and reals have you?

U: Yeah.

A: You know the . . . the difference between them? Can you tell me what the difference is?

U: Er . . . er the real number is just a number by istelf, the integer is if it's got a decimal point.

A: No, in fact that's the wrong way round.

U: It's the wrong way round.

A: Integers are the numbers one, two, three, four, five, etc., and negatives as well of course, and reals are . . . one point nought, one point one; any number with a decimal point in is a real number, O.K.?

U: Yeah.

Explicit checks for understanding are also helpful *before* giving a certain piece of advice, so that its expression and terminology can be adjusted to the user's level of knowledge. In Example 20 the advisor checks the user's knowledge and then tries to modify the advice accordingly. (The user has been inputting data to someone else's program, and cannot understand the error message "Reservation Violation" or what caused it.).

20a. *A*: I can tell you what this means, the most likely thing is that you've got er . . . do you know about dimensions?

U: No.

A: Oh.

A few minutes later:

20b. *A*: The thing is . . . if he has only allowed for 32 sets of data and you've got 74 . . . .

U: Yes.
A: Then that could well do it, because . . . . I don't know how much programming you've done?
U: Well, not much.
A: Well, have you met vectors and matrices?
U: Yes.
A: Yeah, well all   you do in effect . . . you dimension your thing, suppose you call it "X" and if that "X" there says 32 or something . . . .
U: Yes.
A: Allowing for 32 cases, then if you try to go above that it will say . . . aah . . . can't do it, and in fact it will try to do it . . . and it will go into the area of the program, actually programming code, and then will come up with this message to say it's a Reservation Violation, in other words you've gone into a part of the program that you're not supposed to be in.
U: I see, so that could very well be it.

This more tactful and more specific approach to questioning enables the advisor to obtain the necessary information about the user, while at the same time allowing the user to maintain his self-esteem and encouraging further use of the advisory service. It also allows the advisor to adjust his advice to the user's level of knowledge and highlights gaps and inaccuracies in the user's understanding, which the advisor can attempt to remedy by explanation or by referring the user to an appropriate alternative source of information.

4. *The Importance of Clear Instructions*

The giving of confused, or confusing, instructions was another major cause of communication failure between advisors and users at all university sites. However, in this case the difficulty did not necessarily originate with the advisor, because many computing facilities possess features which are either arbitrary or appear arbitrary in the absence of an overall understanding of the system. Nevertheless, advisors did little to dispel these difficulties but often seemed to exaggerate and compound them. Example 21 gives an illustration of some extremely confusing instructions.

21. A: If you . . . you want to remove all records concerning the Smith family from the file, type "T" followed by "C" for record, that's a case, followed by the string "Smith", surrounded by delimiters, any will do of course, though avoid those in the file, and then passover that record with a "P" command, then repeat as often

as necessary. Yes that will get rid of it, but you could do it by numbers, but that would not be as good.

U: Umm.

In this conversation, an inexperienced user wanted to know how to use the GEORGE editor to remove all records relating to the Smith family from his file (a record of club membership). In this instance the advice is not only incomplete but contains many features which could give difficulty even to an experienced user. Some of these sources of possible confusion are:

(i) The use of technical terms which are not necessarily known to the user. Is the *string* "Smith" the same as the name "Smith"? Is a *record* necessarily the same as a case? What is a *delimiter?* The user may or may not know the precise meaning of these terms, but the advisor does not know how much the user knows because he has not tried to find out.

(ii) The omission of relevant information. "Followed by C for record" gives no indication of what the "C" stands for. The user may well believe it stands for "Case" rather than for the "record Containing a certain string of characters".

(iii) The inclusion of irrelevant information. There are two instances of this. The instruction concerned with delimiters is qualified twice—"any will do", "though avoid those in the file"— which is irrelevant and meaningless unless the user already knows the allowable set of delimiters, in which case the qualification is not worth mentioning. The second irrelevance—"you could do it by numbers"—is even more confusing, and questions the validity of the entire set of instructions. However, having confused the user by introducing this alternative, the advisor then informs him that it "would not be as good"; so tempting one to ask why he bothered to mention it at all.

(iv) The switching of contexts between computing terms and applications terms. "Followed by 'C' for record, that's a case, followed by the string 'Smith' ". The case here refers to the user's problem domain, whereas both "record" and "string" are strictly computing terminology. Such sudden shifting of contexts can be extremely confusing because it does not help the user to differentiate clearly between concepts in his problem area and computing concepts. Thus he may well believe that the computer can recognize a case as an entity, which is not the case in a GEORGE file, where a case may well spread over several records. To give good explanations and help understanding it is certainly necessary to relate the computing context to the context of the user's problem, but the distinction must be made explicit and the sudden unsignalled switching of contexts should be avoided.

In addition to all these sources of confusion, which would certainly inhibit correct recall of the information, the advisor omitted to write down the editing instructions for the user. The user was thus expected to remember six distinct items of information ("T", "C" for record, the string "Smith", any delimiters, "P" for passover, repeat as necessary), which is about the limit of memory for unfamiliar information even when presented under ideal conditions (Miller, 1956). Most advisory situations are of course far from ideal, the user usually having to divide his attention between trying to understand the advice and trying to process it for later recall. Moreover, he may be doing this while being distracted by other activities taking place around the advisory desk.

The problems illustrated above were common to very many advisory interactions. They arise from the tendency of advisors to talk as though the user already knew all about the subject area (e.g. editing) but for some reason had temporarily forgotten the information. Advisors tend to make many assumptions (often unconsciously) about what the user already knows, yet it is usually evident that if the user knew half of what the advisor assumed he knew, the user would not have needed to ask his query in the first place. Advisors can minimize these problems by avoiding the sources of confusion outlined above, and by following the principles of clear instruction and communication summarized below:

(i)   ensure that the user knows the contextual meaning of the words used;

(ii) ensure that the user can remember (or keep a copy of) the information being given;

(iii) keep the context of the information consistent (or make changes of context explicit);

(iv) avoid irrelevance.

B. Common Comprehension Problems of Inexpert Users

We have said little so far about which aspects of computing cause most serious comprehension difficulties for inexpert users, as this has not been the focus of our research. However, in the course of our investigations we have obtained information from a variety of sources (observation and analysis of advisory interactions; observation and evaluation of various programming and computing courses; interviews with users; personal experiences), and have acquired some insight into the difficulties which commonly confuse inexpert users, especially novices. We will say nothing about the problems of teaching and learning programming, as du Boulay and O'Shea provide a thorough review of this topic in Chapter 4. However, programming is only one aspect of computing, and it is not necessarily the one that gives novice users the greatest difficulty. We have identified, at a general level, certain categories of problems that confuse novice users, and shall now suggest some ways in which they may be helped to understand and avoid these problems.

1. *The Problem of Context*

We have already commented on the confusion that advisors may induce by suddenly switching between the context of computing and the context of the user's problem. There are also several different operational contexts within a computing system itself, and these can also be a source of many errors and considerable confusion—for some evidence and discussion see Florentin and Smith (1978). One of the commonest experiences in computing is to do the right thing in the wrong place, e.g. to give an editing command when the machine is not in editing mode. This type of mistake is very easily spotted and rectified by an experienced user, but novices find it confusing as it often produces an error message which bears no relation to their intended operation. Moreover, attempts to establish a relationship between the two often lead the user to develop elaborate and erroneous models of the machine's operation. Such models can prevent a novice from acquiring an accurate picture of the machine and can lead to more errors when used to generate further responses to the machine. The problem was well illustrated in Example 18, where the user was confusing commands which are specific to SPSS with general operating system commands.

There are at least three ways in which advisors can help users to avoid this kind of confusion. First, they can explain the functions of the different contexts and make clear the relations between them. The ability to give clear explanations at a general level is not easily defined or acquired, but the use of diagrams often has valuable explanatory power when verbal description fails. Figure 9 shows a diagram that the advisor in Example 18 could have quickly drawn to help the user understand her error. It should be emphasized that such

Sequence of
punched cards:

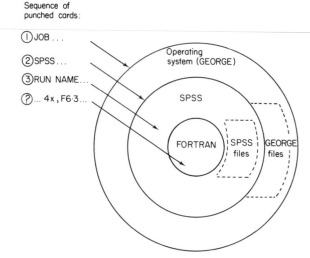

Fig. 9. Rough illustration of different computing contexts. (Note that this diagram applies specifically to the use of SPSS, and does not represent the overall system organization.)

diagrams need not be very accurate, but they can often succeed in conveying concepts when words are cumbersome and ineffective. Alternatively, analogies can be useful for illustrating concepts, again without having to be particularly accurate. For example, the various modes of operation of a tape-recorder (play, record, stop, rewind, etc.) may help a user to understand the different states of an interactive computer system (execution, input, halted, edit, etc.) and the rules which govern them, although it should be pointed out that such analogies will usually break down if they are carried too far.

Secondly, when the user clearly understands the nature of the different computing contexts, the advisor should still indicate the status and function of particular computing instructions. For example, he should state whether a command is to be interpreted by the operating system or by a particular language or package.

Thirdly, advisors can help users to avoid future errors by thinking about the reason for a particular error and diagnosing a general problem rather than just giving a particular solution. For example, if a user has incorrectly punched his data starting in column 7, it will probably be because he has over-generalized the rule that statements in a FORTRAN program should start in column 7. It may also mean that he cannot differentiate between FORTRAN statements and other kinds of information such as operating system commands. A useful piece of general advice to all inexpert users, when trying to trace their own errors, would be to "check the context"; in other words, as well as checking that all the statements and instructions are correct, check that they are in the correct place.

2. The Problem of Procedure

One type of comment frequently made by users was that they knew more or less what they wanted to do and how to do it, but that they weren't sure how to start off, or what order to do things in. For example, when being taught how to use a package, users would be able to grasp the various functions of the package and the instructions for carrying them out, but they were often uncertain how to begin. Many packages have their internal operations and sequences of instructions detailed at great length, but the method of implementing them on a particular machine is often poorly documented. Similarly, on programming courses the details of a particular language are usually discussed at length, but the mechanics of actually running a program on the machine are barely mentioned. Often a sequence of commands is dictated, or maybe pre-punched cards are distributed, which are simply to be added to the program to get it to run. Very little information is given about the functional details of these mysterious additions to the program.

Given this background it is scarcely surprising that users have difficulty in following through their operation from beginning to end. What they require is some form of check-list of *all* the steps to be taken, in the correct order. The level of detail necessary will of course depend on the user's experience and expertise. For novice users, the check-list ought to include physical actions such as where to go to submit a job, what cards to put on the top and bottom of the deck, what tray to put the cards in, and where to collect the output. Such apparently trivial steps are frequently overlooked when instructing new users. Similarly, when explaining more complex procedures to more experienced users, it is easy to overlook the small but critical details at the beginning and end of an operation, yet it is these that tend to give users the most difficult problems and cause them to seek further advice.

Advisors can help users by writing down in order all the steps to be taken in a particular operation (e.g. editing, using a package, running a program), so that the user knows how to start and finish as well as all the intermediate details. Additionally, by outlining the function of each step and so relating the procedure to the context, the advisor can give some idea of what is happening at each stage of the operation, and what part of the system is involved at each point.

3. The Problem of Alternatives

Many computing objectives can be achieved in a variety of ways, but this useful flexibility can be a source of confusion when learning to use a computer system. Novice users often seem to expect there to be one way and only one way of doing things using a computer. Because of this, many of them continue to persevere with the one method they know even though it may become highly inappropriate. On the other hand, presenting users with alternatives before they understand the need for them can be extremely confusing. This is illustrated in Examples 18 and 21, where the advisor presents alternative possibilities even though it is evident that the user needs and wants just one method (the simplest) for achieving his objective. The user in such cases does not want to be faced with an unnecessary choice which he is not qualified to make.

We have observed a student on a FORTRAN course punch all the numbers from 10 to 99 on to cards because they were presented in the problem as data, and he thought that data always had to be read-in using a READ statement. He knew that a number could be assigned to a variable and then incremented, but did not think to do this because he conceived of the data as being necessarily distinct from the program. Obviously this type of situation is to be avoided, but there is no point in presenting all the alternatives before the need for them is perceived by the user. To illustrate the problem, there are at least four ways of getting a FORTRAN program on access data:

(i)   put the data and the program into separate files, and use the operating system to connect the two;
(ii) put the data immediately after the last statement in the program;
(iii) declare the data as variables in the program, and manipulate them as necessary (e.g. by incrementing);
(iv) declare the data in the program via "DATA" statements.

To inform a novice user about all these alternatives would be immensely confusing, yet most users need to know that there is more than one method. The best solution would be to instruct the user in detail about one method only, but to inform him that other methods are available that may be more suitable for more complex problems. The user could then return for further advice when he perceived a need to use one of the alternative methods. As an expert, the advisor or course lecturer should have the knowledge to judge the best method for the user for a particular task, rather than presenting the user with a seemingly arbitrary choice.

4. The Problem of "What Happens in the Machine"

This is a rather vague category of problems that seem to arise from user's ignorance or misconception of what goes on inside the computer. Some understanding of the workings of the machine will help to avoid many errors, and will also help explain rules which otherwise appear arbitrary. For example, if a user knows that editing involves creating a new file rather than altering an existing one, he will understand why certain rules exist, e.g. text that has already been transcribed cannot be altered. Furthermore, if the user has a fairly clear conception of the relevant machine processes, he can deduce rules for himself instead of having to learn them or refer to a document. There are of course various levels of detail at which machine operations can be understood, and for most purposes it is only necessary to have a fairly high-level conceptual understanding of what happens—some idea of the "notional machine". Some ways of characterizing the notional machine to help teach computing concepts have been suggested by du Boulay and O'Shea (1978).

There are no easy solutions to this category of problem. If advisors can identify the cause of a user's error as being due to misconceiving the notional machine, then a rough analogy or conceptual explanation should certainly help, but it seems reasonable to suggest that users should attend an introductory lecture or course to gain some overview of the system before using the computer regularly. Such a course ought to answer elementary questions such as "What happens when I log in?", and "What happens when I run a job?" at a general level, giving the user enough insight into machine processes to use the system competently without overloading him with a mass of detail about machine operations.

There is obviously some overlap between this type of problem and the other categories of problem discussed above, which are by no means independent. A good understanding of machine processes ought to reduce the number of errors in each category, particularly those due to misconstruing the operational context. Even the most thorough comprehension of a computing system will not eliminate errors, but the better the user understands the workings of the system the greater his ability to diagnose and recover from his errors. Error diagnosis is a valuable source of learning for users, and the more advisors can help users to acquire this ability the more they

will help users to help themselves and so help to make experts out of
novices.

VII. OBJECTIVES FOR AN EFFECTIVE COMPUTING
ADVISORY SERVICE

The majority of interactions studied in our investigation of advisory
services were dominated by one of two objectives:
  – the identification of the cause of a failed computation and the
    specification of some remedial action;
  – the provision of advice about either a computation or some
    other programming topic.
All other objectives were subsidiary in the sense that they were not
deliberately and systematically followed, but occurred as a by-
product of these two. For example, conceptual explanations were
not given routinely but occasionally as a bonus when time allowed or
in response to a user's specific question. A positive affective tone to
interactions was not deliberately sought but emerged as a result of a
good cognitive relationship between advisor and user.

Our detailed analysis of conversations has led us to suggest that
advisors can improve the service by broadening their range of objectives, particularly in response to novice or inexpert users. Several
users have confirmed this view, and one of the users interviewed
expressed his feelings about the advisory service so eloquently that
we have decided to quote him at length:

> I use it as a learning process as well. O.K., initially I say, "I think this is
> the problem", but I want him [the advisor] to tell me if in fact I've got
> my understanding correct. Not only do I want him to correct the program,
> I want him to check out my understanding and also to tell me if my under-
> standing is wrong or hopefully for him to explain a little bit more and
> enlarge my understanding. That way you make progress, otherwise it's just
> a Band-Aid job each time . . . . I think an important part of this
> advisory is that they explain why they're doing what they're doing, other-
> wise if the slightest thing goes wrong you've got to go back to them for
> the answer.

And further on in the same debriefing interview:

> The other problem is that he takes too narrow a view. He'll give you the
> absolute minimum of what you ask and won't follow through to any of
> the peripheral aspects, and this is one of the biggest sources of my frus-
> tration with advisory. That's what I find causes frustration, when someone
> just gives you what you ask and doesn't point out the next track on the
> line or the next track back. Now this is dependent on the experience of

the advisor. The more experienced person will know that everyone crashes on the next track because he's met it twenty times before. But this is the source of quite a few of my return trips to advisory.

One of the advisors at the same centre expressed an alternative viewpoint, but at the same time acknowledged the validity of some of these criticisms:

Because a problem is routine, you do tend to . . . you have the answer pat, so it's very easy to sort of say "this is what you do, go away and do it". And that means sometimes that instead of explaining what you're doing you're just giving a recipe. And part of the job is, well I think part of the job is, trying to get people to see, to understand what they're doing. But if you're tired and you've seen that problem four times that day, then I'm afraid . . . hard lines.

If it's a problem which is very technical, which requires a fair amount of experience, then even if the user is fairly competent I would probably just give him a set of instructions, and then try and explain what the instructions were doing. If it's a user who is less competent, or I feel he's less competent, then I would probably just . . . . I wouldn't explain as much, because from his point of view actually getting the technical information in a form which he can follow is probably more important than actually understanding what's going on.

[Some users] don't understand quite often what they're doing, either because they've not done very much computing, or they're using programs which they've been given by various people, people giving courses and so on, in which they don't know what they're doing. They feed in numbers and out come answers, and when they don't get answers or they don't quite get the cards right . . . they can't hope to understand it.

Similar attitudes to these were frequently expressed by other advisors interviewed in our study. They seem to imply that they rarely support operational instructions with explanations because they believe such explanations to be difficult to formulate, time-consuming to give, and not necessarily required by the user. Advisors thus tend to stick to problem-solving objectives, and so gain little practice in giving explanations and do not develop the skills appropriate to a more tutorial style of advice-giving. In order to provide a more successful service for inexperienced users, advisors should aim to help the user extend his skills, knowledge and understanding as part of the broader objective of helping users to help themselves and so reducing their dependence on the advisory service.

A common source of irritation to many users, not only novices, arises from feeling bound to the advisory service for support. This feeling is exacerbated by advisors' failure to help users to be more independent. Advisors can help to reduce users' dependence on the service in the following ways.

- By putting users in touch with alternative sources of information whenever possible and relevant.
- By using the problem to expand the user's conceptual understanding of programming and of the local computer system. This will help him to solve similar problems for himself when they arise in the future, or even to avoid them. It should also help him to use the computer system more efficiently.
- By aiming to improve the user's debugging skills. This could be achieved both by explicitly instructing the user in debugging procedures and the use of debugging tools (e.g. the list of transfers given in the monitoring file), and by keeping the user informed about the advisor's problem-solving procedures. This appears to be achieved more effectively by a review of the problem and its solution at the end of the interaction, rather than by thinking aloud during the process of finding the solution. The review could also be used to help the user improve his programming skills, and to indicate any faults in program design which may have created the problems.

By adopting these new objectives, as well as those discussed earlier such as helping users to feel at ease and to participate usefully in an interaction, advisors would not only help users but would also help themselves by reducing the number of "trivial" queries reaching advisory and so allowing more time for solving the "interesting" problems of expert users. In addition, interactions with inexpert users should become more rewarding, producing an increase in user-friendliness and appreciation.

One of the most worrying characteristics of advisory services which emerged from our study was the relatively low status which most advisors attached to the job of advising. This attitude seemed most noticeable and pervasive at those centres where several programmers worked on advisory in rotation, so that each one was on duty fairly infrequently. These advisors seemed to get very little satisfaction from advising, which was seen as something that "had to be done", and which prevented them from getting on with their "real" work. This attitude is worrying in that it will cause difficulties in motivating advisors to change their method of advice-giving and to improve the educative nature of the service. We have considered this point and feel that in addition to broadening advisory objectives to include those given above, more involvement in the process of information-provision might help.

In the larger university computer centres the advisory service is usually organized separately from the information and education services. This appears to reduce interaction between the three guidance services even though they are functionally complementary, with any weakness in one service increasing the demands placed on the others. For example, inadequate introductory courses will result in novice users placing heavy demands on the advisory service. However, it is rare for information on user difficulties to be fed back to improve courses. We therefore propose that the job of advising could be made more satisfying by involving advisors in the running of an integrated guidance system. In order to achieve such a service advisors would need to be trained both to fulfil the advisory objectives discussed in Section VI and to maintain communication channels between the various services. Such training should include the following activities.

- Sessions should be held with advisors to illustrate the importance of the advisory service and to discuss case-studies of interactions to assist in identifying specific types of users and classes of problem. In this context we would recommend that advisors should be involved in research aimed at evolving effective strategies for answering queries. Such research is particularly necessary with reference to novice users.
- Advisors should, at the end of a session, record the query, the solution and possible reasons for the query (this information would be fed back to the appropriate documentation writers, lecturers or applications programmers).
- Advisors should be closely involved in the writing of documentation and the preparation of courses. Indeed, an integrated approach to guidance services may encourage the writing of advisory or instructional documents aimed at specific groups of users with special needs.
- Regular lectures and seminars about specific aspects of the computing and information system should be organized for advisors to ensure that they have an adequate knowledge of all key facilities.

The research reported in this chapter has indicated that the advisory service has a crucial role among the guidance services provided by university computer centres. The recommendations made above and in Section VI are intended to extend this role and to optimize effectiveness, particularly for inexperienced users. However, given the present state of knowledge regarding the nature of computing skills, most of the recommendations can only be made with reference to the general principles of communication rather than to a theory of computing skills. While this is an entirely satisfactory basis for initiating changes, we feel that in the absence of a sound theoretical foundation their effects should be closely and systematically monitored to ensure they are tuned to a given computing environment. Such a project is currently being undertaken at Liverpool, along with some related research into the effects of various methods of advice—giving on the development of users' computing skills. Results of the work will be built into courses for advisors and will be reported at a future date.

ACKNOWLEDGEMENTS

Research for this paper was supported by Social Science Research grant number HE4421.

REFERENCES

Alty, J.L. and Coombs M.J. (1980). University computing advisory services: the study of the man—machine interface. *Software Practice and Experience* **10**, 919–934.
Austin, J.L. (1962). *How to Do Things with Words*. Oxford: Clarendon Press.
Burroughs, G.E.R. (1971). *Design and Analysis in Educational Research*. Educational Monograph No. 8, School of Education, University of Birmingham.
Coombs, M.J. (1979a). The principal findings of a survey of user computing experience and the use of the Liverpool Advisory Service. *Research Report No. 102*, Computer Laboratory, University of Liverpool.
Coombs, M.J. (1979b). Anatomy of an advisory service: some facts and figures. *Research Report No. 101*, Computer Laboratory, University of Liverpool.
du Boulay, B. and O'Shea, T. (1978). Seeing the works: a strategy for teaching interactive programming. *Proceedings of the Workshop on Computing Skills and Adaptive Systems*, University of Liverpool.
Florentin, J.J. and Smith, B.C. (1978). Guessing the state of a computer. *Proceedings of the Workshop on Computing Skills and Adaptive Systems*, University of Liverpool.
Garrod, S. and Sanford, A. (1977). Interpreting anaphoric relations: the integration of semantic information while reading. *J. Verbal Learning Verbal Behav.*, **16**, 77–90.
Grice, H.P. (1975). Logic and conversation. In P. Cole and J.C. Morgan (eds) *Syntax and Semantics 111: Speech Acts*. New York and London: Academic Press.
Halliday, M.A.K. (1973). *Explorations in the Functions of Language*. London: Arnold.

Hersen, M. and Barlow, D.H. (1976). *Single Case Experimental Designs: Strategies for Studying Behaviour Change*. Oxford: Pergamon Press.

Hymes, D. (1974). Ways of speaking. In R. Bauman and J. Sherzer (eds) Explorations in the Ethnography of Speaking. Cambridge: Cambridge University Press.

Labov, W. and Fanshel. D. (1978). *Therapeutic Discourse: Psychotherapy as Conversation*. London and New York: Academic Press.

Mathiot, M. (1978). Towards a frame of reference for the analysis of face-to-face interactions. *Semiotica*, 24, 199–230.

Mathiot, M. and Gargin, P.J. (1975). The functions of language: a sociocultural view. *Anthropol. Q.*, 48, 148–156.

Miller. G.A. (1956). The magical number seven, plus or minus two: some limits on our capacity for processing information. *Psychol. Rev.*, 63, 81–97.

Osgood, C.E., Suci, G.J. and Tannenbaum, P.H. (1957). *The Measurement of Meaning*. Urbana: University of Illinois Press.

Rogers, C. (1951) *Client-Centred Therapy*. Cambridge, Massachusetts: Riverside Press.

Schegloff, E. and Sacks, H. (1973). Opening up closings. *Semiotica*, 9, 289–327

Sharrock, W.W. and Turner, R. (1978). On a conversational environment for equivocality. In J. Schenkein (ed.) *Studies in the Organization of Conversational Interaction*. London and New York: Academic Press.

Siegel, S. (1956). *Nonparametric Statistics for the Behavioural Sciences*. New York: McGraw-Hill.

Sinclair, N., Forsyth, I.J., Coulthard, R.M. and Ashby, M.C. (1972). The English used by teachers and pupils. Final Report to S.S.R.C., University of Birmingham.

Sommer, R. (1965). Further studies of small-group ecology. *Sociometry*, 28, 337–348.

2. University Computer Users: Characteristics and Behaviour

R. AULD*, K. LANG* and T. LANG†

*Computer Centre, University of Birmingham, Birmingham, England
†Computer Centre, The Polytechnic, Wolverhampton, England

I. INTRODUCTION

The work upon which this Chapter is based was carried out at the University of Birmingham Computer Centre during 1977 and 1978; it was financed by the Social Science Research Council. It emanates from the experience of the project directors over many years of providing computing services to a body of computer users with rather special problems, these users being the staff and students in universities. These user communities have several unusual features. A high proportion of them are transient, in that post-graduate students use the computing facilities for at most three years, and few have any significant initial expertise in computing. Secondly, while quite a number of university users need to become skilled in computing, only a handful will ever become computer professionals: for the great majority, computing, however important and time-consuming, is secondary to their main involvement which is research in their own discipline. Finally, and here their work has much in common with research institutes and R and D departments, very few university applications involve user-written production programs. Standard software packages are, of course, used to good effect in many fields; but in academic computing there is no equivalent of the commercial applications such as payroll and accounting which form the bulk of the work of professional computer users outside universities. Nor are there many at the other end of the scale, where the parallel is with airline reservation clerks, who simply use the application system as given with no control over it or knowledge of its inner workings. The net result of these unusual features has been that, in order for such people to make effective use of the computer, it has been necessary to give them guidance services—documentation, courses, face-to-face advice, machine-based HELP systems—beyond what the manufacturer provides. The provision of these services has typically been undertaken on an *ad hoc* basis. The best ways of providing such guidance cost-effectively have never been examined, and the need to do this was the motive for setting up the project.

The research has been particularly concerned with three tasks:
(a) identifying interactions between users and guidance services within the computing environment;
(b) identifying user characteristics;
(c) evaluating current methods and characteristics of guidance services.

It is assumed that a purely behavioural account would be of limited value: the user's behaviour is regarded as a complex function of his goals and his perception of the computing environment, and an adequate account of his interaction with the computing and guidance services should acknowledge the psychological importance of the subjective environment. Such a user-centred approach, employing observational rather than experimental techniques, directed towards the achievement of an understanding of users' computing behaviour, is intended to yield readily applicable conclusions, relevant to the real-world settings from which data are drawn.

As it is employed here the term "user" refers generally to actual computer users, but also, in most contexts, to potential users who, given adequate guidance, would become able to make effective use of computing resources in the course of their work. In the pages which follow models will be proposed, and will be related to other evidence garnered from the literature. Problems peculiar to computing in the higher education context will be identified and discussed. The guidance requirements of university computer users will be considered in relation to technological, economic, and social factors, and relevant psychological research on learning and instructional methods will be reviewed. As the conceptual model is a multi-level one, this review will span a number of disciplinary perspectives. A selection of applicable research methods will be discussed.

A necessary first stage in this research was the acquisition of a general description of the population of university computer users in terms of academic discipline, computing experience, history of formal instruction in computing, and attitudes towards services. This was achieved by means of a large-scale survey, which will be described later, and which provided a basis for sampling representative computer users to participate in a subsequent longitudinal study, which is also reported here.

II. THE BACKGROUND TO THE PRESENT RESEARCH

A. The Origins and Nature of the Need for Computing Guidance in Universities

The problems of guidance which this research addresses have arisen, paradoxically, because computer use has over time become very much easier, and because computing resources have become more generally accessible. Computer use has thus become feasible for a large population of non-specialists with little technical knowledge.

The development of computers and computing science has been extraordinarily rapid, and the universities have been active participants in the technological and theoretical advances of the last thirty-five years. Throughout this period processors have become faster and more powerful, while computer memories have increased in capacity. The present ubiquity of digital computers has come about as all computing hardware has become cheaper and physically smaller. The penetration of this technology into almost all areas of life has been associated with changes in public awareness of computers and in attitudes towards them.

For the non-specialist the most significant single conceptual development was the displacement of machine-oriented assembly languages by problem-oriented, human-oriented high-level programming languages during the later 1950s (Sammet, 1969). The ability to write programs in FORTRAN in a recognizable approximation to conventional mathematical notation, sufficiently reduced the effort of programming to establish a strain of "amateur" programmers. To a greater extent than previously (or subsequently) released languages, FORTRAN was accepted as a *de facto* standard, and so greatly increased the portability of software, thus reducing the need for users to write their own programs on site. These trends have continued, so that within the universities there is a community of computer users who are able to make effective use of computing resources without the advantage of a full training in computing science. Thus arises the problem of communicating necessary technical information to users lacking such a background.

In universities in particular the computer user has become a client rather than a technician, thanks to the technical developments which have made computing power cheaper, and the conceptual developments which opened up a great diversity of computer applications (Rosen, 1969; Pylyshyn, 1970). Though some departments retain some independent computing resources, at most universities computer centres have been instituted to serve the varied computing needs of a wide range of departments in teaching and research. The computer centre's functions extend beyond the maintenance of computer hardware and software, and include the preparation and distribution of instructional documents on computing, the organization of courses of instruction on the use of computing resources, and the provision of advisory services for computer users.

The last fifty years have seen a continuing exchange of concepts amongst various emergent fields of thought (system theory, cybernetics, programmed instruction, artificial intelligence, computer science) which have common roots in logic, mathematics, and electronics. By virtue of their parallel development these new disciplines have generated a variety of computer applications, and have established a conceptually sophisticated population which readily recognizes potential uses for computers. Therefore, looking beyond the obvious necessity to educate specialist computer scientists, the availability of well-supported resources in universities is essential for students, teachers, and research workers across the disciplinary spectrum.

Within universities, computer scientists now comprise a small (though significant) minority of computer users, the majority being non-specialists who have recognized computers as powerful, widely applicable tools. Providing satisfactory computing services to such a diverse group of users is a formidable problem, and its solution is subject to constraints on financial, administrative, and manpower resources. Particular difficulties arise in planning and managing services to meet these varied requirements during such a period of rapid technical development, in that the criteria upon which decisions rest are themselves changing in response to larger forces in the social system. The risk of planning for the past rather than the future might seem particularly acute with respect to information services for computer users at a time when technological and conceptual change is so rapid. (Iklé (1967) implies that any attempt to plan for a changing future is likely to be conservatively biased.) Empirical studies of *existing* needs and practices cannot, then, provide a wholly adequate basis for designing guidance services, but must complement rational analysis of foreseeable require-ments. However, empirical methods play a part in the investi-gation of the constant perceptual and cognitive human factors which affect computer users' ability to use and apply technical information.

The psychological flexibility of computer users also serves to camouflage many of the inefficiencies and failures of guidance services. Up to a point users are tolerant of such failures (and may not recognize them as such) since they are able to adapt their behaviour to avoid problems, even though such strategies may involve inefficient use of computing resources and of their own time. It should be remembered that chronic inefficiencies in computing may be more costly than acute failures.

At present, then, it is increasingly important that well-supported computing facilities should be generally available within universities, and that the potential users should have ready access to information and guidance to develop the skills which will enable them to derive the intended advantages from the computing resources. Since change is a constant factor in this environment, adaptability is to be desired in the users as much as in the systems themselves. At the present stage of software and hardware development, this requirement justifies some investment of the user's time in acquiring programming skills, to achieve a basic level of computing "literacy".

B. Computing Services and Computer Users: Earlier Research

The studies described in this chapter are intended to lead to improvements in the efficiency of computing within universities, but the criteria for efficiency should not be excessively narrow. Such evaluation requires the adoption of some rule to resolve the relative value of man-hours and machine time to a common basis. No general rule is possible: the economic balance is dependent on local circumstances (e.g. the load on the computer), and may change from time to time. Likewise, savings in effort while preparing a program (e.g. by omitting to document it) may be offset by avoidable difficulties if attempts are made to modify or re-use the program later (Weinberg, 1971).

The effect of programming experience was considered by Youngs (1974): while experienced and novice programmers had similar numbers of errors on the first run of a program, the novices required more runs to remove the errors. This suggests that they were less able to use available information than the experienced programmers.

The supposition that students from different disciplines differ in their performance on programming courses was considered by Mazlack (1975). He found that academic background was not related to performance on an introductory programming course. However, this conclusion was based on observation of under-graduates undertaking a formal course of study, and cannot be assumed to hold for users in other circumstances. A need to provide appropriate assistance to different groups is indicated by a study of inexperienced computer users (Eason, 1976). Eason concluded that user interfaces should be tailored to the groups using them, with regard to task factors, role factors, and personal factors. (Such factors will be further considered in a later section.) Users' attitudes towards computing are considered important by Sackman (1970, p.209), who advocates a greater element of "computer appreciation" in introductory programming courses.

Studies of programming errors and of debugging are numerous. Weinberg (1971) offers an entertaining general discussion, while Gould and his colleagues have presented a series of experimental studies, and have shown differences in the speed with which different types of bugs are traced (Gould and Drongowski, 1974; Gould, 1975). Boies and Gould (1974) have monitored users' programs automatically, but acknowledge the difficulty in dis-covering the proportion of "new" programs which are compiled successfully at the first attempt. Gould (1975) found that for experienced programmers debugging was more efficient when the programmer was already familiar with the bugged program. He presents a cognitive, cyclic model of debugging, functionally similar to the model which will be presented here. It appears, then, that debugging is facilitated if the user has the opportunity to achieve a cognitive representation of the program's structure. Consistent with this is the suggestion by Lukey (1978) that debugging is performed by means of program descriptions which represent program under-standing. Weinberg and Schulman (1974) have shown that, in an experimental study of programming, performance depends on the relative value which the programmer attaches to speed of production and program efficiency. More recently Weinberg (1979) has sug-gested that a checklist may be used effectively to prescribe a systematic error-tracing procedure for programmers.

C. Human Factors in the Design of Man–Machine Systems

A coherent body of research on debugging and programming language characteristics has come from the MRC Social and Applied Psychology Unit in the University of Sheffield. Sime *et al.* (1977b) have found differences in the difficulty of writing and debugging programs when different structures are used for conditional instructions. Sime *et al.* (1977a) found that programming errors involving nested conditional structures could be reduced by prescribing a procedure for writing the programs.

In a study of man–computer dialogue (using interactive systems) Moore *et al.* (1977) described a process of continual redefinition of goals. This becomes more obvious when the time-scale is compressed as it is in interactive use of computers, but a corresponding process is apparent in batch computing.

Under the heading of "human factors", we may also note some research in environmental psychology which has implications for the physical organization of guidance services. Weinberg (1971) indicated anecdotally how a simple environmental change (the relocation of a coffee machine in a computer centre) had an unanticipated adverse effect on the pattern of interaction amongst users. This disruption of informal consultancy threw an additional workload on to the centre's programming advisory staff. More formal studies have given a better understanding of the extent to which the organization of physical surroundings may affect the behaviour of computer users. This is particularly relevant in user–adviser consultations, where co-operation is facilitated by side-by-side seating arrangements, and the absence of barriers (such as desks) between participants (Joiner, 1976). In more obvious ways (e.g. the organization of a computer centre library) the accessibility of information may depend on spatial arrangements, thus affecting the efficiency of the communication links represented in Fig. 1.

Figure 1 is a simplified representation of the formally established communication links between the user and the elements of the computing service. This embodies the relationships among the elements as they were intended to function, and is quite accessible to observation. It may be noted here that the formal system may be complemented by additional informal links. Such adaptations will be considered in a later section, in relation to other social formants of computing behaviour.

As research continues, hardware and software will continue to become easier to use, but this development is complementary to the provision of adequate guidance for users, who in the meantime must have sufficient assistance to help them overcome the demonstrated shortcomings of existing resources. Despite the promise of human factors research in computing, neither hardware nor software can ever be perfectly tailored to the requirements of individuals (if only because these requirements are continually redefined as the problems are worked through), and for this reason suitable adaptive guidance must be available.

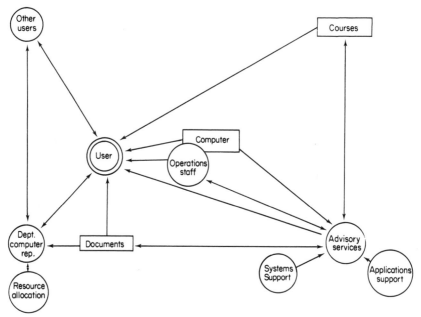

Fig. 1. The flow of information about computing to the computer user.

D. Approaches to the Design of Instructional Methods and Materials

Guidance has much in common with other forms of instruction, but whereas most research on instruction is concerned with the construction and appraisal of structured courses, research on guidance is, in addition, concerned particularly with occasional or incidental learning—the acquisition of small packets of information as the need arises.

Cognitive approaches to instruction have brought a new richness to theory and research in the last decade (Bruner, 1966; Briggs *et al.*, 1967; Atkinson, 1972; Wittrock and Lumsdaine, 1977). Cognitive theory acknowledges the complexity of learning in everyday life, and this has encouraged the development of task analysis. Resnick (1976) distinguishes rational analysis (modelling efficient, idealized task performance, ignoring the information-processing shortcomings of human learners) and empirical analysis (based on observation of actual performance). Such analyses investigate the differences between novice and expert, to discover "ways of arranging experiences that will help novices become experts" (Resnick, 1976, p. 53).

An alternative conceptualization of instruction is distinguished from the mainstream of cognitive theory by its close affinity to theories of artificial intelligence: though somewhat formal, the work of Pask (1975, 1976) has some experimental support. Pask (1975) recognizes that individuals employ different learning strategies and teaching strategies, and suggests that effective learning is conditional on these being matched to the learner's competence. In other words, instruction should exploit the learner's existing aptitudes. Landa (1976) offers a cybernetic approach related to Pask's, and to other versions of task analysis, which involves "algorithmization" of tasks, and thus yields instructional programs to meet individual requirements. This work may indicate that more efficient instruction can be promoted by a sufficiently detailed analysis of the task in question, coupled with an awareness of the user's initial knowledge and abilities. Given the range and complexity of computing tasks, and the diversity of computer users encountered in universities, questions remain about the difficulty which might be involved in applying these methods in this environment.

However, since university computer centres themselves produce a large fraction of the reference documents and instructional texts provided for users, such information may be usefully applied in the evaluation of existing materials and the production of new ones.

Awareness of the varying requirements of individual learners has brought recognition of the advantages in employing various combinations of instructional media, rather than attempting to use a single mode of instruction for all learners and topics, (Briggs et al., 1967; Allen, 1971; Haskell, 1976). However, Bligh (1977) has suggested that some of the claimed advantages of recently developed methods are unproven. While such innovations as visual aids, tape recorders, film, television, and programmed learning may be effective in teaching certain topics to particular classes of students, Bligh's review of the relevant literature indicates that they have more often been un-critically and inappropriately applied. Likewise the value of tape-slide teaching and computer-assisted instruction has yet to be clearly established. In view of the widespread applications of all of these techniques in teaching computing skills, some effort should perhaps be made to assess their effectiveness, and to match the most suitable methods of instruction to the range of skills which are taught.

It is convenient to distinguish a number of separate phases in the user's activity as he applies computing resources to his practical problem. The model shown in Fig. 2 represents, at a rather coarse

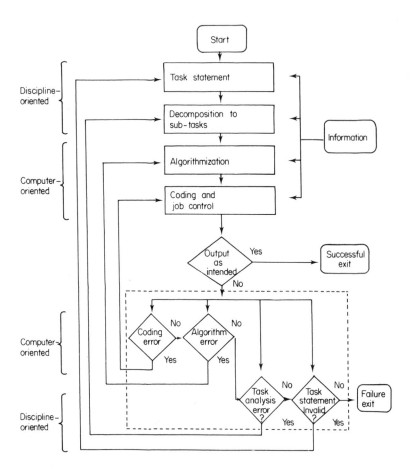

Fig. 2. A cyclic model of computer use.

level of analysis, a set of nested cycles, within which may be recognized various potential failure points. The model may be of some assistance in devising efficient working strategies or as a diagnostic aid in cases of failure.

The sequence of activities implied by this representation is intended to be general, comprehensive and efficient. The model represents the activities of the user: external events are acknowledged only in so far as they impart information and direct the flow of control through the tests and revisions towards an eventual exit, successful or unsuccessful.

The model is composed of two halves, the first representing preparation of a computer job, and the second the debugging/post-mortem following an unsuccessful computer run. (Ideally, the user would never enter the error-tracing phase, but would exit successfully after a single passage through the preparatory phase. In the real world, however, the user will frequently enter the lower half of the model, but will enter successively lower blocks with decreasing frequency.) Both halves of the model are somewhat idealized, in that the sequence of actions represented may not always be strictly adhered to. In the preparatory phase, for instance, the intuitive or impulsive (bottom-up) programmer may embark on coding part of his program before the algorithm as a whole has been designed. During debugging the user may hold some strong concept about the source of his error, and may not, therefore, apply all of the tests specified by the model in the prescribed order. The tests enclosed within the dotted box may be considered to proceed in parallel in some instances, as, for example, in the case of a large modular program, when the several modules may each be scrutinized in turn. Testing different levels in parallel, except in such cases, where the approximate location of the error is known *a priori,* may be less efficient than systematic sequential checking. (However, even when parallel testing is in operation the point in the preparatory phase to which control returns is dependent on the level at which the error is recognized.) Again, the output from the unsuccessful run may provide evidence which would immediately focus attention on checks at a particular level—perhaps by error messages flagging syntax errors ("coding" level), or by a package recognizing logically inconsistent or inappropriate procedures ("algorithm" level). In such instances tests at lower levels may be perfunctory, if applied at all. In a study of programming errors and debugging, Youngs (1974) observed that the errors met on successive runs of a program tend to be at different levels.

An unsuccessful exit implies that the error has not been recognized, and the task has been abandoned. It does not mean that the problem is intrinsically insoluble. A user may pass through the cycle overlooking errors to exit in this way. Such behaviour is attributable to failure to perceive available information, perhaps because of tenacious adherence to an incorrect hypothesis about the nature of the error in which the user has invested effort, or selection of an inappropriate strategy. Pask (1975, p.265) has labelled this tendency "cognitive fixity" (extending the notion of cognitive dissonance), and suggests that it may best be overcome by providing the subject with feedback about his performance, and discouraging misguided strategies.

Efficiency in use of the computer is inversely related to the total "distance" traversed within the model between start and (successful) exit points. Depending on the number of cycles completed this may take a considerable time. Since job-control errors and coding errors are frequent, but are relatively easy to correct (having limited, local expression) they are checked at the beginning of the testing phase. This bottom-up approach to error-tracing allows some economy of effort. Identification of an error at any level generally necessitates corrective action at all inferior levels, and the action required by a single error at the global conceptual level becomes increasingly extensive in scope at successively lower levels. In the absence of contrary evidence it is parsimonious to begin tracing on the assumption that the fault is minor, and that the required changes are of limited scope.

The model thus represents a generalized strategy (or "plan") for the preparation and debugging of computer jobs, which may be executed with varying degrees of efficiency by different individuals. It is closely related to the kind of learning strategies discussed by Pask (1975, pp.263f), and to the TOTE (Test-Operate-Test-Exit) conception of Miller *et al.* (1960).

In practice errors may exist unrecognized within a computer job, if, for example, it produces output which conforms in general characteristics to the user's expectation. Such errors should be sought by running the program with test data, or otherwise checking the output against a solution obtained by some other method of established validity and reliability. If, in running a new program, results are obtained which appear consistent with expectation and intention, the model indicates an immediate successful exit. Nevertheless, there are good reasons for continuing through the complete sequence of checks, given the possibility of concealed latent errors which might be unleashed by different data at some time in the future (when the author has lost recall of his intentions, and requires to refamiliarize himself with the program's logic before he can seek out the error). Again, the identification of a single error in a program does not mean that there may not be other errors co-existing at the same level, or at higher conceptual levels. These may be latent errors whose manifestations would only become apparent after correction of the primary error (especially where the primary error involves the output).

E. Psychological Characteristics of the Individual Computer User

It has been suggested in the previous chapter that there are good reasons for acknowledging the variations in the experience and abilities of computer users. While it would be naive to regard the user population as being ·homogeneous it would be impractical to investigate all of the characteristics in which individuals may differ. It is therefore appropriate to consider evidence from psychological research pertaining to some of the characteristics which might be supposed to have a bearing on individuals' performance as computer users, and their needs for instruction and assistance.

1. *Learning*

Learning is a fundamental psychological process and as such has generated an enormous volume of research literature, and numerous contending theories. In the present context we wish to understand how users memorize facts and procedures, and how they acquire concepts, skills and attitudes. Horton and Turnage (1976) have recently reviewed historical and contemporary approaches to learning, with particular emphasis on verbal learning and the emergence of cognitive theories. Information-processing theory and psycholinguistic theory imply the existence of specific human abilities to extract and organize information from the environment. Horton and Turnage identify meaning and context as central topics in current research on learning, and acknowledge the importance of experiments on rules and rule learning. These investigations will clearly have further significance for the teaching of computing, since effective perform-ance rests on the acquisition of concepts and principles (or rules). Research on learning is increasingly conducted in more natural instructional situations, so that the connection between instructional research and more fundamental psychological research is stronger than formerly, and the distinction is often difficult to maintain (Greeno, 1976; Shaw and Wilson, 1976; Simon and Hayes, 1976; Taylor, 1977). The evidence that learning is dependent on meaning suggests that attention might usefully be turned towards the organization and structure of computing documents. (For example, alphabetical organization of entries in reference manuals may be less effective than organization by topic—for certain purposes at least.)

2. *Skills*

The acquisition of a skill is a relatively complex learning process which involves the incorporation of a number of separate activities into a single co-ordinated sequence. This co-ordination is dependent on perceptual feedback. The work of Miller *et al.* (1960) on the organization of behaviour in so-called TOTE units has been followed and extended by other cognitive theorists such as Neisser (1976).

Reason (1977) has reviewed the literature on skilled performance and proposed a composite model supported by evidence from performance errors in everyday activities, classified according to the point in the behavioural cycle at which failure occurred. Reason's model emphasizes the automatic, habitual nature of skilled behaviour. At least a small proportion of computing errors may arise from inappropriate performance of a habitual behavioural sequence. For example, a user might inadvertently specify his usual routing parameter on a job-control card on the exceptional occasion when he wishes to direct his output elsewhere. Such errors reflect the degree to which skilled behaviour becomes automatic—which may be reassuring to the novice user for whom every parameter and punctuation mark must be considered before it is, very deliberately, punched. Before computing skills can be taught effectively they should be well analysed and understood.

3. *Individual Differences in Intelligence, Cognitive Style and Personality*

Different users, faced with a particular computing task, will follow different courses towards solution: in terms ot the cyclic model, they will differ in the number of times that they repeat particular actions, or the sequences with which they test for errors at different levels, or the extent to which they draw on the various sources of information available to them. Such variations in behaviour are explained partly in terms of differences in experience, and partly in terms of more intrinsic psychological characteristics.

Research on differences amongst individuals in mental aptitudes (e.g. numerical, verbal, and spatial abilities) was long the province of factor analysts (Vernon, 1961) and though their work demonstrates differences in performance on different kinds of tasks, doubts remained about the existence of the specific abilities which were inferred from these observations. More recently, interest has been directed towards differences in cognitive style. Britt (1971) distinguished three "learner types" whose performance on objective tests in an experiment was related to personality characteristics, and suggested that different teaching strategies would be appropriate for such groups. Rotter (1966) found that differences in learning could be related to the subject's perception of effects as being contingent on his actions, or as being due to chance: individuals could therefore be classified according to their tendency to see events as being under their control (internal locus of control) or independent of their actions (external locus of control). Parent et al. (1975) found that "internal" students performed better when teacher discipline was high. Some individuals are thus better able to pursue independent study, while others require more direction. Pask (1976) has distinguished *holistic* and *serialistic* styles in learning to account for individual differences on a range of cognitive tests, and has suggested that such personal biases in cognitive style should be recognized and taken into account in instruction. Pask's concept of cognitive fixity, discussed above, is related to the "rigidity" described by Rokeach (1960), and would explain why some individuals may fail to recognize computing errors because cognitive inflexibility makes it difficult for them to adopt new perspectives on their problems.

The range of variation on the dimension of general intelligence is restricted within the university population, and its significance is therefore reduced. Nevertheless, we would expect to encounter appreciable differences between users in more specific mental abilities, and on the assumption that such differences are related to computing skills a number of tests have been devised to measure "aptitude" for computer programming (e.g. Palormo, 1967).

In view of the relatively small proportion of women using university computing resources, it should be asked whether they encounter particular problems because of cognitive differences between the sexes. Such effects, of course, are in this context confounded with differences between disciplines, and with other social forces (which will be noted later). There is some evidence for the existence of sex differences in specific cognitive abilities (Wilson and Vandenberg, 1978), though this remains an area of dispute.

Personality theorists have devised various systems to explain the observable consistencies in the behaviour of individuals (Hall and Lindzey, 1978). Eysenck's theory suggests that different learning strategies are appropriate to individuals who stand at different points along the dimensions of extroversion and neuroticism (Eysenck and Eysenck, 1969). Other theories treat cognitive aspects more centrally (e.g. Rokeach, 1960).

Nothing has been said so far about the effects of different levels of motivation on performance and problem-solving, though this is clearly relevant. The classic theory of motivation focuses on the gratification which the subject expects to obtain when his goal is attained and his task is completed (Vroom, 1964). More recently, however, there has been wide recognition of the motivating power of intrinsic task factors (Berlyne, 1974; Turney, 1974).

Taking these general findings with the remarks of Weizenbaum (1976) and Weinberg (1971) on the "seductive" pleasures of computer use, we may infer that once the potential user's initial doubt and apprehension are laid to rest by a suitable course in computer appreciation (as suggested by Sackman) he may be sufficiently motivated by the immediate satisfactions of computing to lose sight of the task in which the computer was to serve as a tool. Occasionally appropriate guidance may involve helping the user *not* to use computing facilities, to achieve more efficient use of his own time, as well as computer time.

F. The University Computer User as a Member of a Social System

The psychological factors reviewed above do not by themselves offer a complete explanation for the variations in aptitude and performance which may be observed among computer users in their natural habitat. To achieve a fuller understanding of the conditions which affect the user's performance, we must consider his activity in its social context. By definition the university computer user belongs to a complex, formal organization (the university), and his behaviour is to a considerable degree motivated and constrained by the characteristics of that institution. The computing service may be regarded as a sub-system within the larger organization.

Cyert and MacCrimmon (1968) offer a conceptual review of organizations which considers information flow in relation to organizational goals and the roles defined within the organizational structure. These authors point out that the organization exerts considerable control upon the individual. This fact imposes an obligation on the managers of the computing service (and, less immediately, on the university's decision-takers) to monitor the needs of actual and potential computer users for services and information.

Organizational and individual goals may stand in conflict: a computer centre aims to provide services equitably, while an individual user demands more than his due share of resources. Similarly there may be conflict between the goals implied by the functions of the university and of the computer centre, such that the centre's freedom to meet demands is constrained by the university's pursuit of its educational goals. Payne and Pugh (1971) conclude that individuals perform most effectively when organizational demands are consistent with their own needs, abilities and personalities.

With regard to the research objective of identifying interactions between user and guidance service the concept of role is a useful one, as it defines the individual's relation to the organization and to others within it in terms of rights, responsibilities, privileges and obligations (Sarbin and Allen, 1969). A computer user's behaviour is therefore constrained by the expectations or beliefs which he holds with regard to that role, and by the expectations of other members of the organization (Katz and Kahn, 1978). Since roles are not only defined by the individuals who discharge them, but are established and maintained by "tradition" it can be difficult to change them.

Sex roles may also relate to success in the use of computing services. Setting aside the inconclusive evidence on the existence of genuine cognitive differences between the sexes, it is still clear that there are differences in the social roles played by men and women, even in universities. This is reflected in the marked differences in the proportions of men and women in different departments and faculties. It is, then, reasonable to ask whether the sexes tackle problems in the same ways, and whether their guidance requirements are, in fact, similar.

Social psychology also offers useful information about processes of communication, and the conditions which facilitate or impede the effective transfer of information. This may be dependent on organizational restrictions on the flow of information, and there is a great deal of experimental evidence on the effects of differently structured communication networks on the efficiency of co-operative problem-solving (Shaw, 1964). This leads to the conclusion that the efficiency of communication depends on an interaction between the network's structure and the complexity of the problem: where several persons are engaged on a complex problem the solution is reached more easily when there is free communication in all directions among the participants.

Kelley and Thibaut (1969) observe that the effective channels of information flow are not always those planned for the organization:

where information is not provided an individual may actively seek it for himself. Such informal adaptations within organizations occur when participants set aside the prescriptions of their assigned roles and relate on a personal level. (So a computer user, unable to access required information, may bypass the official advisory services to consult a member of staff who is expected to be able to help.) Informal developments of this kind can be symptomatic of structural inadequacies in communication networks. Evaluation of the effectiveness of guidance services should thus include some observation of the formal and informal communication structures which link users, computer centre staff and academic staff, with a view to the design of structures which will make for efficient transmission of reliable information on computer use.

Social forces also influence the behaviour of the individual computer user through the beliefs (knowledge of "facts") and attitudes (evaluations) which govern his behaviour (Fishbein and Ajzen, 1975). His beliefs are related to his roles, and depend largely on the information reaching him, while attitudes are particularly subject to social influence from the various groups to which the individual belongs. So computer users belonging tq a departmental group may support each other in certain attitudes towards particular computing services, and may consequently show uniform behaviour with regard to these services. The cultivation of positive attitudes towards computing and computing services through appropriate orientation courses for new users (as suggested in an earlier section) should improve users' motivation to exploit available computing services, and aid communication with the computer centre's staff.

Values are related to attitudes, but are fundamental and more enduring. Anderson (1978) reports differences in the values held by social science students and computing science students, which would be consistent with different attitudes towards the use of computers, and therefore with different levels of motivation in computing-related activities.

In some cases it may be straightforward to ease the computer user's difficulties by organizational changes to improve or control the flow of information to him. In other instances where difficulties or inefficiencies arise from bad working habits (e.g. a reluctance to bring problems to the advisory service), an appropriate strategy would be to attempt to change the user's behaviour by changing his attitudes.

Weinberg (1971) enthuses over "egoless" programming, which rests on the existence of a co-operative group, in which programs are not the "property" of individuals but of the group. In such a context the original programmer's self-esteem is unaffected by criticisms of the program. Such group working is also prophylactic against the frustrations of cognitive fixity. However, such programming "project teams" are less common in universities than in commercial organizations, simply because the users are "amateurs" in computing, applying computer power to problems which arise in the course of their work. In some university departments (particularly in the physical sciences) the great majority of staff and students are required to use computers, and there is therefore a reservoir of knowledge and experience which allows some co-operation and mutual assistance with computing. However, since most university computing arises in the course of personal work (except for some larger research projects) the user's self-esteem is involved in the performance of his computing jobs, and the encouragement of "egoless" practices does not necessarily represent a practicable solution.

Still less could it be recommended for users in those departments where computer use is rare. These individuals suffer particularly in that they have far fewer opportunities to discuss their work with others who combine a knowledge of the users' discipline with understanding of computing techniques. Users working under such conditions of "social" isolation share many difficulties with those who are geographically isolated (e.g. working off-campus). Both types are largely dependent for information upon the formal communication system. The "social" isolate often suffers the further disadvantage that his departmental computing representative is no more expert than himself, and does not have a pool of departmental computing expertise to draw on. The situation may be represented in the terms of Fig. 2 as a severe restriction in the input flow of information, causing unnecessary difficulty in the performance of computing tasks. "Social" isolation may also affect the user's motivation, since he is not pressed to conform to a group norm of computing behaviour, and is not exposed to the social facilitation effect of other computer users around him. The isolate may therefore have difficulty in learning the role of "computer user", and may consequently have problems in interacting and communicating with the computing service.

This situation is likely to be self-perpetuating, as the difficulties will tend to discourage greater use of computers in the departments which make little (or no) use of them at present. In consideration of these disadvantages it seems desirable to enquire into the distribution of isolated users, and to discover how well they are served by existing guidance services.

Even where an information-seeker and an information-provider are brought into direct contact, effective communication is not assured. Obvious difficulties arise when a non-expert computer user attempts to describe a problem to a computing professional, or when a professional attempts to explain the remedy. Pearce (1973) reports a study of communication problems between the staff of a data-processing service and the users of the service. The difficulties were attributed to differences between the groups in the understanding of technical terminology. In the university context, communication between computing staff and computer users may also be disrupted by differences in language or cultural background. This frequently degrades communication at both the verbal and the non-verbal level (Argyle, 1969). However, even where differences in language and culture are not present it can be difficult for the advisor to perceive and adopt the user's frame of reference (especially if the advisor employs words in a technical sense not recognized by the user).

G. A Research Strategy

The ascendancy of the "new introspectionism" of cognitive psychology reflects a desire to understand, rather than merely describe, behaviour. This aspiration has stimulated the development of new approaches to research, paralleled in social psychology by the efforts of investigators to escape the artificiality of the laboratory and to tackle the problems of the real world in a theory-oriented way (McGuire, 1969, 1973). There is a trend towards more open and sensitive strategies for the evaluation of instructional schemes, acknowledging the wider values of the context in which the instruction if practised. Parlett and Hamilton (1972) review this trend and discuss the methods of "illuminative evaluation", whereby the investigator first seeks a general orientation within the system being evaluated, then gradually focuses attention on the issues which emerge from this consideration, and finally attempts an explanation which allows particular findings to be interpreted in a more general context. This contrasts with more traditional methods which have focused narrowly on variables selected on purely theoretical grounds, and which have therefore yielded results which are isolated and difficult to relate. Such an approach seems appropriate to the problems of guidance services, given the acknowledged weakness of the initial conceptual models. This strategy also promises more applicable results, though the need for orientation and focusing obviously means that the whole process takes longer than other evaluations.

In evaluating existing guidance services it would be naive and simplistic to attempt to contrive a single index-function of system performance. Parlett and Hamilton point out that evaluative research of this kind is addressed to three groups of decision-makers (participants, sponsors and outsiders) who have different interests (and, hence, conflicting criteria). The authors accept the impossibility of reconciling these interests, and resist the alternative of adopting the criteria of one group:

> Illuminative evaluation thus concentrates on the information-gathering rather than the decision-making component of evaluation . . . . In his report, therefore the evaluator aims to sharpen discussion, disentangle complexities, isolate the significant from the trivial, and to raise the level of sophistication of debate.   (Parlett and Hamilton, 1972, p.30)

The present research is oriented towards the real world of university computing, and must therefore tackle the complex factors—both personal and social—which influence the computer user's behaviour. Thus in considering the well-being of individual users and other potential beneficiaries of computing services the focus of analysis should shift between the individual and the group levels. For this reason a variety of data-collection techniques have been appropriate in handling the various issues implied by the foregoing discussion.

The illuminative approach reduces the risk of most of the problems which Weinberg (1971, Chapter 3) finds common in research on computer use. These include observing the wrong variables, failing to observe the right. ones, overly constrained experiments and wrongly measuring what is simple to measure. There is also danger in artificially isolating variables from their natural context (Burnhill and Hartley, 1975). It is desirable that the investigator's activity should not itself disrupt the behaviour which he seeks to observe (e.g. by boosting the subject's motivation, as in the ill-famed Hawthorne effect: Roethlisberger and Dickson, 1939). The researcher should also try to avoid the possibility that he might inadvertently bias his results to correspond to a preconceived version of the phenomena (Rosenthal, 1966).

In the early phase of research it is useful to try to discover how the situation and activity are described by the subjects under investigation, since this affords evidence about the motives involved, and reveals the concepts which the subjects use in referring to their activities. Structured or semi-structured interviews provide a systematic (though time-consuming) means of obtaining such information (Cannell and Kahn, 1968).

Additional factual and attitudinal data may be collected by that most familiar instrument of psychological enquiry, the survey questionnaire, which may be interviewer-administered, or completed by the subject himself (Selltiz *et al.*, 1976). The self-completion form enables large amounts of data to be obtained from a large number of subjects, using relatively little manpower, though if the data are to be intelligible a great deal of effort must be put into preparation of items which are objective, relevant and unambiguous, and which admit the full range of possible responses. Even so, some recipients may object to intrusive enquiries, while others feel that a question-naire misrepresents and trivializes their complex views (Parlett and Hamilton, 1972, p.22). These attitudes may themselves be reflected in non-response, so that the investigator must consider how failure to respond should be interpreted in the circumstances of his research.

Self-completion questionnaires are particularly well suited for research in the university setting, given the high level of literacy of the subjects, their familiarity with such survey techniques, and their relatively sophisticated (and generally sympathetic) attitudes towards research.

The construction of questionnaires which combine factual enquiry with simple attitude-measurement is a practicable means of obtaining a cross-sectional view of the active computing population of one or more universities at one point in time, though for reasons mentioned above it cannot yield a complete picture and must be supplemented by other techniques. Though users' own reports of their activity (whether elicited in interview or volunteered on a questionnaire) offer some information about the dynamics of their computing over time, other more direct techniques are required to clarify the crude process model of Fig. 2. Such complementary longitudinal studies yield very large volumes of data, and require much analysis. They may only be applied to small numbers of subjects who should therefore be carefully and systematically selected to represent the population as a whole.

Direct and indirect observation of behaviour are necessary complements to the indirect questionnaire methods, and allow some validation of the indirectly obtained data. Direct observation may also be employed to test behavioural predictions based on attitudinal information. The "unobtrusive", or "non-reactive" techniques (Webb *et al.*, 1966) represent a useful attempt to avoid the kind of distorting experimenter effects discussed previously, but they are somewhat restricted in application, and less adaptable than conventional systematic observational methods (Weick, 1968). The dynamic aspects of computing behaviour may also be studied by means of automatic monitoring of users' programs on a particular computer over a period of time. Though this may have appreciable costs in terms of machine resources it permits study of various aspects of computer use without directly interfering with the users' behaviour (Nagy and Pennebaker, 1974; Robinson and Torsun 1976). Such data, however, can be difficult to interpret without additional information (Boies and Gould, 1974).

III. THE CENSUS

At the outset, a primary hypothesis was that the attitudes and perceptions of university computer users with regard to computing in general, and guidance services in particular, were influenced by certain attributes. Initially we postulated five such attributes, namely, length of computing experience, length of discipline experience, amount of computing, regularity of computing, and extent of isolation (both geographical and social).

Length of computing experience refers to the number of months or years for which a user has been using computers as a tool in his work; we predicted that those who had some years' experience in using computers would differ in their perceptions of computing from novice users. Furthermore, since many problems in computing arise from lack of understanding of the interface between a problem expressed in terms of the initiating discipline, and its interpretation in computing terms, users with a good grasp of their own discipline (chemistry or linguistics for instance) might have different perceptions of computing from those who were still novices in their own area. Thus it was predicted that *length of discipline experience* would also be an important attribute.

Using computers involves a degree of understanding of computing techniques and a familiarity with the operating system and procedures of the local computer. We therefore predicted that not only length of computing experience, but also the *amount of computing* and the *regularity of computing* would influence users' perceptions of computing as well as their performance. Finally, much computing expertise is gained through informal sharing of knowledge and experience. We therefore expected that those users who were isolated from others, whether geographically (through being sited some distance from others, e.g. working from home, or through being members of departments in which only one or two people used computers) or socially (through choosing not to take such opportunities as existed for informal contact with other users) would show different patterns of perceptions of computing from those who habitually worked as part of a computing group.

In addition to these five attributes, we also felt we should investigate the impact of age and sex. Computing is an area of marked technological change, and we felt that older people might tend to find this a difficulty, with this effect offsetting the benefits of greater experience. It also seemed likely that the well-documented differences between the sexes with regard to mathematical and mechanical skills might have some impact.

However, no information was in existence when this project began which would even identify users according to all these five attributes. We thus had insufficient information about a suitable sampling frame to sample among users, which led us to opt for a full census of users. We wanted to begin by studying users at Birmingham, and at its partner university in this phase of the project, Liverpool. However, Birmingham and Liverpool have similar user profiles with regard to the discipline mix and to the amounts and kinds of computing being done. It would have been a task beyond the capacity of the project team to extend the census to cover all users at every university. We therefore felt we would have to sample among universities. We constructed a sample of eight universities which between them gave us what we regarded as a satisfactory cross-section with regard to characteristics such as size of university population, discipline mix, and variety and use of computing resources (particularly of facilities geographically remote from the home site). Each registered user at these universities (Aston, Birmingham, Cambridge, East Anglia, Edinburgh, Exeter, Glasgow and Liverpool) was sent a self-completion questionnaire which had been previously pilot-tested at each site. About 35% of these users responded; the only bias amongst non-respondents that could be detected from available figures was a tendency for fewer postgraduate students to respond than the population figures predicted, but this effect was not marked.

The results of the census are described under three main headings: user characteristics, user interaction with the guidance services, and between-university differences. Relationships between variables were analysed using the chi-square test, and measures of significance refer to this test throughout.

A. User Characteristics

One major section of the questionnaire was concerned with identifying each user by means of the five attributes described above. In the course of our analysis using these variables, it became clear that another attribute, the user's primary academic discipline, was also of significant predictive value, and this was therefore added, giving the following set.

1. Length of computing experience.
2. Length of discipline experience.
3. Amount of computing being done.
4. Regularity of computing.
5. Isolation (geographical and social).
6. Discipline (faculty grouping).

Clearly these six attributes, together with the population variables, age and sex, are to some extent interrelated. However, since one aim of this work is to characterize users likely to have particular difficulty with computing and, some characteristics are more easily ascertainable than others, such an overlap may be positively advantageous.

Three measures of users' attitudes and perceptions were also identified; these we refer to as perceptions of computing. They were the user's rating of the adequacy of his own skills, his attitude to computing, and his estimate of the ease of use of the local operating system. Five-point scales of the semantic differential type were used as measures.

The variables used as measures of our attributes were derived directly from the questionnaire. "Experience of discipline" was simply a crude dichotomy between staff and students, while "experience of computing" related to the length of time since the user began to use the computer seriously in his research. "Discipline" was based on faculty groupings, and "isolation" on the number of other users with whom the respondent discussed computing. "Regularity of use" was measured by the longest period in which a user did no computing, and "volume of computing activity" by a five-point scale ranging from "continuously" to "rarely" (which correlated closely with the observed numbers of jobs users had run during the period concerned). When cross-tabulated with the measures of perception of computing, it appeared that all the attributes except the second were significantly associated with perceived adequacy of skill ($p < 0.0001$ in each case). The same five attributes are also associated with users' estimates of ease of use of the operating system ($p < 0.001$ in the case of attributes 3 to 6, $p = 0.01$ for the first). As for enjoyment of computing, attributes 3 to 6 are again significantly related ($p < 0.0001$).

Neither age nor sex proved to have any value as a predictor of *perceptions of computing;* there was no discernible relationship with attitude to computing or estimate of ease of use of the local operating system. Women were much more likely than men to feel that their skills were inadequate ($p < 0.0001$), but of course far more women than men study the arts and social sciences, men commonly being in the majority in the pure and applied sciences. It turned out that this "two cultures" variable was the significant predictor; within each "culture" group sex-differences were largely unrelated to perceived adequacy of skill although among the scientists women were slightly more likely than men to be neutral about the adequacy of their skills.

Initial attempts to elicit and order the independent significant attributes suggest that amount of computing, discipline and length of computing experience together provide an adequate predictor of a user's perceptions of computing, although there remains a substantial element of variance which appears to be due to individual differences.

B. User Interaction with Guidance Services

In this area, users were asked specific questions about guidance services relating to the operating system and to applications software, both on their local computer and on any remote system to which they had access. These included questions on access to advisory services, documentation and courses. Users were also asked about their access to more general facilities such as regular news-letters and notice-boards.

The answers to the questions on the advisory service make possible a sketch of the kind of clientele with which the computer centre must deal. They also show, by way of complement, those users who rely most upon their colleagues in their own departments. Overall, of the 1569 users who stated their most frequent source of advice on the local operating system, 43% asked a friend, 40% went to the computer centre, and the remainder asked a departmental computer representative or programmer; hardly anyone claimed to refer to an operator as the preferred source. The pattern of advice-seeking is similar for FORTRAN, with the tendency to ask a friend being stronger still (48%).

However, with the software which is in widespread use but not quite so "popular", users were much more likely to cite the computer centre as their first port of call. Of the NAG (Numerical Algorithms Group) library users, 58% most often asked the computer centre, as did 51% of users of SPSS (Statistical Package for the Social Sciences). About 30% in each case asked a friend, so that people were more likely to seek help with SPSS than with NAG from an "official" computing source within their own departments. A summary of these findings is shown in Table 1. These findings are borne out to some extent by advisory service records at our own Computer Centre in Birmingham.

TABLE 1

Most likely source of software advice

Software item	Local operating system	FORTRAN	NAG	SPSS
Source of advice				
Computer centre advisory service	627 (40.0%)	410 (37.4%)	244 (55.7%)	171 (50.3%)
Departmental computer representative	156 (9.9%)	93 (8.5%)	36 (8.2%)	36 (10.6%)
Technical assistant or programmer	109 (7.0%)	62 (5.7%)	23 (5.3%)	28 (8.2%)
Computer operator or receptionist	8 (0.5%)	3 (0.3%)	1 (0.2%)	2 (0.6%)
Colleague, friend, or supervisor	669 (42.6%)	527 (48.1%)	134 (30.6%)	103 (30.3%)
TOTAL	1569	1095	438	340

When these data are related to the attributes of users and their perceptions of computing as discussed in the previous section, it becomes clear that the central advisory service provided by the central computing service must deal with a wide diversity of queries, and with great variations in users' perceptions and attitudes. For instance, novice users were as likely as experienced users to give the centre as their first source of advice. So if, as the work on job analysis (see Section IV) suggests, novice users tend to have simple problems and experienced users difficult ones, this finding would imply that the centre advisory service can be expected to have to deal with a widely diverse complexity of queries, not just the more difficult ones, as is sometimes supposed. On the other hand, for all kinds of software, members of staff are much more likely than postgraduate students to consult the centre, so that advisors often have to help users of substantially greater academic standing than their own. The evidence from the data on users' perceptions of computing displays a similar breadth. We have seen that, on average 40% of users gave the computer centre as their most frequent source of advice on the local operating system. However, this average includes 54% of the users who felt their skills completely inadequate and 45% of the completely adequate.

While quite a clear picture can be formed of the service clientele, there is less clarity in the reaction of the users to the advice they get. This is partly because the overall level of satisfaction with the computer centre advisory service is very high, leaving little room for group variations. More than two-thirds of those who ever consulted the service on the operating system or FORTRAN, and more than three-quarters of SPSS questioners, were satisfied or very satisfied with the advice they got. The postgraduate students were slightly less likely to be satisfied with the advice than members of staff, but otherwise the user characteristics were not closely related to satisfaction. Perceptions of computing were, however, rather better indicators. Of those users who felt their skills to be inadequate, 63% were satisfied with computer centre advice, compared with 74% of the adequates ($p<0.05$); while of those who found the operating system hard to use 57% were satisfied with the advice, compared with 78% of those who found it easy ($p<0.001$).

Thus while the overall level of satisfaction is high, it is still higher among the confident users than among the inadequate users who find computing difficult.

As for documentation, while users are in general less satisfied, a similar pattern emerges. Respondents were asked if they owned a copy of the documentation on the software they were using, and how satisfied they were with it. Of the 88% of users who had consulted operating system documentation, 61% were satisfied with it, as against 17% who were dissatisfied. Of the FORTRAN users, 67% were satisfied with the documentation, as were 77% of the SPSS users. These results are summarized in Table 2.

Users' attributes had no discernible relationship with their satisfaction with documentation, but perceptions of computing played some part. As with advisory services, users who rated their skills inadequate were less likely to be satisfied than those who perceived their skills to be adequate. For instance, among the FORTRAN users, 45% of the inadequates were satisfied with the documentation, compared with 69% of the adequates. With regard to operating system documentation, as one might have expected, a smaller proportion (30%) of those who found the operating system hard to use were satisfied with the documentation, compared to 70% satisfied customers among those who found the system easy to use.

TABLE 2

Satisfaction with documents on software

Response	Local operating system	FORTRAN	NAG	SPSS
Very satisfied/ satisfied	826 (61%)	691 (67%)	318 (74%)	258 (77%)
Neither satisfied nor dissatisfied	303 (22%)	259 (25%)	75 (18%)	46 (14%)
Dissatisfied/very dissatisfied	231 (17%)	82 (8%)	36 (8%)	32 (9%)
TOTAL	1360	1032	429	336
Have not referred to documents	187	100	25	9

The most disappointing area of guidance data was on courses; for instance, only about a third of the respondents had been on any kind of course on the operating system, although almost all had the opportunity. Two factors seem to contribute to this. One is that, while many users perceive the need to learn a programming language, few seem to conceive of the operating system as a subject requiring explicit learning, and thus simply try to "pick it up" as they go along. This, paradoxically, is encouraged by the tendency to minimize the impact of the operating system upon novices so that they can concentrate on learning about the language or package which is the prime subject for study in that particular course. Secondly, when a user comes to need a more detailed understanding of the operating system as part of his use of the computer in his research, the need is an immediate one, while courses tend to be put on at considerable intervals. He thus sets about increasing his knowledge, again by "picking it up", and so by the time a course is available he feels he knows all he needs. This lack of initial systematic training has serious implications for the level of expertise in the user community. It may be helped by improving the facilities for self-teaching and by enhancing the "helpfulness" of operating systems and applications software.

C. Between-university Differences

One element in our choice of universities for the census was the variety of attributes their users were expected to display, and this was confirmed by our analysis of the responses. We thus expected major differences in users' perceptions of computing between universities on this basis alone, and in the event perceived adequacy of skill and ease of use of the operating system were significantly related to university of origin ($p < 0.001$ in each case). We therefore assembled eight groupings from the three most important attributes, i.e.,

    (a) the user's academic discipline, categorized as "science" (S) (strictly speaking physical science) or "non-science" (A);

    (b) whether the user ran few (F) or many (M) jobs related to the norm for any period;

    (c) whether the user was a novice (N) or experienced (E) in computing (i.e. whether the user had less than or more than two years' experience).

This gave a total of eight combinations:

AFN: Arts and Social Science/few computing jobs/novices in computing

AFE: Arts and Social Science/few computing jobs/experienced in computing

AMN: Arts and Social Science/many computing jobs/novices in computing

AME: Arts and Social Science/many computing jobs/experienced in computing

SFN: Science and Engineering/few computing jobs/novices in computing.

SFE: Science and Engineering/few computing jobs/experienced in computing

SMN: Science and Engineering/many computing jobs/novices in computing

SME: Science and Engineering/many computing jobs/experienced in computing

The attitude measures were then related to these eight groupings. Within these groups, a complex pattern of relationships among users in the different universities emerges. In two universities of the eight, the AME users were much less likely to feel their skills adequate ($p < 0.001$) than the corresponding group in the other six. In the same two universities, three of the four categories of novice users found it significantly harder to use the operating system (p ranging from < 0.01 to 0.0001). Since the two universities had different computing systems, it may be that there are differences in approaches to new users in these universities. In a different pair of universities, SME users were less likely to feel their computing skills to be inadequate than in the other six universities ($p < 0.005$).

There are also substantial variations among users' attitudes to guidance services in the universities studied. Even within the attribute groups, there was wide variation among the universities in the extent to which users consulted the central advisory service, and in the degree of satisfaction with this service and with documentation. Investigation is continuing to identify the salient features within each university which contribute to these variations.

D. Conclusions

Firm conclusions and consequent predictions about user characteristics are made difficult by such problems as the extent to which users report their perceptions accurately, and by the relation between perception and performance. But some elements stand out. One is the association between the amount of computing and the perceived adequacy and ease of use: this factor is much more important than regularity of use, which implies that a user with a small amount of computing to do should "hoard" it to create a short period of intensive use, rather than run a very small number of jobs regularly. The other interesting conclusion is that users in the arts and social sciences, both men and women, have much greater problems with computing than their colleagues in the sciences, suggesting the need both for further investigation of this problem and the need to give particular support to users in those areas. Finally, while there clearly is a link between isolation, perceived adequacy and efficacy, its nature and causal relationships need further investigation.

In the area of guidance services, the high level of satisfaction among those who use them is clearly cause for some congratulation. There are, however, areas of concern, notably in the difficulties experienced by those who exhibit at least two of the non-science/ few-jobs/novice-user characteristics. These factors clearly play some part in the observed differences between universities, but in both areas much more needs to be done to unravel the complex interactions in order to improve users' satisfaction and efficiency.

IV. A LONGITUDINAL STUDY OF USER BEHAVIOUR

As a complement to the approach of studying the events which occurred at specific interfaces in the computing environment, a longitudinal study was undertaken to follow the detailed sequence of computing events related to a sample of users over a period of about one month. The sample was selected from the population of Birmingham users covered by the census, and stratified according to the primary characteristics as determined from that census, i.e. academic discipline, amount of computing, length of computing experience (see Section III above).

The three characteristics, each with two possible values, thus gave eight different user categories. However, as the study required a fair degree of involvement from users, it was not easy to find volunteers, particularly in the few-jobs/novice-user categories. (None could be found in the non-science/few-jobs/novice-user category.) In all, 17 users were involved (5% of the active user population) and they ran 433 jobs (3% of the total background jobs). As well as using the sample directly for the comparison of the behaviours of the different categories, the results from each category were subsequently weighted to reflect the scaled behaviour of the aggregate local population (i.e. the results obtained for the jobs from each category of users in the sample were scaled in proportion to the number of jobs run by the same category in the full population).

The study involved the users in completing a form reporting on every batch job they had run. (Users could use a terminal for preparing jobs and inspecting results, but no truly interactive computing was covered by this study.) The form was to be completed after the job had run, and they had studied the output and decided what to do next. As well as giving the date, time, and an identification of the sequence of which the job formed part, the users were asked to complete four questions on every job run and a further seven questions if there had been any kind of error. In general each answer simply required a tick in the appropriate box on the form: the form itself was confined to a single sheet of paper. The design of the form layout was of course checked in a pilot run, and significant changes followed this. It proved difficult to arrive at a design which succinctly captured all the relevant data and which allowed for the wide range of possibilities. This in itself gave some indication that even the simple task of running a background job and deciding on the next step according to the results is not actually as straightforward as it might appear.

The very fact that the user completed a form could of course alter to a greater or lesser extent the pattern of his behaviour. In an attempt to monitor this, the computer operating system was modified so that it would, with the users' permission, keep a record of all the work they had run. The monitoring process was started before the form-filling study commenced and was carried on for some time after its completion. The end result was, as we had suspected, far more data than we have as yet been able to analyse. One thing it has already made clear, however, is that it is not possible by automatic processing of the monitor records to collect much of the information which was collected from the form. For example, a program which terminates with an error message can still be counted by the user as successful if that was what he had anticipated, whilst a program which terminated with a success message could still be a failure if either the data was wrong or it was processed in the wrong way. Neither is it possible to decide automatically whether a user felt that an error was trivial or serious, nor whether it was easy or difficult to find.

The study revealed that 74% of all jobs over the full (weighted) population were intended as "production" runs. Our hypothesis had been that many "production" jobs would be optimistic attempts with programs that had not run successfully before. In the event users reported that 75% of such jobs had been run successfully before. Even more interestingly, when comparing the proportions of jobs which were reported as being totally successful, the jobs which had not run previously were almost as successful (62%) as those which had run before (65%). This would suggest that users were more realistic about their expectations than had been expected. (But caution should be exercised: here as much as anywhere the act of completing the report form might be expected to affect the user's behaviour.) Eighteen per cent of jobs were intended for the debugging of the user's own programming (in Birmingham almost all user programming is in FORTRAN), whilst the remainder were "housekeeping" or for exploring new facilities.

Over the total (weighted) population, 56% of all jobs were reported as totally successful, 25% as partially successful, whilst 19% were total failures. The total success rate for packages, 68%, was much higher than for users' own programming, which was 42%. The success rate for imported packages (i.e. obtained by the user himself from a source other than the computer centre) was just a little higher than for packages provided through the centre. It may be that the support from the user's local community for imported packages is balancing the official documentation and advisory service for the centre packages. It is hoped that a follow-up study on the behaviour of users who are socially isolated will throw more light on this.

Where users did their own programming, a noticeable increase in the success rate (from 42% to 58%) was reported where the user had made significant use of a library (e.g. the Numerical Algorithms Group library). There had been speculation as to whether the reduction in programming effort brought about by use of a library would outweigh the increased complexity in interfacing and the frequently weighty documentation associated with it. In the pilot study there was a hint that the use of libraries was not especially beneficial, but this appears to have been contradicted by the full study.

Looking at the relationship between user category and success rate, the dominant factor appeared to be experience in computing. The *more* experienced the user the *lower* his success rate. We found this result surprising, and feel that the dominant factor must be that the more experienced a user becomes the more demanding he is of the computer system. When we discussed this with an experienced user he said he could have told us that without an expensive study! The most successful category was the science/few-jobs/novice-user. (This category did nothing but occasional production work using "imported" packages.)

The users reported that they found 70% of their faults definitely (over the total weighted population), 21% probably, whilst the remaining 9% were located only possibly or not at all. This latter class, which might be termed "serious" faults, corresponded to 4% of all the jobs run. These figures were corroborated by the parallel reports that, when the supposed faults were corrected, 68% of all corrections were totally successful whilst the remainder were at best only a partial success. The non-science and computer-novice categories reported their faults harder to find than the average, but once the correction was proposed, again the computer-experienced categories were the least successful. Apparently experience helps in finding the general area of a problem, but greater demands of the experienced user make it harder to find the absolute cure.

Almost all errors were reported as occurring in the user's own programming, job-control commands, or data or control cards. Hardly any errors were reported as occurring within the facilities provided by the computer centre itself. (Users did report that errors in documentation led them into making 3% of their faults, but no other information source was reported as misleading them.) About a half of all errors in data (over the weighted population) were reported as trivial, but in the other three areas it was very much less than this. More of the serious errors of concept were reported as arising in the user's own discipline rather than in the computing aspects of his work, and most of these discipline errors were found where the user was doing his own programming.

The types of errors reported varied greatly according to the type of user. The overall indications were that the science users matured as they became more experienced, with their success rate falling, probably as they became more demanding. There was no such indication for the non-science users however, suggesting rather that those experienced in computing were in a disjoint set which was perhaps not reached as a natural progression from the novice class.

The provisional conclusions and implications may thus be summarized as follows.

(a) The need for care in the preparation of data should be highlighted.

(b) Positive encouragement should be given to the formation of discipline-oriented sub-routine libraries paralleling the mathematical facilities already available, e.g. from the NAG library.

(c) The use of computing in the non-sciences is evidently still in a state of flux, and deserves special attention.

(d) Experienced users are less "successful" in their computing than computer novices, presumably as the complexity of

their demands increases. (Too much experience is a dangerous thing!)

V. CONCLUSIONS

This chapter has indicated that research findings from a number of
diverse areas are applicable to the problem of providing appropriate
guidance to computer users in universities, and that the illuminative
strategy represents an appropriate means of encompassing the many
facets of the problem. The two studies briefly described are components of a wider investigation, and reflect some of the difficulty of
collecting valid and useful data in such an environment without
thereby disrupting the phenomena under observation. These studies
also demonstrate a degree of complementarity, in that the interpretation of each is assisted by information from the other. Issues
therefore emerge with greater clarity.

The research has confirmed the need for adequate guidance
services for university computer users. At present only about half
of all computer runs are completely successful by the users' own
criteria, and the investigators have observed heavy reliance on
official computer centre advisory services. The research has added
support to the belief that an adequate analysis of the services in
relation to users' requirements must take full account of cognitive
and behavioural aspects.

The use of program packages and sub-routine libraries not only
reduces programming effort, but also reduces the number of
unsuccessful computer jobs. Programs wholly written by the user
himself are the least successful. Where packages are used there is
some evidence that those errors which occur tend to be on the
package/system interface, at the level of job-control language. Some
advantage might be gained by improvements in interface design, and
by wider use of packages and libraries. There is a good case for the
development and implementation of more specialized libraries and
packages.

A user's success in computing is a function of his discipline or
academic background, the amount of computing which he does, and
the length of his experience in computing. Intermittency of use of
computing facilities is not in itself a handicap. These effects appear
uniform across universities. Experienced users do not simply make
fewer errors than the inexperienced: their superior performance
results from their greater success in identifying and correcting their

errors. Users encounter appreciable difficulty in using remote systems: at a time when the use of networks is growing rapidly this observation suggests a need for appropriate compensatory guidance services.

Users rely to some extent on advice from within their own departments. However this pool of expertise is less comprehensive than that provided by the computer centres, and its adequacy varies across departments. Though users report that they seek help from friends and colleagues almost as often as from the official advisory service they also indicate that they regard the informal sources as less authoritative and more dispensable than the official sources. There may therefore be scope for the development of improved self-help capabilities within departmental user groups.

Despite the uniformly high level of satisfaction with computer centre advisory services there are indications that some improvements may be possible if more account is taken of the variations amongst users. The results support the view that university computer users may be legitimately divided into a number of groups on the basis of academic discipline and experience in computing, and that more effective (and efficient) use of computing services might be promoted if instruction, documentation, and advisory services explicitly recognized the differing guidance requirements of these groups.

ACKNOWLEDGEMENTS

The research described in this chapter was supported by Social Science Research Council grant HR4421.

REFERENCES

Allen, W.H. (1971). Instructional media research: past, present and future. *A. V. Communication Rev.*, **19**, 79–87.

Anderson, R.E. (1978). Value orientation of computer science students. *Communications of the ACM*, **21**, 219–255.

Argyle, M. (1969). *Social Interaction*. London: Methuen.

Atkinson, R.C. (1972). Ingredients for a theory of instruction. *Am. Psychol.*, **27**, 921–931.

Berlyne, D.E. (1974). Information and motivation. In A. Silverstein (ed.) *Human Communication: Theoretical Explorations*. New York: LEA (Wiley).

Bligh, D.M. (1977). Are teaching innovations in post-secondary education irrelevant? In M.J.A. Howe (ed.) *Adult Learning*. Chichester: Wiley.

Boies S.J. and Gould, J.D. (1974). Syntactic errors in computer programming. *Human Factors*, 16, 253–257.

Briggs, L.J., Campeau, P.L., Gagne, R.M. and May, M.A. (1967). *Instructional Media*. Pittsburg: American Institutes for Research.

Britt, D.H. (1971). Improved method for instructional development: learner types. *Audiovisual Instruction*, April, 14–15.

Bruner, J. (1966). *Toward a Theory of Instruction*. Cambridge, Massachusetts: Belknap Press of Harvard University.

Burnhill, P and Hartley, J. (1975). Psychology and textbook design: a research critique. In J. Baggaley, G.H. Jamieson and H. Marchant (eds.) *Aspects of Educational Technology, VIII, Communication and Learning*. London: Pitman.

Cannell, C.F. and Kahn, R.L. (1968). Interviewing. In G. Lindzey and E. Aronson (eds) *Handbook of Social Psychology*. (Vol. 2, 2nd Edn.) Reading, Massachusetts: Addison-Wesley.

Cyert, R.M. and MacCrimmon, K.R. (1968). Organisations. In G. Lindzey and E. Aronson (eds) *Handbook of Social Psychology*. (Vol. 1, 2nd Edn.) Reading, Massachusetts: Addison-Wesley.

Eason, K.D. (1976). Understanding the naive computer user. *Computer J.*, 19, 3–7.

Eysenck, H.J. and Eysenck, S.B.G. (1969). *Personality Structure and Measurement*. London: Routledge and Kegan Paul.

Fishbein, M and Ajzen, I. (1975). *Belief, Attitude, Intention and Behavior: An Introduction to Theory and Research*. Reading, Massachusetts: Addison-Wesley.

Gould, J.D. (1975). Some psychological evidence on how people debug computer programs. *Int. J. Man-Machine Stud.*, 7, 151–182.

Gould, J.D. and Drongowski, P. (1974). An exploratory study of computer program debugging. *Human Factors*, 16, 258–277.

Greeno, J.G. (1976). Cognitive objectives of instruction: Theory of knowledge for solving problems and answering questions. In D. Klahr (ed.) *Cognition and Instruction*. Hillsdale, New Jersey: LEA (Wiley).

Hall, C.S. and Lindzey, G. (1978). *Theories of Personality*. (3rd Edn.) New York: Wiley.

Haskell, R.W. (1976). Individual learner variables and the prescribing of instructional methods and media—some preliminary findings. In P.J. Sleeman and D.M. Rockwell (eds) *Instructional Media and Technology*. Stroudsburg, Pennsylvania: Dowden, Hutchinson and Ross.

Horton, D.L. and Turnage, T.W. (1976). *Human Learning*. Englewood Cliffs, New Jersey: Prentice-Hall.

Iklé, F.C. (1967). Can social predictions be evaluated? *Daedalus*, 96, 733–758.

Joiner, D. (1976). Social ritual and architectural space. In H.M. Proshansky, W.H. Ittleson and L.G. Rivlin (eds) *Environmental Psychology*. (2nd Edn.) New York: Holt, Rinehart and Winston.

Katz, D. and Kahn, R.L. (1978). *The Social Psychology of Organizations*. (2nd Edn.) New York: Wiley.

Kelley, H.H. and Thibaut, J.W. (1969). Group problem solving. In G. Lindzey and E. Aronson (eds) *Handbook of Social Psychology*. (Vol. 4, 2nd Edn.) Reading, Massachusetts: Addison-Wesley.

Landa, L.N. (1976). *Instructional Regulation and Control: Cybernetics, Algorithmization and Heuristics in Education*. Englewood Cliffs, New

Jersey: Educational Technology Publications.

Lukey, F.J. (1978). Understanding and debugging computer programs. *Proceedings of the Workshop on Computing Skills and Adaptive Systems*, University of Liverpool.

McGuire, W.J. (1969). Theory-oriented research in natural settings: the best of both worlds for social psychology. In M. Sherif and C.W. Sherif (eds) *Interdisciplinary Relationship in the Social Sciences*. Chicago: Aldine.

McGuire, W.J. (1973). The yin and yang of progress in social psychology: seven koan. *J. Personality Soc. Psychol.*, 26, 446–456.

Mazlack, L.J. (1975). Compatibility of students from different disciplines and semesters. In O. Lecarme and R. Lewis (eds) *Computers in Education*. Amsterdam: North Holland.

Miller, G.A., Galanter, E. and Pribram, K.H. (1960). *Plans and the Structure of Behavior*. New York: Holt.

Moore, J.A., Levin, J.A. and Mann, W.C. (1977). A goal-oriented model of human dialogue. *Am. J. Computational Linguistics*, Microfiche No. 67.

Nagy, G. and Pennebaker, M.C. (1974). A step towards automatic analysis of student programming errors in a batch environment. *Int. J. Man-Machine Stud.*, 6, 563–578.

Neisser, U. (1976). *Cognition and Reality*. San Francisco: W.H. Freeman.

Palormo, J.M. (1967). The computer programmer aptitude battery–a description and discussion. *Proceedings of the Annual Computer Personnel Research Conference*, 5, 57–63.

Parent, J., Forward, J., Canter, R. and Mohling, J. (1975). Interactive effects of teaching strategy and personal locus of control on student performance and satisfaction. *J. Educ. Psychol.*, 67, 764–769.

Parlett, M. and Hamilton, D. (1972). Evaluation as illumination: a new approach to the study of innovatory programs. *Occasional Paper No. 9*, Centre for Research in the Educational Sciences, University of Edinburgh.

Pask, G. (1975). *The Cybernetics of Human Learning and Performance: A Guide to Theory and Research*. London: Hutchinson.

Pask, G. (1976). *Conversation Theory*. Amsterdam: Elsevier.

Payne, R. and Pugh, D. (1971). Organizations as psychological environments. In P.B. Warr (ed.) *Psychology at Work*. Harmondsworth: Penguin.

Pearce, W.L. (1973). Understanding data processing terminology. Ph.D. Thesis, University of Missouri, Columbia.

Pylyshyn, Z.W. (ed.) (1970). *Perspectives on the Computer Revolution*. Englewood Cliffs, New Jersey: Prentice-Hall.

Reason, J.T. (1977). Skill and error in everyday life. In M.J.A. Howe (ed.) *Adult Learning*. Chichester: Wiley.

Resnick, L.B. (1976). Task analysis in instructional design: some cases from mathematics. In D. Klahr (ed.) *Cognition and Instruction*. Hillsdale, New Jersey: LEA (Wiley).

Robinson, S.K. and Torsun, I.S. (1976). An empirical analysis of FORTRAN programs. *Computer J.*, 19, 56–62.

Roethlisberger, F.J. and Dickson, W.J. (1939). *Management and the Worker*. Cambridge, Massachusetts: Harvard University Press.

Rokeach, M. (1960). *The Open and Closed Mind*. New York: Basic Books.

Rosen, S. (1969). Electronic computers: an historical survey. *Computing Surveys*, 1, 7–36.

Rosenthal, R. (1966). *Experimenter Effects in Behavioral Research*. New York:

Appleton-Century-Crofts.

Rotter, J.B. (1966). Generalised expectancies for internal versus external control of reinforcement. *Psychol. Monogr.*, 80, 1–28.

Sackman, H. (1970). *Man–Computer Problem Solving*. Princeton: Auerbach.

Sammet, J.E. (1969). *Programming Languages, History and Fundamentals.* Englewood Cliffs, New Jersey: Prentice-Hall.

Sarbin, T.R. and Allen, V.L. (1969). Role Theory. In G. Lindzey and E. Aronson (eds) *Handbook of Social Psychology.* (Vol. 1, 2nd Edn.) Reading, Massachusetts: Addison-Wesley.

Selltiz, C., Wrightsman, L.S. and Cook, S.W. (1976). *Research Methods in Social Relations.* (3rd Edn.) New York: Holt, Rinehart and Winston.

Shaw, M.E. (1964). Communication networks. In L. Berkowitz (ed.) *Advances in Experimental Psychology.* (Vol. 1) New York and London: Academic Press.

Shaw, R.E. and Wilson, B.E. (1976). Abstract conceptual knowledge: how we know what we know. In D. Klahr (ed.) *Cognition and Instruction.* Hillsdale, New Jersey: LEA (Wiley).

Sime, M.E., Arblaster, A.T. and Green, T.R.G. (1977a). Reducing programming errors in nested conditionals by prescribing writing procedure. *Int. J. Man–Machine Stud.*, 9, 119–126.

Sime, M.E., Green, T.R.G. and Guest, D.J. (1977b). Scope marking in computer conditionals—a psychological evaluation. *Int. J. Man–Machine Stud.*, 9, 107–118.

Simon, H.A. and Hayes, J.R. (1976). Understanding complex task instructions. In D. Klahr (ed.) *Cognition and Instruction.* Hillsdale, New Jersey: LEA (Wiley).

Taylor, F. (1977). Acquiring knowledge from prose and continuous discourse. In M.J.A. Howe (ed.) *Adult Learning.* Chichester: Wiley.

Turney, J.R. (1974). Activity outcome expectancies and intrinsic activity values as predictors of several motivation indexes for technical professionals. *Organisational Behavior and Human Performance*, 11, 65–82.

Vernon, P.E. (1961). *The Structure of Human Abilities.* (2nd Edn.) London: Methuen.

Vroom, K.H. (1964). *Work and Motivation.* New York: Wiley.

Webb, E.J., Campbell, D.T., Schwartz, R.D. and Sechrest, L. (1966). *Unobtrusive Measures: Non-Reactive Research in the Social Sciences.* Chicago: Rand-McNally.

Weick, K.E. (1968). Systematic observational methods. In G. Lindzey and E. Aronson (eds) *Handbook of Social Psychology.* (Vol. 5, 2nd Edn.) Reading, Massachusetts: Addison-Wesley.

Weinberg, G.M. (1971). *The Psychology of Computer Programming.* New York: Van Nostrand Reinhold.

Weinberg, G.M. (1979). Notes for young debuggers. *Datalink*, 8 January.

Weinberg, G.M. and Schulman, E.L. (1974). Goals and performance in computer programming. *Human Factors*, 16, 70–77.

Weizenbaum, J. (1976). *Computer Power and Human Reason.* San Francisco: W.H. Freeman.

Wilson, J.R. and Vandenberg, S.G. (1978). Sex differences in cognition: evidence from the Hawaii family study. In T.E. McGill, D.A. Dewsbury and B.D. Sachs (eds) *Sex and Behavior.* New York: Plenum.

Wittrock, M.C. and Lumsdaine, A.A. (1977). Instructional Psychology. *A. Rev.*

Psychol., **28**, 417–459.

Youngs, E.A. (1974). Human errors in programming. *Int. J. Man–Machine Stud.*, **6**, 361–376.

3. The Needs of the Commercial User

K.D. EASON and L. DAMODARAN

Department of Human Sciences, University of Technology, Loughborough, England

---

I. INTRODUCTION

Commercial computer applications have a wide variety of users. Programmers, systems analysts, system designers and computer scientists form a core of "expert" users. The rest of the user population comprises a range of professional managerial, technical and clerical users as well as a growing number of the public. Apart from the small number of experts, most of these commercial computer users are "naive" with respect to computing—the computer is essentially a mystery to them. Naive users have certain common characteristics which distinguish them from expert users, but of course there are wide variations between individual users. In order to design successful systems it is therefore necessary to take account of both the general characteristics of naive users and the differences between them.

In this chapter we shall focus on the needs of naive commercial computer users, and we begin by presenting a classification of both the general and specific characteristics of these users. The classification of specific characteristics incorporates considerations of the different kinds of requirements the user makes of a system and the consequences if these requirements are not met. In Section V a series of user job-profiles are discussed, which involves a comparison of the way people in different jobs differ on the variables previously described. We also present a classification of those computer system characteristics which are the prime means for meeting user requirements. It is these variables that have to be manipulated in the design process if the naive user is to make effective use of the system.

II. GENERAL ATTRIBUTES OF A NAIVE COMPUTER USER

A naive computer user may be defined as *a person who is not an expert in computer technology but who uses a computer system to assist him in the performance of his task.* This definition focuses attention upon four important attributes of the user.

A. The Task-Tool Relationship

The user will evaluate the system as a tool by virtue of its ability to service his task. The "fit" between tool and task will be his main assessment criterion. It is of little interest to him that the system is a technical masterpiece, or that it serves another user very well; if it serves his task needs poorly, it stands condemned as a poor system.

B. Expertise in Computer Technology

The user's interests and aspirations lie outside computer technology; if he has aspirations for personal development at work he will probably wish to devote his time to becoming more competent in his chosen profession or career. His knowledge of computer technology will be limited and he will be little motivated to extend his knowledge. He will seek to minimize the time and effort he must devote to studying computing and will probably restrict his study to the information and skills necessary to fulfil his tasks (Eason, 1980).

C. Ease of Use

The user will be interested in a computer system as a *means* to an end, not an *end* in itself, and will seek to minimize the time and effort he must devote to operating the system and interpreting output.

D. User Support and Training

By virtue of his limited knowledge of the technology he is using, the naive user is often in need of help. He may face problems in interpreting how the system can handle his task, how to ask it to do so, why it is behaving as it is, and how to recover from errors and breakdowns. The system must make provision for answering these needs and should protect the user from features of the system which are of no concern to him.

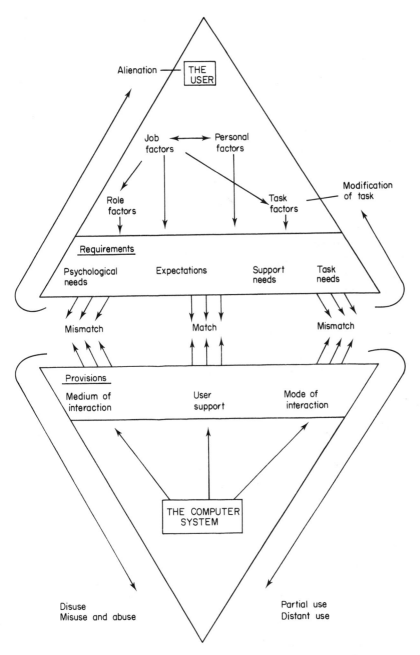

Fig. 1. Critical variables in the match/mismatch of user requirements and system provisions.

III. CRITICAL VARIABLES IN MAN–COMPUTER INTERACTION

The foregoing description of the important attributes of the naive computer user emphasizes the task–user–tool triad of variables which is basic to the success of man–computer interaction. When these variables are in harmony interaction may be successful; when they are not the outcome for one or more of the variables will not be satisfactory, e.g. the user may become frustrated, the task may be distorted to fit the tool, or the tool may be abused, disused or misused.

It is the purpose of this section to:

(i)   identify the task and user variables that cause different users to make different demands upon a system;

(ii)   categorize the different kinds of requirement a user will have of a computer system; and

(iii) identify the consequences if the user's requirements are not satisfactorily met by the provisions of the system.

Figure 1 summarizes the variables and the way they interact.

A. The User and Task Variables

In the parlance of experimental science these factors constitute the independent variables in the causal chain to be described. The nature of the user and the job he has undertaken are the factors which define the requirements the user will have of a computer system. In Fig. 1 four factors are identified. The *job* the person undertakes is a fundamental concern for a number of reasons. First, it defines the relevance of the computer to the user, i.e. whether it is of central or peripheral importance, and secondly, it defines the *task* or tasks for which computer aid is required. The task in its turn defines the specific information or information-processing needs the user will have of the system. Thirdly, the job defines the discretionary powers of the user; the degree to which he can decide for himself what he does and how he does it. The discretion of the user has obvious consequences for decisions to use or not use a computer system. Interlinked with the job the person undertakes is the *role* he plays. While the job is concerned with an organizational function, the work role relates to the behaviour generally expected both by the job occupant and by others. In our society there are, for example, expectations not only about the work of a priest, a policeman, a waiter, etc. but also about how they will do their work and how they will behave in general. In the same way, the work roles of people who are naive computer users can influence the way they and their colleagues expect them to conduct computer-aided tasks. Finally, there are *personal* factors which distinguish one person from another, e.g. personality, attitudes, motives, intelligence, etc. These factors may mean that although two people have identical jobs and tasks to conduct, their requirements of a computer system are not identical.

B. User Requirements of a Computer System

The combination of variables that characterize a user give rise to a specific set of requirements of a computer system. Again in the language of experimental science, these requirements constitute a set of intervening variables, mediating between the independent variables and the critical dependent variable, which is the response of the user to the system he uses. In Fig. 1 four kinds of requirements are identified. The task the person undertakes gives rise to *task needs*, i.e. the particular information or information-processing facilities required to complete the task. This is probably the principal kind of requirement considered in the design of systems but it by no means exhausts the demands of the user. A second need is for *support*. The user comes to the system with his task needs but, because of his "naive" status, he is unlikely to be fully prepared to engage in dialogue with the computer. He may need help understanding what the system can do, how it can be asked to do it, and how to correct errors if he makes them. His support needs define his state of readiness to engage in the kind of interaction necessary to satisfy his task needs.

In addition to these requirements the user also brings to man–computer interaction a set of *expectations* which define what he is and is not prepared to do to achieve his task needs. Some people may be prepared to attend lengthy training courses to learn about the computer system they are to use, others may regard a one-day appreciation course as an appropriate expenditure of time and effort. An important point to note is that expectations are likely to be affected more by job demands than by a realistic appreciation of the effort required to meet task and support needs.

The final set of requirements is for ways to be found to meet the *psychological needs* of the user for an interesting job, autonomy over the decisions that affect his work, appropriate pay for his work and so on, i.e. all of the factors which determine whether a person is satisfied or dissatisfied with his job. As will be discussed later in this chapter, in some circumstances the computer system is virtually irrelevant as a means of satisfying psychological needs, but in others its role in this respect is crucial.

C. The Consequences of a User Requirement—System Provisions Mismatch

The final stage of this analysis of user behaviour is to examine what happens when a specific set of user requirements is matched with the provisions offered by a computer system. The matching of human needs and technological provisions has been of concern to students of human nature since the beginning of the industrial revolution (Klein, 1976). On numerous occasions a potential mismatch has been identified which, in practice, has had few observable consequences because the user has adapted his behaviour to compensate for the inadequacies of the technology. If the same were true of the user of computer technology there would be little purpose in producing this book. However, in a wide range of circumstances, mismatches between requirements and provisions can lead to important consequences. The consequences, as indicated in Fig. 1, may relate to the use of the system, the way the task is undertaken, the feelings and attitudes of the user, or any combination of these factors (Eason *et al.*, 1974).

Probably the most common response is to change one's use of the system. This is typically the response when use of the system is rather peripheral to the important elements of a job and where the user has considerable discretion over the manner in which he conducts his work. In these circumstances the user might adopt one of the following responses. In the extreme case he may stop using the system and it may fall into *disuse*. However, if it has some merits a common response is to make *partial* use of its services, i.e. to select the most useful, most accessible or most easily understood aspects of. the service and to disregard the rest. Frequently this means that potentially valuable facilities remain virtually unused. A third possibility is typical of situations in which the system provides a valued service but demands more time and effort than the user is prepared to give. If the user has the discretion, there is a tendency for him to adopt a *distant* use strategy, in which another person (a "human" interface) operates the system on behalf of the user. This is·a strategy typical of management users who have access to interactive systems. The advantages and·disadvantages of employing a human interface are debated in Chapter 11 "Design

Procedures for User Involvement and User Support".

If the user has little discretion and therefore has to use the system, or if computer aid is indispensable in the performance of his task, the above options are not so easily available. In these circumstances users may seek to mitigate the mismatch between requirements and provisions by a collection of methods which represent *misuse* or *abuse* of the system. For example, if a user has a task which he performs regularly, he will become very frustrated with a system that requires him to answer a series of irrelevant questions before giving him access to the appropriate facilities. It is likely that the user will seek ways of short-cutting this process, some of which may be harmful to the system. In general, if the rules for using a system seem restricting or unnecessary, the user may seek ways of "bending" the rules to accommodate his needs.

The system may not be the only casualty of a mismatch between requirements and provisions because, in many situations, the user may find it expedient to modify the task he is doing to fit the provisions of the system. He is therefore modifying the task to fit the tool. This is particularly the case where there are a variety of ways in which the user may interpret his task and only a few of these interpretations, and not necessarily the best ones, match the provisions of the system. In these circumstances, unless he has a good alternative "tool" available, there will be a tendency for the user to interpret his task in a way which fits the computer system. Sackman (1974) has called this phenomenon "computer tunnel vision". It is a tendency common to many problem-solvers and designers, as shown by Stewart (1977).

It is likely that any mismatch between requirements and provisions is going to have an effect upon the attitudes and feelings of the user. Mismatches will be accompanied by feelings of frustration because the potential value of the tool is not being realized in practice. However, if the user is able to adopt one of the strategies outlined above he will, within his terms, optimize the advantages of using the system and may, in time, dispel his frustrations. This is not the case in situations in which users have low discretion, are forced to use the system to conduct their work and are unable to modify their task to any great extent. A mismatch between requirements and provisions for these users can be a constant source of irritation and may create extra work. For example, such users may have to carry out meaningless activities such as stripping print-outs, throwing away useless output, and entering data that have no meaning. The effect of such activities is to deprive a job of its meaning and to induce an attitude of "Why should I care? There's no logic in it" in the user. These are the classic symptoms of alienation; the separation of a person's interest and commitment from the work that he does. Responses of this kind are characteristic of some clerical users of the computer.

IV. OPERATIONAL EFFECTS OF USER AND TASK VARIABLES

Thus far the presentation of variables important in naive computer user behaviour has focused on the general ways in which they interact. This section examines in greater detail specific aspects of of the task and the user.

A. Task Variables

There are two aspects of the task a person performs which determine his task needs for information and hence the requirements he makes of a computer system.

1. *Information-handling Facilities*

To accomplish his task the user will need to handle specific pieces of information, and to serve these needs the system must provide the user with appropriate information-handling techniques. A given user may require input, output or processing facilities, or a combination of these.

The aspects of the computer system of most relevance to the provision of these needs is the mode of interaction; the set of software facilities which specifies the options available to the user. It will be apparent that for some users, e.g. those who only need input facilities, a fairly limited set of facilities will suffice, whilst users with processing needs may require a complex set of facilities.

2. *Task Structure*

Tasks vary in the extent to which it is possible to predict precisely how they will be conducted. Simon (1960) calls this "task structure" and places tasks on a structured–unstructured continuum. At the structured pole there are tasks for which a complete specification exists of the goals to be achieved (performance criteria), the method to be employed, the sequence of the operations, and perhaps even the timing of operations. The best example is the work of a person on an assembly line whose task is defined even to the extent of the timing of the operations he performs.

At the other end of the continuum none of the task features may be pre-specified. For example, the board of a company may issue a directive that profits are to be doubled in the next year. It is then up to individual managers to transform this non-operational objective into a particular task for their department, e.g. to increase the sales of certain products, and to establish a method for achieving the specified goals. Most tasks lie somewhere between these extremes. Along the continuum, as tasks are examined that are progressively more structured, it is goals that are the first features to be explicitly stated. Normally the method is the next feature to be formulated, then the sequence of operations is fixed and finally, the timing may be established.

If the method of conducting a task is not pre-specified then it is necessary for the task-performer to generate a specification as he proceeds. There are many situations where this is a desirable strategy. The most important situation is one in which there is variation in the input specification to the task, the task-performer being called upon to cope with unusual and new task characteristics. The problem-solver, designer and decision-maker are frequently in this position, but it is not always recognized that this is also a feature of many seemingly routine clerical activities, e.g. the customer in a bank may well make a request to a cashier which he has previously not encountered. The user may have the discretion to choose for himself a way of interpreting his task and a method of conducting it. It is a futile exercise to try to specify how a managing director, a research scientist or a creative artist should go about their work.

There are then good reasons why the methods of conducting many tasks are not pre-specified. It is however, a characteristic of industrial and commercial work that much task performance *is* pre-specified. It is useful to consider the forces that cause tasks to be pre-structured. In most organizations there are supervisors who define the duties of subordinates, and specialists whose function it is to analyse how tasks should be done and to train people to perform in the appropriate way (training departments, work-study engineers, O and M specialists, etc.). Secondly, the act of providing technological support for a task serves to structure to some degree the way it is conducted. In the extreme case of the paced assembly line, the effect of the technology is to structure the task completely. Finally, the more frequently a person performs a task, the more likely he is to provide himself with an habitual way of working; in effect the pre-structuring comes from the individual himself.

This analysis serves to bring into focus a crucial dilemma in task performance. The degree of structure in a task determines the degree to which information needs can be predicted in advance. A person performing a fully structured task will require exactly the same kinds of information every time he performs the task. If the sequence and timing are fixed then the sequence and timing of information needs can be predicted.

The user with an unstructured or semi-structured task requires a system which will permit him to specify his information needs as and when he becomes aware of them. A system which provides fixed information to service such a task is not likely to be acceptable to the user. It is reasonable to hypothesize that the less structured the user's task, the more flexible the computer system needs to be, offering him a progressively wider set of options. The converse is also true, that the more structured the task, the less flexible the system need be. However, there are dangers in the literal interpretation of this statement because the provision for psychological needs may not be entirely compatible with the pre-definition of task needs.

In Fig. 2 the relationship between task structure and information needs is presented more systematically. When the task is entirely

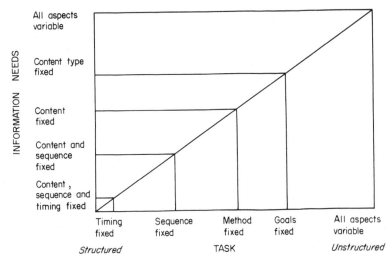

Fig. 2. Relationships between task structure and information needs.

unstructured nothing can be predicted about the information that will be needed. In these circumstances information systems will have to be extremely general-purpose. When the goals of the task are established the type of information or information-processing that will be relevant can be established, but the specific information needs cannot be fixed. The user may need to be able to extract from a wide variety of options the service he requires as he formulates a method of achieving his goal. When the methods as well as the goals are pre-determined, the nature of information needs can be specified in advance. When the sequence of operations is pre-determined, so is the sequence in which information is required, and, if timing of operations is also controlled, the timing of information presentation may also be established.

It is clearly desirable that a computer service matches the degree of structure of the task. If those who commission a system wish to use it as a device for pre-structuring tasks, they have that opportunity. It will be apparent that there are risks to this course of action because it makes assumptions about future task demands. However, consciously taken decisions are one thing; in reality it is likely that the majority of structuring created by a system occurs because designers were unaware of the consequences of their decisions. It is a recurring theme in current research in man–computer interaction that unwanted intrusions of the computer system into the way human beings conduct tasks occur widely in present-day systems.

B. User Characteristics

If two people are given the same task to perform there is no guarantee they will approach it in the same way; one may find the computer facilities available to assist him acceptable and easy to use, whilst another may find them unacceptable. To account for this variability in human response, reference must be made to three groups of factors: job, role and personal factors.

In this section each of these groups of factors is discussed in more detail to indicate how they can affect user responses.

1. *Job Factors*

A job may be defined as the sum total of the responsibilities of an individual in his position of employment. An alternative view is that the job is a collection of tasks, and in most jobs tasks which involve using computer aid are only part of the total task-set of the job. Job factors are therefore important determinants of user responses to computer aid because they define the task, and therefore the task needs, placed on the system as discussed in the previous section. However, there are also more subtle influences which are of concern in this section, such as the user's needs for support in using a system, his expectations of its use, and the extent to which his psychological needs are met by system provisions. The type of job which a computer user has emerges as an extremely pervasive factor in determing the response to computer aid.

(a) Discretion

The responsibilities a person carries in his job are usually related to the degree of discretion he is given; if the person is not to be asked to take responsibility for matters he cannot control he must be given discretion. The individual with discretion will have the freedom to decide for himself how he will approach his work. This has two consequences of particular importance for his use of a computer system. The first is that high levels of discretion mean autonomy over task structure, which has consequences for systems design discussed in the preceding section. The second is that high levels of discretion give the individual the option of using or not using the system. When an individual has a job giving him a high degree of discretion any "tool", including a computer system, is used strictly according to the benefits it brings. It cannot be imposed upon the person and he is unlikely to adapt his behaviour to suit its needs unless it provides a vital service that cannot be obtained elsewhere. The discretionary powers of an individual therefore play a major role in defining the terms on which a computer system will be acceptable, and therefore the *expectations* the user brings to the computer system. The converse of these statements is also true. If an individual has a job giving him little discretion it may well be that he has to accept structured ways of undertaking tasks and is expected to make use of a computer system to do his work. Decisions not to abide by these rules may well be the equivalent of decisions to leave the job and hence are not taken lightly.

(b) Task Frequency

Some jobs require the repetition of the same task many times each day; in others there is barely any repetition. If the tasks for which the computer is used are frequently repeated then the user rapidly becomes an experienced user of the relevant facilities whereas his counterpart who uses the system intermittently remains unpractised in its use. The amount of use of a system has many repercussions for the design of the interface that is appropriate to the user. It defines the state of readiness of the user to engage in appropriate interaction and therefore the amount of *support* he will require. It affects for example, the manner in which options can be offered, the nature of error messages, the verbosity of dialogue, and the complexity of input devices.

Users progress, usually, from being novices in the use of a system to becoming practised, regular users. As they develop, their needs of a software dialogue may change and they may become impatient with the self-explanatory level with which they began. Following this argument to its logical conclusion implies that it may be advantageous to provide more than one level of dialogue verbosity in a system in order that users may graduate from a verbose to a terse form.

A feature of on-line systems which is closely related to the frequency with which computer-oriented tasks are performed is the amount of concern users express about the design of terminal work places, i.e. the screens, furniture, chairs, etc. that comprise the equipment they use. A work place that is not ideal for human use, e.g. uncomfortable chairs, non-availability of storage space, noise, glare from screens, poor lighting, etc. is a minor source of irritation to the intermittent user. He is usually prepared to put up with a little discomfort or inconvenience because it is temporary, although it may lead to more limited use of the system than might otherwise be the case. For the full-time user however these irritations can become issues of major significance because they must be endured throughout the working day. The growing interest in visual display units and visual fatigue emphasizes the importance of these factors.

(c) Computer Discipline and Terminology

To use computer technology one has to accept some fundamental qualities of the technology. The computer is an unforgiving mechanism; it requires rigour, accuracy, precision, total lack of ambiguity and completeness of instruction. There are many people, such as engineers and mathematicians, whose work makes similar demands upon them and who, even if they have never used a computer before, will find these qualities easy to accept. There are many other jobs where these qualities are the reverse of the normal demands made upon the job-holder; in jobs dealing with people (management, social services, politics, etc.) the employee learns to cope with ambiguity and imprecision. The nature of this kind of job does not prepare the individual for the demands that computer use will make upon him, which can cause frustration, impatience or contempt for "the great brain that needs every *i* dotted".

At the same time as naive users are coming to terms with the discipline involved in computer use, they also have to assimilate the technical terms or "jargon" of computer technology. For people in jobs with their own elaborate technical knowledge, the new set of terms may hold few fears, only a desire to assess which of them have to be understood and which can be safely ignored. For those in jobs which have not prepared them for new technological vocabularies, terms like "multi-access", "time-shared", "real-time systems", may be very daunting and can lead to the establishment of mental blocks to computer use.

The nature of the job therefore influences the degree to which the user is, in a general way, prepared to use the system, and as a consequence, the degree of *support* he will require. It also influences the realism of the user's expectations about computer use; someone whose work has not prepared him for this kind of technology may initially have quite unreasonable expectations of what it will and will not do.

(d) The Identification of the Job with the Computer-related Tasks

Some users have jobs which are almost wholly composed of computer-related tasks (e.g. data-preparation clerks). For other users the computer system is a minor component of the total job (e.g. the managing director). The proportion of the job which is devoted to tasks for which the computer is used has important consequences for the attitudes of the user and hence for the design of acceptable systems.

Consider first the attitudes of the user whose job is peripheral to the computer system. He is going to regard the computer system as one of the many tools he uses to do his job. His main concern will be that the system serves his task needs well and that it demands less from him in terms of effort and time than other ways of accomplishing his task. If this is so he can devote his energies to pursuing tasks which he considers to be of central relevance to his job and which, for him, answer his *psychological needs* for interesting, rewarding and satisfying work. The use of the computer system is unlikely to be a major source of satisfaction or dissatisfaction at work.

Consider now the user who is in permanent contact with the computer system. For this person the computer system is an important part of working life and as such it becomes involved in the person's efforts to meet his psychological needs in the work situation. In short, the person for whom there is a strong job–system identification is likely to treat the computer system as an important source of satisfaction or dissatisfaction at work.

To illustrate this point further a distinction can be made between computer users and "computer servants". In some jobs where there is strong job–system identification the user is primarily concerned with data input. The job may be defined as data preparation or data input. In these circumstances the person often sees the computer as a master, controlling and limiting his behaviour and possibly even pacing the rate of work. People in this position rarely express satisfaction with their work unless they have a thorough under-standing of the system and its purpose and have a variety of responsible tasks to perform relating to the care and maintenance of the system. To be acting as servant to a machine you do not understand and cannot control is not a recipe for a rewarding and interesting job (Mumford and Banks, 1967).

There are, however, jobs which, although closely identified with computer systems, are less likely to lead to a loss of job satisfaction. The jobs of the airline booking clerk and the bank clerk, for example, often make extensive use of a computer system but do so not only to provide it with data, but also to access its files. People with jobs of this kind are truly "computer users" because they have tasks to perform which require them to treat the computer as a tool. As such they are able to evaluate it as a tool, in terms of the quality of service it provides, and not as an inhuman master which dominates their working lives. Thus the direction of interaction and the locus of control in man–computer interaction is of central importance if man's psychological needs are to be met in jobs with high system identification.

2. *Role Factors*

A role may be defined as a set of behaviours expected of anyone occupying a particular job. These expectations come from the job-holder himself and from people in jobs which interact with the job in question. People at work come to develop shared expectations about one another's behaviour. These expectations range from fundamental issues, e.g. the goals each person will pursue and the way he allocates his time, to seemingly trivial issues, e.g. how each person will dress and where he will park his car.

The concept of role has been extremely valuable to social

scientists who seek to understand how people behave at work. It helps to explain why two people of very different personalities and disposition will behave in a similar manner when taking on the same job. The concept can therefore be of value to the present discussion because it will enable us to identify why people in similar jobs develop similar *expectations* of the computer systems they will use. Expectations about what is and is not acceptable about computer use vary substantially from job to job, and some of this variance can be attributed to the following factors.

(a) The Task in Job Context

The amount of effort considered appropriate to use and learn to use a computer system will, in part, depend upon how central the computer-aided tasks are to the job as a whole. The issue turns on the amount of discretion the user has over the way he interprets his role, e.g. whether he can decide when and how to undertake tasks, and what order of priorities they should receive. If the user has discretion over these issues he can make the critical assessment of the effort/benefit ratio he will accept. If the user gives the relevant tasks high priority, he may be expected to give his time and energy freely while using the system for these task purposes. If the priority rating is low, the user will prefer to devote his energies to other matters, considering time required by the computer system to be time ill-spent (Eason, 1980). In this context the user obeys Zipf's (1965) "principle of least effort" in trying to minimize the amount of personal effort that must be devoted to the achievement of his goals.

There are, however, a variety of factors which may limit the user's discretion to decide for himself what priority can be accorded the use of a computer system. The job may be tightly structured by organization of work resulting from decisions made by management and staff groups such as O and M and Work Study. In these circumstances the user accords the computer system the priority assigned to it by the job designers. If it is rated high, he will be expected to devote his time and energy to using it; if it is rated low, any time devoted in this direction may be considered wasteful. If the user finds the system demands more time and energy than he has been granted, the limits on his discretion are such as to put him in a difficult and frustrating position.

It is not only the management and the job designers who structure jobs but also a variety of forces and constraints external to the job. The expectations and demands of colleagues, for example, can limit the degree to which the user can decide how much time and energy he may devote to a given task. Another problem is that, during work overload, urgent tasks are undertaken in preference to those of more long-term significance. This factor mitigates against general learning about a computer system because emphasis is given to learning just sufficient to undertake the present task.

Some jobs are characterized by the lack of control the user has over the in-flow of work which demands immediate attention. Process controllers and supervisors have jobs of this kind in which action can be on a minute-by-minute basis and in which it is very difficult to devote time to more long-term issues. In contrast the "back-room boffin" may be no less busy but, because he is working on long-term projects, he is able to exert much more control over the allocation of his own time.

(b) Short-term and Long-term Considerations

In formulating his "principle of least effort", Zipf (1965) defined effort in terms of the probable requirements of present and future tasks. He suggested therefore that a person assessing the amount of effort warranted by a particular task will make this assessment not only in terms of the importance of the current task but also in terms of its likely future repetitions. A little extra effort devoted to the use of a tool, for example, might delay the completion of the current task but may well save considerable time in the future.

The intermittent user who does not see himself becoming a future regular computer user will evaluate the amount of effort warranted by a task strictly in terms of the present needs. If the demands of the computer system are considered too great, the user may well seek a less demanding way of completing his task. This is often the kind of response made by management users.

An alternative view may be taken by a prospective regular user; a person who considers he has found a potentially valuable tool which could be used for a variety of tasks he may undertake in the future. The amount of effort he is prepared to expend may be grossly out of proportion to the needs of the current task because he is exploring the potential of the tool for future use. This kind of attitude is often found amongst scientists and engineers who are prepared to learn a high-level programming language in order to use the computer most effectively in their specialist problem-solving activities.

(c) Status

Roles define how people at work relate to one another. In particular, the respective status of two jobs can have important effects upon the use of a computer aid. This may be illustrated by examples from the high-status job of a senior manager and the low-status job of a junior clerk. For some managers there may be a certain glamour in having a visual display unit placed in their office. But if using this device entails lengthy typing they may quickly decide that this is not an appropriate activity for a senior manager, and either the terminal is operated by a trained operator or it becomes simply a talking point for visitors. In other circumstances senior managers may find themselves having to follow precise computer rules, for example, to obtain information from a system. Being more accustomed to giving than receiving such instructions, they may rebel against seemingly inflexible computer discipline.

At the other end of the scale the junior clerk has so little status that he tends to accept whatever he is asked to do without question (although he may well grumble at the idiocy of it). As a computer user, the clerk may need the help and advice of people who know more about the system but he may be very reticent about asking for help because computer people are more senior and "will not wish to be bothered by the likes of me". The same problem reveals itself in a different form when clerks are asked to contribute to systems design and are reticent because they do not feel that they have any contribution to make. Howie (1975) in a study of two computer systems, found that very few clerks had any expectations of being involved in the system design process although they were the only repository of detailed knowledge of the tasks to be aided by the system.

3. *Personal Factors*

Although they may occupy similar jobs and play similar roles, the behaviour of two users towards a given computer system may still be markedly different. To account for these differences it is necessary to seek psychological differences in the make-up of the individuals concerned. There are a great many such differences, ranging from those with biological roots such as age and sex to those of a more psychological nature such as intelligence, personality and abilities. There are also differences which are often of a more transitory, changeable nature such as attitudes and values. Given a range of variables of this magnitude the problem is to know which ones are likely to be important determinants of responses to computer systems. This section reviews a few variables which have been shown to be of significance although, as research in this area is relatively new, this list is almost certainly not exhaustive.

(a) Attitudes

The relationship between attitudes and behaviour is complex and not well understood but it is probably true to say in the context of attitudes to computers that they will colour a user's response in the following ways. A strong negative attitude may turn minor problems in using a system into major obstacles, examples for the user of what he had been expecting. A strong positive attitude may give a user the will to overcome minor problems without difficulty. Attitudes therefore provide motivational inputs to the task–tool relationships with which the user works, facilitating or constraining it accordingly.

The computer is something few can ignore and most have strong attitudes towards it. For some people the spirit of technological advance, invention and discovery is deeply exciting and the computer is a device of intrigue and wonderment. For others it is a little-understood device which threatens their way of life, taking away jobs, removing the human element in life and replacing it with the inhuman. Potential naive users can therefore be expected to have quite strong attitudes towards computers, whether they be predominately hopes or fears.

Initial attitudes are by definition not based upon personal experience; they are the product of views and arguments presented by the mass communication media, by workmates and by friends. Some insight into the way these rather global attitudes are modified by experience of computer use has been provided by Guthrie's (1974) study of 2000 Canadian managerial computer users. He found that the more experience the manager had of computer use, the more differentiated were his attitudes to computers, i.e. he could specify good and bad features. In general, greater experience also led to a more positive overall evaluation.

If these conclusions are accurate and general then the problem for the designer is the initial attitudes of users; experience of the system, if it is good, will itself look after subsequent attitudes.

(b) Personality

Personality is composed of enduring, i.e. relatively unchanging, aspects of a person which typify his way of behaving, e.g. nervousness, tenseness, introversion, etc. There are numerous such personality variables, but few have been examined in the context of computer use.

One exception is the introversion–extroversion dimension extensively researched by Eysenck (1974). He has shown that high introversion is associated with a preference for low arousal situations and that high extroversion is associated with a preference for high arousal situations.

Folkard et al. (1974) have investigated the relation of this variable to system response time, and conclude that over-arousal is often associated with the use of on-line computer terminals. This condition may therefore be more harmful to the performance of introvert users than to that of extrovert users.

Another personality variable of relevance is the distinction proposed by Little (1969) between "people-oriented" and "thing-oriented" people. A "people-oriented" person, as might be expected, is attracted by and values the human elements in any situation and is sensitive to human needs and problems. A "thing-oriented" person, however, is more attracted by the inanimate elements of a situation and tends to be more interested in efficient means of achieving goals than in any complications that may be caused by the people involved. Prima facie it would appear that computers would appeal to "thing-oriented" people. Malde (1975) proposed a dimension of "person-centred" people and "efficiency-centred" people which may be related to Little's dimensions. Malde found that members of the public who were "efficiency-centred" and computer terminal operators who were "efficiency-centred" found computer systems more satisfactory to work with than did "people-oriented" members of the public or operators. This was not just a question of preference; it was also a question of task interpretation because operators who were "person-oriented" found that the computer system did not enable them to interpret their task as they deemed appropriate.

(c) Intelligence and Cognition

In addition to the enduring qualities of an individual which typify his behaviour, i.e. his personality, there are enduring qualities that characterize the maximum possible level of achievement of the individual, e.g. his intelligence.

There has been little research to date which looks directly at the relationship between intelligence and performance with a computer system, although Carlisle (1974) has investigated the relation of verbal and quantitative intelligence to the complexity of the man–computer interface.

Perhaps of more long-term significance than the study of different levels of intelligence is the study of the characteristic ways in which individuals take decisions, handle information and solve problems. Under the general heading of "cognitive style", a number of authors have recently demonstrated that individuals have characteristic ways of approaching the task of processing information. In categorizing a wide variety of objects, for example, some people use a few categories and others use many, regardless of the nature of the objects. A collection of readings on these topics is to be found in Warr (1970).

Characteristic differences in handling information have relevance to the use of information-processing devices such as computers since it should be possible to present information to a user in a manner that fits the particular information-processing strategies he adopts. To date little work has been conducted on these issues with the exception, once again, of Carlisle (1974) who has investigated the relationship between the cognitive complexity of the user and the complexity of the interface he uses.

V. USER JOB-PROFILES

Most of the variables which have been discussed are directly or indirectly related to the job the user undertakes. This is of considerable importance to the computer system designer because systems are often designed for people in particular jobs, e.g. management information systems. An understanding of the particular characteristics of the jobs of potential users can therefore be used to advantage in system design.

A classification of user job-profiles is presented in Table 1. It gives a value for each job type for each of the variables discussed. This is inevitably a simplified representation. For example, for most variables only three values are used, which does not do justice to the full range of each variable. In addition, some jobs are characterized by a wide range of possibilities on some variables, which are not easy to indicate in tabular form. Nevertheless, the table is worth presenting, despite its simplifications, because it highlights the critical issues concerning each type of user and the critical differences between them.

Management users need flexible information output because task

TABLE 1

User job profiles

User variables	User job types						
	Manager	Clerk A	Clerk B	Specialist	Process controller	The public	Programmer
Task variables							
Content	Output	Input	Input/ Output	Processing	Output/ Input	Output	Processing
Degree of structure	Low	High	Moderate	Low	Moderate	Moderate	Low
Job variables							
Task frequency	Low	High	High	Moderate	High	Low	High
Familiarity with discipline	Low	Low	Low	High	High	Low	High
Job/System identification	Low	High	High	Moderate	High	Low	High
Role variables							
Task priority in job	Low	High	High	Moderate	Moderate	Low	High
Short-term/Long-term benefits	Low	High	High	Moderate	High	Low	High
Status	High	Low	Low	Moderate	Low	?	Moderate

structure is low, but job and role factors suggest they will expect to spend very little time and effort on using the computer. Flexible tools usually require skilled handling but managers have little opportunity to develop the skills.

The *Clerk A* category refers to clerks who are primarily concerned with data input. Here the high degree of task structure and task frequency often produces boring, repetitive tasks and because of the strong job/system identification the search for answers to psychological needs for job interest etc. is focused on the system. In these circumstances job dissatisfaction is often the most important problem.

The *Clerk B* category refers to clerks who use both the input and output facilities of the computer system. They often make frequent use of the system and their tasks, although seemingly structured, often involve unexpected variability, with the consequence that they place demands for flexibility on the system that are sometimes not met. The key problem here is that the tool needs to fit the job very closely because it is much used, and even a slight misfit can be extremely frustrating.

The *Specialist* is someone who by virtue of his professional training has specialist problems to solve, e.g. an engineer, a statistician, an economist, and for whom the computer can be an important tool. Users of this type frequently require fairly specific information-processing facilities, and they need to be able to spend considerable time and effort obtaining and using such facilities. Fortunately many specialists are able and willing to provide such effort but there is a danger that this itself may cause them to examine only problem solutions commensurate with the available computer tools, missing other solutions.

The *Process Controller* has a job in which he has immediate responsibility for a work process which he can control remotely, usually from a centralized control room, e.g. in oil refining, chemical manufacture, railway signalling, power-station control etc. The computer may be used in a variety of ways to give information about the state of the process or to control the process automatically. In these circumstances there is a high job/system identification and also the possibility that the computer may help the controller to develop a better, more accurate understanding of work/system dynamics. However, a poor computer system can serve as a barrier to the user's view of the process rather than as an aid.

A *Member of the Public* using a computer to, for example, book a hotel room, or draw money from a bank account, is the supreme example of a naive user for whom training cannot be provided and knowledge of the system cannot be assumed. The problems of designing very straightforward "foolproof" systems for use in these situations have meant that only a very limited set of facilities are available to the user which may not match the particular task needs of the person.

Finally, the *Programmer* is included in the list, not as a naive computer user, but simply to illustrate the differences between his needs and expectations and those of his fellows. He has a complex programming task to perform (in contrast to most other users), and is strongly identified with the tool he uses for this purpose. It is easy to see the dangers which might befall a programmer who writes procedures for a naive user and tests the system by using himself as a model user.

Further consideration of personal factors, e.g. personality, is not undertaken for two reasons. First, it is easy to place too great an emphasis upon the personal qualities of the user when trying to account for his responses to computer aid. When faced with a particularly hostile response it is easy to say "It's just him, he is always like that." Having made this assessment there is little more that can be done except to work round the obstacle. However, if an effort is made to try and understand the response in terms of the task the user has to perform or the characteristics of his job, a productive way of working with the user may be found. One conclusion that may be derived from the evidence on naive user behaviour is that designers should consider possible explanations in terms of the variables discussed here before they turn to explanations based upon the personal characteristics of the user.

The second reason is that, if it is found that a particular personal characteristic, e.g. cognitive style, means that different individuals need different types of interface, this information is difficult for the designer to use. He cannot select users of only one type to use his system, nor can he easily check the relevant personal characteristics of his potential users and design for the majority. The only possiblity is to design the system to accommodate the full range of user variability. This is perhaps a long-term aim which can only be achieved when research evidence is more conclusive than it is at present.

REFERENCES

Carlisle, J.H. (1974). Man–computer interactive problem solving–relationships between user characteristics and interface complexity. Doctoral Dissertation, Centre for the Study of Organisations, Yale University, New Haven, Connecticut.

Eason, K.D. (forthcoming). A task–tool analysis of manager–computer interaction. In B. Shackel (ed.) *Man–Computer Interaction.* Amsterdam: Sijthoff and Noordhoff.

Eason, K.D., Damodaran, L. and Stewart, T.F.M. (1974). A survey of man–computer interaction in commercial applications. *LUTERG No. 144,* Dept. of Human Sciences, Loughborough University.

Eysenck, H.J. (1947). *Dimensions of Personality.* London: Routledge and Kegan Paul.

Folkard, T., Innocent, P.R., Penn, R.F. and Dallos, R. (1974) Studies of the ease of learning and usage of on-line computer systems. *HUSAT Memo No. 89,* Dept. of Human Sciences, Loughborough University.

Guthrie, A. (1974). Attitudes of the user managers towards management information systems. *Management Information, 3, 5.*

Howie, A. (1975). Clerical user involvement in management information systems design. M.Sc. Dissertation, Dept. of Human Sciences Loughborough University.

Klein, L. (1976). *New forms of Work Organisation.* Cambridge: Cambridge University Press.

Little, B. (1969). Studies of psycho-specialists. *Psychol. Rep. 52.*

Malde, B. (1975). Research into the simultaneous conduct of man–man and man–computer interaction. *HUSAT Memo No. 98,* Dept. of Human Sciences, Loughborough University.

Mumford, E. and Banks, O. (1967). *The Computer and the Clerk.* London: Routledge and Kegan Paul.

Sackman, H. (1974). Stages of problem solving with and without computers. *Report R-1490-NSF,* Rand Corporation, California.

Simon, H.A. (1960). *The New Science of Management Decision.* New York: Harper and Row.

Stewart, T.F.M. (1977) Side-effects of computer problem solving. In A. Parkin (ed.) *Computers and People.* London: Arnold.

Warr, P.B. (ed.) (1970). *Thought and Personality.* London: Penguin.

Zipf, G.K. (1965). *Human Behaviour and the Principle of Least Effort: An Introduction to Human Ecology.* (2nd Edn.) New York: Harper.

Part II
The Nature and Acquisition of Computing Skills

Introduction

Computing is beginning to be adopted as a basic subject in schools and universities, and to be counted as a valued qualification by commerce. This rise in the status of the subject has produced a demand for instruction at a time when little is known either about the nature of computing skills, or about effective methods of teaching them. There is therefore an urgent need for a substantial research effort in this area.

The existing literature is small and consists mainly of small-scale isolated studies many of which were conducted on computer science students, undergraduates or professional programmers. However, some interesting guidelines for teaching non-computer professionals do emerge from this scattered work, which is comprehensively reviewed by du Boulay and O'Shea, (p. 147). These guidelines include such proposals as getting learners to run interesting programs from the start of their course in order to build confidence, providing learners with a model of the notional machine to help them avoid semantic errors, and providing novices with language-specific editors to minimize syntactic errors.

Much of the early work on programming skills was motivated by the need to improve the efficiency of large-scale software projects involving teams of programmers. The main concern was not with the learning of programming skills *per se* but with increasing efficiency by promoting communication between the various team members. However, through this work it was realized that other variables were also important, such as the style of programming adopted and the language used. This initiated the first major research initiative which was directed at identifying the characteristics of a perfect programming language.

Programming language issues are discussed by Green *et al.,* (p.221) who have made a major contribution to the area themselves in their experimental work on the forms of the conditional. Supported by this and other work on diagrammatic languages (Fitter and Green, p.253) they argue that "the intelligibility of a programming language depends on the way programs are presented on the page and how they are structured, not on the particular facilities supported by the language". Furthermore, no language appears to optimally support all of the complex array of skills employed in programming. For example, conventional languages appear to support the answering of sequential or "trace" questions ("What can the program do next after A?"), while decision tables are suited to circumstantial or "taxon" questions ("Under what circumstances can A begin?"). Both types of question will need to be asked during program-writing and debugging, so it is perhaps necessary to design a language to give the best compromise.

Research interest has now shifted from a consideration of language features to the study of programming skills themselves. The relationship between these two areas is discussed in the latter part of the chapter by Green *et al.,* while Lukey (p.201) concentrates in detail on the nature of program comprehension and its role in the skill of debugging. Green *et al.* argue that the structure of a programming language should support good programming practices. For example, it should permit the programmer to write effective programs using only short units of code and should offer perceptual cues to make trails through the code easily visible. The language should also help the user to readily build up a global description of the function—and related structure—of a program unit. Knowledge of such functions will make the program easier to debug and modify by clearly identifying the relationships between individual structures. Lukey considers that knowledge of the comprehension process will itself enhance our ability to teach programming skills. With reference to relevant research, he points out that three approaches have been used for the study of comprehension: an experimental approach, an observational approach and an artificial intelligence approach. Lukey argues that great difficulties face the experimentalist and that the best progress has been made in artificial intelligence, which has furnished valuable descriptions of the classes of information (the segmentation of a program, flow of control, data flow, the changing values of variables) which may well be used by the programmer to understand a piece of code. From such descriptions artificial intelligence workers, including Lukey himself, have built systems which automatically debug a specified range of programs.

A common complaint in the area is the lack of useful theory. However, we would maintain that useful theory is unlikely to emerge while research is conducted as isolated experiments which take little account of related work in other disciplines. Instead of contenting themselves with thorough descriptive research, or approaching experimental work from related background studies, researchers tend to work at the experimental level with low-level and poorly formulated hypotheses. Findings from such work will be unlikely to generalize very far from the original context and the experiments themselves will be prone to artefacts. An example of a descriptive style of research intended to identify fruitful hypotheses is given in the chapter by Coombs *et al.*, (p.289). Here it was decided that in the absence of an adequate theory of computing skill, it was preferable to attempt first to dimension the activity rather than to make assumptions which could well prove erroneous. Appropriate dimensions were sought via the study of naturally occurring individual differences in learning style found among novice programmers learning their first language. The work has provided some support for the frequently made contention that there are considerable individual differences in students' ability to learn to program and for the proposal that there are many advantages in seeking to give a student a sound grasp of the syntax of a programming language in isolation from a given application or application area. The advantages of such teaching are discussed by Boldyreff (p.315), who also describes a computer implementation of a system for teaching syntax.

It is almost universally agreed that empirical work on the nature and acquisition of programming skills has been less than successful. This is largely because the studies often lack adequately defined variables for manipulation and measurement. A further problem is the lack of adequate experimental designs to cope with the complexity of programming, which does not appear to readily decompose into skills which can be studied separately. It is therefore proposed that a new approach is necessary. We would argue that considerably more attention should be paid to developing good descriptions of programming behaviour. This could be achieved by the use of the participant-experimenter techniques which have proved successful in developmental psychology, and by techniques involving the parallel development of a computer simulation of given behaviour and related experiments. The latter approach has proved very successful in the study of memory and in a number of problem-solving situations, including those of equal complexity to programming.

Finally, it is hoped that future research into the teaching of computing will take account of the literature on the teaching of other artificial languages and formal systems, including mathematics. For example, while the important process of presenting examples and exercises to students has been successfully researched in these other areas, there is at present little similar work with reference to programming. It might thus be hoped that future research will examine such contentions as the following.

— The early programming problems should be both easy to understand in themselves and easy to program. This will enable the learner to concentrate on program command structures and on input/output procedures.

— The next examples should be extensions of the previous ones, not *new* problems. These should be used to demonstrate how a program may evolve to encompass an increasingly wide range of circumstances.

— Following the above stage, alternative ways of writing programs should be explained. This will introduce learners to new language features and acquaint them with the principles of a well-formed algorithm. This stage will extend smoothly into the introduction of more advanced programming techniques, such as the principle of sorting and the use of data format statements to break up mixed-mode entries.

Such proposals yield concrete, testable hypotheses and translate easily into teaching strategies.

4. Teaching Novices Programming

B. DU BOULAY* and T. O'SHEA†

*Department of Computer Science, University of Aberdeen, Old Aberdeen, Scotland
†Institute of Educational Technology, Open University, Milton Keynes, England

---

I. INTRODUCTION

Those involved in the task of teaching novices programming face three educational problems, with little empirical evidence to guide them. First, what difficulties do novices encounter in learning to program? Second, what features make a language suitable or unsuitable as a first programming language, and which of the available languages meet the criteria? Third, what is the nature of the skill to be imparted, and how should teaching be organized to best effect? There are no easy answers, and certainly no language may be regarded as a "best buy". Moreover there will be many other constraints, apart from good pedagogy, on both choice of language and organization of teaching.

This chapter is a comprehensive and up-to-date literature review of the empirically established findings about the problems of teaching novices programming. It is divided into sections that address the following questions:

1. What is known about novices' difficulties with programming?
2. What has been established about language design for novices?
3. What is known about the learning of particular languages?
4. What has been established about teaching strategy?
5. What are the important open questions and what empirical studies are possible?

In our analysis of novices' difficulties with programming we divide their activity into three main skills: planning, coding and debugging. We give less consideration to documentation and group activities since, at the novice level, programming tends to be an autonomous activity where the programs are for the novices' own use or for course assessment purposes. By "novices" we mean both naive users, in Eason's (1976) sense of non-experts in computer technology who use a computer system to assist the performance of some task, and learners of their first programming language, who may go on to be professional programmers. This definition covers a very wide range of users. Our focus is mainly on those who are not going to be professional programmers, although much of the empirical evidence comes from studies on computer science under-graduates.

In the second section we examine how different language features affect the ease with which novices master planning, coding and debugging. For example much of the work on coding has concentrated on the way different control specifiers facilitate the construction and comprehensibility of algorithms.

A number of studies of the way novices learn to program using various languages have recorded the frequency with which different constructs were used, the typical errors made and the attempted solutions to programming problems. These studies are summarized in Section IV, which has sub-sections devoted to COBOL, FORTRAN, BASIC, LOGO, PASCAL, APL and an assembly language.

Section V turns from language design to teaching issues. It reviews experiments in teaching programming that have tried to resolve such questions as whether a first language should be high or low level, whether it should be interactive or batch and whether two languages should be taught at the beginning or just one. It also looks at methods of organizing concepts within a course and of organizing students who take the course.

The last section draws the threads together by listing the important open questions about language design and teaching. It then selects from this list those questions amenable to experiment and briefly describes possible experimental methodologies.

II. NOVICES' DIFFICULTIES WITH PROGRAMMING

This section reviews the empirical evidence about novices' ability to plan, code and debug programs. Review articles on aspects of these issues are provided by Furuta and Kemp (1979) and Green *et al.*, (1978).

A. Planning

One of the first things that the novice has to learn is what sub-set of his problems is amenable to computer solution and how his view of a problem has to be altered to allow it to be expressed as a program. Kreitsberg and Swanson (1974) describe the "computer shock" which some novices suffer when attempting this task. Novices have problems in understanding both what a computer program can do for them and its relation to the problem in hand. They also find it hard to organize their algorithms so that they actually carry out the required task.

Teachers often say that writing a computer program is just like giving a person instructions, but it is not. For example, when instructing a person one can rely both on his existing knowledge and on his ability to make inferences, and this reduces the need to be absolutely specific about every eventuality.

Novice programmers' ability to plan algorithms for a limited class of sorting problems has been studied by Miller (1974). The novices constructed programs by selecting from a menu consisting of commands specified in simplified English. Miller found that problems involving a disjunction of sorting attributes (i.e. one attribute *or* another) were more difficult than those involving a conjunction (i.e. one attribute *and* another). Disjunctive programs needed many more modifications and each modification tended to take much longer to carry out. The difficulty of problems was also increased by sorts requiring tests for the absence of an attribute, especially in the case of disjunctive sorts.

Analysis of errors showed that a high proportion concerned the specification of flow of control (by conditional jump to label). Many of the incorrect programs computed a conjunction when a disjunction was required. One difficulty in interpreting the results of this experiment is that we do not know to what extent the form of the laboratory programming language chosen contributed to the students' difficulties.

Part of a novice's difficulty in planning is caused by the disparity between the familiar conventions for specifying a plan to a human being, e.g. a cooking recipe, and a computer program. Miller (1975) found that the fundamental difference between the two was that the specification for human use was often "qualificational" rather than "conditional". He contrasts the more natural formulation "PUT RED THINGS IN BOX 1" with the conditional "IF THING IS RED THEN PUT IN BOX 1". Novices apparently have difficulty in translating from a qualificational mental representation of a problem to an explicit conditional plan. Programming languages do not have to contain conditionals, but can declare the goals and sub-goals of the program and rely on automatic mechanisms to look after the flow of control. PROLOG (Pereira *et al.*, 1978) is an example of such a declarative language.

A typical PROLOG program consists of a series of sentences, each of which consists of clauses, such as P,Q,R and S as follows:

$$P:- Q, R, S.$$

A sentence may be interpreted declaratively (by the programmer) to mean: "P is true if Q and R and S are true". Or the sentence may be viewed procedurally to mean: "To satisfy goal P, satisfy goals Q and R and S".

It would be interesting to see whether novices formulated plans more easily in such a language than in conventional procedural languages. Another aspect of novices' plans observed by Miller (1975) was concerned with their generality. Novices tended to underspecify algorithms, e.g. not describing what to do when a certain set of conditions was *not* satisfied. They also assumed a high degree of contextual information.

Similar observations were made by Hoc (1977) who compared programmers of varying levels of experience in their ability to plan (and code in COBOL) an algorithm to control a change-giving ticket-machine. He found that beginners tended to formulate solutions for specific instances of the problem rather than a general algorithm. This he attributed to the beginner's lack of experience of a machine which could control its own actions. Similar difficulties in children's understanding of general algorithms are reported by Weyer and Cannara (1975). Children were asked to complete a partially specified flowchart for a chocolate-vending machine. Some misconstrued the flowchart as a representation of the action that the machine might take in response to a single specific set of input coins rather than treating it as an algorithm to deal with all possible sets of coins.

B.   Coding

Having represented the problem as an algorithm, the novice must then code the algorithm in the given language. Mistakes occur in this process. We follow Youngs' (1974) classification of errors: syntactic, semantic, logical and clerical. Syntactic errors are incorrect expressions in the language that cause the compiler or interpreter to generate an error message. Typically a novice might not know or not remember the rules for well-formed expressions (like a child's "I have eated my dinner"). Semantic errors try to make the computer carry out impossible or contradictory actions, though the expression is syntactically correct. An example would be the attempt to read a file after it has been closed. Logical errors concern the mapping from the problem to the program. Here the program does not produce the desired result i.e. it does not do the job it was designed to do. These errors can be due to either poor planning of the algorithm, or incorrect expression of the algorithm in code form. Clerical errors are due to carelessness or accident in the coding process, such as a mistyped character. We extend Youngs' classification to include stylistic errors. These are errors of programming style (Kernighan and Plauger, 1974) that make a program hard to comprehend, or very inefficient, though it runs correctly. Dunsmore and Gannon (1978) have tried to quantify the idea of programmer style in terms of measures such as average nesting depth.

Youngs' (1974) study analysed errors in 69 programs, produced by 30 novice programmers and 12 experienced programmers, written in a variety of languages (ALGOL, BASIC, COBOL, FORTRAN and PL/1). He compared the errors made by both groups and found that they each produced about the same number of errors in the first runs of their programs, though their debugging skills were quite different. The distribution of errors between the different classes was different for the two groups. The majority of the novices' errors were semantic, and these they found hard to diagnose. This emphasizes the fact that the novices were still finding out about the properties of the notional machine defined by the language and its implementation. Professionals made syntactic, semantic and logical errors in about equal numbers.

Syntactic errors did not seem to be a great source of difficulty for novices. The frequency of this class of error was not high and they were relatively easily diagnosed, because error messages could usually pinpoint them. The low proportion of syntactic errors is confirmed in a study by Boies and Gould (1974) who found that the vast majority of programs (78% in FORTRAN, 62% in ASSEMBLER and 73% in PL/1) submitted for compilation in a large-scale user system were syntactically correct. Their study did not distinguish the programs from users of different levels of experience. They cite an earlier study (Moulton and Muller, 1967) in which 66% of student-submitted FORTRAN programs compiled correctly.

Friend's (1975) analysis of students' AID programs (a language similar to BASIC) gave a different result. Syntax errors outnumbered semantic and logical errors by about two to one, and 57% of programs were error-free on first submission. Friend makes the important point that many of the syntax errors were "reasonable" in that they "resulted from students misapplying—or overextending—some existing syntactic rule" (p.66). This suggests the need for consistent syntax in a first language. Friend found that semantic errors were frequently associated with the use of variables and with algebra. That is, the students' poor mathematical background contributed to their programming difficulties (in that language with that particular set of programming problems).

Novices' errors are not randomly distributed among language-expressions but tend to cluster around certain constructs (Gannon, 1978) in a language-dependent way, e.g. ALGOL and FORTRAN I/0 formatting statements are a source of a large number of errors (Youngs, 1974). Youngs found that, in gross terms, the most frequent causes of errors in his small sample were assignment and allocation statements, for both novices and professionals. However, when error frequencies were adjusted over statement frequency, the most troublesome statements were conditionals. Friend (1975) came to a similar conclusion.

Various studies have shown that programmers tend to use a small sub-set of a language's constructs very frequently and others infrequently, or not at all. In a study of syntactically correct FORTRAN programs, Knuth (1971) found that most were written using only a small number of statement types and these in a very simple way. Knuth found that assignment, IF, GOTO, CALL and CONTINUE accounted for over 80% of all statements in a sample of 440 professional programs. The ordering of statement frequencies was about the same for a sample of more casual users, except that WRITE and DO replaced CONTINUE to make up 80% of the occurrences. Saal and Weiss (1977) compared APL programs with Knuth's findings. They came to much the same conclusion which was that 80% of the usage was supplied by about 20% of the available operations. Nagy and Pennebaker (1974) found that 17 common PL/1 statements accounted for more than 99% of all program statements in a large sample of students' programs.

Al-Jarrah and Torsun (1979) report that in a static analysis of COBOL programs 17% of the available COBOL statements accounted for 84% of use. Although these studies are concerned with compiler optimization, they have implications for teaching. They suggest that novices can be introduced to a small sub-set of a language's constructs and still be able to write useful programs. The results also support Barron's (1977) language-design goal of "economy of concept", namely that a programming language should embody only a small number of concepts appropriate for a given class of task rather than providing a huge range of constructs which would be more difficult to learn.

Not only do programmers tend to use a small sub-set of the available language constructs but in addition a small number of syntactic error types account for the vast majority of syntactic errors committed. For instance, Litecky and Davis (1976) found that 20% of syntactic error types in COBOL accounted for 80% of the errors committed by 50 students in about 1000 program runs. One of the present authors (du Boulay, 1978) found that only 11 error types account for 96% of the errors of 15 students learning LOGO. Similar results are reported for PASCAL where 10 out of 112 recorded syntax error types accounted for about half the actual errors observed in 589 programs (Ripley and Druseikis, 1978). Ripley and Druseikis note that PASCAL delimiters, especially the semi-colon, were a frequent source of error. More details of the causes of errors in particular languages are given in Section IV. Teachers of programming could make use of this "clustering" of errors to concentrate their teaching effort in those areas that prove troublesome.

It is frequently reported that novices write poorly structured programs, lacking in style and comprehensibility. The difficulty is a combination of lack of experience of the virtual machine on which the program is to be run (semantics), of unfamiliarity with algorithms and flow of control (logic), and of stylistic rules and program techniques that enhance readability of code (style). Hoc (1977) found that beginners translated their plans for a ticket-machine algorithm inefficiently into COBOL code, although they understood the meaning of individual COBOL statements. Florentin and Smith (1978) reported that a proposed analysis of novices' interaction with a computer was abandoned because the researchers could not deduce the purpose of the programs from their code.

Much of the structured programming debate has been concerned with program style as well as with program correctness. This issue will be dealt with in more detail under "debugging" and in Section III in "language design". The central notion of comprehensibility of code (Green *et al.*, 1978) cuts across our coding/debugging and learning/design classification.

C. Debugging

Debugging is the lengthy and difficult process of finding and removing the errors in the program code. Not surprisingly, experienced programmers are better at this than novices, though there is great variability even among professional programmers (Gould, 1975). Chrysler (1978) has shown that a programmer's length of experience with a given language is highly correlated with the time it takes him to develop a program in that language. Youngs (1974) compared the rates at which novices and experienced programmers eliminated different classes of error · from their programs. Professionals quickly dealt with syntactic and semantic errors and spent most of their time dealing with the logical errors. Novices, on the other hand, had great difficulty dealing with both semantic and logical errors.

In addition to observing novices ability to plan sorting programs, Miller (1974) examined their testing and debugging strategies. He found that his novices were fairly good at choosing a necessary and sufficient set of test data for their programs, though all each novice had to do was choose the four correct items from eight presented.

Debugging took about one and a half times as long to complete as the production of the initial version of the program, and was much more protracted for programs involving disjunctive tests. Miller found that novices used a "passive analytical" testing procedure rather than an "active" testing procedure. So clearly debugging, like coding, is a skill that needs to be learnt explicitly.

More light is thrown on this skill by studying experienced programmers' developed strategies rather than novices' naive strategies. Gould and Drongowski (1974) examined how effectively 30 experienced programmers removed bugs in FORTRAN programs given various debugging aids. Each program had one, and only one, bug inserted and the programmers were asked to locate it as fast as possible. Debug times were fast (median = six minutes) but this was probably the result of the experimental set-up, namely that the programmers knew that there was only one bug to find and had been told to work as fast as possible. Instructions on how to proceed with a programming task have a large effect on the way that task is executed (Weinberg and Shulman, 1974). Debugging the same program, but with a different bug inserted, proceeded even faster.

There were no marked differences in debugging speed between the groups given different debugging aids such as (i) a listing only, (ii) listing plus examples of typical input and output, (iii) as for (ii) but with examples of correct output, (iv) listing plus knowledge of the class of bug, and (v) listing plus line number of bug. Programmers in each group appeared to adapt their strategies to the information available. There were large individual differences in debugging speed and accuracy, as well as differences attributed to the class of bug and to the type of program being debugged.

The programmers adopted a simple hierarchical debugging strategy, where they looked for simple bugs first e.g. semantic bugs such as exceeding array bounds (they knew that no syntactic bugs existed in the program). They then moved on to a search for logical errors where location demanded that they understood how the program worked as a whole.

A subsequent study by Gould (1975) showed that access to interactive aids did not improve debugging times in this type of laboratory experiment. Both studies indicated that there were no short cuts to finding the toughest bugs, i.e. those in assignments, and that to reveal those the programmer had to buckle down and work out the logic of the program, a task not much helped by the debugging aids provided.

Surprisingly fast debugging times, typically 15 minutes compared to a program-writing time of 26 minutes, have been observed by Brooks (1977). This result must be treated with caution since he was studying a single experienced programmer only (with a view to constructing a theoretical model of that programmer's skill).

A number of experiments have been conducted that examine how different ways of specifying control in a language help or hinder debugging. These will be described in the next section on language design.

Novices' attitudes to computers are very important in determining how far they are willing to overcome the difficulties of debugging. Eason (1976) has isolated three factors of importance in this connection: what the novice expects and needs from programming; how his job or status will be affected by using a computer; and personal factors such as age and intelligence. We should not underestimate the amount of effort that the novice may have to expend in order to master the system command language and the editor, both of which he may need in order to enter, run or change his program. The system command language is the language used by the programmer to create, edit and move files around as well as compile programs and carry out other actions concerned with the programming system. Embley *et al.* (1978) and Treu (1975) describe methodologies for comparing text editors and argue for more studies to evaluate the ease with which different editors can be used.

Miller and Thomas (1977) provide an excellent review of the empirical evidence bearing on the use of command languages. They emphasize the value of a robust system that has a predictable response time. In this respect predictability of response time is more important than speed of response. They stress the importance of making a system command language easy to use as follows:

> Probably no other feature is more important in determining an individual's effectiveness in using a computer system than this aspect. The user is often placed in the position of an absolute master over an awesomely powerful slave, who speaks a strange and painfully awkward tongue, where obedience is immediate and complete but woefully thoughtless without regard to the potential destruction of its master's things, rigid to the point of being psychotic, lacking sense, memory, compassion and— worst of all—obvious consistency. (p. 512)

III. LANGUAGE DESIGN FOR NOVICES

In the last few years language design has taken more account of human factors. This has come from the recognition that a large proportion of the costs of computing are expended in debugging and extending software, and this makes it essential that programs be comprehensible to human beings as well as to computers.

There have been two areas of development. First, languages have been developed, or existing languages changed, in order to encourage programmers to write in a disciplined way that allows the program's correctness to be considered and its purpose to be seen. Second, languages and constructs within languages have been developed which enable computer programs to be written in a form closer to the standard terminology of the problem domain (e.g. SIMULA). This contrasts with languages where features are largely constrained by the properties of the computer. An excellent, brief review of issues in language design is given by Wasserman (1975). Shneiderman (1978) reviews issues in the design of data-base query languages.

Barron (1977) suggests economy of concepts, uniformity and orthogonality. as design goals for program language design. Weinberg (1971) argues for uniformity, compactness and locality. There are three sources of evidence to support these design goals: psychological research; observation of novices' encounters with existing languages; and controlled experiments on particular language features. This section reviews the evidence.

We classify proposals about the design of languages which are easy for novices to use into those concerned with syntax, those concerned with semantics and those concerned with implementation. Empirical investigations have concentrated on syntactic issues and these will be described first.

A. Flow of Control

Specifying flow of control is central to programming in algorithmic languages and many novices find it very hard. Friend (1975) found that two predictors of problem difficulty in a computer course were the number of conditional commands involved and whether or not loops or sub-routines were required for the solution.

The results of a variety of experiments with novices are summarized by Sime *et al.* (1977a). Sime *et al.* used mini-languages that differed in the way that conditionals were specified. Each language was sparse and restrictive, containing only predicates, action- and control-specifiers. The problem domain concerned cooking. They disallowed the Boolean operators **AND** and **OR** in order to

Statement of problem

Fry: everything which is juicy but not hard
Boil: everything which is hard
Chop and roast: everything which is neither hard nor juicy

(a) **JUMP**
    IF hard **GOTO L1**
    IF juicy **GOTO L2**
    chop roast stop
  L2 fry stop
  L1 boil stop

(b)**NEST-BE**
IF hard **THEN**
    BEGIN boil **END**
ELSE
    BEGIN
    IF juicy **THEN**
      BEGIN fry **END**
    ELSE
      BEGIN chop roast **END**
    END

(c)**NEST-INE**
IF hard: boil
NOT hard:
    IF juicy: fry
    NOT juicy: chop roast
    END juicy
END hard

Fig. 1. Mini-languages, from Sime *et al.* (1977a).

focus on the conditionals, but this traded predicate simplicity for conditional complexity. They tested three styles of conditional (see Fig. 1), (a) the jump using **GOTO**, (b) the nested conditional **IF** . . . **THEN** . . . **ELSE** using the scope markers **BEGIN** and **END** and (c) the nested conditional in which the predicate is repeated.

This experiment produced the following results: first, they were able to train novices to use the languages relatively easily because of their simple semantics and by explaining the languages in terms of a mechanical realization of the virtual machine. Second, they showed that nested conditionals in which the predicate is repeated redundantly produced the lowest number of syntax errors, the highest number of logically correct programs and were the easiest to debug, i.e. the error lifetimes were shortest. Nested conditionals with scope markers produced the greatest number of syntactic errors, were the most difficult to debug, but produced only slightly more logical errors than the conditionals with repeated predicates. Jump instructions did poorly in all counts.

Miller (1975) conducted similar experiments but found that

TABLE 1

Procedure table, from Miller (1975)

LABEL	QUESTION	ACTION(S)	GOTO
A1	ANY CARD IN INPUT BOX? *NO:* STOP	LOOK AT NEXT CARD	
	NAME ON CARD HAS SECOND LETTER AS "NOT-L" OR LAST LETTER AS "N"	PUT CARD IN BOX #3, INCREASE COUNTER 1	A1
	⟶	PUT CARD IN BOX #2	A1

PROBLEM: PUT A CARD IN BOX 3 IF EITHER THE NAME ON THE CARD HAS THE SECOND LETTER *NOT* "L" OR ELSE THE LAST LETTER IS "N" (OR BOTH).

COUNT THE NUMBER OF CARDS IN BOX 3 USING COUNTER 1.
PUT THE REMAINING CARDS IN BOX 2.

NESTED IFs were more difficult to learn than JUMP TO LABEL, and more difficult to use. He believes that the difference between this result and that of Sime *et al.* is due to factors in their experimental set-up, such as automatic indentation, that favoured NESTED IFs. But such favourable conditions can be incorporated into a programming language. In a subsequent experiment, Miller found that novices learned to use "procedure tables" with more facility and success than either JUMP TO LABEL or NESTED IFs (see Table 1). Unlike Sime *et al.*, Miller permitted use of AND, OR and NOT to reduce the number of control statements.

Sime *et al.* point out that debugging requires the extraction from a program of both "sequence information" which describes what the program will do under a given set of conditions, and "taxon information", which describes what set of conditions would cause a program to reach a given point. They explain the superiority of the redundant repetition of predicates for debugging in terms of the extra perceptual clues that the program listing provides about taxon information. This result was confirmed for experienced programmers as well (Green, 1977). Lucas and Kaplan (1976) found that restricting the use of GOTO made code easier for students to update.

Mayer (1976a) tested the effects of different forms of program representation on its comprehensibility. The novices were not asked to write programs but to interpret and answer questions about a sporting competition expressed in various "verbal" program-like forms (see Fig. 2). Overall error rates were high, but Mayer found (in

(a) **JUMP** (Verbal)

(1) If Indiana defeats Michigan go on to next step, otherwise go to step 7.

(2) If Ohio defeats Michigan go on to next step, otherwise go to step 6.

(3) If Indiana defeats Ohio go on to next step, otherwise go to step 5.

(4) You win prize F.

(5) You win prize E.

(6) You win prize D.

(7) If Ohio defeats Michigan go on to next step, otherwise go to step 9.

(8) You win prize C.

(9) If Indiana defeats Ohio go on to next step, otherwise go to step 11.

(10) You win prize B.

(11) You win prize A.   (continued)

(b) JUMP (Flow)

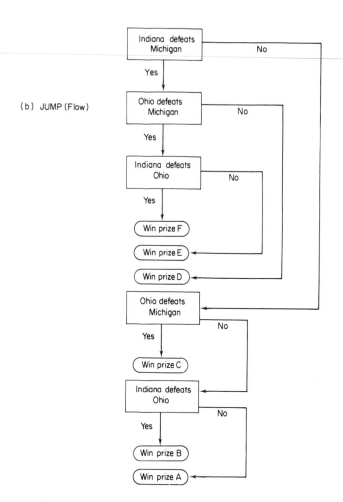

(c) **NEST** (Verbal)

If Indiana defeats Michigan then
    If Ohio defeats Michigan then
        If Indiana defeats Ohio then you win prize F.
        Otherwise you win prize E.
    Otherwise you win prize D.
Otherwise

    If Ohio defeats Michigan then you win prize C.
    Otherwise
        If Indiana defeats Ohio then you win prize B.
        Otherwise you win prize A.   (continued)

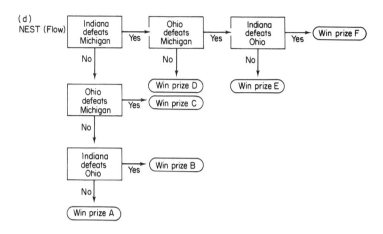

(e) **SHORT-JUMP** (Verbal)

(1) If Indiana defeats Michigan go to step 2, otherwise go to step 4.

(2) If Ohio defeats Michigan go to step 3, otherwise you win prize D.

(3) If Indiana defeats Ohio you win prize F, otherwise you win prize E.

(4) If Ohio defeats Michigan you win prize D, otherwise go to step 5.

(5) If Indiana defeats Ohio you win prize B, otherwise you win prize A.

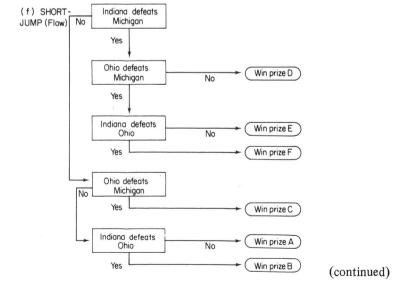

(continued)

(g) **EXAMPLE** (Flow)

Winner of Game 1	Winner of Game 2	Winner of Game 3	Prize you win
Indiana v Michigan	Ohio v. Michigan	Indiana v Ohio	

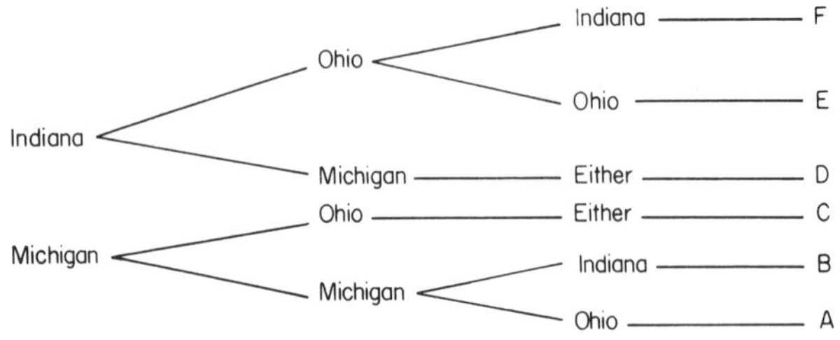

(h) **EXAMPLE** (Verbal)

There are three games: (1) Indiana v. Michigan, (2) Ohio v. Michigan; (3) Indiana v. Ohio.

If the winners are (1) Indiana, (2) Ohio, (3) Indiana, then you win prize F.

If the winners are (1) Indiana, (2) Ohio, (3) Ohio, then you win prize E.

If the winners are (1) Indiana, (2) Michigan, (3) either team, then you win prize D.

If the winners are (1) Michigan, (2) Ohio, (3) either team, then you win prize C.

If the winners are (1) Michigan, (2) Michigan, (3) Indiana, then you win prize B.

If the winners are (1) Michigan, (2) Michigan, (3) Ohio, then you win prize A.

Fig. 2. Problem representations, from Mayer (1976a).

common with Sime *et al.*) that a nested organization produced better performance than two forms of **JUMP TO LABEL**. Mayer found that "sequence" questions which asked students to trace forwards through the programs could be answered in the jump format, but those demanding backwards tracing ("taxon" questions) proved hard in this format.

The most effective representation was a fourth, called **EXAMPLE**, which presented the same information on a set of possible outcomes, as a kind of decision table rather than as an algorithm. The harder the question, the greater was the superiority of this representation.

Mayer also tested the efficiency of a diagrammatic representation (see Fig. 2). In the **EXAMPLE** format, students given a written listing did better than those given a matching diagram. For other groups, working with **NESTED** or **JUMP** formats, the matching diagrams (various forms of flowchart) produced better results. This suggests that the written **EXAMPLE** form is effective in enabling students to grasp the overall structure of the program. Fitter and Green (1979) review the issues surrounding diagrammatic languages. (See Chapter 7 of this volume.)

Love (1977) compared novices' ability to memorize short programs written in various forms, with and without indentation and with or without simplified control. All the programs were written in standard FORTRAN. He gave students three minutes to memorize each program and four minutes to reconstruct it from memory. He found no difference in their ability to reconstruct the programs of different form. Although he was interested in comprehension of the programs, the result suggests that students did not attempt to examine the meaning of the program so much as learn it by rote. This conjecture is supported by the fact that more experienced programmers, under the same conditions, did better with simplified control. Indentation (i.e. paragraphing of conditionals) made no difference to either group. Shneiderman (1976) showed that novices were only marginally better at recalling working programs than recalling scrambled programs, and argued that the ability to recall a program is a good measure of the extent to which the program is comprehended.

But cognitive style may play an important role here, as in other aspects of programming. A distinction in cognitive style between operation learners and comprehension learners is due to Pask (1976). It may be characterized informally as follows. Operation learners tend to concentrate on the details of complex subject matter and work "upwards" to a more general understanding, while comprehension learners attempt to construct a more global picture and then fit the details in later. Coombs *et al.* (1979) found that inexperienced student programmers who were operation learners were much better at sorting out a scrambled FORTRAN program than those who were comprehension learners (see Chapter 8 of this volume). Certain languages and certain methods of teaching programming may well be more in tune with one style than another. As far as we are aware, the question of whether successful, experienced programmers tend to exhibit a particular cognitive style has yet to be investigated.

Embley (1978) argues that the ALGOL control specifiers **if . . . then . . . else, while** and **case** can be unified into a single new construct called a "selector". An example of a selector used in simple

CAI answer-judging is compared with an ALGOL-like encoding in Fig. 3.

Embley tested the comprehensibility of two programs, where each was written in two versions: using either conventional control or the selector. He found that students answered questions about both versions of the programs with equal facility, but that they thought they understood the selector versions slightly better (this sort of experimental result has the ring of a Hawthorne effect).

There is some difficulty in knowing how far experiments on minilanguages can be generalized to full-scale programming languages. Supposing Sime *et al.*'s (1977a) recommendation on conditionals were implemented, it is not clear what the repercussions would be for other language features. For example, given a language with the Boolean operators **AND** and **OR** that allowed complex predicates to be expressed, it is not clear whether that complex predicate should

(a)
```
present_question;
answer_ok←false;
while not (answer_ok) do
   accept reply;
   if match (reply, answer_1) then
      response_1;
      answer_ok←true;
   elseif match (reply, answer_2) then
      response_2;
      answer_ok←true;
   elseif
   . . .
   elseif match (reply, answer_n) then
      response_n;
   else response_for_unanticipated_answer;
   fi;
od;
```

(b)
```
present_question;
[accept reply; if reply
   |matches answer_1:response_1;
   |matches answer_2:response_2;
   . . .
   |matches answer_n: response_n; again
   |else: response_for_unanticipated_answer: again;
];
```

Fig. 3. (a) ALGOL-like control and (b) "selector" control, from Embley (1978).

be repeated, as in:

IF tall **OR** (green **AND** hard) : boil
NOT tall **OR** (green **AND** hard) : grill
END tall **OR** (green **AND** hard)

At least Sime *et al.* have done the experimenting where others have simply made (often plausible) pronouncements. For example Kovats (1978) suggests, without empirical evidence, that the block structure of programs is revealed by distinctive closing keywords (e.g. **endcase** for **case** and **endif** for **if**) and prefix-style intermediate keywords such as **then** in **if . . .then. . .else.**

Consistency of syntax and choice of instruction names have not been the subject of sufficient empirical research. Miller and Thomas (1977) examine these issues for system command languages but not for general-purpose languages. Both Barron (1977) and Weinberg (1971) regard syntactic consistency as a desirable design goal, and Friend's (1975) observation of students' "reasonable" syntactic errors confirms this. But in some cases there will be a trade-off between consistency and readability. For example, greater consistency can lead to long typing sequences and unreadability of text, as in pure LISP. Another aspect of language design is that the same symbol ought to mean the same thing in different contexts. In this respect BASIC does badly because the "=" sign is used to denote assignment, successive assignment, identity in function definition and as an infix predicate that checks whether two items are equal. Weinberg (1971) provides a number of other similar examples from FORTRAN and PL/1. Denvir (1979) gives a more detailed discussion of this issue.

It seems sensible to choose the names of language instructions so that any common English connotations correspond to notional machine actions. Kennedy (1975) gives an example where novices learning how to use a computerized hospital filing system mixed up two filing instructions because the everyday meaning of the instruction names did not match their internal function. Professional computer scientists tend to hold strongly one of two contradictory views on what the "tail" of a list is. The LISP (tadpole) view is that the tail is everything except the head (first item). The ALGOL-68 (donkey) view is that the tail is only the last item and that removing the tail leaves the head and body. But success in capitalizing on the ordinary connotation of instruction names can cause difficulties because students may be beguiled into typing in English rather than in the formal syntax of the programming language. Green *et al.* (1978) observed this difficulty and found that certain forms of conditional statement provoked mistakes because students mistook the programming language for English. Plum (1977) gives various examples of the way programming languages can "fool" their users. He argues for small, systematic languages and against languages which give a superficial appearance of naturalness that entices naive users to type in English. Such languages are appropriate only when systems are developed with the wide knowledge and powers of inference necessary to cope intelligently with such input.

This view is echoed by Thomas (1978) who argues that man–computer dialogues should be modelled on human dialogues (a point also argued by Kennedy, 1974), though he does not suggest how the consequent programming problems would be solved. Naur (1975) uses the analogy between programming languages and other forms of artificial language (e.g. mathematics and Esperanto) to predict little hope of removing FORTRAN and COBOL from their pre-eminent position, whatever better alternatives are developed.

Weinberg (1971) claimed to be able to tell what programming language a person first met as a novice by examining the style of his programs (and his errors) in whatever language he currently used.

Many programming languages have their grammatical roots in English. Commands are often in the imperative form of the verb, e.g. "PRINT<file>". Adapting programming languages for novices whose first or only language is not English can be difficult and is not just a matter of a one-to-one translation of keywords. This is because the grammar of the user's own language may not match the English-influenced grammar of the programming language. Curado and Valente (1978) provide an interesting discussion of these issues in the case of LOGO "in" Portuguese.

B. Semantics

There have been rather fewer experiments on program semantics than on syntax. Two studies have compared complete, working languages rather than isolated features in mini-languages.

Gannon and Horning (1975) compared the errors made by the same group of 25 experienced programmers using two languages: TOPPS and TOPPSII. The languages were "expression-oriented" and designed to teach "the concepts of asynchronous processes and interprocess communication". The differences between the two languages are reproduced in Table 2.

Because Gannon and Horning were dealing with complete programming languages, they found many points of comparison. This is both a strength and a weakness of their approach compared to that

TABLE 2

Comparison of TOPPS and TOPPSII, from Gannon and Horning (1975)

TOPPS	TOPPSII
(1) Expression evaluation right to left with equal precedence among operators	Expression evaluation left to right with "traditional" operator precedence
(2) Assignment operator	Assignment statement
(3) Logical operators ∈ and |	Logical functions **all** and **any**
(4) Semicolon as separator	Semicolon as terminator
(5) Selection statements: if	Selection statements: **if** and **case**
(6) Repetition statements: **repeat**	Repetition statements: **repeat** and **for each** (element of an array)
(7) Brackets used to close compound expressions: **end** and parentheses	Brackets used to close compound statements: **end**
(8) Automatic inheritance of environment	Inheritance of environment only upon specific request
(9) Constants: literals	Constants: literals and named constants

of Sime *et al.* (1977a) using mini-languages. One of Gannon and Horning's results was that the restrictions on "inheritance of environment" (No. 8 in Table 2, i.e. restrictions on the access to global variables from inside a procedure body) reduced the persistence of some errors in TOPPSII, though this language produced its own crop of persistent subtle errors. Other results (concerning syntax) were that the TOPPSII use of a semi-colon as a statement terminator (No. 4 in Table 2) led to many fewer errors than the TOPPS use of it as a separator. Studies of PASCAL errors came to much the same conclusion (see Section IV). Gannon and Horning also found that errors involving the use of ":=" to make assignment in TOPPS were persistent. This was due to the similarity between this operator and "=". The authors favoured the use of a completely different symbol to mark assignment, such as " ← " in APL.

Gannon (1977) compared total errors and error persistence of novices and experts in a typed and typeless language. In the typed language, data were associated with identifiers statically, through an explicit declaration. For example, once a particular variable had been declared as an integer, say, then any attempt to assign a real number value to it would cause an error. By contrast, in the typeless language there were no such associations or declarations. He found that the statically typed language caused fewer errors and less error persistence for the single test problem, though the majority of these errors were associated with the more complex representation of data in the typeless language. Novices had the greatest difference in performance using the two languages.

Part of the difficulty faced by some novices, such as arts students, is that the first language they learn is best suited to solving problems of a mathematical nature. These students may have neither the ability nor the inclination to solve such problems, so various writers have suggested that they use a text-processing language as a first language (see for example Brown, 1972; Raskin, 1974; Axford *et al.*, 1979). Snark (1973) has proposed a data-base query language for ethnologists learning to program. The whole question of whether programming can or ought to be de-mathematized needs empirical study. Even languages designed to manipulate text may retain sufficient mathematical flavour, e.g. in their use of symbols, to deter arts students.

C. Implementation

Questions of implementation are closely related to questions of teaching strategy because both are concerned with the presentation of language concepts to the student. Thus the desirability of basing one's teaching of a language on an explicit notional machine, may well depend on the extent to which the language implementation supports this strategy, e.g. by helping students to see selected parts of the "works" of this machine (du Boulay and O'Shea, 1978).

Apart from providing "windows" on to important internal aspects of the machine, good language design can ensure that the notional machine is functionally simple. That is to say, it can be considered as a small set of mechanisms and their interactions. This idea is developed by Mayer (1979) who gives a simple characterization of a BASIC notional machine in terms of the "transactions" it can carry out. This is a level of representation of the computing system that lies somewhere between a hardware description of the computer and a definition of the semantics of the language.

The workings of the notional machine can be revealed by augmenting the programming language so that certain hidden actions are accompanied by external changes. Barr *et al.* (1976), in their BIP system for teaching BASIC, make flow of control visible on a display by showing pointers which move around the program text as it is executed. They also provide the user with the facility of slowing down the execution of his program, or even of single-stepping through it. Hidden side-effects such as assignment can be shown dynamically on another part of the screen. Similar systems for FORTRAN are described by Shapiro and Witmer (1974). for PASCAL (Nievergelt *et al*., 1978) and for assembly languages (Schweppe, 1973; Shapiro and Witmer, 1974).

A device which nicely demonstrates flow of control is the "slot box" (Hillis, 1975) and has been used to teach very young children how to program (Perlman, 1974). The novice inserts tokens into slots in the box. Each token has an instruction name written on it and a code that the machine can read. The slots represent a simple linear address structure. A light next to each slot comes on as the instruction in the slot is executed. Program modification is accomplished easily by rearranging tokens manually in the slots. In the language LOGO, flow of control can be revealed by the movements of a drawing device, a small floor robot called "a turtle" (Papert, 1972) which has a pen attached to it. Commands from the student cause the turtle to either rotate or translate. Flow of control through a stored sequence of commands is shown by the visible trail which the turtle leaves behind it on the floor as it moves. If the student is using a button box as a simple input device, this trail can be matched to the buttons which light up in turn as each stored instruction is executed (du Boulay and Emanuel, 1975).

Various additions to language implementation have been made to decrease the possibility that novices type in incorrect code. Sime *et al*. (1977b) found that they could dramatically reduce the incidence of syntax errors in their mini-language consisting of nested conditionals and scope markers. This was achieved by having the computer automatically constrain the programmer to fill in subsequent slots in a template, once he had started to specify a conditional. This method did not increase the number of logical errors or error lifetimes. A similar system is employed in the language SOLO, learned by novices at remote terminals at Open University study centres where there is little chance to ask for help. Having typed in the "if" part of a conditional, the interpreter automatically sets up the lines for the "then" and the "else" branches into which the student types the desired actions. This sytem has been successfully used by large numbers of Open University students (Eisenstadt, 1979).

A more extreme solution using typing amplification is adopted in the language FLOW (Raskin, 1974). Typing the first letter of a command causes the whole command to be duplexed on the display screen. Typing a character that would lead to a syntactic error produces no visible output on the screen—so the random key presses of a baby or monkey would eventually produce a syntactically correct, if logically useless program. A more sophisticated interactive error-detection system is proposed by Davis *et al.* (1975), that would have the capability of giving the user hints about how to correct the errors it discovers, both at compile time ánd run time.

Various experiments have been conducted to test the utility of automatic debugging aids. Biermann, *et al.* (1975) found that in-experienced and expert programmers were more successful than medium-skilled programmers in finding non-syntactic bugs in an assembly listing using a trace of the instruction leading up to the error compared with using a relatively raw core dump. Medium-skilled programmers were also helped by the trace, but not to the same extent. These results can be reconciled with those of Gould (1975) and Gould and Drongowski (1974), mentioned earlier, since they found that both the type of bug and the type of program had more effect on debugging time than the type of debugging aid.

Lemos (1979a) has shown the advantage (at least in teaching students COBOL) of having them debug each other's programs away from the machine but following a set procedure. Gould and Drongowski (1974) and Gould (1975) analysed the debugging behaviour of experienced programmers. They came to the conclusion that highly motivated, experienced programmers, debugging FORTRAN programs in which they knew there was exactly one bug, were able to debug as efficiently when given only the program listing as when given other aids such as specimen input and output or inter-active debugging aids. This result is slightly suspect because of the artificial condition of one and only one bug. Myers (1978) found a large amount of variability in experienced programmers' ability to find errors in PL/1 programs. He also found that the mean number of errors located was only about one third of the total (his subjects did not know how many errors to expect in each program). The large variability led to the result that the most efficient debugging method was to have two programmers work on the same program independently. He concluded that computer-based testing is as effective as manual code walk-through and inspection, though the latter took people longer to complete.

One problem that motivated a large number of empirical studies was the question of whether batch languages were preferable to interactive languages. Most of the studies summarized in Sackman (1970) have shown that interactive languages have a slight edge, in terms of man-hours spent on problems, over batch equivalents, but that this advantage is gained at the expense of greater machine time. Skelton (1972) found that students learned FORTRAN equally well under a batch system as under an interactive one. The batch students had slightly more positive attitudes towards the computer. He concluded that a batch service is a much cheaper, and just as effective means of teaching programming as an interactive service. This result is rapidly being overtaken by events and the much greater access to interactive facilities. A recent study (Lee and Shneiderman, 1978) has revived the issue and tried to relate programmers' preference for batch or interactive styles of working to personality factors such as assertiveness, but with mixed results.

IV. EXPERIENCE OF PARTICULAR LANGUAGES

This section describes studies that have investigated novices' experiences of particular languages, such as FORTRAN. Not enough of these studies have been conducted and so the empirical evidence is patchy. Inevitably the main focus is on what the novices found hard rather than on what they found easy. Since some languages have generated more of this type of study than others the sections devoted to the more frequently investigated languages appear more critical than those concerning the less frequently investigated languages. Most of the work on individual languages is based on theoretical considerations or personal experience. Empirical studies are usually concerned with questions of relative efficiency of different languages from the viewpoint of machine time or space rather than from the programmer's viewpoint. Barron (1977) and Higman (1977) provide useful overviews of the properties of different languages, together with comments about their faults, some of which are likely to confuse novices.

Studies of novices' experience of individual languages have focused on the errors novices made and on the difficulties they face in solving programming problems. Several studies have analysed the syntactic and semantic errors in samples of novices' (usually students) programs. These sorts of error are amenable to simple automatic methods of data capture, where logical errors require a more intelligent analysis of the programming task and of the novice's attempted solution.

Analysis of syntactic and semantic errors provides two useful pieces of data. First is the overall frequency of different types of error, and the evidence is that a small number of error types usually account for a vast proportion of all errors. Second is the measure of *error-proneness*. This is the propensity for certain features of a particular language to cause errors. It is calculated by dividing the error frequency of an error type by the number of times the language feature associated with this error is used in total (both correctly and incorrectly). On this basis Youngs (1974) found that conditionals were highly error-prone even though they accounted for a relatively small number of actual errors. In other words novices were highly likely to make an error when coding a conditional even though they did not have many conditionals in their programs. The causes of error-proneness include internal inconsistencies or arbitrary restrictions within the language (e.g. the rules for array subscripts in some dialects of FORTRAN), clashes with natural language usage (e.g. delimiters in PASCAL) or psychological mismatches between a construct and the task it is to do (e.g. the nested conditional "goto" controversy).

Analysis of the rate at which errors are eliminated from programs provides a measure of *error persistence*. Errors with high persistence are hard to diagnose and put right. As in the case of error-proneness, error persistence can point to ambiguities in the language and to the need for special emphasis when the language is taught.

A. COBOL

Despite COBOL's importance in commercial programming very little research on novices' experiences of learning this language has been done.

Litecky and Davis (1976) classified 1777 errors from 1400 program runs of 73 students learning COBOL into 88 classes. They found that 20% of these classes accounted for 80% of all the errors. Their table of this "top twenty" per cent is given in Table 3.

The vast majority of errors in this list are syntactic, and many are concerned with delimiters of one sort or another. This points to a difficulty for novices using COBOL that can be only partially alleviated by adopting Litecky and Davis's suggestion of implementing a compiler sensitive to students' most frequent errors. Their suggestion is a curative rather than a preventative measure.

One very important issue described by Litecky and Davis is that the compiler they used was only able to give "accurate" error messages in about 20% of the cases. By an accurate error diagnosis they mean one that points to the source of the error rather than to

TABLE 3

"Top twenty" per cent of COBOL errors, from Litecky and Davis (1976)

Rank	No. of errors	Description of errors or grouped errors
1	253	Misspelling of non-structurals
2	176	Hyphenation error
3	154	Period missing
4	117	Name not defined
5	89	Reserved word used as data name
6	88	Period added
7	81	Data description error
8	67	Multiple definition of name
9	58	Incompatible class in arithmetic statement
10	47	Misspellings of structural
11	46	B margin coded to left of column 12
12	42	Invalid word delimiters, e.g. comma without a space
13	38	Incompatible class in move statement
14	37	Words run together without blank as delimiter
15	34	A margin coded to right of column 8
16	32	Keypunching shift error, e.g. numeric instead of alphanumeric
17	28	Continuation error on alphanumeric literal
18	27	Coding beyond column 72

TOTAL 1414 (= 79.6% density)

N = 88 error classes (20% $\times$ N = 18)

an incidental side-effect. Writing a compiler that has the requisite internal model of the programmer and his task needed to accomplish this sort of diagnosis would be extremely difficult.

Litecky and Davis found four constructs that were error-prone. These are reproduced in Table 4. Notice that the three most error-prone constructs concerned delimiters.

Litecky and Davis did not analyse error persistence or logical

TABLE 4

Error-prone COBOL constructs, from Litecky and Davis (1976)

Rank	Description of error	Errors per 10 000 usages
1	The period added after "FE file-name"	509.3
2	The use of commas as word delimiters	124.6
3	The period required after "01 record name"	88.2
4	The computational class requirement of arithmetic statements	84.5

errors in their study.

Al-Jarrah and Torson (1979) provide statistics derived from a static analysis of a large sample of commercial and industrial COBOL programs. They do not report on the errors in the programs but give detailed figures on the frequency with which different constructs were used. Programs in their sample tended to use a small sub-set of the available constructs, e.g. the most popular data description clause was the PICTURE and of these over 92% were numeric. Their argument is that compilers should be adapted to work most efficiently on those constructs that occur frequently. The difficulty with this is that it may make the compiler run more quickly but at the expense of its own internal structure. Parts of the compiler dealing with closely related constructs might be in widely separated places because although logically connected they could be used with quite different frequencies.

Youngs (1974) studied a small number of programs (some in COBOL) submitted by twelve programmers. He found some evidence that allocation was troublesome in COBOL, because of both the lack of defaults and the complexity of syntax.

B. FORTRAN

The lack of empirical evidence about novices' experience of FORTRAN mirrors the situation for COBOL. There is one major static analysis of FORTRAN programs (Knuth, 1971) and a few mentions of specific difficulties as part of their studies.

Knuth's study looked at syntactically correct programs only, and compiled statistics about frequency of usage of different constructs.

Like the other studies which followed it, this showed that programmers tend to use a small sub-set of constructs very frequently, and also tend to use these in simple ways.

Syntactic errors in FORTRAN programming were studied by Boies and Gould (1974) who came to the conclusion that syntactic errors were not a major bottleneck in programming. Unfortunately their study does not provide a breakdown of different types of syntactic error nor of other classes of error, e.g. semantic or logical. Youngs (1974) found that I/O formatting statements caused a large number of errors, but that (in contrast to COBOL) allocation errors were infrequent. PASCAL has been compared to FORTRAN as an introductory language by Nutt (1978). He found that PASCAL was superior, but presents no detailed evidence about students' experiences of each language.

Both Weinberg (1971) and Barron (1977) describe certain non-uniformities in FORTRAN, e.g. the rules about subscript expressions, but neither presents empirical evidence that these cause novices difficulty.

C. BASIC

The conventional wisdom is that BASIC is easy to learn, but that its naming, control and other restrictions make programs hard to read and understand as well as leading novices into bad programming habits. As far as we are aware no study has looked at what happens to students as they learn BASIC, at what they find difficult and at what they find easy. Mayer's (1979) work on BASIC has been concerned with methods of presenting the language to students, e.g. with or without a concrete model, and not with a detailed analysis of the programs students write.

Our best source of information on students' BASIC programs is the study by Friend (1975) that observed, in great detail, 40 students' programs in AID. This is an algebraic language similar to BASIC. Friend was interested in both the logical organization of the students' solution to a set of 25 programming problems and in the syntactic and semantic errors in their code.

Friend found 1090 errors in the 7063 commands typed by the students. Her basic distinction was between syntactic and semantic errors. Clerical errors were counted as a sub-class of syntactic errors. There is a marked difference between her results and those of Youngs (1974) (see Table 5).

It is impossible to say whether this difference is due to the

TABLE 5

Patterns of error: Youngs (1974) compared with Friend (1975)

	Friend (AID)%	Youngs (Various languages)%
Syntactic + Clerical	68	17
Semantic + Logical	32	76
Other	0	7

different languages employed in the two experiments, to the types of problems set, or to other factors such as the small sample sizes or differences in decisions about classification of errors.

Friend also recorded the features that determined whether the students found a programming problem difficult. These were the expected proportion of conditional commands, and whether or not loops or sub-routines were required. Friend found that her students' knowledge of algebra was poor and this contributed to their difficulties.

D. LOGO

LOGO is an interactive procedural language derived from LISP. It was developed for use by children by Feurzeig *et al.* (1969) and has primitives for data manipulation as well as for the control of a wide variety of peripheral devices, the most well known of which is the "turtle" (Papert, 1972).

Given its development as an educational tool, there have been rather more studies of how novices learned this language than there have been for other languages. This accounts for the more detailed comments on this language, which should not necessarily be interpreted as evidence that it is "worse" than other languages. Most of the novices who have been observed were children.

The most detailed account of children's difficulties is that of Cannara (1976) which includes much of the data from an earlier experiment (Weyer and Cannara, 1975). Cannara taught children (aged from nine to fifteen) in two experiments designed to investigate how children learned programming. It is plausible that some of the difficulties he observed were caused by the immaturity of his subjects, although Austin (1976) and Statz (1973) suggest that adults make the same kind of mistakes as children when both are beginning to learn LOGO.

Some of the children's difficulties can be traced back to their misunderstanding of the underlying notional machine. Cannara summarizes their problem as follows:

> The two most common, virtually universal misunderstandings of all the students were: (1) misunderstandings of linguistic/computational context [the particular virtual machine with which the student is communicating], and (2) ill-defined intents. The former applying to both storage/passing of information within their programs and their interaction with the interpreters. The latter, or fuzzy program specifications, amounts to wishful thinking, wherein the particular interpreter was expected to read the student's mind and run correctly even though, for instance, a command had been left out. (p. 109)

Thus some students attempted to run a program while it was being edited or vice versa. Difficulties with "storage" included the belief that the computer stored partial results automatically and that these results could be retrieved for use in later computations. Students also had difficulties with the filing system.

There were also a number of difficulties associated with the name/value distinction. Some students thought that procedure names *had* to describe their action in order to work, or thought that variable names were computationally related to their values. Difficulties with control included misunderstandings about the recursion/iteration distinction, binding of argument values, result-passing and command-parsing. Syntactic difficulties included use of predicates, use of the abbreviation " : " for VALUE, use of VALUE, use of infix operators and invention of illegal "noise" words.

Cannara also notes that students were not very good at problem-solving in programming. They did not break down problems into sub-problems nor did they match the problem decomposition to the available language constructs. They also failed to use old solutions in new problems and wrote inelegant procedures.

Statz (1973) briefly mentions some of the difficulties she observed among the eleven- and twelve-year-old children, in her experiment. There were wide variations among the children, caused by differences in ability or in maturation. She noted that some children had difficulty with filing and with editing. Others were defeated by "small mechanical errors" (later she mentions the difficulty some of the children had with spelling and typing). She also notes that children sometimes structured their procedures badly, as had children in Cannara's experiment. Milner (1973) in his experiment with eleven-year-old children mentions a difficulty they faced associated with the input of numerical values to procedures. Subsequent associated difficulties were the use of a variable as a counter to terminate a recursion and the definition of a procedure with two or more arguments.

Austin (1976) reports that the student teachers he taught suffered from many of the same problems as the children in Cannara's experiment. He lists difficulties with editing, filing, breaking down problems appropriately and the construction of syntactically correct commands and procedures. Brown and Rubinstein (1974) report that social science students whom they taught also had difficulty in problem-solving. Some of the solutions to the problems set were so short that the students solved them either immediately or not at all. There was no way for them to refine an initial attempt gradually. For other problems, students tended to use procedure "templates" (e.g. a simple recursion) when they were not appropriate. Their students were confused by the scope of variables.

Statz mentions that some of the undergraduates she taught were "frightened away by initial problems" with the computer and that others "dealt with LOGO in a pedantic fashion". Particular programming difficulties were encountered in terminating a recursion using a stop rule and understanding conditionals in general. Many also had difficulty with result-passing. Others had formed the impression that "input" (arguments) and "output" (results) referred to user-typed input and computer-typed output. This is a good example of the wrong connotation being brought to bear because of the choice of name or term. Cannara also mentioned a similar difficulty and proposed a change in the terminology to reduce the difficulty. Statz also compared the programming performance of teachers with that of the children. She noted that they made the same kind of mistakes as children but were better able to recover from them. This is similar to Youngs' (1974) finding, in his comparison of naive and experienced programmers. The teachers, like Cannara's children, confused procedure execution with procedure definition, as well as making mistakes in the definition such as omitting line numbers. They also treated the machine as "intelligent", for example by answering error messages. Syntactic mistakes were also made with spaces and quotation marks. The causes of the last two errors probably lie in the form of the LOGO implementation used. There

TABLE 6

Most frequent LOGO errors, from du Boulay (1978)

Rank	Description of error	%	Histogram
1	Call undefined procedure	28	****************************
2	Insufficient arguments	16	****************
3	No line number	11	***********
4	Extra text	10	**********
5	Turtle off drawing area	10	**********
6	Variables misused	6	******
7	Wrong type of argument	4	****
8	Command leaves a value	3	***
9	Device claiming violation	3	***
10	Number too large	3	***
11	Stack overflow	2	**

were command names constructed from concatenated English words such as IFTRUE, IFFALSE, TYPEIN, PENUP, PENDOWN, which would not be interpreted if typed with a space inserted.

One of the present authors (du Boulay, 1978) analysed 2400 error messages from 19 000 LOGO commands issued by 15 student teachers. He found that 11 error messages accounted for 96% of the total number—these are given in Table 6.

The students' most persistent difficulties were concerned with variables. There were also difficulties with syntactic markers, especially the quotation mark. Mistyping caused many errors, especially mistyping involving the space character.

E. PASCAL

PASCAL has attracted a fair amount of comment (e.g. Habermann, 1973; Lecarme and Desjardins, 1975; Welsh *et al.*, 1977) but only two empirical studies of users' experiences have been carried out. Ripley and Druseikis (1978) who were interested in error recovery strategies for compilers, have studied the syntactic errors of two classes of graduate computer science students. They found that 64%

of the programs compiled by students experienced in PASCAL were syntactically and semantically correct, while 58% of the programs written by those first encountering the language were correct. Of the errors found about 60% were puncutation errors, with the great proportion centring around the use of the semi-colon. Syntactic errors were classified into those involving a missing token, those involving an extra token, those where the wrong token had been used and those in which the error involved several tokens. Ripley and Druseikis' data are reproduced as Tables 7–10.

Ripley and Druseikis found that spelling and key punch (i.e. clerical) errors were fairly infrequent, accounting for only 8% of the total.

The most error-prone construct in PASCAL was the semi-colon, which was, for instance, often used in place of a comma to separate actual parameters, since formal parameters are separated by semi-colons. Declarations formed another error-prone area because of restrictions on the ordering of declaration keywords. Missing **begins**

TABLE 7

Missing token errors in PASCAL, from Ripley and Druseikis (1978)

No. of errors	%	Missing token
83	48.5	;
18	10.5	**end**
13	7.6	**begin**
8	4.7	Identifier
7	4.1	:
7	4.1	=
6	3.5	)
6	3.5	# (String delimiter)
5	2.9	(
5	2.9	**do**
< 4	7.7	(Miscellaneous tokens

TOTAL 171 (=41.4% density)

TABLE 8

Extra token errors in PASCAL, from Ripley and Druseikis (1978)

No. of errors	%	Extra token
10	30.3	**var**
7	21.2	;
3	9.1	Identifier
3	9.1	**type**
2	6.1	]
< 2	24.2	(Miscellaneous tokens)

TOTAL 33 (=8.0% density)

and **ends** were another troublesome point, and Ripley and Druseikis argue for uniquely bracketed control construction such as **if** and **endif**.

Pugh and Simpson (1979) conducted a less detailed study of students' errors. They reiterated Ripley and Druseikis's point about the semi-colon and also argued for **endif**. Their students made a large number of errors in various aspects of I/O.

F. APL

There has been no detailed study of novices' experiences of APL in the manner of Litecky and Davis's (1976) study of COBOL. Saal and Weiss (1977) have conducted a static analysis of the usage of APL constructs but have not concerned themselves with errors. Their main result is that programmers tend to write their programs using only a small sub-set of the available APL constructs.

G. Assembly Languages

The only work that we know of that has studied novices' experience of assembly language programming is that of Cannara (1976). He taught schoolchildren SIMPER, a simulated decimal machine language. He characterizes the most common difficulty of the pupils as one of understanding "context". For example, pupils

TABLE 9

Wrong token errors in PASCAL, from Ripley and Druseikis (1978)

No. of errors	%	Incorrect and correct token
21	13.1	,;
15	9.4	:= =
12	7.5	"#
8	5.0	= :=
7	4.4	'#
6	3.8	*(*
6	3.8	;,
5	3.1	([
5	3.1	in identifier
4	2.5	: =
4	2.5	: :=
3	1.9	)]
3	1.9	];
3	1.9	;·
2	1.3	;]
2	1.3	.)
2	1.3	until to
2	1.3	;:
2	1.3	input identifier
2	1.3	label identifier
2	1.3	_[
2	1.3	]= :=
2	1.3	* *)
2	1.3	# = :=
2	1.3	[(
2	1.3	? #
2	1.3	wrteln writeln
< 2	19.2	(Miscellaneous pairs of tokens)

TOTAL 160 (38.7% density)

TABLE 10

Multiple token errors in PASCAL, from Ripley and Druseikis (1978)

No. of errors	%	Description of error
17	34.0	Declaration out of order
5	10.0	Conditional expression not allowed in PASCAL
3	6.0	Extra array information in parameter declaration
3	6.0	**Go to** in place of goto
2	4.0	Missing **of** type
2	4.0	Extra **step** constant
2	4.0	Extra label: preceding **begin**
< 2	32.0	(Miscellaneous other errors)

TOTAL 50 (=12.1% density)

would try to edit a program while it was running. He found that most pupils did not grasp the distinction between editing commands and assembler instructions.

V. TEACHING STRATEGY

This section reviews experiments on strategies for teaching programming. Austing *et al.* (1977) provide an extensive survey of the literature (mostly from ACM sources) on computer science education. Surveys of courses for arts students in the USA are given by Bowles (1971) and Allen (1974). Lemos (1979b) describes a number of approaches to teaching programming. There is discussion of teaching issues in Turski (1973) but little empirical evidence.

A. Which Language to Use

Almost every programming language seems to have a band of dedicated users who argue that it is the best language to teach novices. Tagg (1974), in a review of many popular first languages, was unable to select any "best buy". Part of the difficulty is the wide variation in novices' expected use of their programming skill (see e.g. Eason, 1976). There are two basic language choices for those who intend to teach programming. First: should a high- or low-level language be used? Second: should one or more than one language be introduced at the start?

The advantages of a low-level language are that both its syntax and semantics are likely to be simple, it is amenable to simulation on a large machine in a way that can illustrate the contents of registers and store locations, and it involves students directly in such programming concepts as names, addresses and values that have repercussions in high-level languages. The low-level language brings the student closer to the computer. The high-level language on the other hand is intended to bring the student closer to the problem. Its advantages are that it enables the programmer to solve realistic problems, it relieves him of a number of tedious jobs, and it is more likely to lead to disciplined and comprehensible programs.

We are aware of only one experiment which has examined whether both a high-level and a low-level language should be presented together (Weyer and Cannara, 1975). They taught children both LOGO and SIMPER, and found that children who were taught LOGO first did better than those taught SIMPER first, but better results were obtained when both languages were taught simultaneously. Although the children did mix up the commands in the two languages occasionally, it seemed as if each language was helping the other by providing a contrasting view of the machine and the business of programming. This is an area that needs further research.

B. Characterizing the Notional Machine

One of the difficulties that face the novice is understanding what is going on inside the computer in response to his program. As we saw in Section III, a certain amount can be done by enhancing the language implementation to reveal certain otherwise hidden actions such as variable assignment, by explicit external changes. Where such facilities are unavailable the teacher can help novices considerably by providing a manipulable, concrete, working model of the notional machine. Mayer (1975, 1976b) showed that novices who had been taught a simplified version of FORTRAN, using a model of the FORTRAN machine, were better able to read and write programs than those who had learnt without the model. The advantage was greater where the problems required more interpretations on the part of the students. Miller (1974) was able to teach novices a special-purpose language using a similar model. Statz and Miller (1978) give a detailed description of an "egg-box" computer to illustrate BASIC. Baecker (1975) and Tracs (1974) describe the use of films for the same purpose.

Various works (e.g. Kugel, 1975; Weyer and Cannara, 1975) cite the use of games, anthropormorphic metaphors and other aids to understanding programming as factors in their success in teaching programming. One effect is to make programming more fun to learn and to increase the amount of peer-teaching that occurs. The other is to provide analogies, drawn from the experience of the novices, that illustrate some of the novel concepts. A certain amount of care is needed in matching analogies to the students. It has been our experience that inexperienced adult programmers reject anthropomorphic metaphors that work well with children (du Boulay and O'Shea, 1976) because they perceive them as babyish. It is not that they reject all metaphors and analogies, but only those that seem to be condescending. For a whole-hearted attempt to inject humour and employ everyday analogies for computing ideas, see *The Fortran Colouring Book* (Kaufmann, 1978) or *Illustrating Basic* (Alcock, 1979).

There is controversy about the value of using flowcharts. Despite their popularity in teaching texts, Mayer (1975) found that flowcharts only helped novices learning a simplified FORTRAN when the problems were extremely simple and directly related to the examples given in the teaching, but hindered them in dealing with more complex problems. Shneiderman *et al.* (1977) found no difference in the performance at composing or comprehending FORTRAN programs of novices who had learned the language using flowcharts and those who had not used flowcharts. This is not to say that diagrams are a "bad thing", only that the particular class of flowchart used in these experiments did not appear to help. Brooks (1978) explained Shneiderman *et al.*'s result by suggesting that flowcharts contained inappropriate information and, for example, did not explain what variables were in use by the program. In an experiment with experienced programmers, Brooks found that a variable dictionary was a more effective aid to understanding FORTRAN programs than a flowchart. Providing both types of aid did not give better results than the variable dictionary, but this is probably explained by the simplicity of the flow of control of the programs used.

C. Working in Groups

While novices very often write and debug their programs on their own, professional programmers are usually part of a team and will have to hand over their programs in a form suitable to be understood, run or modified by other users (Weinberg, 1971). Suggestions have been made that programming should be learnt under more realistic (commercial) conditions and that working in groups gives students a better understanding of programming. But changes in technology (e.g. interactive terminals) keep altering patterns of programmer organization. It will be very surprising if the current ways of producing software are still practised in twenty years time.

Lemos (1978) found that students who debugged their COBOL assignments in small groups became more favourably disposed towards programming. He also found (Lemos, 1979a) that this method aided students' comprehension of COBOL. Cheney (1977) has shown that students who worked in pairs on their programming assignments did much better in a programming examination than those who worked individually. Snark (1973) provides anecdotal evidence about the value of an "egoless" approach in training for experienced programmers. The most likely explanation of these results seems to be the benefit of both hearing other people's perceptions of a problem and explaining issues to others. It is a commonplace experience of demonstrators in computer science programming sessions that students start to explain about a program whose bug they cannot find only to break off the conversation because they now "see" the answer—often it is not necessary for the demonstrator to say anything at all. Working in groups would provide the opportunity for many other people to act in this way.

D. Order of Concept Presentation

Bork (1971) argued that novices should be taught programming using a "whole program" approach rather than a "grammatical" approach. The whole program exposes students to complete programs from the start. The notion is that although they will not fully understand all the constructs within the program the students will at least see their role in relation to the program's task. By contrast, the grammatical approach teaches about the constructs in a bottom-up fashion before allowing students to write programs. The validity of this argument was tested by Lemos (1975) but he found no significant differences between groups taught FORTRAN using each strategy. A synthesis of these two strategies is presented by Shneiderman (1977b) who argues that each on its own is inadequate. His "spiral approach" attempts to provide both the syntactic and semantic understanding of programming that he believes a novice needs, though he presents no empirical evidence of the success of this method. In any case students of different cognitive style may prefer one approach rather than another.

Programming may be regarded as a special form of problem-solving, and Fisher *et al.* (1973) argue that certain classes of novice, e.g. arts students, lack the problem-solving skills and experience necessary to appreciate programs as solutions to problems. In consequence they suggest that an initial programming course should be split into two parts, the first to deal with problem-solving as such and the second to impart knowledge of programming. It is argued that this course of action enables the student to concentrate on problem-solving issues while not worrying about intrusive programming details. This idea has not been empirically tested but experience in mathematics teaching, see e.g. Kilpatrick (1978), suggests that teaching problem-solving skills is a very difficult task. This method further ignores the fact that programming can itself be an effective vehicle for improving problem-solving skills (Papert, 1972). Both the activities involved in programming, such as planning and debugging, and the objects produced by programming, such as plans and programs, are concrete embodiments of the very skills and concepts that such users are said to lack. Certain programming languages encourage good problem-solving habits more than others, and the need to split a first course in this way may well depend on the programming language chosen. Description of courses or languages that are believed to promote these habits are numerous (see for example Gries, 1974; Goldberg, 1976; Hoare, 1976; Holt *et al.*, 1977; Friedman and Koffman, 1978).

E. Automatic Tutors

Some researchers seek the solution to the problems of teaching novices in automatic tutors (e.g. Danielson and Nievergelt, 1975). The problems are formidable, because any system that is to provide helpful comments on a student's programming must have an internal model of that student, an internal model of the skill of programming and an internal model of the skill of teaching. Such systems must steer uneasily between making intelligent responses and ensuring that the novice does not attribute so much intelligence to the system that he attempts to communicate with it in English.

The best working system is probably the BIP system for teaching BASIC at Stanford (Barr *et al.*, 1976). In the BIP system the novice can define a BASIC program and ask the BASIC interpreter to run it using the monitor instruction RUN. By typing the instruction MORE he can ask the computer tutor to appraise his program to see if it meets the task specification. The messages that the novice receives come either from the BASIC interpreter, from the monitor or from the computer tutor, and this multiplicity is a potential source of confusion. Another difficulty is that a computer-based tutor with one particular problem-solving method (e.g. top-down, see Goldstein and Miller 1976) would find it hard not to bully a student into adopting this and only this strategy.

The authors of the BIP system devised a method for automatically selecting the next most appropriate programming problem to give to the student. But tests showed that students did no better with this method than when BIP selected problems from a pre-determined sequence. This may mean that whoever chose the problem order did a good job, or that problem order is not crucial.

One problem that automatic programming tutors must overcome is deciding whether the program submitted by the student solves the given problem. In BIP the student's program is tested against pre-defined input/output values, but this method can only provide a pass or fail decision and cannot point to bugs in his program. An alternative strategy is to attempt to match the student's program against a specimen answer program. Clearly this matching cannot just be one-to-one and so various program transformation rules need to be applied (Adam and Laurent, 1979).

VI. CONCLUSIONS

In this final section we summarize what has been established empirically and make suggestions for the directions of future research.

A. What has been Established

The lack of empirical evidence in Weinberg's (1971) book showed how much needed to be done to put the psychology of computer programming on a secure footing. How much has been achieved since then? The honest answer is not much. We seem little further forward in terms of predictive theories about any aspect of the programming process, nor do we have much in the way of reliable and confirmed empirical data. Many of the experiments on programmers have encountered wide variation in individual performance, and this has made it difficult to detect the effect of the experimental conditions under scrutiny. Many of the studies can also be criticized on methodological grounds (Ragsdale, 1978). Part of the problem of interpreting the experimental evidence is knowing how far one can generalize the results to other groups of novices, using different languages to solve other problems under different conditions. It is also unclear how far one can reliably predict performance in "real" computer languages from experiments in mini-languages.

Bearing in mind these reservations, it is clear that all aspects of programming cause novices difficulty, including typing, planning, coding, testing and debugging. Many novices are frightened away right at the start by the amount of arbitrary and detailed information that they have to remember, as well as by the problems of typing accurately and quickly. Languages in which the novice can very quickly start writing and running interesting programs (e.g. LOGO) have a definite advantage in that early success breeds confidence.

In general, during the planning stage novices have difficulty in formulating an algorithm for two reasons. First, they are unfamiliar with the level of generality expected in a computer program, and tend to deal with an over-specific set of conditions from the problem—for example they forget to specify actions when these conditions do *not* hold. Second, they quite reasonably model their algorithms on more familiar sets of instructions such as those found in recipes. This leads to a qualificational rather than to a conditional formulation of the task that will be at odds with most current languages. There seem to be two possible solutions to these difficulties. One is to devote more teaching effort to the qualificational/conditional distinction, the other is to employ languages where control mechanisms are closer to human (and natural language) usage.

Novices certainly make many mistakes in the second stage of the process, namely turning their algorithms into code. The syntactic/semantic/logical/clerical and stylistic classification of errors is useful but it is not clear yet which class, if any, predominates. There is some evidence that semantic errors (concerned with syntactically correct but unexecutable instructions) cause novices particular difficulties.

Here the strategy of providing the novice with a model of the notional machine may well be helpful. This model can be either descriptive, concrete, or derived from a commentary from the computer itself about certain of its own actions, e.g. through diagrams on the VDU screen.

Despite studies which show that, in general, syntactic errors are not the critical bottleneck in programming, detailed studies of novices' programs show that errors in this class are frequently committed. The particular types of syntax error are language-dependent e.g. delimiters in PASCAL, and studies of error-proneness show that conditionals cause particular problems. Evidence is accumulating that omitting "goto"s does actually lead to more comprehensible code that is easier to write and to debug. There is also evidence that increasing the perceptual redundancy, e.g. by indentation, blocking and repeating the predicate, also helps. Some syntactic errors committed by novices are "reasonable" and are derived from over-generalizing a syntactic rule. One solution is to remove non-uniformities in language syntax and give particular symbols the same meaning in all contexts. Another solution may be to teach novices to program using language-specific editors (see e.g. Eisenstadt, 1979) that both prompt the novice and constrain him to typing in the syntactically appropriate piece of program.

The logic of novices' programs often leaves much to be desired. This can be improved by giving them more experience of programming and by prescribing methods for program-building that encourage sound structure. As one would expect the difficulty of a problem for a novice is related to the corresponding program's length, its need for loops and sub-routines and the number of conditionals. One difficulty is that the commonly used introductory language, BASIC, has little in it to guide novices in a good programming style that exposes the logic of their programs.

Debugging is a lengthy process for both novices and experienced programmers. Syntactic errors tend to get debugged fairly easily because the compiler (or interpreter) points to them, or at least near to them. Logical and semantic errors are more tricky, and the work on mini-languages suggests that programs without "goto"s are easier to debug. Only one study that we know of has examined novices' ability to test programs and this used the rather artificial condition of asking novices to select the four most appropriate test-values from a set of eight. Novices were good at this highly constrained test.

Some studies have shown that provision of automatic and other debugging aids does not speed up or improve debugging. This is not to say that these aids are not useful; only that there is no substitute for hard work at a desk to gain an intimate understanding of a program if elusive logical errors are to be tracked down.

There have been surprisingly few studies that have observed novices' experiences with particular languages. We have a "top twenty" per cent list of errors for COBOL and corresponding lists for AID (similar to BASIC) and LOGO, but no such list for other languages. We also have a measure of error-proneness for COBOL constructs, but not for other languages.

Studies of individual languages have tended to concentrate on a static analysis of the frequency with which different constructs are used rather than looking at errors and difficulties. From these studies we have tables of frequently used constructs in FORTRAN, COBOL and APL. These all show that programmers tend to work within a small sub-set of the available constructs.

The quality of the programming environment plays a key role. Novices need a robust system that responds in a predictable time, without large variations. Sudden slowness of response is much harder to accept than a reliably slow system. The qualities of the command language which the novice may have to use to enter, run and edit his program are also important. Novices do not always appreciate the difference between instructions in the command language and instructions in the programming language. A poorly designed command language makes the novices' task much harder.

Studies of teaching programming point to the value of providing novices with some sort of model of the notional machine. There is some evidence that learning both a high-level and a low-level language simultaneously is better than learning them sequentially. Providing ways for the computer to "comment" on its own action, e.g. the "turtle" illustrating flow of control, seems to help.

Investigations of the role of personality traits and cognitive style in learning programming have barely started but there is some evidence that conventional methods of teaching FORTRAN favours those who are "operation" learners. Work on automatic programming tutors have yet to demonstrate any pedagogic advantage in this approach.

Getting novices to work in small groups is beneficial, not only because it is good training for commercial programming, but also because the resultant peer-teaching helps them to understand the ideas better.

Our own work in teaching LOGO suggests that coordinating the language implementation with the teaching materials is useful. This is because error messages (and other comments from the machine) can refer to the machine in the same terms, using the same analogies as are used in a primer (say). It is also possible to choose instruction names that convey the appropriate connotation about the notional machine. This strategy enables one to invite students to make certain errors *deliberately*, as part of learning about the machine, in the secure knowledge that the machine's reaction will be understood. One can also arrange that certain otherwise hidden events are accompanied by comments at the user's terminal, so that he has more information about the state of the machine.

B. The Future

Given our lack of understanding of both programmers and programming, most questions one could ask are "open". So in this section we confine ourselves to selecting some issues that are amenable to experiment. We divide these into three areas, current languages, programming process and teaching methods.

First and foremost we need much more data on how novices cope with existing programming languages. We need to know what mistakes are made, what features of each languages are prone to error and what types of errors are hard to debug. Tables of error type can be fairly readily constructed by augmenting a compiler or interpreter to keep records, in the style of Litecky and Davis (1976). Error-proneness can also be determined in the same way. Error persistence is more problematic and requires that the history of the development of an individual program be recorded. This is much more difficult to automate (because of the problem of deciding equivalence of programs), and may only be amenable to hand analysis of small samples of programs, as was done by Youngs (1974).

Experiments on individual features of language design should continue, e.g. Sime *et al.*'s (1977b) study, but these should be augmented by evaluating the repercussions and benefits of incorporating likely features into full-scale languages. The difficulty of this is that it then becomes hard to isolate the effect of the feature concerned, but some success in this direction has been achieved by Gannon (1977). One such issue that needs investigation is whether a logically redundant repetition of the predicate in conditional statements (Sime *et al.* 1977c) can be beneficially implemented in a real programming language.

The second area of concern is the programming process. We need to know much more about novices' preconceptions of programming, about how they set about planning algorithms, about their perception of the task and about the difficulties they encounter. Small-scale case studies are needed here, and Miller's (1978) work points the way. Similar studies are needed of how novices code, debug and test programs for us to understand their strategies and decide what aids should be provided.

Teaching programming is the third area for investigation. More work needs to be done to develop descriptions of notional machines that explain the actions of the computer executing a program. Mayer's (1979) "transactions" provide a useful descriptive tool for BASIC that may have application in other languages. We also need to extend and evaluate the computer's power to comment on certain of its own hidden internal events. That is, does the provision of "windows" into the machine help novices? Systems that could provide the basis for such work are the BIP system for BASIC at Stanford (Barr *et el.*, 1976) and the PASCAL system at San Diego (Bowles, 1979), both of which illustrate flow of control dynamically.

One question that continues to cause argument is whether a high- or low-level language should be taught first. This is probably only an important issue in the tuition of those novices who will go on to be professional programmers, since others will want to know only how to work the particular language they require. A related question concerns the value of introducing both types of language at once. Weyer and Cannara's (1975) study of children could be repeated for adults.

The relation between preferred cognitive style, personality traits and programming capabilities needs further investigation. One question that needs answering is whether the correlation between learning style and success in problems based on FORTRAN (Coombs *et al.*, 1979) is an effect of the way the language was taught or an effect of the language itself. In this respect, Pask (1976) has demonstrated the effects of a mismatch between a student's learning style and a teacher's teaching style.

Given our lack of understanding, it is not surprising that tests which are claimed to predict aptitude for programming are not very reliable (see e.g. Bell, 1976; Mazlack, 1980). All in all we require a much more detailed knowledge of what makes programming impenetrable for some and a delight for others.

ACKNOWLEDGEMENTS

We would like to thank David Hall, Ken Johnson and Mike Sharples who commented on a draft of this paper, Margaret Pithie who typed it, and the S.S.R.C. who provided financial support for Benedict du Boulay.

REFERENCES

Adam, A. and Laurent, J.P. (1979). A debugger to teach programming to students. Paper presented at 8th World Computer Congress.

Alcock, D. (1979). *Illustrating BASIC.* Cambridge: Cambridge University Press.

Al-Jarrah, M.M. and Torsun, I.S. (1979). An empirical analysis of COBOL programs. *Software-Practice and Experience*, 9, 341-359.

Allen, J.R. (1974). The development of computer courses for humanists. *Computers and the Humanities*, 8, 291-295.

Austin, H. (1976). Teaching teachers LOGO: The Lesley experiments. *A.I. Memo No. 336,* Artificial Intelligence Laboratory, Massachusetts Institute of Technology, Cambridge, Massachusetts.

Austing, R.H., Barnes, B.H., and Engel, G.L. (1977). A survey of the literature in computer science education since curriculum '68. *Communications of the ACM,* 20, 13-21.

Axford, T.H., Burkhardt, D., Dodd, W.P., Laflin, S., Parkyn, D.G. and Ramsay, P. (1979). ATOL: A simple language with powerful data structuring facilities. *SIGPLAN Notices*, 14, 5-15.

Baecker, R. (1975). Two systems which produce animated representations of the execution of computer programs. *SIGCSE Bull*, 7, 158-167.

Barr, A., Beard, M. and Atkinson, R.C. (1976). Stanford BIP Project. *Int. J. Man–Machine Stud.*, 8, 567-595.

Barron, D.W. (1977). *An Introduction to the Study of Programming Languages.* Cambridge Computer Science Texts 7. Cambridge: Cambridge University Press.

Bell, D. (1976). Programmer selection and programming errors. *Computer J.,* 19, 202-206.

Biermann, A.W., Baum, R.I. and Silverman, M. (1975). Trace information as an aid to debugging. *SIGCSE Bull.,* 7, 44-49.

Boies, S.J. and Gould, J.D. (1974). Syntactic errors in computer programming. *Human Factors*, 16, 253-257.

Bork, A.M. (1971). Learning to program for the science student. *J. Educ. Data Processing*, 8, 1-5.

Bowles, E.A. (1971). Towards a computer curriculum for the humanities. *Computers and the Humanities*, 6, 35-38.

Bowles, K.L. (1979). *Microcomputer Problem Solving Using PASCAL.* New York: Springer-Verlag.

Brooks, R. (1977). Towards a theory of the cognitive processes in computer programming. *Int. J. Man–Machine Stud.*, 9, 737-751.

Brooks, R. (1978). Using a behavioural theory of program comprehension in software engineering. *Proceedings of the 3rd International Conference on Software Engineering*, Atlanta, Georgia.

Brown, J.S. and Rubinstein, R. (1974). Recursive functional programming for students in the humanities and social sciences. *Technical Report No. 27*, Dept. of Information and Computer Science, University of California, Irvine, California.

Brown, P.J. (1972). SCAN: A simple conversational programming language for text analysis. *Computers and the Humanities*, **6**, 223–227.

Burstall, R.M., Collins, J.S. and Popplestone, R.J. (1971). *Programming in POP-2*. Edinburgh: Edinburgh University Press.

Cannara, A.B. (1976), Experiments in teaching children computer programming. *Technical Report No. 271*, Institute for Mathematical Studies in the Social Sciences, Stanford University.

Cheney, P.H. (1977). Teaching computer programming in an environment where collaboration is required. *J. Assoc. Educ. Data Systems*, **11**, 1–5.

Chrysler, E. (1978). Some basic determinants of computer programming productivity. *Communications of the ACM*, **21**, 472–483.

Coombs, M.J., Gibson, R. and Alty, J.L. (1979). An approach to the analysis of computing skills. *Research Report No. 105*, Computer Laboratory, University of Liverpool.

Curado, R. and Valente, J.A. (1978). Some problems of translating LOGO into a romance language. *SIGCUE Bull.*, **12**, 11–29.

Danielson, R.L. and Nievergelt, J. (1975). An automatic tutor for introductory programming students. *SIGCSE Bull.*, **7**, 47–50.

Davis, A., Tindall, M.H. and Wilcox, T.R. (1975) Interactive error diagnostics for an instructional programming system. *SIGCSE Bull.*, **7**, 168–171.

Denvir, B.T. (1979). On orthogonality in programming languages. *SIGPLAN Notices*, **14**, 18–30.

Du Boulay, B. (1978). Learning primary mathematics through computer programming. Ph.D. Thesis, Department of Artificial Intelligence, University of Edinburgh.

Du Boulay, B. and Emanuel, R. (1975). LOGO without tears. *D.A.I. Working Paper No. 11*, Department of Artificial Intelligence, University of Edinburgh.

Du Boulay, B. and O'Shea, T. (1976). How to work the LOGO machine. *D.A.I. Occasional Paper No. 4*, Department of Artificial Intelligence, University of Edinburgh.

Du Boulay, B. and O'Shea, T. (1978). Seeing the works: a strategy for teaching interactive programming. *D.A.I. Working Paper No. 28*, Department of Artificial Intelligence, University of Edinburgh.

Dunsmore, H.E. and Gannon, J.D. (1978). Programming factors—language features that help explain programming complexity. *Proceedings of the ACM Annual Conference*, Washington D.C.

Eason, K.D. (1976). Understanding the naive computer user. *Computer J.*, **19**, 3–7.

Eisenstadt, M. (1979). A friendly A.I. software environment for psychology students. *AISB Q.*, **34**, 11–12.

Embley, D.W. (1978). Empirical and formal language design applied to a unified control construct for interactive computing. *Int. J. Man–Machine Stud.*, **10**, 197–216.

Embley, D.W., Lan, M.T., Leinbaugh, D.W. and Nagy, G. (1978). A procedure for predicting program editor performance from the user's point of view. *Int. J. Man–Machine Stud.*, **10**, 639–650.

Feurzeig, W., Papert, S., Bloom, M., Grant, R. and Solomon, C. (1969). Programming languages as a conceptual framework for teaching mathematics. *Report No. 1889.* Bolt Beranek and Newman, Cambridge, Massachusetts.

Fisher, P., Hankley, W. and Wallentine, V. (1973). Separation of introductory programming and language instruction. *SIGCSE Bull.*, **5**, 9–14.

Fitter, M.J. and Green, T.R.G. (1979). When do diagrams make good computer languages? *Int. J. Man–Machine Stud.*, **11**, 235–261.

Florentin, J.J. and Smith, C. (1978). Guessing the state of a computer. *Proceedings of the Workshop on Computing Skills and Adaptive Systems,* University of Liverpool.

Friedman, F.L. and Koffman, E.B. (1978). Teaching problem solving and structured programming in FORTRAN. *Computers and Education,* **2**, 235–245.

Friend, J. (1975). Programs students write. *Technical Report No. 257,* Institute for Mathematical Studies in the Social Sciences, Stanford University.

Furuta, R. and Kemp, P.M. (1979). Experimental evaluation of programming language features: implications for introductory programming languages. *SIGCSE Bull.*, **11**, 18–21.

Gannon, J.D. (1978). Characteristic errors in programming languages. *Proceedings of the ACM Annual Conference,* Washington D.C.

Gannon, J.D. and Horning, J.J. (1975). Language design for programming reliability. *IEEE Transactions on Software Engineering*, **1**, 179–191.

Goldberg, P.C. (1976). Structured programming for non-programmers. In D. Bates (ed.) *Structured Programming.* Maidenhead, Berkshire: Infotech International.

Goldstein, I.P. and Miller, M.L. (1976). A.I. based personal learning environments: Direction for long term research. *A.I. Memo No. 384*, Artificial Intelligence Laboratory, Massachusetts Institute of Technology.

Gould, J.D. (1975). Some psychological evidence on how people debug computer programs. *Int. J. Man–Machine Stud.*, **8**, 151–182.

Gould, J.D. and Drongowski, P. (1974). An exploratory study of computer programming debugging. *Human Factors,* **16**, 258–277.

Green, T.R.G. (1977). Conditional program statements and their comprehensibility to professional programmers. *J. Occupational Psychol.* **50**, 93–109.

Green, T.R.G., Sime, M.E. and Fitter, M. (1978). Thoughts on behavioural studies of programming. *AISB Q.* **30**, 8–15.

Gries, D.(1974). What should we teach in an introductory programming course? *SIGCSE Bull.*, **6**, 81–89.

Habermann, A.N. (1973). Critical comments on the programming language PASCAL. *Acta Informatica*, **3**, 47–57.

Higman, B. (1977). *A Comparative Study of Programming Languages.* (2nd Edn) London: MacDonald and Jane's Computer Monographs.

Hillis, D. (1975). Slot machine: Hardware manual. *LOGO Working Paper No. 39*, Artificial Intelligence Laboratory, Massachusetts Institute of Technology.

Hoare, C.A.R. (1976). Structured programming in introductory programming courses. In D. Bates (ed.) *Structured Programming.* Maidenhead, Berkshire: Infotech International.

Hoc, J.-M. (1977). Role of mental representation in learning a programming language. *Int. J. Man–Machine Stud.,* **9,** 87–105.

Holt, R.C., Wortman, D.B., Barnard, D.T. and Cordy, J.R. (1977). SP/K: A system for teaching computer programming. *Communications of the ACM,* **20,** 301–309.

Kaufmann, R. (1978). *The Fortran Colouring Book.* Cambridge, Massachusetts: M.I.T. Press.

Kennedy, T.C.S. (1974). The design of interactive procedures for man–machine communication. *Int. J. Man–Machine Stud.,* **6,** 309–334.

Kennedy, T.C.S. Some behavioural factors affecting the training of naive users of an interactive computer system. *Int. J. Man–Machine Stud.,* **7,** 817–834.

Kernighan, B.W. and Plauger, P.J. (1974). Programming style. *SIGCSE Bull.,* **6,** 90–96.

Kilpatrick, J. (1978). Research on problem solving in mathematics. *School Science and Mathematics,* **78,** 189–192.

Knuth, D.E. (1971). An empirical study of FORTRAN programs. *Software-Practice and Experience,* **1,** 105–133.

Kovats, T.A. (1978). Program readability, closing keywords and prefix-style intermediate keywords. *SIGPLAN Notices,* **13,** 30-42.

Kreitsberg, C.B. and Swanson, L. (1974). A cognitive model for structuring an introductory programming curriculum. *Proceedings of the AFIPS National Computer Conference,* **43,** 307–311.

Kugel, P. (1975). How to make abstract ideas more concrete. *SIGCSE Bull.,* **7,** 191–195.

Lecarme, D. and Desjardins, P. (1975). More comments on the programming language PASCAL. *Acta Informatica,* **4,** 231–243.

Lee, J.M. and Shneiderman, B. (1978). Personality and programming: time-sharing vs. batch preference. *Proceedings of the ACM Annual Conference,* Washington D.C.

Lemos, R.S. (1975). FORTRAN programming: an analysis of pedagogical alternatives. *J. Educ. Data Processing,* **12,** 21–29.

Lemos, R.S. (1978) Students' attitudes towards programming: the effects of structured walk-throughs. *Computers and Education,* **2,** 301–306.

Lemos, R.S. (1979a). An implementation of structured walk-throughs in teaching Cobol programming. *Communications of the ACM,* **22,** 335–340.

Lemos, R.S. (1979b). Teaching programming languages: a survey of approaches. *SIGCSE Bull.,* **11,** 174–181.

Litecky, C.R. and Davis G.B. (1976). A study of errors, error proneness and error diagnosis in COBOL. *Communications of the ACM,* **19,** 33–37.

Love, T. (1977). An experimental investigation of the effect of program structure on program understanding. *SIGPLAN Notices,* **12,** 105–113.

Lukas, M.C. and Kaplan, R.B. (1976). A structured programming experiment. *Computer J.,* **19,** 136–138.

Mayer, R.E. (1975). Different problem-solving competencies established in learning computer programming with and without meaningful models. *J. Educ. Psychol.,* **67,** 725–734.

Mayer, R.E. (1976a). Comprehension as affected by structure of problem representation. *Memory and Cognition*, **4**, 249–255.

Mayer, R.E. (1976b). Some conditions of meaningful learning for computer programming: advance organizers and subject control of frame order. *J. Educ. Psychol.*, **68**, 143–150.

Mayer, R.E. (1979) A psychology of learning BASIC. *Communications of the ACM*, **22**, 589–593.

Mazlack, L.J. (1980). Identifying potential to acquire programming skill. *Communications of the ACM*, **23**, 14–17.

Miller, L.A. (1974). Programming by non-programmers. *Int. J. Man–Machine Stud.*, **6**, 237–260.

Miller, L.A. (1975). Naive programmer problems with specification of transfer-of-control. *Proceedings of the AFIPS National Computer Conference*, **44**, 657–663.

Miller, L.A. (1978). Behavioural studies of the programming process. *Research Report RC 7367*, IBM Thomas J. Watson Research Laboratory, Yorktown Heights, New York.

Miller, L.A. and Thomas J.C. (1977). Behavioural issues in the use of interactive systems. *Int. J. Man–Stud.*, **9**, 509–536.

Milner, S. (1973). The effects of computer programming on performance in mathematics. *ERIC Report ED 076 391*. Educational Resources Information Center.

Moulton, P.G. and Muller, M.E. (1967). DITRAN: A compiler emphasising diagnostics. *Communications of the ACM*, **10**, 45–52.

Myers, G.L. (1978). A controlled experiment in program testing and code walkthroughs/inspections. *Communications of the ACM*, **21**, 760–768.

Nagy, G. and Pennebaker, M.C. (1974). A step toward automatic analysis of student programming errors in a batch environment. *Int. J. Man–Machine Stud.*, **6**, 563–578.

Naur, P. (1975). Programming languages, natural languages and mathematics. *Communications of the ACM*, **18**, 676–683.

Nievergelt, J., Frei, H.P., Burkhard, H., Jacobi, C., Pattner, B., Sugaya, H., Weibel, B. and Weydert, J. (1978). XS-∅: A self-explanatory school computer. *SIGCSE Bull.*, **10**, 66–69.

Nutt, G.J. (1978). A comparison of PASCAL and FORTRAN as introductory programming languages. *SIGPLAN Notices*, **13**, 57–62.

Papert, S. (1972). Teaching children to be mathematicians versus teaching about mathematics. *Int. J. Math. Educ. Sci. Technol.*, **3**, 249–262.

Pask, G. (1976). Styles and strategies of learning. *Bri. J. Educ. Psychol.*, **46**, 128–148.

Pereira, L.M., Pereira, F.C.N. and Warren, D.H.D., (1979). User's guide to DEC system-10 PROLOG. *D.A.I. Occasional Paper No. 15*, Department of Artificial Intelligence, University of Edinburgh.

Perlman, R. (1974). TORTIS: Toddler's own recursive turtle interpreter system. *LOGO Memo No. 9*, Artificial Intelligence Laboratory, Massachusetts Institute of Technology.

Plum, T. (1977). Fooling the user of a programming language. *Software-Practice and Experience*, **7**, 215–221.

Pugh, J. and Simpson, D., (1979). PASCAL errors—empirical evidence. *Computer Bull.*, **2**, 26–28.

Ragsdale, R.G. (1978). Evaluating curricula for the teaching of programming. *Topics in Instructional Computing*, 11–19.

Raskin, J. (1974). FLOW: A teaching language for computer programming in the humanities. *Computers and the Humanities*, **8**, 231–237.

Ripley, G.D. and Druseikis, F.C. (1978). A statistical analysis of syntax errors. *Computer Languages*, **3**, 227–240.

Saal, H.J. and Weiss, Z. (1977). An empirical study of APL programs. *Computer Languages*, **2**, 47–59.

Sackman, M. (1970). *Man–Computer Problem Solving*. Princeton: Auerbach.

Schweppe, E.J. (1973). Dynamic instructional models of computer organisations and programming languages. *SIGCSE Bull.*, **5**, 26–31.

Shapiro, S.C. and Witmer, D.P. (1974). Interactive visual simulators for beginning programming students. *SIGCSE Bull.*, **6**, 11–14.

Shneiderman, B. (1976). Exploratory experiments in programmer behaviour. *Int. J. Computer Information Sci.*, **5**, 123–143.

Shneiderman, B. (1977a). Measuring computer program quality and comprehension. *Int. J. Man–Machine Stud.*, **9**, 465–478.

Shneiderman, B. (1977b). Teaching programming: a spiral approach to syntax and semantics. *Computers and Education*, **1**, 193–197.

Shneiderman, B. (1978). Improving the human factors aspect of database interactions. *ACM Transactions on Database Systems*, **3**, 417–439.

Shneiderman, B., Mayer, R., McKay, D. and Heller, P. (1977). Experimental investigations of the utility of detailed flowcharts in programming. *Communications of the ACM*, **20**, 373–381.

Sime, M.E., Arblaster, A.T. and Green, T.R.G. (1977a). Structuring the programmer's task. *J. Occupational Psychol.*, **50**, 205–216.

Sime, M.E., Arblaster, A.T. and Green, T.R.G. (1977b). Reducing programming errors in nested conditionals by prescribing a writing procedure. *Int. J. Man–Machine Stud.*, **9**, 119–126.

Sime, M.E., Green, T.R.G. and Guest, D.J. (1977c). Scope marking in computer conditionals—a psychological evaluation. *Int. J. Man–Machine Stud.*, **9**, 107–118.

Skelton, J.E. (1972). Time-sharing versus batch processing and teaching beginning computer programming: an experiment. *J. Assoc. Educ. Data Systems*, **5**, 91–97 (part 1) and **5**, 103–111 (part 2).

Snark, R.H. (1973). Diverse approaches to teaching programming: three projects. In W.M. Turski (ed.) *Programming Teaching Techniques*. Amsterdam: North Holland.

Statz, J. (1973). Syracuse University LOGO Project: Final Report, Syracuse University, New York.

Statz, J. and Miller, L. (1978). The egg series: using simple computer models. *The Mathematics Teacher*, **71**, 459–467.

Tagg, W. (1974). Programming languages for school use. *Computer Education*. **16**, 11–22.

Thomas, J.C. (1978). A design-interpretation analysis of natural English with applications to man–computer interaction. *Int. Man–Machine Stud.*, **10**, 651–668.

Tracz, W. (1974). The use of ATOPSS for presenting elementary operating system concepts. *SIGCSE Bull*, **6**, 74–78.

Treu, S. (1975). Interactive command language design based on required mental work. *Int. J. Man–Machine Stud.*, **7**, 135–149.

Turski, W.M. (ed.) (1973). *Programming Teaching Techniques.* Amsterdam: North Holland.

Wasserman, A.I. (1975). Issues in programming languages design—an overview. *Proceedings of the AFIPS National Computer Conference*, **44**, 297–299.

Weinberg, G.M. (1971). *The Psychology of Computer Programming.* New York: Van Nostrand Reinhold.

Weinberg, G.M. and Schulman, E.L. (1974). Goals and performance in computer programming. *Human Factors*, **16**, 70–77.

Welsh, J., Sneeringer, W.J. and Hoare, C.A.R. (1977). Ambiguities and insecurities in PASCAL. *Software-Practice and Experience*, **7**, 685–696.

Weyer, S.A. and Cannara, A.B. (1975). Children learning computer programming: experiments with languages, curricula and programming devices. *Technical Report No. 250*, Institute for Mathematical Studies in the Social Sciences, Stanford University.

Youngs, E.A. (1974). Human errors in programming. *Int. J. Man–Machine Stud.*, **6**, 361–376.

5. Comprehending and Debugging Computer Programs

F.J. LUKEY

Logica Limited, London, England

I. INTRODUCTION

Program comprehension plays a very significant role in the production and maintenance of programs. This point has been emphasized both by experimental psychologists (Green *et al.,* 1978) and by computer scientists (Dijkstra, 1972). However, there has been relatively little progress towards a satisfactory explanation of program comprehension. This chapter reviews the progress that has been made and tries to abstract some general principles that may help to guide future research.

The chapter also reviews research concerned with debugging. Debugging is closely related to program comprehension in that the removal of a non-syntactic bug requires some understanding of the program being debugged. This intimate relationship is reflected in the fact that much of the research on debugging also deals with comprehension. Thus, it is appropriate to discuss these two programming skills together.

Three methods of systematically studying programming skills may be distinguished. The *experimental* approach (discussed in Section II) involves constructing a theory and testing it experimentally. The *artificial intelligence* approach (discussed in Section III) involves constructing a theory and testing it by designing a computer system that embodies the theory. The *observational* approach involves gathering and interpreting data about naturally occurring programming behaviour.

Observational studies are a valuable source of reliable data and can be an effective antidote to anecdotal evidence. However, observational methods have not yet had a great deal of impact on our

understanding of program comprehension. Moreover, the observational approach has been discussed at some length in Chapter 4.
Therefore, this chapter focuses on the experimental approach and
the artificial intelligence approach.

II. THE EXPERIMENTAL APPROACH

There is considerable and growing interest in the application of the
techniques of experimental psychology to the study of computer
programming. This stems from the realization that we need objective
evidence about programming tools. However, as the following
discussion will show, it is important not to expect too much too
soon. As anyone familiar with experimental psychology will realize,
there are tremendous difficulties involved in the experimental study
of any intellectual task.

A. Comprehension

Experimentalists studying programming were quick to spot the
importance of program comprehension and there have been several
experimental studies devoted to it. Unfortunately, program
comprehension is not very amenable to experimental investigation
and, so far, experimental studies have not given us the sort of insight
originally expected. Some researchers, recognizing the immense
difficulties they faced, opted for experiments aimed at developing an
appropriate methodology. For example, Weissman (1974) attempted
to find a satisfactory method of measuring program comprehension.
Since an adequate method of measurement is a prerequisite for useful
experiments, it is appropriate to take a detailed look at Weissman's
work.

A method of measuring comprehension that Weissman tried, and
discarded, involved asking subjects to fill in the blanks in a paragraph
describing the program. Another method that he found unsatisfactory involved measuring how well subjects could hand-
simulate the program. (Hand-simulation involves tracing through
the execution of a program for a set of example input values, keeping
track of the values of all variables.) Interestingly, Weissman argued
that, although the ability to hand-simulate a program is not a good
measure of how well the program is understood, hand-simulation can
make an important contribution to one's understanding of a
program. This argument was supported by the results of some of
his experiments, although some subjects objected to the method on

the grounds that they could have understood the program better using other techniques.

After a total of five experiments, Weissman felt that he had found a reasonable method of measuring program comprehension; this involved combining the results of a quiz about the program with subjects' self-evaluation of their understanding. This method seems intuitively reasonable but it is not yet the sharpest of research tools. It is pertinent to ask exactly what sort of questions need to be in the quiz and precisely how much account should be taken of self-evaluation.

Green's (1977) study is highly relevant to the problem of deciding which sort of questions adequately test comprehension. Green was comparing different types of conditional construction using "micro-languages" which allowed only conditions and action. He argued that two different facets of comprehension could be tapped by using appropriate questions. Questions such as "What action will be performed given these input values?" tested the ability to hand-simulate. Questions such as "Under what circumstances will this action be performed?" were more concerned with the perception of program structure. The work of Green and his colleagues is discussed at greater length in Chapter 6.

Shneiderman (1976, 1977) suggested that there is a close link between how well one can understand a program and how well one can remember it. If this is so, and few would dispute it, then measuring how well a program is remembered indirectly measures how well the program was understood. Shneiderman's experiment indicated that well-structured programs were easier to remember than badly structured programs; he concluded that well-structured programs were more easily understood. This method of measuring comprehension is very useful because of the relative ease with which one can measure how well someone remembers a program. However, remembering a program and understanding a program cannot be equated; a full understanding of a program requires insight into the plan on which the program is based and this insight is not necessarily tapped by measuring how well someone can remember the detailed implementation of the plan. Thus, Shneiderman's method is not completely satisfactory.

B. Debugging

It is tremendously difficult to design a useful experiment in which programmers debug their own errors. This is because there is no good way of controlling the errors which will be made. Subjects in such an experiment would be likely to make a wide range of errors and, quite probably, no two subjects would be performing exactly the same debugging task. Because of this, most experiments on debugging have involved the debugging of programs prepared by the experimenter.

This approach was adopted by Gould and Drongowski (1974) in an experiment which compared the utility of different debugging aids. One group of subjects was given a listing of the program to be debugged (the listing included a description of what the program should achieve); a second group was given the listing plus an example set of input values and the resulting output; a third group was given the same materials as the second plus the output that the correct program would have produced; a fourth group was given the listing and told the class of bug that the program contained ("iteration", "assignment" or "array").

The results of this experiment were most surprising; the various types of aid did not increase the probability of a bug being found, nor did they reduce the time needed to find a bug. Gould and Drongowski explained the results in terms of programmers' ability to successfully adapt their strategies to whatever information was available. To back up this explanation they noted certain differences in approach between the groups of subjects. For example, the group which was given an example input–output pair seemed more selective in the statements they attended to than the group which was given the listing only.

Although cautious about the generality of their findings, Gould and Drongowski seemed to accept the validity of their results a little too readily. It seems unreasonable to accept such counter-intuitive findings on the basis of a single experiment. Rather, we should ask if there were any special features of Gould and Drongowski's study which might explain the results. For example, all the input and output statements had been removed from the programs used and this may have reduced the usefulness of example input–output pairs.

Gould and Drongowski's experiment was concerned with other variables besides debugging aids. For example, they compared performance for different types of bug and found that bugs such as endless loops, foolish flow of control and array elements going out of bounds were detected more quickly than bugs which could only be found given an understanding of exactly how the program achieved its goal. They suggested that subjects began their search for a bug by checking the "grammatical" correctness of the program, an interpretation which was supported by subjects' introspections.

Shneiderman and McKay (1976) reported several experiments on debugging and, as with Gould and Drongowski, some of their findings are quite surprising. For example, Shneiderman and McKay found that flowcharts did not seem to be of any use to subjects during debugging. (In fact, they found that flowcharts did not seem to be useful during any stage of the programming process.) Although their study was very thorough, they recognized that more experimental data were needed before a final assessment could be made as to whether flowcharts aid debugging. In particular, they thought that "macro" flowcharts, which describe a program at a relatively high level, merited further study.

Shneiderman and McKay also reported experiments concerning the role of comments in debugging and concluded that they seemed to be ignored during debugging. However, the failure to demonstrate the utility of comments may be connected to the size of program used; the largest was only thirty lines long. It may be that comments are only useful for debugging when a programmer finds a program difficult to understand and, in general, short programs are easier to understand than long ones. A study of program comprehension by Newsted (1974) lends some support to this explanation; his experiments indicated that comments were only useful for relatively complex programs.

C. Difficulties Facing the Experimental Approach

The preceding discussion of experimental studies illustrates that, as yet, we have made relatively little progress towards understanding program comprehension and debugging. This section will try to explain this state of affairs by elucidating some of the many difficulties facing researchers.

From an experimental point of view, one of the most daunting features of programming behaviour is the great variability between programmers. Sackman (1970) found that the typical difference in performance between individual programmers was an order of magnitude greater than the typical difference attributable to batch versus interactive modes of operation. If individual differences were limited to quantitative factors such as speed and accuracy then the experimentalist could cope without too much difficulty. However, programming is such a complex intellectual task that it is reasonable to expect considerable qualitative differences between individuals. Thus, a straightforward search for those elements of programming behaviour common to most programmers might not produce much of interest; it would certainly be difficult to discover high-level strategies using this approach.

Another problem facing experimentalists is the lack of theories about programming behaviour. Many people voice their prejudices concerning the way programs are, and should be, produced and maintained but there has been no real attempt to produce a sophisticated, comprehensive theory of programming behaviour. Indeed, given the small amount of objective evidence available, it would probably be premature to try to construct such a theory. However, the point to bear in mind is that the experimentalist has very little theoretical framework to guide him and, typically, he must supply his own theories, starting more or less from scratch.

There are also many practical difficulties in setting up experiments on programming. For example, it is normally very expensive to conduct experiments using professional programmers as subjects. Using advanced computer science students is a reasonable alternative but it would be inappropriate to use them to the exclusion of professional programmers. Another problem relating to choice of subjects is how to control for experience and ability. One way round this tricky problem is to use novice programmers but this has the drawback that, because subjects are still learning to program, results may not be applicable to programming in general.

The desirability of deriving generally applicable findings raises other problems. For example, the programming language used in an experiment may well influence the results. Program size is another relevant factor. When a programmer deals with a very large program, a key factor is his ability to abstract and manipulate high-level descriptions of the program. It may be that this aspect of programming is not adequately tapped by experiments which use small programs. Unfortunately, setting up and controlling experiments involving very large programs would pose immense practical and theoretical problems. Finally, we must remember that the type of program used in an experiment is an important variable. For example, the production and maintenance of list-processing programs may involve behaviour which does not occur for other types of program.

The list of difficulties presented above should explain why experimentalists are not yet producing results which are reliable and generally useful. However, most of these difficulties will probably be circumvented. We must be patient and wait for an appropriate methodology to evolve.

III. THE ARTIFICIAL INTELLIGENCE APPROACH

An artificial intelligence (AI) theory is intended to provide a precise and detailed explanation of how to produce some type of intelligent behaviour. Of secondary importance is the extent to which the theory accurately explains the way people behave. (Indeed, some AI researchers are not at all concerned with modelling human behaviour.) These priorities are reflected in the way in which AI theories are tested; to test an AI theory one designs and implements a computer system which embodies the theory and observes whether the system produces the behaviour that the theory is supposed to explain.

With regard to the testing of AI theories, it must be admitted that some of the AI research projects discussed below have not produced fully implemented systems. In some cases implementation efforts are continuing. In other cases researchers seem content to produce a specification for a system along with some indication of how the system could be implemented. However, it seems unwise to ignore ideas simply because they have not yet been rigorously tested, especially as we know so little about program understanding and debugging.

An important difference between the AI approach and the experimental approach is that the use of the AI paradigm naturally leads to the construction of theories which, compared to the experimentalist's theories, are rich and complex. This is because the AI researcher is not constrained to mirror human behaviour, nor is he constrained to produce theories which can be experimentally tested.

A. Comprehension

A key point that has emerged from recent AI research is that program comprehension can usefully be viewed as the construction of several different types of description. These types of description include:

(a) the segmentation of a program;
(b) the description of data flow;
(c) the description of the flow of control;
(d) the description of the values of variables;
(e) teleological commentary.

These descriptions should not be constructed independently of each other. For example, the description of data flow should indicate the data flow links between the segments of code produced by the segmentation process, rather than data flow links between arbitrary pieces of code. A full understanding of a program is produced by integrating the different types of description so that one can see how the different aspects of the program relate to each other.

1. *Segmentation*

The vast majority of programs are too large to be understood as a single unit. It is normally necessary to apply the principle "divide and rule", that is, to divide a program into segments of code that will form useful units of analysis. The syntactic structure of a program provides a starting point for segmentation. A program is divided into sub-programs (procedures, functions, sub-routines, or whatever), a sub-program is divided into statements, and statements are divided into parts such as labels, variables, expressions and conditions. Although this syntactic segmentation is very useful, it does not always provide groupings of code that are ideal units of analysis.

Goldstein's (1975) system uses a program's specification to enhance syntactic segmentation. The underlying idea is to discover which part of the specification each piece of code is concerned with and to group together all code concerned with the same part of the specification. This approach is obviously useful, although its success depends on the availability of a detailed specification.

Waters' (1976) approach involves using comments and program layout to augment syntactic segmentation. For well-written programs, comments and program layout provide a very useful guide. However, program understanding systems should eventually be able to cope with badly written programs and therefore it is undesirable for a segmentation process to rely too heavily on such sources of information.

The search for an appropriate basis for segmentation is often simplified when conducted in parallel with the construction of other types of program description. For example, Rich and Shrobe (1976) and Waters (1976) have pointed out that the recognition of familiar plans can help in the identification of suitable groupings of code. This is because a group of statements which implement a known plan (for example, a linear search of an array) is almost certain to correspond to a component of the program's conceptual structure. However, even if the segmentation process is conducted in parallel with the construction of other types of program description, there will still be cases where one's initial partition turns out to be inappropriate. Therefore, as one's understanding of a program grows, one should bear in mind that a different segmentation may help to simplify one's program descriptions.

2. *Data Flow*

A key step in the understanding of a program is the identification
of the inputs and outputs of the program segments. This principle is
already well established for sub-programs and it can usefully be
applied at other levels of segmentation. Researchers at Massachusetts
Institute of Technology (Goldstein, 1975; Rich and Shrobe, 1976;
Waters 1976) have proposed a distinction that is very useful when
giving a precise description of segment inputs and outputs. An
intrinsic description of a segment describes the segment in isolation
from any particular context. In contrast, an *extrinsic* description
describes the segment in terms of its use within a particular context.
The following segment of code may be used to illustrate this
distinction:

$$j := 1;$$
$$sum := 0;$$
$$\textbf{while } (j \leqslant n) \textbf{ and } (a[j] > x) \textbf{ do}$$
$$sum := sum + a[j];$$
$$j := j + 1$$
$$\textbf{enddo}$$

where j is given the value within the segment and thus is an intrinsic
output of the segment. However, j may be a "local variable" for the
segment; that is, the value held by j when control leaves the segment
may not be referenced subsequently. If this is the case then j is not
an extrinsic output. Note that finding the extrinsic outputs of a
segment gives some indication of the purpose of the segment. For
example, assuming that *sum* is the only extrinsic output we may
deduce that the segment has the sole purpose of setting the variable
sum.

Having found the extrinsic inputs and outputs of all segments
within a sub-program, one can build a higher level description of
data flow which indicates where each input derives from and where
each output is used. Such a description indicates how the segments
within a sub-program interact and can be very useful during debugging. Further details of this type of description may be found in
Lukey (1980).

3. *Control Flow*

The superficial analysis of control flow within a program can be
performed in a relatively straightforward manner. Optimizing compilers often perform such analysis. However, problems arise when

one tries to produce a description of the flow of control that is integrated with other types of program description. Ideally, a description of control flow should be constructed in such a manner that it can make a contribution to the construction of other types of description. For example, the segmentation of a program should take account of the flow of control within the program. Finding appropriate groupings of sub-programs is greatly simplified if the description of control flow allows the easy identification of a "family" of sub-programs, the members of which do not call sub-programs outside the family.

When producing a description of control flow, useful information from other types of program description should not be ignored. For example, a description of the values of variables can be used to refine a description of control flow. Constraints on the values of variables may be such that some control paths can never be executed. For example, the **then** clause of a conditional beginning "**if** $(x>0)$ **then**" will never be executed if x is never greater than zero. Of course, some level of description of control flow will be needed before one can construct a description of the values of variables, but this does not mean that the control flow description cannot be improved using information in the description of the values of variables.

Rich and Shrobe (1976) and Waters (1976) argue that an important preliminary in the analysis of a program is to identify those pieces of code which constitute "control flow connective tissue". An obvious example is the "goto" statement. The idea may be developed so that certain parts of statements are identified as control flow connective tissue. For example, in the FORTRAN statement 'DO 10 I=1,N' both the word DO and the label 10 may be regarded as control flow connective tissue.

Rich and Shrobe (1976) further argue that all control flow links between segments of code may be described in terms of three basic relations: "next", "invokes" and "returns". This has the advantage of stripping away some implementation details. Rich and Shrobe find a control flow description in these terms a useful stepping stone to a teleological description.

4. *Values of Variables*

Producing a description of the values of a program's variables is a tremendously difficult task. In order to be generally useful a description must be valid for all values of program inputs and therefore the description must be in terms of these inputs. The ultimate aim is to describe the program's outputs in terms of the program's inputs.

A complete description of the values of variables would involve having a description of each variable's value at every point where the variable is accessed. The formal proof of a program's correctness depends on the ability to construct a description at this level of detail. Research directed towards formal program verification will not be reviewed here. This is partly because good reviews of such work already exists (Elspas *et al.*, 1972; Brady, 1977); it is also partly because such work is only concerned with one type of program description (the description of the values of variables) and this chapter has tried to show how understanding a program involves constructing several types of description.

Other types of program description can be very useful when describing the values of variables. It is of great assistance to know the key points in a program's execution and the key variables at these points. An appropriate segmentation of a program, linked with a sophisticated description of data flow, supplies this information and thus provides a framework within which to describe the value of variables. This approach is described in greater detail in Lukey (1980).

Knowledge of commonly occurring programming constructs can be very helpful when describing the values of a program's variables. If a piece of code is recognized as an instantiation of a known type of plan (for example, a count or linear search of an array) then it is often a simple matter to deduce everything necessary about the values of variables. AI systems which know many common plans and are able to recognize instantiations of these plans probably offer the best prospects for future success in the description of the values of variables. Of particular interest is the work by Waters (1976) who has precisely defined many plan types, ranging from the simple concatenation of pieces of code to the "interleaved loop", where two conceptually independent loops have been combined into one. The recognition of plans plays a large part in the ability of Waters's system to understand programs. The same is true of Rich and Shrobe's (1976) system.

5. *Teleological Commentary*

Novice programmers are often advised that comments in programs should describe the purpose of a piece of code rather than simply describe what the code does. This is sound advice; one can (normally) deduce what a piece of code does by inspecting it but, in order to deduce its purpose, one must be able to relate the code to its context, which is often a very difficult task. Moreover, deducing the purpose of the segments of code within a program is a key step towards understanding the program.

Artificial intelligence researchers at Massachusetts Institute of Technology have recognized the significance of teleological commentary as an aid to program comprehension, and much of their research focuses on its use (Goldstein, 1975; Sussman, 1975; Rich and Shrobe, 1976; Waters, 1976; Rich *et al.*, 1978). For example, the key feature of Goldstein's (1975) program understanding system is the identification of the role played by each line of code in achieving the program's specification.

Sussman's (1975) problem-solving system solves a problem by proposing a program and then debugging this program until it works. The success of this technique depends on the use of *purpose links*, which describe the purpose of each piece of code in the proposed program. Sussman distinguishes two types of purpose link, these being (a) a *prerequisite* link, to describe situations in which a segment achieves a prerequisite of a subsequent segment, and (b) an *achieve* link, to describe situations in which a segment achieves a sub-goal of an embedding segment.

Rich and Shrobe (1976), building on the work of Goldstein and Sussman, designed a system capable of deducing purpose links for certain types of LISP program. Their system first deduces the *surface plan* of a program by analysing control flow and data flow. It then constructs a *deep plan* which is independent of implementation details, the segments of the deep plan being conceptual units rather than pieces of code. The segments of the deep plan are related to each other by purpose links.

B. Debugging

Artificial intelligence research has not yet made as much progress with debugging as it has with program comprehension. This is partly because debugging relies heavily on program comprehension, which means that it cannot be adequately explained until satisfactory theories of comprehension are available. It is also worth noting that AI studies of debugging have almost completely ignored the removal of syntactic bugs, which is generally easier than the removal of non-syntactic bugs and is less dependent on program comprehension.

Even though debugging is not yet understood as well as program comprehension, some interesting ideas about debugging have emerged from recent studies. These ideas, which are discussed in detail below, include:

(a) spotting violations of the general constraints that apply to all correct, rational programs;

(b) using bug classifications which are geared towards debugging;

(c) extending the program verification paradigm to cope with debugging.

1. *General Constraints on Programs*

There are certain general constraints which apply to all correct programs and which are independent of the particular goals of any program. An example of such a constraint is that all loops should always terminate. There are also general constraints that apply to all rational programs, that is, programs which are written in a sensible and reasonable way. For example, a conditional statement is irrational of its condition always evaluates to the same truth-value.

The general constraints on correct, rational programs play an important role in debugging. Identifying a violation of a constraint on correct programs is equivalent to spotting a bug and a violation of a constraint on rational programs is often indicative of an error. Moreover, the removal of an error must be guided by the constraints on correct, rational programs; otherwise one is likely to introduce one or more new bugs in getting rid of the old bug.

Artificial intelligence systems for program understanding and debugging have made good use of these general constraints. Goldstein's (1975) system takes note of any irrationalities in the program it is analysing. If the program needs to be debugged Goldstein's system is able to use its notes recording irrationalities to help guide debugging.

Ruth's (1976) system, which is concerned with the recognition of known algorithms, is able to recognize certain types of irrationality. Before trying to recognize a program, it checks that the program is rationally organized and refuses to attempt the recognition of an irrational program.

Lukey's (1980) system makes considerable use of the general constraints on programs. When understanding a program the system continually checks for violations of these constraints. Normally violations are noted for possible later use if the program needs to be debugged. However, sometimes the system will edit a program on the basis of a violation of a constraint without completing its understanding of the program. For example, consider the piece of code:

```
i:=10;
while (i>0) and (a[i]>x) do
    i:=i+1;
enddo
```

Here the increment of the variable i is inconsistent with the relationship between its initialization and its use in the loop exit condition. Lukey's system, on spotting such a piece of code, would immediately change "$i:=i+1$" to "$i:=i-1$". The advantage of this style of debugging is that one does not waste time describing a program that is obviously incorrect or grossly irrational. This style of debugging has much in common with the checking for "grammatical" correctness that Gould and Drongowski (1974) observed in their experiment on debugging.

Lukey's system, in common with Goldstein's, is keen to pick up any information that might help debugging and takes note of "suspicious" code, even if there is no guarantee that such code is either irrational or incorrect. For example, a piece of code may be considered suspicious if it involves a variable called COUNT which is not used to count anything. Although such a piece of code may occur in a rationally organized correct program, the unusual usage of the variable name may well be a useful debugging clue.

2. Bug Classifications

As noted above, Sussman's (1975) system (HACKER) solves a problem by proposing a program and then debugging it until it works. HACKER's debugging mechanism uses a classification of bugs based on underlying causes. For example, one class of bug is called "prerequisite missing". Such a classification is far more useful than one based on bug manifestations such as execution errors; each type of execution error may have any number of underlying causes. HACKER's competence in classifying bugs according to underlying causes is based on the use of the teleological commentary attached to all the programs with which HACKER deals. For each class of bug HACKER has an appropriate method of patching the relevant code.

Sussman takes great pains to emphasize that programming knowledge, including debugging knowledge, can be expressed independently of any domain. While this claim is undoubtedly true, Sussman's bug typology is quite limited and seems greatly influenced by his domain (the "blocks world" previously used by Winston (1970) and Winograd (1972)). HACKER knows only four bug types and three of these are concerned with a piece of code prematurely undoing the effect of a previous piece of code.

Miller and Goldstein (1976, 1977), who built on Sussman's work, pointed out the most important drawback of Sussman's approach; his theory of planning (as expressed in HACKER's program-writing mechanism) is largely independent of his theory of debugging. Miller and Goldstein set out to produce an integrated theory of planning and debugging. Their theory is expressed in terms of concepts from computational linguistics, and an augmented transition network (Woods, 1970) is used to define the gross structure of a problem-solving system. The linguistic analogy is also applied to debugging and the following classification of bugs is suggested.

A *syntactic* bug involves a violation of the planning grammar. (This type of bug should not be confused with the violation of programming language syntax.) A *semantic* bug involves a violation of the problem specification within a syntactically well-formed plan. A *pragmatic* bug involves an inappropriate selection from a set of mutually exclusive disjuncts during planning. A *circumlocution* bug involves a plan that is successful but inefficient. A *slip-of-the-tongue* bug involves errors such as mis-spellings and abuse of programming language syntax.

Miller and Goldstein's classification of bugs indicates the extent to which they view debugging within the context of a particular theory of planning. The debugging techniques that they propose all presuppose detailed knowledge of the planning decisions which led to the bugged plan. They argue that these planning decisions can often be inferred by using a planning grammar to parse the protocol that led to the bugged plan. As with Sussman, the important point is that Miller and Goldstein's classification is geared towards debugging; having identified the cause of a bug with respect to the program's plan, it is often relatively simple to correct it.

3. *Other Approaches to Debugging*

Earlier it was argued that the program verification paradigm was an unsatisfactory method of studying program understanding because it focused on a single type of program description (the description of the values of variables). However, it must be admitted that the work of Katz and Manna (1975, 1976), who extend the program verification paradigm to deal with debugging, is of considerable importance. Katz and Manna describe how the logical analysis of programs can be extended to cope with both correct and incorrect programs; previously program verification research had concentrated on correct programs. Katz and Manna also show how the logical analysis of an incorrect program can be used as a basis for debugging the program. They suggest that, when trying to verify a program, a record should be kept of the source of each assertion used. This record may be used in conjunction with a proof of incorrectness (or a failed proof of correctness if a proof of incorrectness cannot be found) to debug the program.

Katz and Manna's proposals have not yet been expressed in terms of a design for a system. However, Manna has collaborated with Dershowitz to produce a system which will do some automatic debugging (Dershowitz and Manna, 1977). This system takes as input (a) a program, (b) assertions describing what the program does, and (c) assertions describing what the program should do. A comparison of (b) and (c) is used to indicate which transformation to apply to the program so that it will achieve its specification. Emphasis is placed on the use of global transformations that are applied throughout the program. Whilst this system is quite interesting, it does not approach the sophistication of Katz and Manna's suggestions.

Lukey's (1980) approach to debugging has something in common with Katz and Manna's suggestions. Lukey's system takes as input a program and a brief specification for the program. It builds several types of program description, culminating in a high-level description of what the program does. A discrepancy between this high-level description and the specification indicates that the program is bugged. A bug is removed by (a) identifying the piece of code responsible for the bug, (b) generating a specification for this piece of code, and (c) editing the code on the basis of the difference between this specification and the piece of code's description.

A drawback of Lukey's system is that it ignores a very commonly used debugging strategy. This strategy involves focusing on the fate of a particular set of values for a program's inputs. Typically, these values will have produced the wrong output or led to an execution error. The problem with this strategy is that it is easy to lose sight of general considerations relating to the whole range of valid inputs. However, given the relative ease of reasoning about a particular case, this strategy has much to commend it.

C. Programming Knowledge

The ability to understand and debug programs is firmly rooted in considerable programming knowledge. The description of data flow depends on a knowledge of the way in which variables and parameters may be used to transfer information. The description of control flow depends on knowing the effect on each type of statement that influences the flow of control. The effective description of the values of variables is based on a knowledge of commonly occurring plans. Successful debugging requires knowledge of the general constraints on correct, rational programs.

Attempts to study program understanding and debugging which do not take much account of programming knowledge are doomed to failure. This is particularly unfortunate for experimentalists studying programming skills because it is very difficult to control for a factor such as programming knowledge. Artificial intelligence researchers are more fortunate because the AI paradigm actually encourages the incorporation of knowledge into one's theories and system. Artificial intelligence studies of program understanding and debugging have made significant progress towards discovering, and making effective use of, the programming knowledge on which these skills are based. Particularly impressive in this respect is the work of Waters (1976), who investigated a range of common plans, and Rich and Shrobe (1976), who not only deal with common plans but also suggest how a system can be given useful knowledge about different types of data structure.

IV. CONCLUSIONS

The foregoing discussion has demonstrated that, although the systematic study of program comprehension and debugging is still in its infancy, important progress has been made. Experimentalists have sensibly concentrated on the development of an appropriate methodology and have established firm foundations for subsequent research. Of particular importance is the attention devoted to identifying good methods of measuring program comprehension. The experimental approach has also produced some interesting findings, such as Shneiderman and McKay's (1976) results indicating that flowcharts do not significantly aid debugging. Whilst such results need to be replicated before they will be generally accepted, they illustrate how objective experimental evidence will eventually be used to resolve some of the controversial issues within computing.

Artificial intelligence research has also made useful progress. In contrast to the experimental approach, most of this progress has been theoretical rather than methodological. The AI analysis of program comprehension, which emphasizes the importance of several types of interrelated program description, is sophisticated and impressive.

Although the AI approach has had less success with debugging, interesting themes are beginning to emerge. In particular, researchers have stressed how rich program descriptions are needed to guide debugging. Another key theme is the recognition of the significant role played by programming knowledge.

The success of the AI approach is somewhat marred by the lack of fully implemented, robust systems capable of understanding and debugging a wide range of programs. One of the major contributions of my research (Lukey, 1980) was to demonstrate that such systems are within our reach. My system, which embodied much of the theory discussed earlier, was capable of understanding and debugging non-trivial PASCAL programs. Its significant limitation was the range of programs with which it could cope. There seems every reason to believe that future systems will significantly extend this range.

As yet, there has been little cross-fertilization of ideas between experimentalists and those working within the AI paradigm. This is understandable in view of the different problems currently facing the two approaches. To take one important example, those in AI are stressing the importance of programming knowledge and trying to describe its role; experimentalists usually want to control for it. However, it is to be hoped that in future more cross-fertilization will occur. AI theories could provide a useful stimulus for experimentalists, whose theories and results could help AI researchers to generate theories applicable to human programming behaviour.

REFERENCES

Brady, M. *Theory of Computer Sciences.* (1977). London: Chapman and Hall.

Dershowitz, N. and Manna, Z. (1977). The evolution of programs: a system for automatic program modification. *Proceedings of the Fourth ACM Symposium on Principles of Programming Languages,* Los Angeles.

Dijkstra, E.W. (1972). Notes on structured programming. In O.-J. Dahl, E.W. Dijkstra and C.A.R. Hoare, *Structured programming.* London and New York: Academic Press.

Elspas, B., Levitt, K.N., Waldinger, R.J. and Waksman, A. (1972). An assessment of techniques for proving program correctness. *Computing Surveys, 4,* 97–147.

Goldstein, I.P. (1975). Summary of MYCROFT: A system for understanding simple picture programs. *Artificial Intelligence, 6,* 249–288.

Gould, J.D. and Drongowski, P. (1974). An exploratory study of computer program debugging. *Human Factors, 16,* 258–277.

Green, T.R.G. (1977). Conditional program statements and their comprehensibility to professional programmers. *J. Occupational Psychol., 50,* 93–109.

Green, T.R.G., Sime, M.E. and Fitter, M. (1978). Thoughts on behavioural studies of programming. *AISB Q.,* **30,** 8-15.

Katz, S.M. and Manna, Z. (1975). Towards automatic debugging of programs. *SIGPLAN Notices,* **10,** 234-245.

Katz, S.M. and Manna, Z. (1976). Logical analysis of programs. *Communications of the ACM,* **19,** 188-206.

Lukey, F.J. (1980). Understanding and debugging programs. *Int. J. Man-Machine Stud.,* **12,** 189-202.

Miller, M.J. and Goldstein, I.P. (1976). SPADE: A grammar-based editor for planning and debugging programs. *Technical Report No. 386,* Artificial Intelligence Laboratory, Massachusetts Institute of Technology, Cambridge, Massachusetts.

Miller, M.L. and Goldstein, I.P. (1977). Structured planning and debugging. *Proceedings of the Fifth International Joint Conference on Artificial Intelligence,* Cambridge, Massachusetts, 773-779.

Newsted, P.R. (1974). FORTRAN program comprehension as a function of documentation. Research Report, School of Business Administration, University of Wisconsin-Milwaukee.

Rich, C. and Shrobe, H.E. (1976). Initial report on a LISP programmer's apprentice. *Technical Report No. 354,* Artificial Intelligence Laboratory, Massachusetts Institute of Technology.

Rich, C., Shrobe, H.E., Waters, R.C., Sussman, G.J. and Hewitt, C.E. (1978). Programming viewed as an engineering activity. *A.I. Memo No. 459,* Artificial Intelligence Laboratory, Massachusetts Institute of Technology.

Ruth, G.R. (1976). Intelligent program analysis. *Artificial Intelligence,* **7,** 65-87.

Sackman, H. (1970). *Man-Computer Problem Solving.* Princeton, New York: Auerbach.

Shneiderman, B. (1976). Exploratory experiments in programmer behaviour. *Int. J. Computer System Sci.,* **5,** 123-143.

Shneiderman, B. (1977). Measuring computer program quality and comprehension. *Int. J. Man-Machine Stud.,* **9,** 465-478.

Shneiderman, B. and McKay, D. (1976). Experimental investigations of computer program debugging and modification. *Technical Report No. 48,* Computer Science Dept., Indiana University.

Sussman, G. (1975). *A Computer Model of Skill Acquisition.* New York: American Elsevier.

Waters, R.C. (1976). A system for understanding mathematical FORTRAN programs. *A.I. Memo No. 368,* Artificial Intelligence Laboratory, Massachusetts Institute of Technology.

Weissman, L. (1974). Psychological complexity of computer programs: an experimental methodology. *SIGPLAN Notices,* **9,** 25-36.

Winograd, T. (1972). *Understanding Natural Language.* Edinburgh: Edinburgh University Press.

Winston, P.H. (1970). Learning structural descriptions from examples. *Technical Report No. 76,* Artificial Intelligence Laboratory, Massachusetts Institute of Technology.

Woods, W.A. (1970). Transition network grammars for natural language analysis. *Communications of the ACM,* **13,** 591-606.

6. The Art of Notation

T.R.G. GREEN, M.E. SIME and M.J. FITTER

MRC/SSRC Social and Applied Psychology Unit, Department of Psychology, University of Sheffield, Sheffield, England

"What we find difficult about mathematics is the formal, symbolic presentation of the subject by pedagogues with a taste for dogma, sadism and incomprehensible squiggles". (Gordon, 1978, p.29).

I. INTRODUCTION

In the proliferating shelves of libraries there are notations to describe myriad activities; notations which are concise or prolix, readable or opaque, easy or nearly impossible to learn; but curiously little has been written on notations in general. Each new one seems to have been invented *de novo* with little reference to its precursors—an unfortunate tradition of ancestor-snubbery, for most notations appear to have been the work of gifted minds. Happily that tradition has expired in the programming world. Here, repeated efforts to solve the same problem have encouraged the dissemination and discussion of good ideas from any source, and there have been essays in comparative notation (e.g. Barron, 1977) taking the main requirements of a programming language one by one and exhibiting the solutions offered by various languages. There have also been essays in "cognitive ergonomics" or "software psychology", attempting to uncover the reasons why some notations succeed. A few general lessons can now perhaps be offered.

The intelligibility of a programming language depends on the way programs are presented on the page and on how they are structured, not on the particular facilities supported by the language—although these facilities, it is true, are sometimes intimately related to how the programs are presented; for instance it would be hard to design a language with a wide variety of event-driven loops (such as **while**)

221

unless it also supported Booleans. But we do not find one style of language for numerical analysis and another for symbol-processing. We find instead that there are schools of languages—ones with jump-style control structures, ones with more sophisticated control structures, and ones with more sophisticated data structures—and within each school there are languages for numerical analysis, for symbol-processing, for everything else. Our interest here is with the "design schools", not with the particular domain of the language. We hope to keep that clear by reserving the term "notation" for these aspects of a language, and also to achieve some generality, for programming languages have much in common with other notations describing processes, such as knitting patterns, flowcharts, recipes, keystrokes on calculators, musical notations, and algebraic formalisms.

In the current state of knowledge, understanding programming notations and their pros and cons is a bit like mapping a town by seeing where blindfolded people bump into walls. First we discover some major facts, later we think up possible patterns. The literature at present consists mainly of studies of individual features related tenuously at best to other studies; although authors dutifully mention each other's work, integrating it into a whole is something harder. Fortified by the thought that in these conditions even a patchy attempt is better than none, we shall see what we can do.

II. SOME ASPECTS OF STRUCTURE

To understand a text of any length, readers must be able to impose a *macrostructure* on it. There is too much detail to comprehend it all, so the reader will remember the gist of each chapter in a book, perhaps the gist of the sections within a chapter, occasionally the paragraphs within a section. Macrostructures are important in at least three ways: allowing the reader who is searching for a particular feature to discard a whole unit as irrelevant ("Well, it won't be in this chapter"), allowing the reader to reconstruct certain material so that he or she has no need to remember all of it, and making it easier to work out the purpose of particular activities in the overall process. One's first guess is that macrostructures are groupings or clusterings of text in its correct sequence, as with the divisions of a book, but as we shall eventually see there are important relationships that cannot be captured so simply.

The macrostructures of a program do *not* simply coincide with its division into components according to flow of control—a procedure here, a loop there. The term has a distinct meaning, which is lifted from the field of discourse analysis and text processing, e.g. van Dijk (1977):

Macro-structures are assumed to be semantic structures of discourse whose meaning and reference is defined in terms of their constituents' meanings. . . . Each macro-proposition must be interpreted with respect to other macro-propositions.

Thus the macrostructure of a program (if we knew how to extract it!) would reveal not only the control flow and the data flow, but also the relationships between components.

In contrast there is also a *micro*structure, corresponding to the parsing of individual components. If we take some particular statement, e.g.

$$a := (b + c) * (c + d)$$

then we can see that it has an internal microstructure. But we are still at a loss as to what the statement is "about": perhaps it is computing an intermediate value in a sequence of arithmetic computations, or perhaps it will be tested in a loop, such as

$$\text{while } a > 20 \text{ do } . . .$$

or perhaps it is to be used to index an array, or perhaps (especially in the more primitive languages) it is part of a cumbersome way of doing Boolean algebra using zero and non-zero for false and true. It may even be an irrelevant assignment, with a never being used. Each of these would be a possible macrostructure, uniting a number of statements and allowing them to be interpreted as a group.

Within a program the reader must be able to find *signposts* and follow *trails*. The trivial case here is the subject index, where for example the entry "Herpetology, 7" is a signpost and the trail is just one step from the index to page 7. In researching a series of references one might follow a more typical trail: a cites b, b cites c, etc. Observe that this trail, like many others, is *asymmetrical*—given a we can find c much more readily than the reverse. Only by using special aids, such as the Science Citations Index with its backward-pointing signposts (c is cited by b, b is cited by a) can the trails be followed backwards at all readily.

Why on earth should we wish to follow trails backwards? At first sight it may seem surprising that a notation such as a programming language is designed expressly to denote sequences of events over time. Consider, however, the sorts of questions we often need to answer about programs. There are *sequential* ("trace") types of question, e.g. "What can it do next after *a*?" or "Given that the input is *x*, *y*, *z*, . . . what actions will it perform?" And there are circumstantial ("taxon") questions such as "Under what circumstances can *a* happen?" The circumstantial question would typically be answered by finding *a* (the first backward-pointing signpost) and following the trail backwards, collecting facts as we go. Circumstantial questions arise often—whenever programs need to be modified, debugged, or understood. Indeed, since programming demands frequent checking and monitoring as the program is created (the equivalent of feedback in a motor skill), circumstantial questions will continually arise during the act of creation.

One tends to think of programmers as tubes of toothpaste. Squeeze one end and code comes out of the other. But they are not so simple: they start with a mental representation of a problem, then they program a chunk of it, and then they need to "deprogram" it back again to make sure that it does what it should. Thus it is vital that circumstantial questions can be answered swiftly and accurately in a good notation. Unfortunately, conventional programming languages make it much easier to follow trails forwards than to follow them backwards; the asymmetry of information flow is very marked indeed. One conclusion that our arguments lead to is that if these notations were made as easy to follow backwards as they are to follow forwards, programming would be made simpler.

It might be difficult to arrive at a sharp distinction between sequential information and circumstantial information in a formal account, although it will be amply illustrated in the course of this chapter, but fortunately a formal distinction is not really necessary because the important difference is not in the type of information but in the manner of obtaining it.

Certain systems, such as production system notations and decision tables, reverse the asymmetry. Instead of the usual practice of writing out the actions to be performed in their order of occurrence, with conditional branches where necessary, in these systems one writes out a list of possible circumstances and states the appropriate action to be performed in each condition. Here, we suggest, discovering sequential information may be extremely difficult, whereas extracting circumstantial information should be very straightforward.

We suggest, then, that some notations make the macrostructure clear while others fail to; and that some make the trails easy to follow in both directions, while others obscure the trails in one direction or the other. A third aspect of notational structure is the complexity of *mental operations*. While following a trail, say to extract circumstantial information, it is necessary to pile the facts won from the program depths into a mental shopping basket. Some facts are given explicitly if we ask "When can caracol occur?", and the trail starts

$$\text{if } x > 1 \text{ then } caracol$$

we can immediately put the condition "$x > 1$" into our mental shopping basket. Other facts are less explicit. If the trail had started

$$\text{if } (x > 1) \text{ or } ((y < 1 \text{ and } y < x) \text{ impl } x > z) \text{ then } prance \text{ else } caracol$$

we would have quite a bit of work to do. There is more work, of a different sort, when further conditions have to be added to the shopping basket; remembering which conditions are positive and which negative, which are conjunctive and which are disjunctive; or in a sequential search, which action always (or sometimes) occurs before which other action. All this creates a mental load while the trails are being followed and increases the probability of mistakes. Reducing mental load by keeping mental operations few in number and simple in kind must therefore be another goal. We must cut down on mental "shopping".

Many of these points are illustrated in Fig. 1. Surely the jump-style version of the algorithm displays the macrostructure more clearly than the others, although they are equivalent algorithms and therefore have the same underlying structure. On the other hand the circumstantial question "When do you go for help?" is harder to answer in the jump-style program than in the decision table. Where the decision table seems to fail is with the sequential questions, e.g. "After pushing the starter, what actions could occur next?" (answer: drive off, go for help, or adjust choke).

The flowchart is particularly interesting when examined in this light. The arrows should make the trails equally easy to follow in either direction, at least at a local level. The poor display of

(a)

(Prelude)

ignition on

(Body)

LOOP: push starter
IF going, **JUMP TO LABEL** 1
IF battery flat, **JUMP TO LABEL** 2
adjust choke
jump to **LOOP**

(Postlude)

LABEL 1: drive off
LABEL 2: go for help

(b)

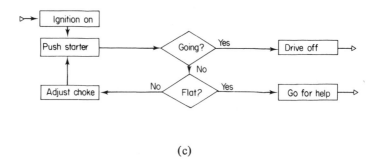

(c)

(Do column 0 actions first. Thereafter, do whichever of columns 1, 2 . . . etc.
matches the conditions. "Repeat" means do that again.)

	0	1	2	3
Going?		Y	N	N
Battery flat?		—	Y	N
Adjust choke				X
Ignition on	X			
Push starter	X			X
Drive off		X		
Go for help			X	
Repeat				X

Fig. 1. Equivalent algorithms for starting a car in three notations. (a) Jump style;
(b) flowchart style; (c) decision table style.

macrostructure should nevertheless make it harder to answer sequential questions in realistically sized programs compared to the jump-style program in Fig. 1a, because the reader would not be able to capitalize on the chunking. Circumstantial questions would be rather easier in a flowchart than in the jump-style program, because the backward trails would be easier to follow, yet decision tables should yield the answers more easily still by eliminating the need for "shopping". The merits of flowcharts can therefore be expected to depend on the particular task. That is also the conclusion reached empirically by Wright and Reid (1973) and it may go some way towards explaining the remarkably diverse judgements on flowcharts quoted in this volume by Fitter and Green (Chapter 7). Table 1 summarizes our predictions.

Finally the *coupling* of sub-structures must also be mentioned. The problem with the car-starting algorithm is that the loop can terminate in two different ways, either with the car going or with the battery flat, and in the postlude it is necessary to know how the loop terminated in order to take appropriate action. It is therefore necessary for one sub-structure, the loop, to send information to another, the postlude. This kind of coupling, a message from the past, is far and away the commonest in programming, although other kinds, involving messages from the "present", are found in programs where different processes are executed concurrently. Messages from the past can be transmitted along various channels. The jump-style program on Fig. 1a transmits information by means of location: if the postlude is entered at **LABEL** 1, then the car is going. To understand this program one therefore has

TABLE 1

How clearly information is displayed by certain notations, or how much mental load is created

	Macrostructure	Sequential	Circumstantial	Shopping
Jump-style program	**	**	—	—
Flowchart	—	*	*	—
Decision table	—	—	**	**

** = clear display or little mental load
* = middling
— = poor

(Prelude)

        ignition on

(Body)

        WHILE not going and battery not flat **DO**
           push starter
           IF battery not flat **THEN** adjust choke **END-IF**
        END-WHILE

(Postlude)

        IF car going **THEN** drive off
        ELSE go for help
        END-IF

Fig. 2. The car-starting algorithm in a "structured" form, with one entrance and exit to each sub-component. Messages from the past are now sent via states to be examined, not by the location of labels as in Fig. 1a.

to discover what conditions take it to **LABEL** 1, which means following the trail backwards—the hard direction.

A message from the past could also be sent along a different channel. In Fig. 2, instead of using jumps to special places in the code, the postlude directly examines the state of the car and the state of the battery. As a result the program follows the precepts of the structured programming school (every sub-component has one entrance and one exit) and if they are to be believed, it should be much easier to understand. Certainly one would expect that circumstantial questions could be answered with less following of backward trails and with less associated "shopping". In a real program the car and the battery would not be physically available of course, and so the message from the program body to the postlude would have to be transmitted by an assignment to an identifier.

Although it has often been noted that it is harder to understand structures when the sub-structures are coupled in complicated ways, little has been proposed beyond the very reasonable suggestion that any one sub-structure should receive messages from as few others as possible. There has not even been much examination of the various ways in which messages can be transmitted, apart from the notable paper on complexity by McClure (1978). One feels that at least some discussion of the two most important methods of transmission, by location and by assignment (Figs. 1a and 2), is due.

III. SOME EMPIRICAL COMPARISONS

In this section we present informal reports of two empirical studies. Although each of these may in its way be regarded more as a preliminary report than as a complete investigation, they serve one of the major purposes of empirical enquiry, the refinement of the terms of discourse. What they do not allow, despite the fact that three different notations were compared in each study, is the conclusion that one style is best. For such a conclusion we would have needed to be completely certain that each style was the optimal variety of its species and to have searched for as wide a variety of test conditions and tasks as possible. But, though that type of conclusion is tempting and must be desirable to the practitioner, it does not concern us while we attempt to untangle the art of notation as a whole. If we can cope with the differences between *some* notations in *some* tasks, however restricted, we shall be pleased.

Both of these studies—one dealing with linguistic notation, one with diagrammatic notation—were aimed at elucidating the effects of asymmetry in information flow between circumstantial and sequential questions. In addition the second study considers the further problem of messages from the past and how they are to be transmitted.

A. Nesting and De-nesting: Three Linguistic Notations

Elsewhere in this volume du Boulay and O'Shea describe our experiments at Sheffield on various forms of conditional structure, in which we compared jump-style conditionals, notations with nested conditionals of the usual sort (NEST-BE or PLAIN NEST, as we have called this dialect), and nested conditionals with added cues to help the reader (NEST-INE). By and large these experiments have favoured the NEST-INE dialect, and Green and Arblaster (1980) have examined at some length the relationship between the pattern of results and the principles of good notations, extending the arguments put forward in earlier papers from the Sheffield group. Essentially they argue that the problems with these notations arise in extracting circumstantial information, and that NEST-INE wins because it combines perceptual cues about structure (indenting to show the scope of each "if") with explicit statement of the negative arms of predicates, thus making "shopping" far easier.

However, it has been argued by a number of influential authors that nested structures—especially nested "if"s—should be avoided (Kernighan and Plauger, 1974a, 1974b; Weinberg, *et al.*, 1975; Richards, 1976; Barron, 1977). Their arguments are not explicitly stated but are based on the belief that "humans are not good at stacking information, and quickly lose track of the pending *elses*"

(Barron, 1977, p. 46). This is interesting because we see no reason from our analysis why nesting should necessarily be difficult; all we predict is that if the programmer has to follow a long and difficult trail, performance will suffer. Since received opinion disagrees with us on this point it will make a good test case.

The usual recommendation is that we should avoid "bushy" conditionals like this one:

> if *a* then
> if *b* then *x* else *y*
> else if *c* then ... else ...

The conditional on *b* is nested inside the one on *a*. The code should be reorganized, we are told, in the "skinny" form:

> if *d* then *x*
> else if *e* then *y*
>   ...
> else ...

The "skinny" structure has been completely de-nested. Unfortunately the price is that the conditions are rather more complex, with *d* and *e* needing to be presented (in terms of *a*, *b*, and *c*) as

> if *a* and *b* then *x*
> else if *a* and not *b* then *y*
>   ...

This, nevertheless, is the recommended method.

To test whether the de-nested structure was better or worse than the nested one, Richards *et al.* (1979) compared three programs— one written in **NEST-INE** (Fig. 3a), one written in **PLAIN NEST** (Fig. 3b) and one that was de-nested (Fig. 3c). The question, given these three programs, is what to compare? Richards *et al.* chose to compare mental-processing times by asking people questions and measuring the time taken to answer them. Two kinds of questions were used: the forwards (sequential) and backwards (circumstantial) questions mentioned above. Furthermore, two different types of sequential questions were used: "Terse Forwards" and "Narrative Forwards" (Fig. 4). In real programming, the answer to every question cannot always be found easily, and so the Narrative Forwards condition was designed to resemble a task in which each

(a) **NEST-INE** *program*
IF time limited:
    IF conveying baggage: Flying Saucer
    NOT conveying baggage:
        IF cost limited:
            IF distance > 10 orbs: Hyperdrive
            NOT distance > 10 orbs: Satellite
            END distance > 10 orbs
        NOT cost limited:
            IF distance > 10 orbs: Superstar
            NOT distance > 10 orbs: Cosmocar
            END distance > 10 orbs
        END cost limited
    END conveying baggage
NOT time limited
    IF liable to space-sickness: Astrobus
    NOT liable to space-sickness: Space-cycle
    END liable to space-sickness
END time limited

(b) **PLAIN NEST** *program*
IF time limited **THEN**
    IF conveying baggage **THEN** Flying Saucer
    ELSE
        IF cost limited **THEN**
            IF distance > 10 orbs **THEN** Hyperdrive
            ELSE Satellite
        ELSE
            IF distance > 10 orbs **THEN** Superstar
            ELSE Cosmocar
ELSE
    IF liable to space-sickness **THEN** Astrobus
    ELSE Space-cycle

(c) **FULL STATEMENT** *program*
IF time limited **AND** conveying baggage **THEN** Flying Saucer
IF time limited **AND NOT** conveying baggage **AND** cost limited **AND** distance > 10 orbs **THEN** Hyperdrive
IF time limited **AND NOT** conveying baggage **AND** cost limited **AND NOT** distance > 10 orbs **THEN** Satellite
IF time limited **AND NOT** conveying baggage **AND NOT** cost limited **AND** distance > 10 orbs **THEN** Superstar
IF time limited **AND NOT** conveying baggage **AND NOT** cost limited **AND NOT** distance > 10 orbs **THEN** Cosmocar
IF NOT time limited **AND** liable to space-sickness **THEN** Astrobus
IF NOT time limited **AND NOT** liable to space-sickness **THEN** Space-cycle

Fig. 3. Each subject in the Richards *et al.* study saw one program and only one, and used it to answer questions such as those in Fig. 4.

(a) *Terse Forwards question*

    Time is unlimited
    Not conveying baggage
    Cost is unlimited
    Distance > 10 orbs
    Liable to space-sickness

(b) *Narrative Forwards question*

A safe-cracker, renowned both for his skill at opening safes and for his crippling attacks of space-sickness, has just pulled a job on the planet Phrygia. He was disappointed to find no money in the safe but the police are after him and he feels it important to get away, even though he is empty-handed. If he pawns his pocket computer he can probably afford a ticket to nearby Bacchus, less than 10 orbs away.

(c) *Backwards question*

    Taking a space-cycle—
      time limited?
      liable to space-sickness?

Fig. 4. The three types of question. Subjects answered 10 each of the Terse Forwards and Narrative Forwards questions, by placing the card with the question into a bin labelled "SPACE-CYCLE", "ASTROBUS" etc., and they answered 6 Backwards questions, placing each card into a bin labelled "BOTH YES", "ONE YES, ONE NO" or "BOTH NO"

truth-value has to be hunted out.

As for the subjects, they were real-life programmers: people who walked into the Sheffield University Computing Centre whose first language was English. They mostly had a year or more experience of programming. Fourteen people were given the **PLAIN NEST** program, fourteen the **NEST-INE** program, and fourteen the **FULL STATEMENT** program, and all were then asked the same set of questions. (It is of course vital that each group was asked the same questions about their programs; the only factor that varied was the language in which the programs were written.) Questions were presented on cards, and each question was "answered" by putting the card into the appropriate bin. By measuring the time taken to work through a pack of cards the average time per question could be obtained.

Results are shown in Fig. 5. In the Terse Forwards condition the three programs did not differ significantly, but in the Narrative Forwards condition the **FULL STATEMENT** notation was by far the worst. Backwards questions gave the **FULL STATEMENT** program a slight edge, with the **PLAIN NEST** program taking the longest time.

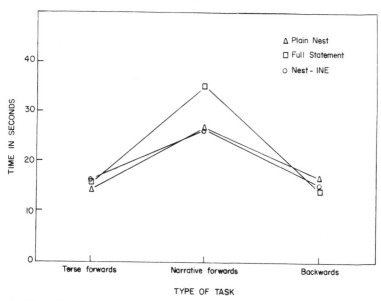

Fig. 5. Mean time per question for three dialects and three types of question in the Richards *et al.* study.

It seems clear from these results that the proponents of de-nesting have a difficult case on their hands (Green, 1980a). The issue before us here, however, is not so much how programs should ideally be written, but rather whether the aspects of structure that we have identified above are sufficient to account for the results. We would argue that the macrostructure of the two nested dialects is made very clear, because of the indenting. In the **FULL STATEMENT** dialect it is obscured, filled up with text; white space in the nested dialects become cluttered with repetitiveness in the **FULL STATE-MENT** condition. The effect is that when following through the program to extract sequential information (i.e. when answering a Forwards question) the reader has to use a "mental finger" as a place-keeper in the **FULL STATEMENT** notation, whereas in the nested dialects the reader can just hop down the page following the indenting. The problem is only present when dealing with predicates with negative values—"*else*" branches of their equivalents in the other dialects—since it is only then that the reader's eye has to move quickly on to another point in the text; but the implications are severe, and they become apparent in the Narrative Forwards condition. The purpose of using a narrative was to force the subject to use up one mental finger for keeping place in the story. It turns out that subjects apparently only have one mental finger. It can be used to keep place in the program (Terse Forwards condition with **FULL STATEMENT** dialect), or it can be used to keep place in the list of truth-values when presented as a story (Narrative Forwards condition, nested dialects), but it cannot do both, and so the **FULL STATEMENT** dialect becomes unworkable in the Narrative Forwards condition.

So much for the two forwards conditions. Turning to the backwards questions, the problem for the subjects here was to follow trails backwards and accumulate circumstantial information. In the **PLAIN NEST** dialect the trail extended from the designated outcome back to the start of the program, and each passage through an "else" required the mental operation of locating the relevant predicate and negating it before adding it to the accumulated set of conditions. NEST-INE was expected to be easier for this task because, although the trail was just as long, the predicates were explicitly negated where required. Finally, **FULL STATEMENT** presented all the predicates, without forcing the subject to follow any trail at all, and was expected to be easiest. These predictions were confirmed with statistically significant outcomes.

The analysis presented above is therefore comfortably able to account for all the effects observed in the Richards *et al.* study, if we add the reasonable postulate that keeping one place with a mental finger is not very hard but keeping more than one place is much harder.

B. Static and Dynamic Processes: Three Diagrammatic Notations

By way of contrast to the linguistic study of Richards *et al.*, the second study compared three notations that were diagrammatic in nature, with the hope that the principles outlined above would also apply to these notations. This diagrammatic study will be fully reported elsewhere, but the method and results are outlined below.

Two of the notations used in the study, the decision table and the conventional flowchart, have been illustrated in Fig. 1. The third notation was the structure diagram, a form of flowchart in which the vocabulary of symbols is increased to include specific symbols for conditionals, loops, etc. In Chapter 7 of this book Fitter and Green discuss some pros and cons for one type of structure diagram, devised by Jackson (1975), but for the empirical study a different sort was used, the "dimensional flowchart" of Witty (1977). Figure 6 shows how these diagrams work.

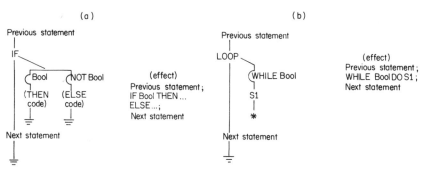

Fig. 6. The bare essentials of one type of structure diagram, the "dimensional flowchart" of Witty (1977). (a) Notation for conditionals. The completion symbol "⟂" sends control back to the most recent branch, or in its absence halts the program. (b) Notation for one kind of loop. The repetition symbol "*" sends control back to the start of the loop until it terminates.

Although decision tables are often recommended as useful aids to programming, they seem to be unsatisfactory when the conditions are liable to change during the course of a program. Dynamic programs of this kind had not been studied by Richards *et al.,* nor indeed in any of the previous Sheffield studies, and with their introduction comes the need to transmit messages from the past—

Sample questions

Sequential: "What rate does a senior working at the weekend get?"
Circumstantial: "Can both seniors and non-seniors receive rate B?"

Pay rates	1	2	3	4	5	6
Week day?	Y	Y	Y	Y	N	N
Overtime?	Y	Y	N	N	–	–
Senior?	Y	N	Y	N	Y	N
Rate A	X					
Rate B		X		X		
Rate C			X			X
Rate D				X		
Draw Pay	X	X	X	X	X	X

Fig. 7a(i)   (continued)

(ii)

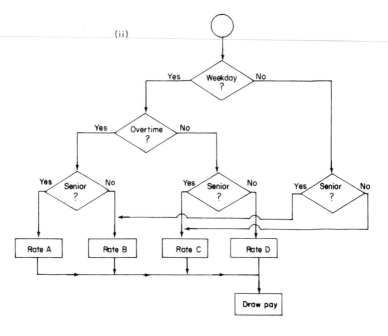

(iii)   Pay rates

Decide time of week

IF

Weekday   Non-weekday

Decide time of day   Decide rank

IF   IF

Overtime   Not   Senior   Not
            overtime   senior

Decide rank   Decide rank   Rate B   Rate C

IF   IF

Senior Not   Senior Not
        senior   senior

Rate A Rate B Rate C Rate D

Draw pay

Sequential: "After what acts does stirring take place?"
Circumstantial: "Under what conditions is the mayonnaise finished?"

Mayonnaise	0	1	2	3
Enough eggs?		Y	Y	N
Enough oil?		Y	N	–
Add egg yolk	X			X
Add oil			X	
Stir	X		X	X
Repeat			X	X
Serve out		X		

(ii)

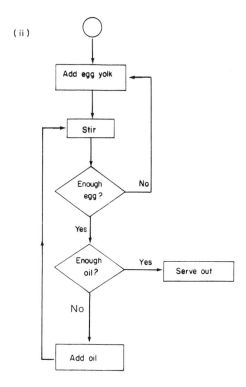

(continued)

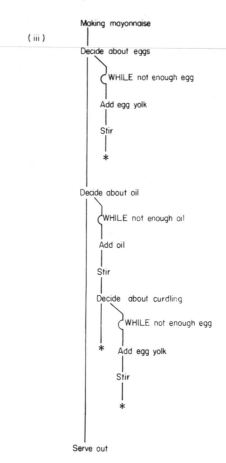

Fig. 7. (a) A static problem used by Fitter and Richards, shown in each of the three notations. (b) A dynamic problem used by Fitter and Richards. (i) Decision table; (ii) flowchart; (iii) structure diagram.

and the associated problems of whether to use a code based on location and jumps to labels, or one based on assignment to variables. To gauge these effects we presented both static and dynamic programs in each notation, and set both sequential and circumstantial questions in each case. In the static programs (Fig. 7a) the structure is identical in each notation, but in the dynamic ones there is variation. The structure diagram notation forces the programmer to use the assignment technique of Fig. 2, in which messages from the past are passed in variables to be tested as needed. The other notations allow more freedom; in particular, using the conventional flowchart, information can be passed from one sub-structure to another either by a location code or by an assignment code, as desired. We chose to use the location code, which produces "unstructured" flowcharts, because we believed that many users of flowcharts would do likewise: the location code allows the flowchart to be constructed with fewer boxes. The mayonnaise example of Fitter and Green (which was one of the problems used in the present study) illustrates how much more compact the "unstructured" version, in their Fig. 8, is than the "structured" version in their Fig. 9. Despite criticisms that can be levelled against unstructured flowcharts, it seems likely that most programmers adopt the principle of fewest boxes. In short, the aim was to compare the most natural solution in each of the three notations. Figure 7b presents the mayonnaise problem and some of the questions put to subjects. Other problems used in this study dealt with choosing a car (a static problem), space travel (a static problem similar to those in the Richards *et al.* study), counting print characters in text (dynamic) and running a bath to the correct temperature by controlling two taps (dynamic).

The subjects in the study were engineering students from Sheffield University, a population with a fairly homogeneous background including some experience in flowcharting and elementary computing. Subjects' answers were again timed by the experimenter, giving a measure of difficulty.

The pattern of results was not simple, with strong interactions among the three variables of notation, of static versus dynamic problems, and of circumstantial versus sequential questions. Moreover the design of the experiment did not include precise matching of difficulty between static and dynamic problems (indeed, it would be hard to see how that could be achieved), nor between circumstantial and sequential questions, so that while comparisons between notations are safe, comparisons within notations must be treated with circumspection.

Taking the static problems first, it is notable that times to answer (Fig. 8a) were much longer when sequential information was to be extracted from decision tables. All the other five points in Fig. 8a are much the same, visually and statistically, with a slight edge for structure diagrams.

In the dynamic problems (Fig. 8b) the first observation is that decision tables fare very badly. The second observation is rather harder to interpret: in all three notations the sequential questions took longer to answer than the circumstantial; but is that a property

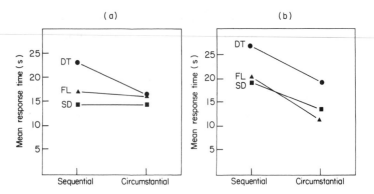

Fig. 8. Mean response times in the diagrammatic study. DT = decision table, FL = flowchart, SD = structure diagram.

of the particular questions used or a property of the particular notations studied? There can be no immediate answer from a single experiment. The problems were roughly matched, in terms of the number of items (predicates and events) involved, which suggests we should infer that in these particular notations dynamic sequential information is hard to extract; but to make a cast-iron case we ought to find a notation in which the effect was reversed, and dynamic sequential information was *easier* to extract than dynamic circumstantial information, still using the same problems.

These results must not be swallowed too credulously, but we shall assume that they are veridical as far as they go. What we are trying to attain, it must be remembered, is not some assertion, however useful, like "decision tables are worst", nor even "decision tables are worst in certain circumstances", but an informed understanding of *why* they are sometimes worst.

In the static case, decision tables function much like the **FULL STATEMENT** condition of the Richards *et al.* study, and the same reasoning may well apply. Whereas the flowchart and the structure diagram break up the decisions and let the subject take each as it comes, the decision table presents them in a solid block and forces him or her to use a mental finger for place-keeping. At the same time another "finger" is also needed to cope with the questions, when these are similar in style to the Narrative Forwards questions used by Richards *et al.* The problems of decision tables could thus be seen as a shortage of mental fingers, or more generally as the problem of trying to cope with the information presented in one order (the question), and demanded in another order (the decision table), with no built-in serializing devices in the notation (whereas in flowcharts one looks at one decision box, then at the next, and so on).

The problems for decision tables in the dynamic case are just as acute, but there are further ones as well. In the problems it may well be necessary to repeat the application of the table, and the trails of sequential information will be obscure, whereas in the other notations there are arrows to be followed.

There is also a negative result to consider. Why were structure diagrams not much better than flowcharts? One reason is no doubt that more has to be learnt about the notation. Structure diagrams contain more types of symbol than flowcharts, and each symbol conveys more information. Other possible effects here are that the structure diagrams do not in fact make the macrostructure more visible, contrary to our expectation, and that in one problem, the mayonnaise one illustrated in Fig. 8b, the structure diagram forces a proliferation of code, with the action "stir" presented three times, which obviously makes trail-following different and maybe harder. Which is better—one complex trail or three simple trails? There can be no absolute answer. Moreover it must be remembered that using different notations, different tasks or larger problems might have revealed more differences—although Brooke and Duncan (1980) found, like us, little difference between flowcharts and structure diagrams, this time using Nassi–Shneiderman notation (see Fitter and Green, this volume) and a debugging task. We can at least conclude that "structure" does not automatically improve performance.

IV. WHAT'S BEHIND THE SEEN?

In the light of these experiments and others in the Sheffield series we can now be reasonably confident in asserting that performance will improve when:

(i)   trails are made shorter;
(ii)   perceptual cues are used to make trails visible;
(iii) mental operations during trail-following (e.g. explicit negation of predicates) are reduced in number and complexity.

We cannot yet be confident about macrostructures. The results of the second experiment surprised us—we had expected structure diagrams to be better—and the implication is that the method of passing messages from the past created additional mental load.

This result raises a number of issues. The adherents of structured programming have written as though the only alternatives were strictly hierarchic structures on the one hand, and utter chaos on the other. Obviously that excludes the middle, to wit any of the other possible principles for organizing programs and similar notations, and since the second experiment offers the suggestion that all may not be well with strictly hierarchic structures, we ought to consider other possible principles. The evidence is weak—more an innuendo than a suggestion—but other evidence of the same sort has been found: Miller (1975) has reported some difficulties with nest-style programming, both van de Wolde (1980) and the Sheffield group have found that non-hierarchic problems, even when static, were harder to solve in nest-style programming, and Sheppard *et al.* (1979) found small deviations from strict structures were not detrimental. Alternative organizations have been found to be reasonably successful by Arblaster *et al.* (in preparation; summarized in Arblaster *et al.*, 1979, Experiment 4).

Choosing one type of macrostructure rather than another as the basis of programming has at least three types of effect: making the programs more alike or more distinct to the eye, making the reader better able or less able to construct what he doesn't know or to reconstruct what he hasn't remembered, and simplifying or complicating coupling between sub-structures.

A. Discriminability

Fitter and Green conclude their chapter in this volume with the notion of programs as points in a perceptual space, and claim that much of the problem is to get the points well separated in order to reduce the risk of confusion. The perceptual distance between programs can be increased either by introducing perceptual cues to magnify the differences between programs, or by eliminating some of the programs. *One effect of an organizing principle is to eliminate a sizeable percentage of programs from the world.* Programs that do not conform to the principle are declared "unacceptable" or even "ungrammatical", and in their absence the remaining programs are effectively spread further apart in the perceptual space (Fig. 9).

This corresponds precisely with the notion of discriminability Psychologists have long known that the discriminability of visual stimuli depends jointly on how different they are and how many of them there are (see Fig. 9). Green (1980b, p. 314) stresses the role of

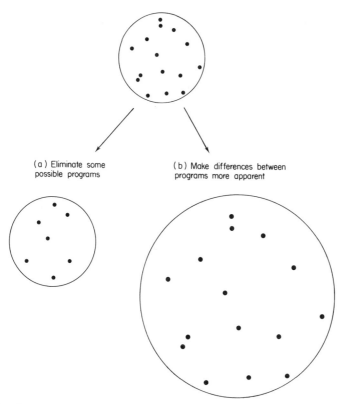

(a) Eliminate some possible programs

(b) Make differences between programs more apparent

Fig. 9. Programs as points in a perceptual space. To increase discriminability one can (a) keep the notation unchanged and rule that some possibilities (such as non-hierarchical structures) are unacceptable, or (b) keep the possibilities unchanged but make the notation clearer. Ideally both methods could be used.

discriminability:

Does this test here take part in a conditional or a loop? Easy to tell in a high-level language, hard in a flowchart or an assembly language [Fig. 10]. Is this loop event-driven or count-driven? Easy to tell in modern languages, hard to tell in some older ones. Under what conditions can this action occur? Easy to tell in decision tables, ...hard with conventional languages. Discriminability can be increased by introducing synonyms, so that the test is not full of repetitions: synonyms are unnecessary for objects like plus signs, but would be a great help with discontinuous constructions such as pairs of brackets, where each bracket's partner has to be discriminated from the heap of candidates and the use of square and round brackets as synonyms would make it that much easier. Discriminability can be increased by clear signalling to identify

(a)

(b)

```
q := 0;
for j := 1 to 10 do
    begin
    read (p);
    if p > 1 then q := q + 1
    end
write (q);
```

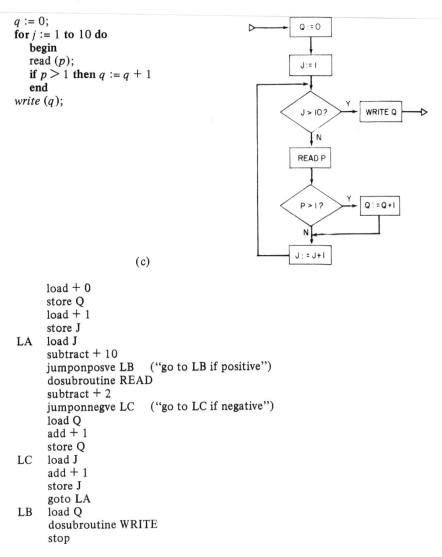

(c)

```
        load + 0
        store Q
        load + 1
        store J
LA      load J
        subtract + 10
        jumponposve LB    ("go to LB if positive")
        dosubroutine READ
        subtract + 2
        jumponnegve LC    ("go to LC if negative")
        load Q
        add + 1
        store Q
LC      load J
        add + 1
        store J
        goto LA
LB      load Q
        dosubroutine WRITE
        stop
```

Fig. 10. The same program in three languages: "Read 10 numbers and count how many are greater than 1". Its structure, a conditional inside a loop with a simple statement at each end, seems to get more obscure as we go from (a) to (c). PASCAL (a) signals the loop and the conditional quite explicitly; in the flowchart (b), we have to examine the contents of the boxes and how they are linked to determine whether the test boxes control conditionals or loops; and of the pseudo-machine (c), the less said the better.

each syntactic construction distinctively.... Discriminability can also be increased by having fewer constructions to identify, but the evidence suggests—at least to my eye—that people can cope with as many constructions as desired, as long as they are well signalled; what people need to do is to determine each construction's role in the behaviour of the program, which they may do better if there are many different constructions each identified with only a few possible roles, rather than one or two incredibly general-purpose constructions.

Once granted discriminability, then in principle the programmer's job should be much more straightforward. Reading a program will be easier, if the programmer knows the basic repertoire of program types—"Oh, it's one of *that* sort"—and that will be true at all levels for the sub-components will also be more easily recognized. On the same basis it will be easier for the programmer to check the working while a program is being written, since the "deprogramming" operation will be easier, and the program that *has* been written will be more easily discriminated from the program that *should* have been written.

B. Generability

In the presence of an organizing principle it is easier for the programmer to reconstruct or to construct—in short to generate—material to fill lacunae. The effect of this has been noted now on many fronts. Du Boulay *et al.* (1980) developed the idea of the "notional machine", an internal model of the computer which is sufficiently concrete and precise to allow the learner to apply analogies with success. Mayer (1979) reports a number of experiments on this theme. Carroll (1980) reports that learners do better with "congruent" sets of commands, using pairs such as "advance"/ "retreat" rather than "advance"/"move-robot-backward". In all these cases, if the learner has some of the information he or she is well placed to generate the rest. In reading text it has been repeatedly shown that active processes of inference and organization take place, and preliminary models to describe the mental operations have been developed with some success (Kintsch and van Dijk, 1978).

Increasing the discriminability of programs will certainly make the macrostructures more visible. The programmer will more readily be able to recognize an instance of a known class of programs— "Oh, yes, it's doing a sort here"; it will be easier to segment the program into sub-components, and it will be easier to fill in lacunae—

"Well, if it's sorting there must be an interchange somewhere, where is it? Oh, yes, there it is." The importance of this type of reasoning has probably been seriously underestimated. We can devour normal text at about 300 words per minute, with all its inferences and reasoning and guesswork; surely programs, at which we stare for many minutes, are the subject of far more inferences.

C. Tractability

When the sub-component can fairly readily be removed from the whole and a new one inserted, or when the order of executing sub-components can fairly readily be altered, we say the program is "tractable". How can we achieve tractable structures?

The now-classical answer is: by using hierarchical constructions. Each component has a single entry point and a single exit, and can therefore readily be snipped out and replaced. A lot can be said for this method (Green and Arblaster, 1980). However, it is only the control flow that is usually organized into a hierarchical structure; once data flow is considered we rapidly see that different components at quite different levels need access to the same data object, and snipping out one component may be much less easy than one hoped. Thus in Fig. 11 we could not be fully confident about snipping out the loop component until the role of the initialization statement, "$x:=0$", was exposed. Pursuing trails looking for references to a given identifier is a frequent activity and a very time-consuming one, and to impose a hierarchical structure on the control flow does not alleviate it. Moreover those trails may be very long: Elshoff (1976) reports that in a sample of actively used commercial programs no less than 13% of all spans between successive references were longer than 100 statements. Here we probably have another parallel with reading ordinary text. Green and Jackson (1976), looking for a measure of the complexity of a text, developed a coefficient of the degree to which a text harked back to earlier topics, and later Jackson (1977) showed that as the coefficient rose (meaning more harking back or

$$
\begin{aligned}
&x := 0; \\
&j := 1; \\
&\textbf{loop: if } a[\text{j}] = < 0 \textbf{ then } x := x + a[j]; \\
&j := j + 1; \\
&\textbf{if } j = < n \textbf{ then goto loop};
\end{aligned}
$$

Fig. 11. A simple counting program. Notice how related components are physically separated.

harking back over longer spans) comprehensibility fell.

A notational device has now been found to reduce these long spans, and to collect together statements of a program that are related by data flow. This gives what might well be regarded as the "real" macrostructure. Waters (1979) describes a technique developed at MIT for representing programs in a different domain. Instead of the domain of time (*"Do A then B"*) he uses the domain of control (*"A has control over B"*). Figure 12 illustrates this interesting development.

Unfortunately Waters' technique, like the structure diagram notation, forces the programmer to adopt one particular solution to

1. *Remove an "augmentation" chunk,*   *leaving:*

    A. $x := 0$;
       $x := x + a[j]$;

                         . . .
                         $j := 1$;
     loop: **if** $a[j] \leqslant 0$ **then**
                         $j := j + 1$;
                         if $j \leqslant n$ **then goto loop;**

2. *Remove a "filter" chunk,*   *leaving:*

    B. **if** $a[j] \leqslant 0$ **then** . . .

                         . . .
                         $j := 1$;
     loop: . . .
                         $j := j + 1$;
                         if $j \leqslant n$ **then goto loop;**

3. *Remove a "termination" chunk,*   *leaving:*

    C. *loop:* . . .
         if $j \leqslant n$ **then goto loop**

                         . . .
                         $j := 1$;
                         . . .
                         $j := j + 1$;
                         . . .

4. *Remove a "counting" chunk,*   *leaving:*

    D. $j := 1$;   (nothing)
       $j := j + 1$;

(Each of these chunks controls the next one: D $\Rightarrow$ C $\Rightarrow$ B $\Rightarrow$ A)

Fig. 12. Changing the notation from a sequential domain, in which the relation exhibited is "this happens before that", to a domain exhibiting the relation "this chunk controls or sends data to that one". D sends to C the numbers 1, 2, 3, ...; C terminates the stream at n and sends them on to B; B discards those numbers that fail a test, and sends the ones that pass to A; A fills up the bucket, x. Although several chunks contain more than one statement, it must be remembered that the statements are merely listed—they do not form a sequence. Thus D comprises two statements, $j := 1$ and $j := j + 1$, but putting them side by side does not mean "do this one and then that one". (After Waters, 1979.)

messages from the past—the method of coding by assignment (Fig. 2) rather than by location (Fig. 1a). This may result in increasing the mental load while following certain trails, it seems, although at present it is far too soon to be sure of that.

On balance, we would say that of the three topics of discriminability, generability and tractability, it is the third that is in most need of attention, but also probably the third that is most promising. Alternative techniques for coupling sub-components and passing information from one to another, and alternative notational devices for displaying the coupling, do not seem to be beyond our reach. Experimentation ought to reveal which styles impose most mental load.

V. HOW TO DO IT

In conclusion we propose to offer a handful of working principles about the Art of Notation. Nobody is likely to master all the information in the psychological literature that might, just possibly, be relevant, so we shall go to the other extreme and offer too little instead of too much. Our principles certainly will not come as a surprise but they are few and simple; they agree with the main body of psychological knowledge, and could be supported by appeal to empirical findings if need be; they have withstood exposure to our own research; and they appear to be applicable to many different notations. They should all the same be applied with good will and scepticism.

(i) *Perceptual cues beat symbolic cues; symbolic cues beat no cues*
If you want to convey information, think first about typographical or diagrammatic codes. Even when the same information is available symbolically it is often helpful to provide a "redundant restatement" using a perceptual code. The standard example is indenting: it clearly displays the program structure, but the actual text contains the same information.

(ii) *Short trails are better than long trails*
When information is not immediately manifest but has instead to be deduced from the text, look at the various points in the text which the reader has to traverse. The fewer stepping stones the better. Not too many sub-routines—not too many conditionals—not too many layers of data structure.

(iii) *Following a trail should demand few mental operations*

Examples of mental operations include checking a label to see if it is the target: "shopping"—accumulating a list of conditions governing some aspect of program behaviour; explicitly negating a conditional expression for an **else** branch; keeping track of changing names as data passes through parameters and common blocks; noting assignments to variables as messages from the past, and so on. All these should be avoided as far as possible. Sometimes one can choose between a short complex trail and a long simple one—e.g. with complex conditional expressions—and probably one should aim for the happy mean.

(iv) *Only one mental finger should be necessary*

A mental finger may be needed to mark the place when a person is checking off truth-values against conditional tests, or the operations in one sub-routine against those in another, or in general checking off one piece of text against another. When there are strong perceptual aids (such as flowchart arrows) mental fingers are probably unnecessary. If neither of the texts has perceptual aids then the information should at least be in the same order in each text; one mental finger can serve for both. But if the texts have no percentual aids *and* the information is in different orders, each text will need its own place-keeper and performance will suffer dramatically.

(v) *Ensembles and orderings should be generable*

The ensemble of commands should be formed by simple rules, or should be strongly related to analogies (the "notional machine"), so that the user can construct or reconstruct anything unknown. If arguments have to be supplied in a particular order there should be simple rules to generate the order.

(vi) *Macrostructures should be visible and tractable*

The components of the program should be clearly separated and their relationships should be immediately apparent. No poking around to find out where this value is initialized or whether that identifier can be accessed elsewhere or whether this component is used before that one. Coupling should be tractable, which means that the arrangement can readily be altered, but also it should be possible to follow the trails easily: thus messages sent by assignment coding may be more tractable than location coding but the "shopping" may be harder.

REFERENCES

Arblaster, A.T., Sime, M.E. and Green, T.R.G. (1979). Jumping to some purpose. *Computer* J., **22**, 105–109.

Barron, D.W. (1977). *An Introduction to the Study of Programming Languages.* Cambridge: Cambridge University Press.

Brooke, J.B. and Duncan, K.D. (1980). Experimental studies of flowchart use at different stages of programming debugging. Unpublished Manuscript, Dept. of Applied Psychology, UWIST, Cardiff.

Carroll, J.M. (1980). Learning, using, and designing command paradigms. *Report RC 8141*, IBM Thomas J. Watson Research Center, Yorktown Heights, New York.

Du Boulay, B., O'Shea, T. and Monk, T. (in press). The black box inside the glass box: presenting computing concepts to novices. *Int. J. Man–Machine Stud.*

Elshoff, J.L. (1976). An analysis of some commercial PL/1 programs. *IEEE Transactions on Software Engineering*, **2**, 113–120.

Gordon, J.E. (1978). *Structures, or Why Things Don't Fall Down.* Harmondsworth: Penguin.

Green, T.R.G. (1980a). IFs and THENs: is nesting just for the birds? *Software-Practice and Experience*, **10**, 373–381.

Green, T.R.G. (1980b). Programming as a cognitive activity. In H.T. Smith and T.R.G. Green (eds) *Human Interaction with Computers.* London and New York: Academic Press.

Green, T.R.G. and Arblaster, A.T. (1980). As you'd like it: contributions to easier computing. *Memo No. 373*, MRC Social and Applied Psychology Unit, University of Sheffield.

Green, T.R.G. and Jackson, P.R. (1976). "Hark-back": a simple measure of search patterns, *Br. J. Math. Statist. Psychol.*, **29**, 102–113.

Green, T.R.G., Sime, M.E. and Fitter, M.J. (in press). The problems the programmer faces. *Ergonomics.*

Jackson, M. (1975). *Principles of Program Design.* London and New York: Academic Press.

Jackson, P.R. (1977). The reconstruction of interviews as a function of harkback. *Memo No. 235*, MRC Social and Applied Psychology Unit, University of Sheffield.

Kernighan, B.W. and Plauger, P.J. (1974a). *The Elements of Programming Style.* New York: McGraw-Hill.

Kernighan, B.W. and Plauger, P.J. (1974b). Programming style: examples and counter-examples. *Computing Surveys*, **6**, 303–319.

Kintsch, W. and van Dijk, T.A. (1978). Toward a model of text comprehension and production. *Psychol. Rev.*, **85**, 363–394.

Mayer, R.E. (1979). A psychology of learning Basic. *Communications of the ACM*, **22**, 589–593.

McClure, C.L. (1978). A model for program complexity analysis. *Proceedings of the 3rd International Conference on Software Engineering*, Atlanta, Georgia.

Miller, L.A. (1975). Naive programmer problems with specification of transfer-of-control. *Proceedings of the AFIPS National Computer Conference*, **44**, 657–663.

Richards, M. (1976). Programming structure, style and efficiency. In *Structured Programming*. An Infotech State-of-the-Art Report, Infotech, Maidenhead.

Richards, V.G., Green, T.R.G. and Manton, J. (1979). What does problem representation affect: chunk size, memory load, or mental process? *Memo No. 319*, MRC Social and Applied Psychology Unit, University of Sheffield.

Sheppard, S.B., Curtis, B., Milliman, P. and Love, T. (1979). Modern coding practices and programmer performance. *Computer,* 12, December, 41–49.

Van de Wolde, J. (1980). Programmeren in NEST or JUMP? Enkele psychologische aspecten van het werken met conditionele structuren. Subfakulteit Psychologie, Vakgroep Funktieleer en Methodenleer, Vrije Universiteit, Amsterdam.

Van Dijk, T.A. (1977). Semantic macrostructures and knowledge frames in discourse comprehension. In M.A. Just and P.A. Carpenter (eds) *Cognitive Processes in Comprehension*. New York: Wiley.

Waters, R.C. (1979). A method for analyzing loop programs. *IEEE Transactions on Software Engineering,* 5, 237–247.

Weinburg, G.M., Geller, D.P. and Plum, T.W.-S. (1975). IF-THEN-ELSE considered harmful. *SIGPLAN Notices,* 10, 34–44.

Witty, R.W. (1977) Dimensional flowcharts. *Software-Practice and Experience,* 7, 553–584.

Wright, P. and Reid, F. (1973). Written information: some alternatives to prose for expressing the outcomes of complex contingencies. *J. Appl. Psychol.,* 57, 160–166.

7. When do Diagrams Make Good Computer Languages?

M.J. FITTER and T.R.G. GREEN

MRC/SSRC Social and Applied Psychology Unit, Department of Psychology, University of Sheffield, Sheffield, England

I. INTRODUCTION

Recently there has been increasing interest in diagrammatic computer languages, of which the flowchart is probably still the best-known example. Too often, however, it is taken for granted that a diagrammatic notation will be easier to read than a conventional one, an assumption that is not by any means always correct. Some diagrammatic notations are very good, some are not. In this chapter we attempt to identify some of the principles that the designer of a notation should bear in mind, illustrating them by a number of examples from a wide range of applications.

Some of the design principles are likely to conflict with one another and it is difficult to see how such conflicts could be resolved in any ultimate theory-based way. Although the principles will give the designer a degree of guidance, he is in no danger of being replaced by a theory of design that will mechanically generate a new notation as required; our principles should be viewed partly as guidelines and partly as criteria for evaluating new notations, preferably by empirical tests—a form of behavioural quality control.

There can be no doubt that diagrams are often stunningly successful. Many of the diagrammatic conventions can be learnt very swiftly and indeed many are already known to the man in the street, so that they make an excellent communication medium for computer-naive people. But some are less successful. One of our favourite examples comes from the owner's manual for the Vauxhall Viva car, showing how to locate and undo the nut for draining the radiator (Fig. 1): a perfectly standard hexagonal nut is illustrated, with an arrow showing that it unscrews in the standard direction . . . and *nothing*

Fig. 1. Diagram accompanying instructions for draining a car engine cooling system. (From the owner's handbook for the Vauxhall Viva Model HC, 1972 edition.)

else, no landmarks of any sort. At least, like the Bellman's perfectly blank map in *The Hunting of the Snark,* it does not confuse you. Can the same be said of Fig. 2? Can it even be said of Fig. 3, though it comes from the august pages of *Scientific American* where every effort is made to present information palatably?

Fig. 2. Diagram for his analysis of the strength of a beam from Galileo's *Discorsi e Dimonstrazioni Matematiche intorno à due nuove scienze,* Leyden, 1638. (From J.D. Bernal, *Science in History.* London: Watts, 1969.)

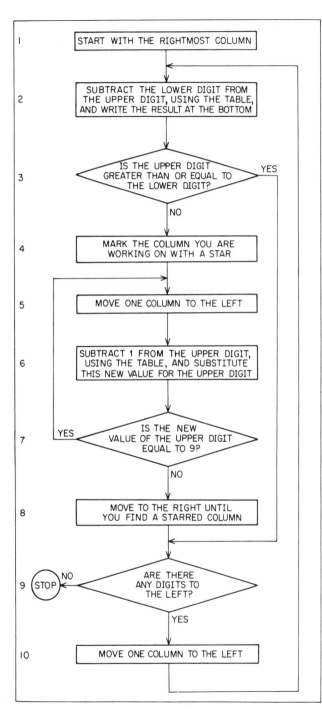

Fig. 3. Algorithm for the subtraction of whole numbers defines an explicit procedure that can be followed without any need for intuition and even without an understanding of the significance each step has to the operation as a whole. The algorithm, which is assumed to incorporate the table of differences shown here, can be applied to an infinite number of subtraction problems. Other algorithms are equally effective. A method of subtraction taught in European schools, for example, differs in the treatment of borrowing where it specifies that 1 should be added to the lower digit instead of being subtracted from the upper one. (From H.R. Lewis and C.H. Papdimitriou, The efficiency of algorithms. *Scientific American,* January 1978.)

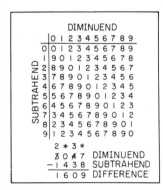

These diagrams illustrate different kinds of problem. Figure 1 quite simply fails to supply the required information. Instructions of any kind, including diagrams, can only be successful when the instructor has the right image of the pupil, and in this particular case it is quite likely that the pupil can already recognize a nut and may even know how to undo it, but wants to know which nut to undo. Lewis and Cook (1969) make the more general point that instructions are a form of telling, which is "a feedforward control process, based on a predictive model of [the receiver's] characteristics" (p. 136). Figure 2 illustrates the difficulty that the perceptual codes used in diagrams cannot carry as much information as symbolic codes can, so that irrelevant material quickly makes them cluttered. Figure 3 is the most questionable example, since many would regard it as excellent. We shall say a lot more about flowcharts later: for the time being, it is sufficient to point out the difficulty of discovering why some columns should be marked with a star, and what might be the purpose of doing so; or the difficulty of discovering by looking at the diagram (rather than by experiment) what will happen using this method if the second number is bigger than the first, giving a negative difference.

The problems raised by Fig. 3 are specific to diagrams that describe a *process*. It is with processes that computing is largely concerned, and many of the diagrammatic notations we shall mention are to do with explaining processes. Descriptions of processes raise special problems, whether they are couched in a diagrammatic notation or in the archetypal computing medium of a programming language, and such problems can be summed up as those of *tractability* of structure and *visibility* of structure. It should be possible to break the description up into pieces that are small enough to be reasoned about, and the interrelationship of the pieces should be clearly visible. Proponents of structured programming have had much to say on this matter:

> A desirable feature of a language is that it should assist the programmer to produce programs that are "nicely structured", in the sense that the structure of the program reflects directly the structure of the problem, and is perspicuous, in the sense that they can be read rather like a mathematical textbook. In seeking nicely structured programs we are not pursuing elegance for its own sake. Such programs will be easier to follow: they are less likely to contain errors, and the errors that they contain will be easier to find.   (Barron, 1977, p. 7)

The chief means to promote tractability proffered by structured programming is to restrict the notation to a small number of standard components that can be linked in standard ways, and we shall in due course see how the notation of diagrams can be restricted in such ways and discuss what the gains might be.

In addition to the tractability and visibility problems raised in describing processes, diagrams also create their own special problems of perceptual obviousness. The whole point of using a diagrammatic notation rather than a symbolic one is to make its meaning perceptually obvious, and the inherent possibilities and limitations of the medium greatly influence the success. We must therefore say something about the perceptual codes that can be used in diagrams before going on to say how the designer of a notation ought to use them.

II. PERCEPTUAL CODING OF INFORMATION

The difference between a perceptual code and a symbolic one is exemplified by comparing a map, which presents its information coded into the dimension of spatial location, and a list of grid references. The differences defy any simple definition (but see Sloman, 1971, who draws the distinction between Fregean or symbolic representations and analogical ones, such as spatial codes). One might argue that symbolic representations require conscious cognitive processing, whereas analogical or pictorial information is perceived immediately, but AI and cognitive psychology have shown us that one cannot make a sharp distinction between perception and cognition. Luckily, everyone knows what we mean when we say that information can be presented in a perceptual code!

There are many perceptual codings in common use, spatial coding in maps, colour coding of mains electric cables, auditory coding of the dialling/ringing/etc. states in the telephone system. Some of them are very ingenious, such as the perceptual property of "insideness" used in Venn diagrams to code the relation of inclusion (Fig. 4), giving a less confusing notation than natural language (Thomas, 1976). It is possible in principle to develop notations that are purely perceptual, like a scale model, but these are of no more practical interest than a purely symbolic notation would be, an unbroken stream of text without any typographical aids to legibility whatsoever—no paragraphs, no capitals, etc. Usable notations always contain both symbolic and perceptual elements. Sometimes the two codes are independent, one conveying one type of information and the other conveying another type, as in Fig. 4 where the perceptual code gives information about relations between sets while the symbolic code, in the form of labels, tells the reader what the sets are. Another case is where the perceptual component is logically speaking, redundant, because the information it conveys can already be extracted from the symbolic component. Programs can be made more legible by using indenting and other spatial conventions (see Van Tassel, 1974, for some good examples) and similarly mathematicians usually adopt layout conventions to make algebra and predicate calculus more readable. We call this "redundant recoding", where the same information is presented both symbolically and perceptually. And at times indeed, it would be hard to decide what information was presented symbolically and what was presented perceptually and how they interrelate, as in the staff notation of music.

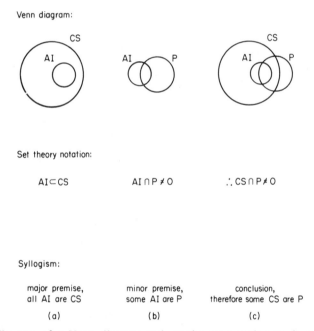

Venn diagram:

Set theory notation:

$AI \subset CS$ $AI \cap P \neq 0$ $\therefore CS \cap P \neq 0$

Syllogism:

major premise,	minor premise,	conclusion,
all AI are CS	some AI are P	therefore some CS are P
(a)	(b)	(c)

Fig. 4. The use of a Venn diagram and set theory notation to demonstrate a syllogism of the form "If all Artificial Intelligentsia are Computer Scientists and some Artificial Intelligentsia are Psychologists, then some Computer Scientists are Psychologists".

Perceptual codes are severely limited in vocabulary size, because there are not many codes available. Spatial location and insideness have been mentioned. Flowcharts use connectedness. Varying the size of symbols makes another useful code, and so does using solid, dotted and dashed lines. Musical notation employs another and very ingenious code: the shorter the note the more ink it requires, giving a very clear relation between how black the page looks and how fast the music is moving. Moreover, not only are there rather few types of code, but their resolution is usually rather coarse for example, it would be no help at all to indent a program by millimetre steps. (We are restricting ourselves in this chapter to what is visually presentable, although our other senses should not be forgotten. One possibility that needs much more investigation is the use of auditory output from interactive computers, using hoots and whistles and even the clattering of teleprinters.)

Perceptual dimensions are therefore a scarce resource to the designer of a notation, and some of the information must be presented symbolically. It is up to him to ensure that the most appropriate choice is made of what to present symbolically and what to present perceptually, whether the two will be independent or will overlap to give "redundancy recoding", and all the other choices—remembering, as well, that the result must be tractable as well as visible.

III. FIVE PRINCIPLES FOR DIAGRAMMATIC NOTATION

Given the limited vocabulary of perceptual dimensions, and the limited amount of resolution available on each dimension, the first principle of a diagrammatic notation is that the information that is encoded perceptually rather than symbolically should be *relevant*. Notations should *restrict* the user to forms that are comprehensible; they should *redundantly recode* important parts of the information; they should *reveal* the underlying processes that they represent, preferably in a *responsive* interactive system which permits manipulation of the diagrams; and finally they should be readily *revisable*. We will discuss these principles in the context of actual notations, and in that manner attempt to illuminate them. Like all good principles, it is difficult to measure up to all of them at once, and to a large degree the designer of a new notation would have to use his intuition in seeking a compromise.

A. Relevance

The Gantt chart is a kind of timetable, in which time is the horizontal axis. Up the vertical axis are a number of rows, each representing one entity, and each column of the chart shows the states of all the entities at one instant of time. Figure 5a shows a Gantt chart representing the progress of school classes from teacher to teacher (or equivalently of steel batches through a job shop, from machine to machine; or data through a suite of programs; or whatever else you will). Each row represents one resource (a teacher), and the entry for a given teacher at a given time shows which entity (class) he is taking. Figure 5b *contains* the same information; this is the dual figure, in which rows represent entities (classes) and entries represent resources (teachers). Although the diagrams are formally identical the information that they readily convey is quite different. For example, in Fig. 5a free periods of classes are readily apparent (the blank cells) whereas in Fig. 5b teachers' free periods are most readily perceived.

(a)

Period

Teacher	1	2	3	4	5	6	7
P	A	A	C	B		D	D
Q	B	B	A		D		
R	D	D		C	A	A	A
S		C	C		A	B	B

(b)

Period

Class	1	2	3	4	5	6	7
A	P	P	Q	S	R	R	R
B	Q	Q		P	S	S	S
C	S	S	P	R			
D	R	R			Q	P	P

Fig. 5. Two types of Gantt chart containing equivalent information. Type (a) is more suitable for showing teachers' free periods and type (b) for classes' free periods. (a) The classes (A, B, C, D) timetabled to be taught by teachers (P, Q, R, S) throughout the seven periods of a day. (b) The teachers (P, Q, R, S) timetabled to take classes (A, B, C, D) throughout the seven periods of a day.

The use of Gantt charts and other sophisticated visual aids for planning was relatively common during the Second World War and earlier. It is our belief that early computing, with its lack of facilities for the manipulation of complex visual displays, had a detrimental effect on the development of planning techniques. Present-day technology now permits the development to continue afresh and take full advantage of interactive computing.

A quite different illustration of the relevance of competing representations is offered by the grammar of the PASCAL programming language, which is presented by Jensen and Wirth (1975) in two different forms: the linear notation of Backus-Naur Form (BNF) and a diagrammatic notation using networks (or syntax diagrams) to show the same information. The first author of this chapter made an empirical comparison of these two notations, using small portions

$\langle$ TYPE $\rangle$: : = $\langle$ NAME 2 $\rangle$ |
 ARRAY ($\langle$ NAME 2 $\rangle$ [, $\langle$ NAME 2 $\rangle$]) OF $\langle$ TYPE $\rangle$ |
 FILE OF $\langle$ TYPE $\rangle$ |
 RECORD $\langle$ FIELD LIST $\rangle$ END

 $\langle$ FIELD LIST $\rangle$: : = $\langle$ RECORD SECTION $\rangle$ [; $\langle$ RECORD SECTION $\rangle$]
 $\langle$ RECORD SECTION $\rangle$: : = $\langle$ NAME 1 $\rangle$ [, $\langle$ NAME 1 $\rangle$] : $\langle$ TYPE $\rangle$ |
                             $\langle$ EMPTY $\rangle$
 $\langle$ NAME 1 $\rangle$: : = HOUSE | GARDEN
 $\langle$ NAME 2 $\rangle$: : = DOG | CAT | MAN | GIRL
 $\langle$ EMPTY $\rangle$: : =

(a)

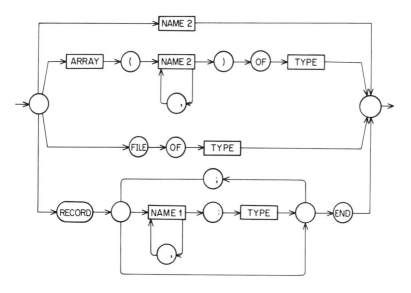

NAME 1 : : = HOUSE | GARDEN

NAME 2 : : = DOG | CAT | MAN | GIRL

(b)

Fig. 6. The syntax (based on the syntax of Pascal) used in the most complex problem in Fitter's study. Each notation apparently has some advantages. (a) Syntax expressed in rewriting rules ("Backus-Naur form"); (b) syntax expressed diagrammatically.

extracted from the grammars with the names of the objects changed from "identifier", "variable", etc. to more familiar entities like "man", "house". Figure 6 shows the most complex problem given to the subjects in each of the notations used. Tests of the speed with which subjects could find mistakes in sample sentences showed that the network notation was clearly better by a substantial margin. Any one experiment is generalizable only within strict limits, of course, but the population from whom the subjects were drawn, engineering students with limited experience of programming, is a fair example of the sort of semi-naive computer user for whom computers ought to be made more accessible than they presently are.

The main point about the study, however, is that it showed that the networks were better for spotting errors in sample sentences, a task that necessitates *tracing through* the grammar. Subjects were also asked questions about the grammar which required a knowledge of its *structure* rather than merely an understanding of sequential information. In these questions the superiority of the network did not appear; in fact for some questions there seemed to be a slight (but not significant) advantage in the BNF representation. The network notation encodes the relation "A follows B" into the perceptual property of connectedness, which is fine when that is the relevant information that the user wants to obtain. When it isn't, the diagrammatic notation becomes less convenient. Examining the notations further leads one to speculate that BNF has particular advantages of its own. For example, by expanding certain BNF rules into further rewriting rules it may be possible to clarify the structure of the grammar. The possibility needs empirical investigation although Steele (1977) has made a similar suggestion for increasing the comprehensibility of procedural languages.

The relationship between BNF and the network representation parallels the relationship between decision tables and flowcharts. Bingham and Davies (1972) make a very reasonable comparison between these two notations, arguing that decision tables are better for showing logical relationships, that they can be modified and checked more easily, and that they are more easily understood by non-specialists—but that flowcharts are better at showing procedural flows. "It is therefore convenient to use flowcharts for the procedural parts of analysis and design, and decision tables to express the logical relations", they say. (Bingham and Davies, 1972, p.67). In a lucid introduction to decision tables, Montalbano (1974) points out that decision tables keep the condition and action parts of a

procedure clearly distinct and facilitate checking of the preconditions for any given course of action.

Nevertheless, there is a serious difficulty with using decision tables
as alternatives to flowcharts. If a flowchart and a standard decision
table are to be regarded as equivalent, it must be the case that the
tests are unaffected by the actions, because in flowcharts the tests
and actions are arranged in a sequence while in decision tables all
tests are made before any of the actions are performed. Only rarely
can we be sure that the actions *cannot possibly* affect the tests. After
a meal, a diner may find himself thirsty after steak but not after fish,
and in the flowchart it is easy to take care of that possibility by post-
poning the test "thirsty?" until after the main course (Fig. 7a); at the
same time this takes care of other diners who find that it is fish, or
soup, that makes them thirsty. To put the same generality into a
decision table, we have to use sub-tables to separate earlier tests from
later ones (Fig. 7b). Maes (1978) makes this point forcefully and
considers a number of decision table notations intended to allow the
tests to depend on the actions, but he concludes that

> none of them, to our knowledge, is able to represent any flowchart-like
> structure while maintaining the combinatorial power and the transparency
> of the original decision table conventions. Therefore, it is our belief that,
> in spite of the ability of the condition part to represent the test predicates
> of a program . . . the syntactical scheme offered by the decision table is an
> inadequate tool for representing algorithms described (and designed) by
> means of classical flowcharts. (p. 294).

He does, however, recommend the decision table as a tool for problem specification.

Certainly it is true that in many cases the interesting questions
about a program turn out to be questions abouts its "trajectory",
such as how often one action is performed before another one, and
in these cases it seems that the flowchart's perceptual coding of
procedural flow is a definite advantage. (Although it may not be the
best method. The next section describes some possible improvements.) A study by the Central Computing Agency (1974) confirms
this, using programs of a realistic size expressed as flowcharts, as
decision tables, and as narrative English. The decision tables were
significantly harder to use, both for answering trajectory questions
and, interestingly enough, for modifying the program to behave
differently, in contradiction to the quite plausible assertions of
Bingham and Davies and others.

Thus the rather scanty evidence suggests that decision tables are
weak when they are used to describe a process of a highly sequential

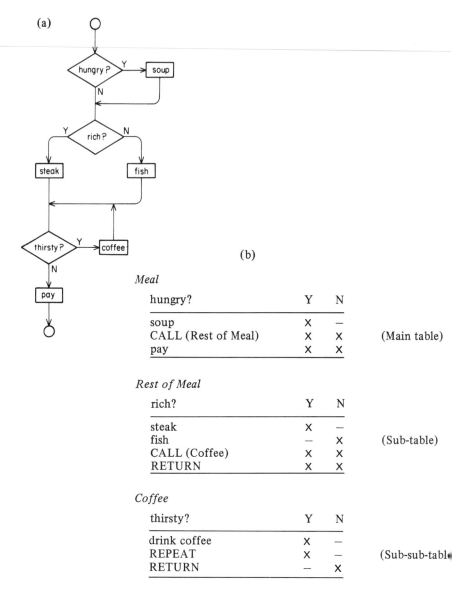

(a)

(b)

Meal

hungry?	Y	N	
soup	X	—	
CALL (Rest of Meal)	X	X	(Main table)
pay	X	X	

Rest of Meal

rich?	Y	N	
steak	X	—	
fish	—	X	(Sub-table)
CALL (Coffee)	X	X	
RETURN	X	X	

Coffee

thirsty?	Y	N	
drink coffee	X	—	
REPEAT	X	—	(Sub-sub-table)
RETURN	—	X	

Fig. 7. Flowchart and decision table notations. (a) Flowchart notation for having a meal in a restaurant; (b) decision table notation for having a meal. Because the flowchart interleaves tests and actions it allows the result of a test to depend upon previous actions, most obviously in the loop for drinking coffee until no longer thirsty. Obtaining an equivalent effect in a decision table notation, as in (b), requires the use of sub-tables making it difficult to read.

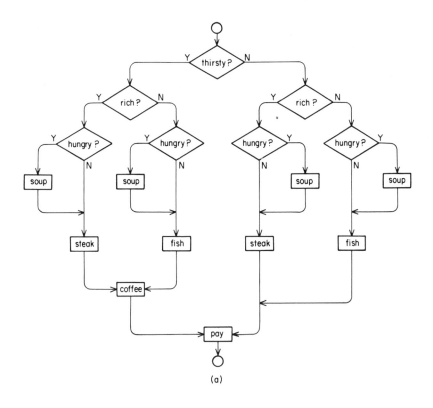

(a)

Meal

hungry?	Y	Y	Y	Y	N	N	N	N
rich?	Y	Y	N	N	Y	Y	N	N
thirsty?	Y	N	Y	N	Y	N	Y	N
soup	X	X	X	X	—	—	—	—
steak	X	X	—	—	X	X	—	—
fish	—	—	X	X	—	—	X	X
coffee	X	—	X	—	X	—	X	—
pay bill	X	X	X	X	X	X	X	X

(b)

Fig. 8. In this comparison the algorithm of Fig. 7 has been modified so that actions depend solely on initial values of conditions, which makes the flowchart harder than the previous version and the decision table easier. Flowcharts are better suited to highly sequential processes and decision tables to processes where order is not critical. (a) Flowchart for having a meal; (b) decision table for having a meal.

nature, because they cannot conveniently show the effects of actions in changing initial conditions. The CCA's study could have been more persuasive than it was; their programs included many iterations, which inherently require the program's actions to change the initial conditions sooner or later (or else the loop will never terminate), and so a more useful study would have examined some of the various notational devices developed to express iteration within decision tables (e.g. Metzner and Barnes, 1977). Nor must we overplay the evidence we do have. Not all processes are highly sequential, and indeed sometimes it is necessary to make the actions performed in a process depend solely on the initial conditions and not upon any subsequent happenings. Then the flowchart, in its turn, becomes rather weak and clumsy, as we see in Fig. 8a, while the decision table is very lucid (Fig. 8b).

The moral in a perfect world would be to find out what types of information were relevant to users' needs and to present each type perceptually. That is very unlikely to be possible, because so few perceptual dimensions are available, as we have remarked. Another approach then is to present the same information in two different notations side by side, as Jensen and Wirth do with the grammar of PASCAL (making quite sure that it really *is* the same information!). When that too is impossible, being uneconomic in all sorts of ways, the designer of a notation should, we suggest, make a careful and deliberate choice of the information that is to be presented perceptually. Is it relevant to the users' needs? Is there any other information where mistakes would be more costly? If one of the users' tasks is made simpler by presenting the relevant information perceptually while other tasks are left to be done symbolically, does it turn out that the ones left are the ones that must be done when the user is hurried, overloaded, or otherwise stressed?

One might conclude that the decision to use a symbolic description is a cautious and safe one; that it will allow the user to interpret the information into a form which meets his needs, albeit that the interpretation may take him a noticeable time and be prone to human error. The increasing availability of on-line computer systems allows alternative representations, directly selected to suit the user's current purpose, to be produced and displayed automatically. We believe the availability of alternative representations will become increasingly common provided that the alternatives can be produced from good design principles.

B. Restriction

Of all the diagrammatic notations for expressing procedures, the flowchart is the best-known. Comparing different opinions is intriguing:

The good

> The flowchart is an essential tool in problem solving. . . . The person who cannot flowchart cannot anticipate a problem, analyse the problem, plan the solution, or solve the problem. (Bohl, 1971, p. 53)

The bad

> The flowchart is a most thoroughly oversold piece of program documentation. Many programs don't need flowcharts at all; few programs need more than a one-page flowchart . . . the detailed blow-by-blow flowchart is an absolute nuisance, suitable only for initiating beginners into algorithmic thinking. (Brooks, 1975, p. 167)

The empirical

> Shneiderman *et al.* (1977) observe that of 45 FORTRAN texts, 14 used flowcharts extensively; 19 occasionally; and 12, not at all. In a number of experimental studies looking at composition, comprehension, debugging, and modification of programs, either with or without flowcharts, they found that in most circumstances flowcharts gave no advantage and in some circumstances they were a disadvantage. By way of control it is interesting that Wright and Reid (1973) found that flowcharts were better than the other formats they studied for conveying information about a complex decision. Similar results were obtained by Blaiwes (1974) and Kammann (1975).

What explanation can we find for these quite conflicting views? The answer seems to depend on how restricted the flowcharts are. In the studies by Wright and Reid, Blaiwes, and Kammann the flowcharts were expressions of sequences of decision which, though fairly lengthy, were just trees in structure; branches attached to branches. There is only one way to get from the root to any particular point, assuming one can only travel forwards. In Shneiderman *et al.*'s study, on the other hand, the flowcharts expressed loops and jumps. The flowcharts now form networks, not trees, and any point in the program can potentially lead you to any other point. So to understand what is going on at point A, it is necessary to search through the whole program and make sure that you have tracked down every single path that can lead to point A. Moreover, at point A it is quite likely that there is a bit of program that will only work if certain preconditions have been fulfilled, such as setting a register to a number which is the maximum number of attempts to be made at finding a given datum in a list, so it is *also* necessary to make sure that every path that leads to A meets the preconditions of A.

To sum up the case against flowcharts:

> Flowcharts look like spaghetti, and therefore encourage spaghetti-like programs. In particular, they provide irresistible temptations to jump into the middle of otherwise working constructions, violating their pre-conditions and generating untraceable bugs.   (Lindsey, 1977, p.36)

The spaghetti problem is illustrated in Fig. 9 which shows the art of making mayonnaise. The process is quite economical–nothing is duplicated–but it is not "structured" in the sense used by the structured programming school. In fact if closely examined it will be seen to be made out of two repetition loops which have been en-twined. One loop deals with adding egg and stirring, the other with adding oil and stirring. Mixing mayonnaise is a tricky art because it curdles if the oil is added too quickly, so the second loop may have to be interrupted to add more egg in a hurry. To achieve economy the designer has overlapped the loops, making "stir" mean both "stir in egg" *and* "stir in oil", and making "need more egg?" mean both "Have I got the right number to start with?" and "Has it started to curdle?".

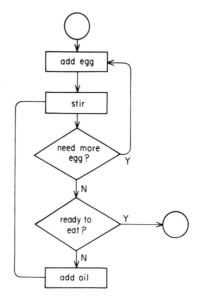

Fig. 9. Mixing mayonnaise. Take enough egg yolks, stir, then add some oil, stir, add some more oil, stir again, and so on until the mayonnaise has reached the right consistency and there is enough for your purposes. But if it starts to curdle, because the oil was added too much at one time, you will hurriedly need another egg yolk.

In Fig. 10 we see exactly the same process, but this time it has been made up strictly from a *restricted set of building blocks*. As a result it is a good deal less economical, using eight boxes instead of five, a 60% increase. On the other hand, at least according to the structured programming school, it ought to be rather easier to understand. They reason that one can first understand what happens within each building block, and then understand how the blocks are

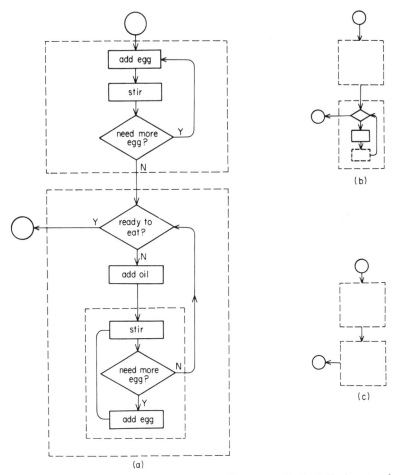

Fig. 10. Mixing mayonnaise by a "structured" process. Each dotted rectangle in (a) encloses a repetition block. Since it has one entrance and one exit, each repetition block can be viewed as a simple action box, as in (b) and (c). In this way the divide-and-rule policy can be applied and the action of the process can be understood a bit at a time. Notice, however, that more boxes are used than in Fig. 9, even though the same actions and tests are performed in the same order.

combined into bigger blocks; or if preferred one could work the other way, first understanding the overall structure and then looking inside each block at the smaller blocks within. In either case the policy is to divide and rule. But when the loops are allowed to overlap, as in Fig. 9, it becomes impossible to divide the process into parts; one must understand it all at one gulp or never.

The problems of unstructured flowcharts come to a head when we try to modify Fig. 9. in even an apparently trivial way. Many recipes for mayonnaise call for a single pinch of mustard after adding the eggs and before adding the oil. Where can we put this action in Fig. 9? The reader will soon discover that there is no point in Fig. 9 that will do; except for the start and stop points, every line in the flowchart may potentially be traversed several times so that mustard might get added several times. Figure 10 has no such difficulties, and there is a clear "cut-point" separating the eggs from the oil. Figure 10, is, in a word, tractable.

A "structured" flowchart, such as Fig. 10, can only be produced if the building blocks that are used have one entry and one exit; they can then be nested hierarchically within each other. That is what makes the divide-and-rule method of understanding them possible, because any combination of blocks can be regarded as another block. Figure 11 shows a set of building blocks with the necessary properties, sufficient (at least in principle) to describe any process.

Whether there is a substantial gain to be had from restricting flowcharts to these building blocks is not yet a matter that has been empirically tested, but it is certainly widely believed that divide-and-rule is such a powerful approach that there must be a gain. There is a price, however. In order to rebuild the mayonnaise process in a structured form, some of the boxes had to be duplicated, which must surely make it harder to extract some kinds of information from the chart. This price is worrying but not as steep as it looks. First, the 60% increase was obtained by deliberately choosing a severe example: normally the amount of duplication would be much less. Second, using sub-routines makes it unnecessary to duplicate any really long stretches. Third and most telling, the apparent duplication may often turn out to be separate parts of the process that are in truth conceptually distinct. In Fig. 9 we have one loop telling us to add enough eggs and stir, but we can get there for two entirely different reasons—i.e. the test, "need more egg?", can mean two entirely different things: "Are there enough eggs for the amount of mayonnaise you need?" or "Has it curdled?".

In short, the mayonnaise example shows that the apparent economy achieved by avoiding duplication is illusory, at least in this one instance. Wrapping up two tests in one will make it harder to answer the question "Under what conditions will I need to add eggs?"; will make it hard to make modifications, such as adding mustard; and will

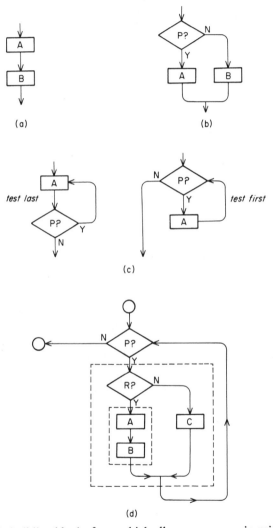

Fig. 11. Basic building blocks from which all programs can, in principle, be constructed. Restricting oneself to the constructions (with the possible addition of sub-routines) is claimed to make for easy understanding—but sometimes it is hard to preserve the property of being "well-structured" when revisions are necessary (cf. Figs 17 and 18). (a) Sequence; (b) selection; (c) two kinds of repetition; (d) combining the basic building blocks in a flowchart.

also make it difficult to follow through the flowchart in a simple manner, because it is necessary to remember what the test means each time one comes to it. (It is easy to visualize a beginner producing curdled mayonnaise because he didn't realize what the test meant the second time; the whole point of flowcharts is that even beginners should be able to follow through their instructions without going wrong.)

If the arguments for using a restricted set of blocks are accepted one can go a step further. Each of the blocks in Fig. 11 has to be identified by examining the configuration. They can instead be given an identifying symbol. There is then no further need to use the connectedness of flowcharts to indicate procedural flow; what has to be coded instead is the hierarchical relationships between blocks. Two different perceptual codes have been proposed. Nassi and Shneiderman (1973) devised a method using "insideness", while Jackson (1975) uses connectedness (Fig. 12).

Both insideness and connectedness have their adherents at present as suitable perceptual codes. Our own preference is for connectedness, because when boxes have to be drawn inside each other one has to be clever enough to start out with a big enough box at the very beginning, instead of just going on down the page as one can using the connectedness code. It is also probably easier to modify diagrams using Jackson's notation. Whichever code is used, however, these "structure diagrams" have grasped an important principle: by restricting the user to a few higher order blocks, instead of giving him very small blocks with which he can create whatever structures he likes, it becomes possible to use *names*. Instead of having to deduce the properties of a larger structure from its component pieces, one can recognize its name and recall its properties.

This aspect of restriction also has its disadvantages, which in a way echo the problems of duplicating boxes. Conventional flowcharts use very few symbols; for everyday purposes one can get away with start/stop boxes, actions boxes, and test boxes. (Flowcharts of big programs often use more, and an old IBM template of ours has twenty-three different symbols on it, but three is a minimum.) These boxes are very easy to explain and a beginner can learn the rules in a few minutes. Structure diagrams, however, use more complex symbols that take more effort to understand, and there are also more symbols to learn. How many different symbols can we afford to have, and of what degree of complexity, before the notation becomes too cumbrous for casual users?

The Venn diagram of Fig. 4 provides a further example of restric-

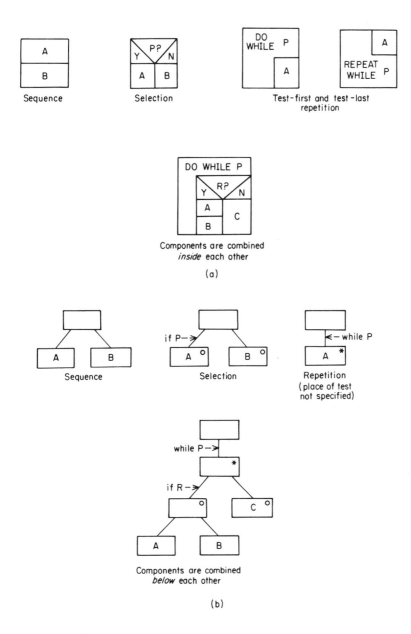

Fig. 12. Two forms of notation for the basic building blocks. (a) Nassi and Shneiderman's notation; (b) Jackson's notation.

tion which can demonstrate a syllogism. If one set is a sub-set of another (Fig. 4a) which overlaps with a third set (Fig. 4b), then it follows that the first set must also overlap (or be included in) the third (Fig. 4c).

This inference is "forced" by the perceptual properties of the diagram and does not require an understanding of set theory notation. Karnaugh maps, which can be used to express multi-dimensional Boolean relationships, provide a more practical application of the use of restriction facilitated by perceptual coding (see for example, Maley, 1970, p.24). Even the designer of complex systems can benefit from restriction offered by diagrammatic notation. Misunas (1973) concluded that Petri nets are of considerable advantage because the diagrams make it easy to grasp the circuit being modelled, and the constraints imposed by the diagram have a mathematically valid underpinning. However, Petri nets are of limited usefulness, and a well-structured language for the design of complex systems is still awaited (although De Remer and Kron, 1975, have made an impressive advance towards the static description of complex systems).

C. Redundant Recoding

This feature occurs most naturally not so much in "pure" diagrammatic notations as in enhancements to essentially linear notations. When one particular type of information is highly relevant to the user's task, it is helpful to present at least the bare bones in a perceptually coded form, meanwhile presenting the fully clothed bones in a symbolic form for a closer examination; thus the same information is coded in two ways, one of which is strictly speaking redundant.

In an experiment that we have ourselves carried out on problem-solving strategies we discovered that the form in which information was represented had a marked and significant effect on solution time. In one condition the subjects saw a set of statements of the form "From A you can get to B", and were required to select a sequence of statements which would join a starting and finishing place. Another condition which was identical to the first except that statements were of the form "You can get to B from A" was considerably more difficult, although it did not produce any significant changes in solution strategy. In other words, subjects could manage better when the information read like this: "J→P P→M M→C", than when the same information read: "P←J M←P C←M". It is quite surprising that such a trivial change could measurably affect performance, and shows that language designers need to be extremely careful about even the tiniest details.

The indentation of program text is a very familiar example of redundant recoding. In the previous section we showed how the property of nestedness could be displayed in flowcharts and structure diagrams; exactly the same property can be displayed in programs by means of indentation. But in a program the symbolic code already contains all the necessary information, and logically speaking the indentation is entirely unnecessary. The perceptual effect of indentation, however, can hardly be denied—see Fig. 13— and it is quite plain that when indenting is used, it is much easier to answer questions about whether one point in a program is heavily nested or not. Whether that is a *relevant* question in many situations is another point: Kernighan and Plauger (1974, p. 123) give a simple decision-tree as an example where indenting the *if* statements is irrelevant to the important question of how a particular branch may be reached. Although some empirical studies have been reported they are not good enough to cite.

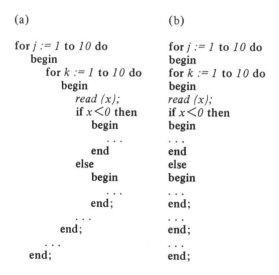

    (a)   (b)

```
(a)                           (b)

for j := 1 to 10 do          for j := 1 to 10 do
   begin                     begin
      for k := 1 to 10 do    for k := 1 to 10 do
         begin               begin
            read (x);        read (x);
            if x<0 then      if x<0 then
               begin         begin
                  . . .      . . .
               end           end
            else             else
               begin         begin
                  . . .      . . .
               end;          end;
         . . .               . . .
      end;                   end;
   . . .                     . . .
end;                         end;
```

Fig. 13. (a) A heavily indented program. (b) The same program without indenting. Does the indenting convey information relevant to the programmer's needs?

We can, however, report empirical studies on the effect of adding redundant recoding in symbolic form on top of indentation already present. This work forms part of a series of investigations into the design of conditional constructions for computer languages, which are reviewed elsewhere in this book (see Chapter 6) and which we need therefore only outline cursorily. Figure 14a shows a hierarchy of conditional constructions with appropriate indentation in a language we called **NEST–BE**. Figure 14b shows the same hierarchy expressed in a language called **NEST–INE** which is logically identical but contains unnecessary restatement of where the various adjectives start to apply and stop applying. When beginners learnt this second language, their programs were more often correct and they found their mistakes faster (Sime *et al.*, 1977b); when professionals answered questions about programs written in the two languages, they could answer one type of question very much faster in the second language—that being, of course, the type of question which called for the information that had been redundantly recoded. In another type of question, calling for different information, there was no statistical difference between the two languages (Green, 1977).

```
        (a)                    (b)

IF hard THEN           IF hard peel
BEGIN peel               IF green roast
    IF green THEN          NOT green grill
    BEGIN roast           END green
    END                  NOT hard
    ELSE                   IF tall chop fry
    BEGIN grill           NOT tall
    END                    IF juicy boil
END                        NOT juicy roast
ELSE                       END juicy
BEGIN                    END tall
    IF tall THEN        END hard
    BEGIN chop fry
    END
    ELSE
    BEGIN
        IF juicy THEN
        BEGIN boil
        END
        ELSE
        BEGIN roast
        END
    END
END
```

Fig. 14. The two styles of nested conditionals used by Sime *et al.* (1977b). Under some conditions, the redundancy in style (b) aids comprehension. (a) **NEST–BE**; (b) **NEST–INE**.

In our opinion, the fact that a considerable boost in performance can be obtained from redundant recoding expressed *symbolically*, as in **NEST–INE**, can only indicate that a much larger boost could be obtained if the information were to be carried *perceptually* instead. At present there is no data on that, although it will be fascinating to see what use can be made of the new developments in colour displays to give information.

D. Revelation and Responsiveness

The Gantt charts mentioned earlier can also be judged on their ability to reveal the underlying process that manipulates them. The dynamic changes inherent in a process may be revealed by using the appropriate representation. That is, if the schedule is being manipulated and developed according to some rules, the underlying process of development will appear more comprehensible and "natural" in the appropriate representation (Fitter, 1979). Furthermore, the importance of the display changing under the direct control of the user (possibly with the aid of a joystick or light-pen) has been stressed by Brooks (1977): "Moving images on a screen have great power to inform, images that move *in response* to one's manual manipulation seem to be perceived more as real things and studied more intently. Such systems achieve a high degree of transparency" (p. 629). Clearly interactive displays provide an important problem-solving tool in many diverse applications where an appreciation of the dynamics of the process is essential (e.g. computer-aided circuit design, air traffic control, financial forecasting, or simulators for perceptual-motor skills).

The need for a "conceptual window" into underlying processes has been argued by Sime and Fitter (1978). In the context of teaching children to program in the LOGO language, du Boulay and O'Shea (1978) have also discussed techniques for revealing underlying processes using plotting devices, turtles, tune boxes, etc. They point out that it is all very well to present the computer as a drawing machine as long as the child is controlling it by very simple commands which relate directly to the actions of the plotting device; but when the child is controlling it by a LOGO program it is no use at all to give error reports of the form "The pen has gone off the paper", because what is "really" wrong is in a different world—a sub-routine has been given invalid parameters, say. In other words, if the child is working at the level of a programming language, with all the various happenings that can occur in a program, the very devices that were intended as aids can actually obscure what is going on, because they are not rich enough in their behaviour to give a conceptual window into what the program is doing.

Revelation has become a critical issue in the design of data-base query languages. Many of these are based on relational algebra (Codd, 1970), but there seems to be a clear division of opinion about how best to present the data structure and access mechanisms to the user. One camp prefers a natural language interface, using for example conceptual graphs (Sowa, 1976) or alternative methods (Heidorn, 1976), while the other prefers to reveal the underlying structure by devising an interface language which reflects it.

For the first camp, Sowa argues:

> Conceptual graphs are precise enough to support logical inferences and data-base accesses, yet they are rich enough and flexible enough to serve as a semantic basis for natural languages. As a formal notation, the graphs can be used directly by the data-base designer for representing and analysing relationships between various domains in the data-base; displays and plotters could present the graphs for a two-dimensional view of the data-base. The designer could see the graphs as a display, but the end-user would not be aware of them. Instead, conceptual graphs could support an interface that would let the user talk about familiar data in a familiar terminology without the need for special query languages and computer-oriented conventions. *(op. cit., p. 3560)*

In contrast, others have argued that the user language should reveal the underlying structure of the data-base. Opinion has differed on how that is best achieved. For example, SQL (Denny, 1977), formerly called SEQUEL, uses a structured language with quite a rich syntax (presented to users as formula-like templates). Query-By-Example (Zloof, 1975), on the other hand, represents the relational tables directly to the user in two-dimensional pictures of tables, business forms, and reports. Two basic concepts are fundamental to Query-By-Example:

(i) "programming" within two-dimensional skeleton tables— filling-in the appropriate table spaces with an example of a possible solution;

(ii) the distinction between a "constant element" and an "example element" or variable, which is made by underlining the example elements.

Figure 15 contrasts the same query, "Find the names of employees whose salary is greater than their manager's salary", in SQL and in Query-By-Example.

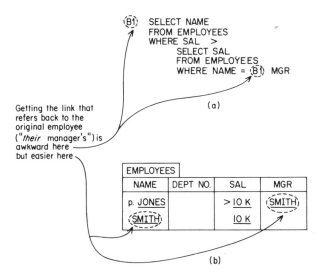

Fig. 15. The data-base query "Find the names of employees whose salary is greater than their manager's salary", expressed in two notations. (a) SEQUEL notation: (b) Query-By-Example notation.

Query-By-Example is an attempt to code the underlying mechanisms in a perceptual form. It appears to be more successful, as a beginner's language, than SQL, since, although no direct comparisons have been made, subjects performed better in an evaluation study of Query-By-Example (Thomas and Gould, 1974) than in an evaluation of SEQUEL (Reisner *et al.*, 1974). The importance of making the perceptual code match the semantic relationships inherent in the data was shown in further work by Durding *et al.* (1974), who found that subjects worked much more slowly when the match was destroyed.

Our conclusion is that if a graphic notation can reveal the structure inherent in the underlying data or the process by which entities are manipulated, then it will b'e superior to a linear symbolic language.

E. Revisability

Not every description of program is correct first time, and even when the bugs are out users frequently have that sudden afterthought—wouldn't it be nice if . . .?

Revising or modifying their work is an important part of users' lives, and so the notation must allow it to be done easily and accurately. It is a sad fact, but at this point some of what seemed so desirable for other purposes starts to seem rather less desirable. The problem is quickly outlined by returning to the topic of indenting program text. The indentations help by giving an elegant restatement of the nestedness information that is also conveyed by the words of the program. Now suppose the program has to be changed slightly (see Fig. 16). Precisely because the information is being conveyed twice, once by words and once by indenting, the program has to be changed in two ways—the words have to be changed and the indenting has to be corrected. Altering the indenting of a large section of text is a tedious job on most text editors, and all too often mistakes are made because each line has to be done separately and accurately. But the mistakes will be invisible to the compiler; they will only be seen by the user, who will find, if he has produced Fig. 16c instead of Fig. 16b, that the perceptual coding has now become a source of confusion hiding the truth about the program. It is difficult to ignore a perceptual coding in favour of a symbolic one, at least in that situation, so unless the perceptual coding is telling the truth it is a positive hindrance. Whereas if there had been no indenting in the first phase, life would have been that much easier, at least clerically. (A few automatically indenting compilers are now available, a development to be applauded.)

(a)	(b)	(c)
if a then	if a then	if a then
begin	begin	begin
$p; q;$	$p; q;$	$p; q;$
if b then $r;$	end;	end;
if c then s	if b then $r;$	if b then $r;$
else t	if c then s	if c then s
end	else t	else t

Fig. 16. Revising an indented program can be trying. In (a) the test on a controls the whole program. If the programmer decides the test should only control p and q, he ought ideally to change his program to (b), in which the last three lines have been realigned. (He should also remove the semicolon after q, in an ideal world.) It is tempting to save trouble by producing (c), where end has been moved and nothing else has been changed—but this version implies by its indenting that it is (a), so henceforth the indenting that was intended as an aid to comprehension has become a hindrance.

On turning to a more diagrammatic notation, such as the flowchart, we find that these problems of revisability are quite general. When a conventional flowchart has to be altered, all that is necessary is to rub out a few lines and put a few others in,

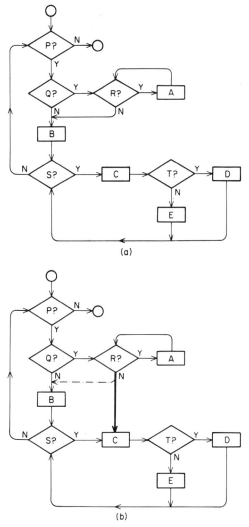

Fig. 17. A flowchart (a) and a modified version (b). The modification requires minimal clerical labour but whereas version (a) is "well-structured"—i.e. composed solely of nested components—the structuring has been destroyed in (b).

possibly altering some boxes here and there. Deciding whether the result works may be tricky, but at least the purely clerical aspects of making the change are straightforward enough. Figure 17a is readily converted to Fig. 17b. But what happens when the equivalent structure diagram has to be revised? Figure 18 shows

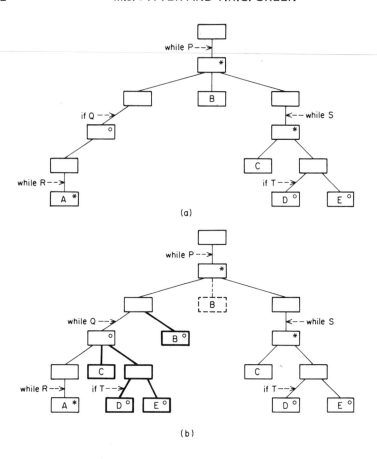

Fig. 18. Skeleton structure diagrams corresponding to the flowcharts of Fig. 17. (Normally boxes are not left empty in Jackson's notation, but are given a label showing what role they play, such as "Process a good card".) In (b) bold lines are additions, dotted lines are deletions. The property of being "well-structured" has been preserved but the modification requires far more clerical labour than the corresponding flowchart modification. Does that make it hard to discover the correct modification to make?

the changes necessary in Jackson's notation, and clerically speaking it is clearly a harder task to make the changes.

When we want to modify an indented program we pay the price of redundant recoding by having to make two sets of modifications, one of them redundant given the other. When we want to modify a restricted notation like a structure diagram, we pay a price for the restrictions, because more change is necessary. One last example, from Shneiderman (1977). When a tree-structured model of a data set is used to design a data-base query language, many-to-many relationships can be expressed in two ways, either by building two separate trees that are logically paired or by having redundant fields in segments. Once again, the notation that is clearer to use, the redundant fields, is harder to update.

In general, if the amount of structure in a notation is increased, it appears that it is harder work to modify it.

IV. CONCLUSIONS

We have described five principles concerning diagrammatic notations. A good notation should present relevant information in a perceptual form, or should use redundant recoding to present important parts of the symbolic information in perceptual code as well; it should restrict users to objects that can readily be understood; it should reveal the underlying mechanisms and be responsive to manipulation; and it should allow easy and accurate revision. There has been disappointingly little hard data to quote to show the effects of doing things one way rather than another, but it does seem plausible that the effects could be very large indeed.

Much of what data there is on the comparison of notational styles comes from linear, symbolic styles, particularly programming languages. A good deal of what we have said about diagrammatic notations applies equally to linear notations. Revisability is an obvious need. Restriction to "nicely structured" forms, as Barron puts it, is the principal plank of the school of structured programming. And redundant recording we illustrated from studies using purely symbolic coding. However, the overlap is not complete between diagrammatic and symbolic styles. Diagrams avoid the problems of "hark-back" created by the sequential nature of symbolic codes, but on the other hand they have problems of their own, notably the need to introduce a vocabulary of special symbols to enhance the small number of perceptual codes that are available to contemporary reproductive techniques.

Assessing the relative effects of these difficulties and advantages is no easy matter. The importance of vocabulary size, for example, will vary from one user population to another. Laboratory studies can help by giving some estimate of the maximum size of an effect in conditions that are carefully chosen, but they can do no more. To make matters particularly awkward some of our requirements appear to be contradictory!

The existence of contradictions is not an accident, not (as we see things) a phenomenon limited to our present state of knowledge and technique. For much of what we have said could be reduced to the principle that *different programs should be perceptually as different as possible.* If we consider them as points in some kind of imaginary space, then the effect of using perceptual codings is to spread the points out farther away from each other, reducing the risk of confusing one with another (i.e. of thinking that a program does something other than what it really does); and the effect of restricting the choice available to the user is to reduce the number of points that exist in the space, which is another way to increase their discriminability. Fine. But there is an inescapable conflict between those ideals and the ideal of revisability, for if we pursue the spatial analogy then revising a program means getting it from one point in that space to another point. *The further apart the points are, the more work has to be done to get from one to another.* There is no way to get away from that, so long as the analogy with a perceptual space holds good—and such analogies, which have been successfully applied in the psychology of perception, should be taken seriously.

In practice the increased cost of changing very distinctive programs is counterbalanced by the fact that they will need changing less often because they will less often be wrong. Nevertheless, in the ideal world programs would be simultaneously very distinctive and very easy to change. The only way we can expect that state of affairs is by much greater use of software aids.

In an important paper summing up her extensive research experience in pure and applied psycholinguistics, Wright (1978) arrived at the important conclusion that while applied psychology can offer some guiding principles, they will always be tentative, common-sense principles. What applied psychology can offer, that common sense cannot, is quality control: the testing of new designs to see how well they work. Very similar conclusions were reached by Brooks (1977), examining his experiences in designing various software tools for interactive graphics. There was no way, both authors concluded, to lay down principles that would ensure a good fit between objectives, human abilities and the performance of the system; all that could be done was to eliminate the misfits.

While that may be a depressing view for anyone who hopes to discover design principles of the same stature as Newton's Laws, it is a very reasonable one in the present context. It would be difficult to see how some of the conflicts we have mentioned could be resolved in any ultimate, theory-based way. Should one use structure diagrams with many symbols or with few? It will all depend. The principles we have outlined are enough for any designer to chew over; they are not enough, nor will they ever be enough, to replace the designer by a theory of design. But if the designer is necessary he is not sufficient on his own. One can aim at principles like the ones we have suggested, yet miss because of some unexpected quirk. Empirical techniques of quality control will continue to be necessary to evaluate new schemes before they become old problems.

REFERENCES

Barron, D.W. (1977). *An Introduction to the Study of Programming Languages.* Cambridge: Cambridge University Press.

Bingham, J.E. and Davies, G.W. (1972). *A Handbook of Systems Analysis.* London: Macmillan.

Blaiwes, A.S. (1974). Formats for presenting procedural instructions. *J. Appl. Psychol.,* **59**, 683–686.

Bohl, M. (1971). *Flowcharting Techniques.* Chicago: Science Research Associates.

Brooks, F.P. (1975). *The Mythical Man-Month.* London: Addison-Wesley.

Brooks, F.P. (1977). The computer "scientist" as toolsmith: studies in interactive computer graphics. In Gilchrist (ed.) *Information Processing 77.* Amsterdam: North Holland.

Central Computing Agency. (1974). *Evaluation of Programming and Systems Techniques: No. 6. Decision Tables.* Civil Service Dept. London: HMSO.

Codd, E.F. (1970). A relational model of data for large shared data banks. *Communications of the ACM,* **13**, 337–387.

Denny, G.H. (1977). An introduction to SQL, a structured query language. *Technical Report RA93,* IBM, Yorktown Heights, New York.

De Remer, F. and Kron, H. (1975). Programming-in-the-large versus programming-in-the-small. *Proceedings of the International Conference on Reliable Software,* Los Angeles.

Du Boulay, B. and O'Shea, T. (1978). Seeing the works: a strategy for teaching interactive programming. *Proceedings of the Workshop on Computing Skills and Adaptive Systems,* University of Liverpool.

Durding, B.M., Becker, C.A. and Gould, J.D. (1974). Data organization. *Technical Report RC 4956,* IBM, Yorktown Heights, New York.

Fitter, M.J. (1979). Towards more "natural" interactive systems. *Int. J. Man-Machine Stud.,* **11**, 339–350.

Green, T.R.G. (1977). Conditional program statements and their comprehensibility to professional programmers. *J. Occupational Psychol.,* **55**, 93–109.

Heidorn, G.E. (1976). Automatic programming through natural language dialogue. *IBM J. Research Dev.,* **20**, 302–313.

Jackson, M. (1975). *Principles of Program Design.* London and New York: Academic Press.

Jensen, K. and Wirth, N. (1975). *PASCAL User Manual and Report.* New York; Springer-Verlag.

Kamman, R. (1975). The comprehensibility of printed instructions and the flowchart alternative. *Human Factors,* 17, 183–191.

Kernighan, B.W. and Plauger, P.J. (1974). *The Elements of Programming Style.* New York: McGraw-Hill.

Lewis, B.N. and Cook, J.A. (1969). Towards a theory of telling. *Int. J. Man–Machine Stud.,* 1, 129–176.

Lindsey, G.H. (1977). Structure charts: a structured alternative to flowcharts. *SIGPLAN Notices,* 36–49.

Maes, R. (1978). On the representation of program structures by decision tables: a critical assessment. *Computer J.,* 21, 290–295.

Maley, G.A. (1970). *Manual of Logic Circuits.* Englewood Cliffs, New Jersey: Prentice-Hall.

Metzner, J.R. and Barnes, B.H. (1977). *Decision Table Languages and Systems.* London and New York: Academic Press.

Misunas, D. (1973). Petri nets and speed independent design. *Communications of the ACM,* 16, 474–481.

Montalbano, M. (1974). *Decision Tables.* Chicago: Science Research Associates.

Nassi, I. and Shneiderman, B. (1973). Flowchart techniques for structured programming. *SIGPLAN Notices,* 8, 12–26.

Reisner, P., Boyce, R.F. and Chamberlin, D.D. (1974). Human factors evaluation of two data base query languages: SQUARE and SEQUEL. *Technical Report RJ 1478,* IBM, Yorktown Heights, New York.

Shneiderman, B. (1977). Improving the human factors aspects of database interactions. *Technical Report No. 26,* Information Systems Management, University of Maryland.

Shneiderman, B., Mayer, R., McKay, D. and Heller, P. (1977). Experimental investigations of the utility of detailed flowcharts in programming. *Communications of the ACM,* 20, 373–381.

Sime, M.E. and Fitter, M.J. (1978). Computer models and decision making. In P.B. Warr (ed.) *Psychology at Work.* (2nd Edn.) Harmondsworth: Penguin.

Sime, M.E., Arblaster, A.T. and Green, T.R.G. (1977a). Structuring the programmer's task. *J. Occupational Psychol.,* 50, 205–216.

Sime, M.E., Green, T.R.G. and Guest, D.J. (1977b). Scope marking in computer conditionals—a psychological evaluation. *Int. J. Man–Machine Stud.,* 9, 107–118.

Sloman, A. (1971). Interactions between philosophy and artificial intelligence: the role of intuition and non-logical reasoning. *Artificial Intelligence,* 2, 209–225.

Sowa, J.F. (1976). Conceptual graphs for a data base interface. *IBM J. Research Dev.,* 20, 336–357.

Steele, G.L. (1977). Debunking the "expensive procedure call" myth or, procedure call implementations considered harmful, or lambda: the ultimate goto. *A.I. Memo No. 443,* Massachusetts Institute of Technology, Cambridge, Massachusetts.

Thomas, J.C. (1976). Quantifiers and question-asking. *Technical Report RC 5866,* IBM, Yorktown Heights, New York.

Thomas, J.C. and Gould, J.D. (1974). A psychological study of Query-by-Example. *Technical Report RC 5124*, IBM, Yorktown Heights, New York.
Van Tassel, D. (1974). *Program Style, Design, Efficiency, Debugging and Testing.* Englewood Cliffs, New Jersey: Prentice-Hall.
Wright, P. (1978). Feeding the information eaters. *Instructional Sci.*, 7, 249–312.
Wright, P. and Reid, F. (1973). Written information: some alternatives to prose for expressing the outcomes of complex contingencies. *J. Appl. Psychol.*, 57, 160–166.
Zloof, M.M. (1975). Query-by-Example. *Proceedings of the AFIPS National Computer Conference*, 44, 431–438.

8. Acquiring a First Computer Language: A Study of Individual Differences

M.J. COOMBS, R. GIBSON and J.L. ALTY

Computer Laboratory, University of Liverpool, Liverpool, England

I. DESIGNING SOFTWARE FOR THE UNIVERSITY USER

Until recently software designers and applications programmers have concentrated almost exclusively upon efficiency and robustness in designing and producing operating systems and applications packages. While such activities are of vital importance, the changing nature of the computing environment, and the relative shifts in costings between the different factors that contribute to the total cost of a package or system, have resulted in interest in other areas such as the user interface (e.g. Meurs and Cardozo, 1977), quality of error messages (e.g. Plum, 1977), documentation (e.g. Brown, 1974) and simplicity of use (e.g. Eason, 1976). A recent workshop at the University of Liverpool, for example, revealed a considerable spread of interest and activity in these areas (Alty and Coombs, 1978).

One of the most important alterations in the environment has been a rapid change in the type of user being served, particularly the increasing importance of users not skilled in computing, though expert in other areas such as medicine, social science, environmental studies and some commercial fields. This has led to an increasing demand for easy-to-use applications packages with error messages which can be readily understood by the non-technical user, and which can be documented comprehensibly and concisely. Another major change to the environment has been the move to interactive working, exposing the operating system designer to a host of problems which were previously shielded from him by expert data-processing departments. He himself now has to cope with a wide range of user demands and expectations (Miller and Thomas, 1977).

Although the need for computer systems which are sympathetic to the user has been recognized for some time, the designing of such systems is not a simple matter. There are a number of questions the designer must ask which do not have obvious answers. What constitutes a "good user interface"? Should the software reveal to the user the workings of the system when solving his problem, or should it present an interface which simulates methods used in his own discipline? What are the characteristics of good documentation? Does the simplification of error messages make complex problems easier to solve? Finally, how can users best be educated to recognize their difficulties and how may they be advised in an economical and effective manner?

Within the computing community there is no shortage of "folk theories" concerning each of the above questions, but such "theories" need to be applied with care. Although they often seem attractive, leading to straightforward proposals for helping the user, they can usually work effectively only under very limited circumstances. The use of three such "theories" may be presented to illustrate this point.

Following a discussion of good programming practices by Weinberg (1971), the authors of introductory texts routinely advise that mnemonics should be used for variable names and procedure calls. This makes good psychological sense both as an aid to memory for the program writer and an aid to understanding for the end-user. However, the extensive use of mnemonics in a data-base language such as ROBOT (Software Sciences, 1977) in which mnemonic variables names are intended to be run together into sentences, without differentiation, can lead to confusion. The following string is correct code but meaningless English:

FOR EACH UNREPORTED AGAINST REVISE INVOICE PRODUCING REP-DETAIL

It is clearly the case that, if mnemonic variable names and procedures are to be written in sequence, it is necessary to provide a syntactic system to ensure the resulting string is coherent. It would also, of course, be necessary to provide the usual safeguards to prevent users from using the names of procedure calls as variables.

A second principle often expounded by computer professionals is that computer programming languages and control languages which look like English are easier to use. Research conducted at the MRC Social and Applied Psychology Unit at the University of Sheffield indicates potential problem areas here. In a series of experiments (reported in Green et al., 1978) the Sheffield group tested the ease

with which novice programmers could write various forms of computer conditional. In one comparison it was found that a format
which approximated to English (Fig. 1a) was less prone to error than
an ALGOL-type condition (Fig. 1b). The most frequent problem with
the ALGOL conditional arose from the matching of the scope markers
BEGIN and END. However, any advantage that the natural English
type of conditional may have had when expressing a single condition
disappeared when conditions were nested two or more deep (Fig. 1c).

(a)   (b)

IF green **THEN** chop fry   IF green **THEN**
ELSE roast   **BEGIN** chop fry **END**
END   (c)   **ELSE**
                                                    BEGIN roast **END**

    IF green **THEN**
      IF juicy **THEN** boil
      ELSE chop fry
      END
    ELSE roast
    END

Fig. 1. Two forms of conditional (after Green *et al.*, 1978).

A final example is the assertion that a user may best be able to
learn to use a programming language if he knows about the basic
workings of a computer. Mayer (1976) devised some experiments to
teach novice programmers to write FORTRAN both with and without
a model. It was found that while the less able students found the
model of great value, the more able students found that it hindered
their learning.

From the above examples it may be argued that the simple application of "folk theories" to systems design may have unexpected and
undesirable results. It is perhaps better that they should be used to
stimulate experimentation rather than to provide ready-made solutions. However, many of the results which have emerged from
empirical research to date are also narrowly prescriptive, and it is
not possible for the designer to wait for a comprehensive set of
principles for the writing of sympathetic software (Alty, 1977) to
emerge. This leaves systems designers and applications programmers
in a very unsatisfactory position. While the long-term solution to the
problems of the non-professional computer user is undoubtedly the
development of more friendly systems, there remains the immediate
problem of helping a rapidly expanding user population to use

conventional computer systems.

II. INDIVIDUAL DIFFERENCES IN THE ACQUISITION OF COMPUTING SKILLS

It is a common observation that there are great differences in people's ability to make use of conventional computing facilities. Early studies in programming, for example, found large discrepancies in performance, even at the professional level (Weinberg, 1971). In universities it has been observed that some individuals make more effective use of facilities than others who have undergone the same training and whose needs are just as great. Of those attending post-graduate courses, some individuals require little more than a manual and a user number, while others require careful explanation before they are able to complete even the simplest task. This discrepancy is particularly interesting in a university environment because it suggests that some factors other than general intelligence (motivation, prejudice, etc.) are operating.

It is proposed that the study of such individual differences in the learning of computing skills would provide valuable insights into ways of effectively supporting computer users. First, an analysis of the contrasting learning strategies used by successful and unsuccessful students should provide data on the nature of computing information itself and the cognitive skills required for its acquisition. This would aid in the design of documentation, machine-based "help" systems and training courses. Secondly, it would be helpful to be able to identify in advance those individuals needing special attention so that they can either be given an individual training program or be instructed at an early stage in the relevant basic learning skills.

There are various methods available for establishing the approaches people take to acquiring computing information and for assessing those which are most successful. It would be possible, for example, for subjects to be given some computing task and to record the actions they take or the thoughts they have while completing it. Such so-called "protocol" analysis has been undertaken successfully in classic studies both by Bruner *et al.* (1956) in a study of concept formation and by Newell and Simon (1972) in a study of problem-solving. However, we considered that this method would be unsatisfactory for our purposes. Any realistic computing task would require a very diverse range of activities, hence the protocols would be expected to be very complex and so difficult, if not impossible, to analyse without some well-established theory of programming to help identify significant details. As stated above, no suitable theory exists.

We have adopted an alternative approach. Subjects are presented with two tasks—a "target" task and an "indicator" task. The objective of the method is the characterization of subject performance on the target task about which little is known, and this is achieved by careful choice of a "formally" derived indicator task which is expected to have some predefined relationship with the target task. Information from the indicator task will then be used to generate hypotheses about strategy and performance on the target task. These hypotheses can then be tested in a conventional manner. This chapter confines itself to the first stage of this approach concerned with the generation of hypotheses on the acquisition of computing skills. The second stage, the testing of such hypotheses, is currently in progress at Liverpool and will be reported elsewhere.

A. The Programming Tests (Target Task)

The computing tasks selected for the present study were concerned with programming itself. This was not only for the obvious reason that programming is central to all computing activity but also because a user with significant programming skill should find debugging simpler (Youngs, 1974) and should find it easier to search for relevant information in documentation. Unlike other researchers (e.g. Mayer, 1976; Sime et al., 1977), it was decided not to devise a special learning task but to study the learning of a widely used language (FORTRAN) by a normal intake of novice university users. The course was fairly typical of the FORTRAN courses taught in most computer centres. Save for the early introduction of the concept of the subroutine, emphasis during lectures was placed on the description of language structures. Students were encouraged to practise the use of these structures on standard problems at the end of each lecture.

The devising of a method for assessing learning raised a number of problems. The measurement of programming skill offers the investigator a heterogeneous set of variables ranging from individual language structures to the logic of the final program. Thus it might be concluded that an adequate test of learning would need to be very complex. However, it is often found in learning experiments that subjects' ability to handle complex sets of variables is determined by a small number of different underlying skills. In previous work by Coombs (1977), for example, into the learning of physical manipulative procedures, it was found that ability to recall the units of a procedure was independent of ability to recall them in the correct order. These two capabilities proved to be the product of two very different coding strategies.

Following a consideration of the standard programming tasks students were expected to be able to perform at the end of a FORTRAN course, it was observed that there were strong parallels with the manipulative procedures studied by Coombs (1977). Most importantly they both involved:

(i)   learning about a large number of individual operations;

(ii) the assembling of these operations in a particular order so as to achieve some given processing objective.

It was therefore decided to test separately for the above two activities in our assessment of programming skills. This decision was supported by programming professionals at Liverpool who maintained that some students had difficulty in assembling logical units into a working program even though they were able to grasp the workings of individual units. Two target tests were accordingly devised to assess the sequential and the non-sequential attributes of programming. These were known as the "Logic Test" and the "Statement Test".

The Statement Test consisted of three short FORTRAN programs, together with a specification of the functions of each (Fig. 2). The

```
THE PROGRAM READS A TIME IN THE FORMAT OF A 24 HOUR
CLOCK, FOR EXAMPLE: 1436
AND OUTPUTS THE RESULTS IN THE FORMAT OF A 12 HOUR
CLOCK, FOR EXAMPLE: 2 36 P.M.

+ + + + + + + + + + + + + + + + + + + + + + + + + + + + + + + + + + + + + + + + + + + + + + + + + + + + + + + + + + + + +

       SUBCALL TIME(TVALU,HRS,MINS,PERIOD)
*  INPUT DATA IS TUVALU THE TIME AS 24 HR. CLOCK,
C  OUTPUT DATA IS THE HRS AND MINS OF 12 HR. CLOCK,
C  WIITH INDICATION
C      PERIOD=1 FOR A.M.
C  (ISE)    =2 FOR P.M.
       INTEGER TVALU,HRS,MINS, -PERIOD
       MINS=TVALU-(TVALU/100)*100
       HRS=TVALU-MINS
C  DETERMINE IF A.M. OR P.M.
       IF (HRS.G.E.13 GOTO WELL
       5PERIOD=1
       RETURN
10     HOURS=HRS=12
       PERIOD=2
       RETURN
       END
```

Fig. 2. A sample question from the Statement Test.

instructions were in the correct order to run the program, but contained a number of clerical and syntactic errors (21 in 56 lines of code) randomly distributed throughout the complete test, but no more than one per line. The errors were all contained within a single statement. The programs were presented on standard computer cards, the statements being presented at the top of the cards.

The Logic Test (Fig. 3) consisted of three short (19-line) FORTRAN programs which were also punched and printed on cards. Each deck comprised a complete set of correctly written instructions but supplied in random order. Working from a specification of the program's operation (including the function of the sub-routine), the subject had to reconstruct the original. Any permissible deviation from the "standard" order was allowed, although the programs were written so as to minimize the number of variations.

> The problem is to produce a program which reads the three lengths of the sides of a triangle, and decides if it is a right-angled triangle. The input data comprises the three lengths of the sides and an acceptable tolerance (or error) such that
>
> $$|A^2 - B^2 - C^2| \leqslant \text{Error}$$
>
> for a right-angled triangle, where A is the length of the largest side and B and C are the lengths of the other sides.

```
      MASTER MAIN
      READ(5,100) A,B,C,ERR
      BIG=A
 C    PUT THE LARGEST VALUE (SIDE) IN BIG
      IF (B.GT.BIG) BIG=B
      IF (C.GT.BIG) BIG=C
 C    EVALUATE THE TEST CONDITION FOR RT. ANGLE TRIANGLE
      TEST=2.0*BIG*BIG-(A*A+B*B+C*C)
      IF (ABS(TEST).LE.ERR) GOTO 10
 5    WRITE(6,200) A,B,C
      STOP
 10   WRITE(6,300) A,B,C
      STOP
 100  FORMAT(4F10.1)
 200  FORMAT(1X,11HNO TRIANGLE,3F10.1)
 300  FORMAT(1X,11HTRIANGLE OK,3F10.1)
      END
      FINISH
```

Fig. 3. A sample program from the Logic Test (statements were presented in random order).

B. The Search for an Indicator Task

It is reasonable to assume that individual differences in the learning of computing skills are related to the strategies adopted by the learner in handling computing information. A pattern of such strategies will make up an identifiable cognitive style.

The literature on cognitive style is extensive, although most writers make their definitions in terms of polar dispositions which seem to be variations on a theme. Examples of these are:

convergent thinking	– divergent thinking	(Hudson, 1966)
vertical thinking	– lateral thinking	(de Bono, 1967)
analytic	– gestalt	(Levy and Sperry, 1968)
verbal	– spatial	(Paivio, 1971)
sequential	– simultaneous	(Luria, 1966)
field independence	– field dependence	(Witkin *et al.*, 1962)

It may be tempting to add, from within computer science, the distinction between "bottom-up" and "top-down" approaches to programming (e.g. Dahl *et al.*, 1972; Hoc, 1977).

The above dichotomies appear to have many features in common but they are by no means identical. Each can be described in terms of two contrasting modes of cognitive functioning: (a) a mode that is active, analytical, articulated, specific and critical; (b) a mode that is passive, global, vague, diffuse and uncritical. However, as is pointed out by Wallach (1962), mental operations given an identical interpretation on this scheme do not always correlate and similar correlational tests yield evidence for a given theoretical placing on one occasion but not on another. It was therefore considered important that any attempt to assess the correlation of computer users' cognitive style with computing performance should use a test of style which had some features in common with the computer learning task.

One writer who has devised a classification of individual differences in cognitive style, using tasks which are in some measure similar to our programming tasks, is Pask (1976a, b). Pask has described two basic dimensions of human information-processing: (a) a dimension concerned with the management of data selected from the world (attention); (b) a dimension concerned with the mental representation of that data (mental model-building). The attention dimension draws the binary distinction between the local features of a subject material and the global features. The representation dimension draws the distinction between the representation of information as a system of rules (what it does) and as a description (what it is). By relating the two dimensions we get four cognitive modes (Fig. 4).

Pask (1976c) argues that rule-building is most effectively undertaken using low-level, local information, and description-building is most effectively undertaken with attention to global features. Hence, learners tend to polarize to operating primarily within two of the quadrants. Learning activity within the rule-building/local quadrant is termed "Operation Learning" and learning activity within the description/global quadrant is termed "Comprehension Learning." In addition to the systematic learning processes identified as Operation and Comprehension Learning, with their characteristic effects on recall, Pask allows for a third class of learning. This is seen as independent of style and is thus described as "incidental" in the sense that it does not result from a systematic method of working through the learning material. The outcome of such learning will be memory for surface, and to some extent isolated, items of information.

Fig. 4. Schematic representation of information-processing dimensions (after Pask, 1976c).

The sequential nature of computing provides a conceptual link between a student's approach to learning and the two programming tests described above. FORTRAN is usually taught by first introducing students to individual language structures (DO loops, conditionals, etc.) and then requiring them, without significant assistance, to assemble the structures into a logical order to solve a problem. This latter activity is not formally taught. It was our contention that students who were primarily Operation Learners would have a dual advantage on the Logic Test but would have no advantage on the Statement Test.

With reference to the Logic Test, the Operation Learner would be expected to pay close attention during the learning of individual language structures to their internal logic, testing for himself their operation under varying conditions. The Comprehension Learner, on the other hand, would only attempt to remember the global features of the structures as given, making no close distinction between their essential features and those arising from their illustrative context. For example, an Operation Learner given illustrations of the use of the DO loop in which the counter variable was always incremented by one would be likely to infer that this may not necessarily be the case and so ask a question to test the inference. However, the Comprehension Learner would be expected to accept the example as given and always work within that framework until he was presented with a different example. The Operation Learner would thus have an advantage when faced with the Logic Test, having a clear idea of the essential features of the structure independent of context. Structures could therefore be readily assembled, without interference, to complete the problem computation. It was also expected that the Operation Learner would gain a second advantage by applying an Operation strategy to the problem itself which would help him to isolate *its* essential structure. The Comprehension Learner, on the other hand, would be expected to have stored global features of the learning context in his representation of the language structures, which would make his performance less flexible owing to interference with the context of the Logic problems.

It was proposed that the Statement Test would not be sensitive to learning style. All errors were contained within individual statements and were not related to the logic of the programs (many were typical typing errors). It was therefore expected that they could be identified from incidental learning of the surface features of the language. They would not "look right" to anyone who had been exposed to FORTRAN, irrespective of the student's understanding of the workings of the language or of its global organization.

C. The Spy-ring History Test—A Candidate for the Indicator Task

Pask provides an instrument for assessing the mix of Comprehension/Operation Learning a student uses to complete a complex learning task. It is called the "Spy-ring History Test". The test is completed in one session of some length (2½ hours), the time being divided between a learning phase and a test phase. The learning material concerns changes in a communication network between five spies in three countries over three years. In the learning phase some background information relating to the character of each of the spies and the political economic situation in each of the countries is given to the subjects and this is followed by representations of the communication network between the spies. The information is presented one year at a time in both the form of a sample list of eight successive transactions and a directional graph showing the channels open between the five spies. The lists are of the form shown in Fig. 5.

From	*To*
Dryden (T)	$\longrightarrow$ Euclid (O)
Euclid (O)	$\longrightarrow$ Caesar (T)
Byron (R)	$\longrightarrow$ Ajax (R)
Dryden (T)	$\longrightarrow$ Euclid (O)
Euclid (O)	$\longrightarrow$ Caesar (T)
Byron (R)	$\longrightarrow$ Ajax (R)
Caesar (T)	$\longrightarrow$ Dryden (T)
Ajax (R)	$\longrightarrow$ Byron (R)

Fig. 5. Representation as a transaction list (1986).
R = Ruritania; T = Transylvania; O = Olympia.

The first three transactions would be interpreted as "The spy Dryden, in Transylvania, sent a message to Euclid, in Olympia; then Eyclid passed this message to Caesar, in Transylvania; then Byron, in Ruritania, sent a message to Ajax, also in Ruritania". Information concerning who can send to whom (as deduced from the occurrences of actual transmissions in the lists) can also be represented as a directed graph (see Fig. 6).

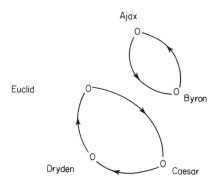

Fig. 6. Representation as a directed graph (1986).

In this representation the order information is lost. Lists and graphs are presented simultaneously on an overhead projector.

Each subject is asked to reproduce both the list and the graph correctly as soon as it is removed from view. It is unlikely that subjects can do this after only one exposure as they are deliberately overloaded with information, with the intention that they should explore alternative representations and adopt one convenient to themselves. Subjects are thus given as many exposures as they wish in order to learn each year's list and graph to a criterion of one perfect recall. With group administration this poses something of a problem, if, as is likely, the subjects learn at different rates.

Following the learning phase, subjects are asked to complete the test booklet. The questions test for rote learning of background information, reproduction of lists and graphs, and ability to make deductions from the lists and graphs (which may well have been forgotten).

III. THE INITIAL PROGRAMMING STUDY

A. Method

Subjects were all volunteers from a standard two-week Introductory FORTRAN Course run by the Computer Laboratory, University of Liverpool for staff and postgraduates (five two-hour sessions each week). The 28 people attending the course were asked on their first day to volunteer to take part in the study, which could "help the Laboratory design better programming courses". Sixteen people agreed to participate, although only 11 people completed both the Spy-ring History Test and the computing tasks. All 16 had no previous experience of computing and were all scientists or engineers.

The Spy-ring History Test was administered to small groups of 3–5 people during the first four days of the course and the programming tests were administered on the final day. Half the people attending on the final day completed the Statement Test first, while the other half completed the Logic Test. Subjects were given a maximum of 30 minutes to complete each test. Three subjects who were identified as being strongly biased towards Operation Learning and three subjects who were biased towards Comprehension Learning (two of them strongly biased) were observed closely during the practical sessions and were interviewed in some depth at the end of the course.

B. Results

The Statement Test was scored using the $P(\overline{A})$ measure employed in signal-detection theory (McNicol, 1972, pp. 31–40). This measure took a line of text as a unit, a line containing an error being regarded as a "signal" trial and one which did not as a "noise" trial. Any line marked as containing an error was taken as a "yes" response, the absence of such a declaration was taken as a "no". A mark on a line containing an error is thus a "hit", and a mark on a line containing no error is a "false alarm". These variables were used to compute a non-parametric measure of sensitivity $P(\overline{A})$. Being a measure of probability the range of possible scores was from 0–1.

The Logic Test was scored using a measure based upon transitional error (Coombs, 1977). The cards returned by each subject were numbered according to their position in the original program. The error score was then calculated by counting the number of incorrect transitions in the program, e.g. the following permutation of the first five integers contains three incorrect transitions: 1 2 4 3 5. Total transitional errors for all three test programs were then expressed as a proportion of possible transitions using the following formula

$$(\text{max. TE} - \text{observed TE}) / \text{max.TE}$$

(where TE = transitional error score; the max.TE for a list of length $n = n-1$).

This method of scoring only takes into account the first-order sequential dependencies. Furthermore, it does not take account of possible reasons for misplaced cards, nor does it rate the "grossness" of any individual error. However, what it lacks in sensitivity it makes up for in objectivity and ease of scoring. This method of scoring has also been found to be most adequate in connection with serial order recall in the learning of manipulative procedures.

The scoring of the Spy-ring History Test is complex. The scoring scheme provided with the test provides for summarization at two levels. Raw scores to sets of individual questions are combined to give seven sub-scores, and these are in turn combined to give four main scales: Neutral score (incidental learning); Operation Learning; Comprehension Learning; and Versatility (the ability to employ either strategy as appropriate). All scores are expressed as a proportion of the maximum possible score.

Means and standard deviations for the two FORTRAN tests and the four Spy-ring scores are given in Table 1. Comparisons were made between the four Spy-ring scores and the two FORTRAN tests using the Pearson r correlation (Table 2). There proved to be no significant correlations between the Statement Test and any of the Spy-ring measures. However, scores on the Logic Test correlated with Operation Learning and Versatility at greater than 0·01 level. It was also noted that there was no significant correlation between the two FORTRAN Tasks (Pearson $r = 0.30$, ns).

TABLE 1

Summary of test scores for the initial programming study

Scores	$\bar{x}$	s
Statement Test	0·92	0·050
Logic Test	0·58	0·180
Neutral	0·70	0·193
Operation Learning	0·57	0·132
Comprehension Learning	0·63	0·138
Versatility	0·16	0·160

All scores range from 0–1 ($N = 11$).

C. Discussion

It can be seen from Table 2 that our hypotheses concerning the Logic Test were supported, the Operation Learning score of the Spy-ring test being correlated with it sufficiently at above the 0·01 level. On the other hand, there was no significant correlation between the Logic Test and either Comprehension Learning or the Neutral score. It therefore appeared reasonable to seek guidance on the psychological requirements for the sequential aspect of programming from the theoretical basis of the Operation/Comprehension distinction. It may also be noted that there was a significant correlation at the 0·01 level between Versatility and the Logic Test. This does not contravene any particular expectation. Although Versatility was intended to represent an ability to use either of the learning strategies as appropriate, the Spy-ring data indicated that the Operation Learning component predominates.

TABLE 2

Summary of comparisons between the programming tests and the Spy-ring scores

Comparisons	r	Significance
Statement Test with		
Neutral	0.40	ns
Operation Learning	0.44	ns
Comprehension Learning	0.11	ns
Versatility	0.14	ns
Logic Test with		
Neutral	0.11	ns
Operation Learning	0.83	$p < 0.01$
Comprehension Learning	0.13	ns
Versatility	0.74	$p < 0.01$

$N = 11$; $df = 9$

The results concerning the Statement Test were less clear. While there was no significant correlation between the Test and either of the two styles of learning, there was also no significant correlation with the Neutral score (incidental learning). However, it was noted that Operation Learning and the Neutral score were both correlated with the Statement Test at a higher level than Comprehension Learning, although the two correlations were well below the 0·05 level of significance. It could thus be concluded that the Operation and Neutral scores tapped a greater proportion of the learning attributes that contributed to success on the Statement Test than Comprehension Learning but the variance accounted for was small. There could be two reasons for these correlations and it is not possible to choose between them on present evidence. The first concerns the operation of a ceiling effect on the Statement Test— it may be noted from Table 1 that the mean success was 92%— while the second concerns the presence of a fourth learning factor not measured by Spy-ring. Given this problem it was decided to delay further interpretation of the results until we had tested their reliability by a replication on a second group of FORTRAN learners.

IV. A REPLICATION OF THE PROGRAMMING STUDY

A. Method

The study was repeated using a second standard Computer Laboratory FORTRAN Course. Twenty-one users attended the course, all of them being completely new to programming. The backgrounds of the students were similar to those in the first study—they were mainly physical scientists. All tests were administered by a different investigator to the initial study.

The only modification made to the test materials was the presentation of the Statement Test on a sheet of computer print-out rather than on cards. The three programs were listed in order down the page, subjects being asked to underline errors on the sheet.

The drop-out rate unfortunately proved to be greater than in the initial study. Only 12 people stayed to complete the course and of those only 8 had taken all our tests. We therefore had just sufficient numbers to serve as a replication but with much smaller numbers than intended.

B. Results

The scoring of all tests was identical to that used in the inital study. A summary of results is given in Table 3.

TABLE 3

Summary of test scores for the replication programming study

Scores	$\bar{x}$	s
Statement Test	0·69	0·210
Logic Test	0·43	0·240
Neutral	0·49	0·295
Operation Learning	0·60	0·166
Comprehension Learning	0·64	0·226
Versatility	0·16	0·148

All scores range from 0—1 ($N = 8$).

Comparisons between the two programming tests and the Spy-ring scores were again made using Pearson correlations. All comparisons are summarized in Table 4.

The replication again found that there was a significant correlation between the Operation Learning score and the Logic Test but not between the Comprehension Learning score and the Logic Test.

TABLE 4

Summary of comparisons between the programming tests and Spy-ring scores

Comparison	r	Significance
Statement Test with		
Neutral	–0·17	ns
Operation Learning	0·74	$p < 0.05$
Comprehension Learning	0·22	ns
Versatility	0·58	ns
Logic Test with		
Neutral	0·03	ns
Operation Learning	0·74	$p < 0.05$
Comprehension Learning	0·47	ns
Versatility	0·49	ns

$N = 8$; df $= 6$

However, it also produced a significant correlation between the two programming tests ($r = 0.83$, $p < 0.01$), and between the Operation Learning score and the Statement Test.

C. Discussion

The above replication may be judged to be partially successful. Both studies revealed a significant positive correlation, as hypothesized, between the Operation Learning scale of the Spy-ring History Test and the test requiring the ordering of statements to form a working program (Logic Test). However, on this occasion the correlation between the Logic Test and Versatility failed to reach significance at the 0·05 level.

Following the definition of Operation Learning provided by Pask (1976c), it may be concluded that the successful completion of a FORTRAN programming course (at least, of the type usually offered by university computer centres) is in some measure associated with attention to local detailed information and the representation of that information in rule form. The student must concentrate on learning the rules governing the relationships between low-level logical units. Students applying such a strategy will succeed on such a course, while those seeking to obtain a general, global description of the computing structures presented on the course will fail (or it will take them longer to get started).

Although both samples supported the predictions made with respect to the Logic Test, and the initial study yielded no significant correlation between the two FORTRAN tests, the replication presents a more confusing picture. In particular it was found that the Statement Test (error-spotting) score correlated significantly with the Logic Test itself and was uncorrelated with the Neutral score.

Taken alone the replication may be considered to provide less-than-convincing support for the hypotheses proposed. Nevertheless, it does not negate the findings of the initial study; it suggests the usual picture of complications and qualifications absent from the first set of data. Overall, it does seem that the Spy-ring History Test does isolate a component of cognitive performance which is relevant to computing skills research. That it is able to do this with such a heterogeneous sample population is quite surprising. Given these problems in interpretation, it was necessary to further continue our analysis. However, because of the complexities encountered in interpreting performance on the Statement Test, it was decided to reserve further consideration of this task for future investigation. We therefore concentrated on the Logic Test.

The two studies potentially generated rather more data than is reflected in the gross scores, in the form of the individual items of the Spy-ring History Test. The author of Spy-ring provides for a set of rather tentatively labelled sub-scales but the nature of the test is such that the relationship of the individual items to the theoretical distinctions they purport to assess is often less than obvious. A further analysis of the Spy-ring History Test was therefore undertaken to clarify such relationships.

V. A FACTOR ANALYSIS OF THE SPY-RING HISTORY TEST[1]

Advantage was taken of the availability of raw scores on individual question items of the Spy-ring test to investigate its internal

[1] All analyses in this section were performed using the Statistical Package for the Social Sciences (SPSS), Version 5, implemented on the 1906S at the University of Liverpool Computer Laboratory.

structure. The sub-scales in the official scoring scheme are to some extent hypothetical, so it is of considerable interest to see if they are statistically valid. A total sample of 19 subjects was obviously inadequate for such an investigation. Although these were the only subjects for which computing skills scores were available, many more Spy-ring Tests had been administered at Liverpool. A number of these were collected together to make a total sample of 34. This gave a 34 x 47 matrix which is, of course, not analysable by factor analysis. However, the 47 raw scores were easily reduced to 23 by elimination of some items (where questions gave scores which were perfectly correlated) and others could be summed (where grouping seemed both acceptable on *a priori* grounds and was supported by correlational data).

The 34 x 23 matrix was analysed using a principal components analysis followed by a varimax rotation using SPSS. Unity was used for the estimated communality for each variable. This produced nine factors (criterion: $\lambda 1 \cdot 0$); a scree test did not strongly indicate that the number of factors should be limited further, so this full set was retained.

Consideration of the factor loadings gave rise to the following interpretations.

Factor 1: *Recall of both lists and graphs for the first two years of the spy-ring* —there were wide variations in patterns of recall performance over the three years. This factor may discriminate between individuals who failed to find a suitable representation for the information, and suffered from increasing interference, and those who found a representation after some practice and improved their recall over the years (see Factors 7 and 8)—19·5% of variance.

Factor 2: *Declared use of uninterpreted patterns and symmetries* — this factor loads mainly on two questions asking the subject to declare whether he looks for "patterns and symmetries in the spy-rings . . . using them to work out the type of patterns which would occur later"—11·3% of variance.

Factor 3: *Rated use of message lists rather than graphical information* —this factor again loads mainly on two variables. The main one of these is a declaration that the subject treated the test as "a memory task relying upon message lists and their ordering"—10% of variance.

Factor 4: *Declared use of the rules governing the transmission of messages*—the main loading is on the declaration that the subject used "the rules for transmitting messages between spies in a given year"—8·7% of variance.

Factor 5: *The rote learning of background information making up the Neutral score*—7·7% of variance.

Factor 6: *Interpreted systematic changes over time*—this factor mainly loads on a set of questions concerned with changes in the spy-ring over time—6·3% of variance.

Factor 7: *Use of systematic representation based on lists*—this factor loads on recall of the list for the final year and the generation of a list for the fourth year on the spy-ring—5·7% of variance.

Factor 8: *Systematic representation based on graphs*—this factor loads on recall of the final graph—5·3% of variance.

Factor 9: *Declared insight into the rules governing temporal changes*—4·6% of variance.

The groupings of Spy-ring History Test items within the nine factors is in no way similar to the groupings that make up the sub-scales in the official scoring scheme. It was therefore necessary to reassess the relationship between performance on Spy-ring and the computing skills tests, particularly the Logic Test. To do this the Factor Score Coefficients were used to compute factor scores for each of the 19 students in the two studies and these were correlated with the Logic Test and Statement Test scores. A summary of results is given in Table 5.

TABLE 5

Correlations between factor scores and the Logic Test

Factor Scores	Logic Test	
	r	Significance
1	0·21	ns
2	0·10	ns
3	0·04	ns
4	0·43	ns
5	−0·24	ns
6	0·19	ns
7	0·55	$p < 0.05$
8	−0·04	ns
9	−0·12	ns

$N = 19$; df $= 17$

It can be clearly seen from Table 5 that Factor 7 correlates with the Logic Test at above the 0·05 level and Factor 4 correlates at just below the 0·05 level. It may be recalled that Factor 7 is labelled as the "use of systematic representation based on lists", and Factor 4 is labelled as the declared "use of rules governing the transmission of messages". We thus find additional support for our former interpretation of the significant correlation between Operational Learning and the Logic Test.

VI. FURTHER DISCUSSION

Sufficient information has been collected in the two studies already reported, in the factor-analysis and in interviews with subjects taken at the end of the FORTRAN courses to attempt a characterization of the behaviour of both successful and unsuccessful learners of the programming and Spy-ring material. This will be mainly done with reference to users showing a distinct bias towards Operation or Comprehension Learning. Performance on the Spy-ring History Test will be considered first.

Observations of subjects taking the Spy-ring Test indicated that they all relied principally upon rote learning for the first-year graphs and lists; they looked for simple patterns in the materials and constructed mnemonics. Subjects with a strong Operation bias, however, soon abandoned this method and sought to reduce the complexity of material, while subjects with a strong Comprehension bias occupied themselves with the construction of increasingly elaborate mnemonics. These mnemonics were often constructed with reference to the graphical representation, although this was by no means always the case.

The extreme Operation Learners appeared to pursue the reduction of complexity as a conscious goal rather than as a result of some other goal such as mnemonic building. They were also fairly uniform in their methods of reduction, which usually fell into two stages. First, they abandoned any attempt to remember the real-world scenario, including the names of spies, early in the test and concentrated upon learning an abstract version of the lists. Secondly, they sought to reduce the abstract lists to a small number of types of transactions between spies and a set of transformation rules which would generate the complete lists from the list of transaction types.

Contact with students during the FORTRAN courses again indicated that those with a strong Operation bias differed in definable ways from those with a strong Comprehension bias. These were most easily observed during the practical sessions where:

- Operation Learners completed more of the exercises than Comprehension Learners;
- Operation Learners accepted the problems as given and solvable while Comprehension Learners often questioned the validity of the problems;
- Operation Learners often extended the problems once they had solved them as presented, while Comprehension Learners rarely experimented with the language outside the set exercises;
- Operation Learners rarely asked general or conceptual questions about the computer, while these were common from Comprehension Learners.

It is possible to explain all of the above differences in terms of the different coding strategies adopted by Operation and Comprehension Learners on the Spy-ring material. The application of an Operation Learning strategy to FORTRAN information presented during lectures would produce a representation of language structures which was more abstract, and so less bound to the context of specific examples, than a Comprehension strategy. It would therefore be expected that the Operation Learner would be more flexible in his problem-solving. He would thus be more likely to be able to solve a problem in the form given; the abstract nature of his representation of a language structure would also make him more likely to "play" with different applications of the structure. The Comprehension Learner, on the other hand, would be expected to represent the language structures in relatively concrete terms, often with some detail from the examples used during instruction. Such representations would be difficult to apply to new problems. This may account for the questioning by Comprehension Learners of the validity of the problems themselves. The request for conceptual information could be seen as an attempt to obtain criteria for abstracting the critical features of language structures prior to attacking the problems.

VII. CONCLUSIONS

The studies reported in this paper allow us to make four assertions about the learning of a first computer language:

(i)   It is possible to define at least two different learning styles in a population of novice computer users.

(ii) Students exercising one of the styles—Operation Learning—are more successful at assembling language structures into an effective algorithm.

(iii) The successful learning style is defined by close attention to detail and a preference for procedural representation.

(iv) Success in the correct identification of individual language structures is independent of learning style.

However, these results beg a number of important issues which need to be resolved before they can be applied with confidence to helping computer users. In particular, detailed information is needed on the strategies students used to select and integrate computing material during the FORTRAN course and on the nature of the rule-based representation used by successful students. Information is also needed on the effects of adopting a Comprehension or Operation approach to learning computing over a long period of time. The initial advantage of an Operation approach may not be sustained when the programmer becomes more experienced and begins to write more complex programs. Finally, we know little of the interactions between the two learning styles and the teaching methods adopted on the Liverpool courses.

The proposals made above and in Section VI are intended as an indication of the different types of processing activity employed by computer users while learning FORTRAN. Although it is not certain that they represent in detail the mental activities involved, the foregoing research has established the relevance of an Operation strategy to learning a computer language. Further work will test the validity of the detailed characterization of strategies and it is hoped that this will lead to a general description of the activities that are likely to result in effective and efficient acquisition of computing skills. These could then be available to guide the design of courses and to help lecturers diagnose and resolve the problems of individuals.

ACKNOWLEDGEMENTS

We would like to thank Brian Walsh of the Computer Laboratory, University of Liverpool for preparing problems for the programming tests.

Research for this paper was supported by Social Science Research Council grant number HR4421.

REFERENCES

Alty, J.L. (1977). Software futures. Paper given at the OR Society Conference, Oxford.

Alty, J.L. and Coombs, M.J. (eds) (1978). *Proceedings of the Workshop on Computing Skills and Adaptive Systems*. Computer Laboratory, University of Liverpool.

Brown, P.J. (1974). Programming and documentary software projects. *Computing Surveys*, **6**, 213–220.

Bruner, J.S., Goodnow, J.J. and Austin, G.A. (1956). *A Study of Thinking*. New York: Wiley.

Coombs, M.J. (1977). Modality and order recall in learning from television, with reference to teaching medical procedures. Ph.D. Thesis, University of Liverpool.

Dahl, O.-J., Dijkstra, E.W. and Hoare, L.A.R. (1972). *Structured Programming*. London and New York: Academic Press.

De Bono, E. (1967). *The Use of Lateral Thinking*. London: Jonathan Cape.

Eason, K.D. (1976). Understanding the naive computer user. *Computer J.*, **19**, 3–7.

Green, T.R.G., Sime, M.E. and Fitter, M. (1978). Thoughts on behavioural studies of programming. *AISB Q.*, **30**, 8–15.

Hoc. J.-M. (1977). Role of representation in learning a programming language. *Int. J. Man–Machine Stud.*, **9**, 87–105.

Hudson, L. (1966). *Contrary Imaginations*. London: Penguin.

Levy-Argesti, J. and Sperry, R. (1968). Differential perceptual capacities in major and minor hemispheres. *Proceedings of the National Academy of Sciences*, U.S.A., **61**.

Luria, A.R. (1966). *Higher Cortical Functions in Man*. New York: Basic Books.

McNicol, D. (1972). *A Primer of Signal Detection Theory*. London: Allen and Unwin.

Mayer, R.E. (1976). Some conditions of meaningful learning for computer programming: advance organizers and subject control of frame order. *J. Educ. Psychol.*, **68**, 143–150.

Meurs, J. van and Cardozo, E.J. (1977). Interfacing the user. *Software-Practice and Experience*, **7**, 85–93.

Miller, L.A. and Thomas, J.C. (1977). Behavioural issues in the use of interactive systems. *Int. J. Man–Machine Stud.*, **9**, 509–536.

Newell, A. and Simon, H.A. (1972). *Human Problem Solving*. Englewood Cliffs, N.J.:Prentice-Hall.

Paivio, A. (1971). *Imagery and Verbal Processes*. New York: Holt, Rinehart and Winston.

Pask, G. (1976a). Conversational techniques in the study and practice of education. *Br. J. Educ. Psychol.*, **46**, 12–25.

Pask, G. (1976b). Styles and strategies of learning. *Br. J. Educ. Psychol.*, **46**, 128–148.

Pask, G. (1976c). *Conversation Theory: Applications in Education and Epistemology*. Amsterdam: Elsevier.

Plum, T. (1977). Fooling the user of a programming language. *Software-Practice and Experience*, **7**, 215–221.

Sime, M.E., Green, T.R.G. and Guest, D.J. (1977). Scope marking in computer conditionals—psychological evaluation. *Int. J. Man–Machine Stud.*, **9**, 107–118.

Software Sciences Products Ltd. (1977). ROBOT: The Organisational Information Management System.

Wallach, M.A. (1962). Commentary: active-analytical vs. passive-global cognitive functioning. In S. Messick and J. Ross (eds) *Measurement in Personality and Cognition.* London: Wiley.

Weinberg, G.M. (1971). *The Psychology of Computer Programming.* New York: Van Nostrand Reinhold.

Witkin, H.A., Dyk, R.B., Faterson, H.F., Goodenough, D.R. and Karp, S.A. (1962). *Psychological Differentiation: Studies of Development.* London: Wiley.

Youngs, E.A. (1974). Human errors in programming. *Int. J. Man–Machine Stud.*, **6**, 361–376.

9. Generating a Programming Environment for Learners

C. BOLDYREFF

South West Universities Regional Computer Centre, University of Bath, Bath, England

I. OVERVIEW

In the mid-1960s, in order to study "rule learning", Professor G.A. Miller at Harvard Center for Cognitive Studies, in a project entitled "Grammarama", programmed a computer to conduct experiments with artificial grammars (Miller, 1970). In 1965 Donald Norman and John Schneider (referred to by Miller, pp. 169–173) used computer programs to study the most effective way to decompose a grammar into rules so that it might be learned by identifying correct and incorrect productions. The work to be described here has been concerned with teaching students how to apply the syntactic rules of the class of artificial languages known as "programming languages"; it is not expressly concerned with the problem of how they might discover these rules, although it has been useful to draw on the methodology of Miller's Grammarama.

The prototype system was a program to teach first-year computing students how to form logical expressions using a notation for these derived from the PL/1 programming language. The program introduced itself as a game in which the student could opt to be either the producer of expressions for checking by the program or checker of program-produced expressions. A score was kept by the program; this was summarized when the student decided to finish. The rules for forming logical expressions were available throughout each session. The program was capable of entering an explanatory mode in which it explained how it produced expressions from the rules and how it checked them, if the student's responses suggested this would be helpful. At this stage, the program was simply an extended version of

Miller's Polish notation program used in the Grammarama Project. It was tested with first-year undergraduate computing students, and found to be satisfactory within its limited goals.

During these studies, it became apparent that such a system could be used to teach almost any formal language syntax provided that the sub-programs for rule presentation, expression production and syntax checking were slotted into the original program. To automate this process, a program has been developed which works from a definition of the syntax of a programming language and generates appropriate sub-programs to be used in the framework of the original syntax game program.

The sub-program generator was tested with the SEQUEL language as described by Chamberlin and Boyce (1973). The resulting program to teach SEQUEL brought out the need to clarify exactly how expressions of specified difficulties can be produced, and from these studies there developed a use of production systems to describe the general teaching strategy. Thus the method of syntax game programs has been generalized, so that both the programming language to be taught and the teaching strategy to be used in the production of examples are both expressed by sets of production rules. The use of production rules to describe the teaching strategy allows the syntax game programs to act as test-beds for different teaching strategies.

The production rules which form the input to the sub-program generator are expressed in Van Wijngaarden notation. The sub-program generated to present the rules may translate the rules if desired into another notation, Backus Naur Form (BNF) or syntax diagrams; this flexibility allows for experiments to be carried out using different notations, for example to determine notation preferences if any exist.

The student must come to understand the notation of the rules as well as learning the language defined by the rules. Students' individual differences may predispose them to learning one notation rather than another.

The purpose of these studies has been to provide systems for generating programs which can be adapted easily to individual students' needs. Some students may benefit from the elegant richness of the full two-level Van Wijngaarden notation while others only require the modest economy of BNF notation. Readers unfamiliar with the grammars cited here should consult Cleveland and Uzgalis' thorough introduction to grammars (1977).

While it is not particularly worthwhile to attempt to teach the complete syntax of a programming language in this way, the complexity of expressions presented and checked would not be suitable for presentation and checking in an interactive mode. For simple languages and for sub-sets of more complex languages, a syntax game is a useful learning vehicle. It not only introduces students to the syntax of a particular language, it also familiarizes them with the use of a formal definition.

II. HISTORICAL BACKGROUND

Miller's interest in artificial languages arose out of work undertaken in the late 1950s with Noam Chomsky. In 1957, they collaborated in a study of algebraic systems which Chomsky then called "finite state grammars". These were thoroughly described in Chomsky's work, *Syntactic Structures*, published in 1957. Chomsky drew on the branch of mathematics concerned with the formal properties and generative capacities of various grammars and made an original contribution to the study of formal systems, providing a definition and hierarchical classification of Phrase Structure Grammars (PSGs) (Lyons, 1970).

Miller assumed that when people learn a natural language, they do not memorize all the particular sentences that comprise it; rather they learn rules for producing and interpreting any sentence. In order to investigate "rule learning", he began to experiment with artificial languages. He described his method as inductive in that the subject could only obtain information about which sentences were part of the language and from this, by induction, had to learn the rules. In Miller's case, these were PSG production rules.

Miller was quick to see the advantages of automating his experiments. It was found from the start, for example, that human experimenters were simply not fast enough or accurate enough to run the experiments if grammars of any complexity were used. In addition to speed, Miller noted that the subjects had great faith in the computer and appeared to believe it would not trick or cheat them:

> I find it remarkable that an intelligent college student will let a machine tell him repeatedly that he is wrong without losing either heart or face; if a human experimenter told him the same thing, he would seethe with indignation.   (Miller, 1970, p. 159).

In evaluating his automated experiments, Miller had the insight to distinguish between people learning a language and people learning to make the machine respond in a certain way. It is, of course, possible to do the latter without a complete understanding of the language; and it is important to bear this distinction in mind when assessing the claims of any automated teaching system.

As the complexity of the grammar increased to the point where it became impossible to learn (inductively) the whole grammar at once, Miller considered using the strategy of teaching the rules one by one and combining them later. Some work was done along these lines by Norman and Schneider, who used a context-free grammar and found that Polish notation was more easily learned when the rules were learned individually. The three rules they taught were:

$$(P1) \ S \rightarrow P$$
$$(P2) \ S \rightarrow NS$$
$$(P3) \ S \rightarrow ASS$$

or in BNF:

$$<S> ::= P | N<S> | A<S><S>$$

Miller postulated that decomposing the grammar to be learned into a regular grammar with infinite rules would be of little help to learners; to Miller, a grammar with infinite rules was ridiculous. At almost the same time, such a grammar, the so-called "W-grammar" form, was being developed and used to describe the then new programming language, ALGOL 68 (Van Wijngaarden, 1976).

Grammars have been used to describe programming languages since the late 1950s. In 1959, John Backus, a designer of ALGOL 60, developed a grammatical form equivalent in descriptive power to Chomsky's Type 2 PSG, which was used to describe the context-free syntax of ALGOL 60. Cleaveland and Uzgalis claim that Backus notation, commonly BNF, has been used in the description of every major programming language since ALGOL 60.

Since their inception, context-free grammars describing programming languages have provided a useful teaching aid. Because of their similarity in form to dictionary definitions, most people find the use of a context-free grammar almost intuitive, and so refer to it naturally as they would a dictionary to settle exactly how any particular notion in the language has been defined.

III. SCOPE OF THIS WORK

Miller's inductive method of rule learning may be compared with the way in which many people approach learning a programming language. For the most part, beginning programmers have no understanding of explicit grammatical rules for describing the languages in which they are programming. Like Miller's subjects, they submit their attempts at program production to the compiler and it responds by identifying correct productions and signalling errors if any occur.

Beginning programmers may be concerned only with getting results and may not wish to gain any more of an understanding of the language than is necessary for their immediate goals. This attitude is acceptable for "one-off" programmers but encourages a dangerous dependency if maintained over a programming career of any length. The following slogan appeared on a Christian Aid collection envelope: "Give a hungry man a fish, and you feed him for a day. Teach him to fish and you feed him for life". In the context of programming, a distinction might equally be made between the benefits of imparting specific information of limited utility and those which accrue from imparting more general information applicable in a wide range of cases. Where possible, specific information should be derived as an instance of a more general principle; such an approach enables students to gain a more systematic understanding of the programming language. In contrast, experienced programmers learning a language use the language definition as an independent source of information, deriving programs from it. While the experienced programmers may use the compiler to check their understanding of the definition, they also make use of the definition as an independent check on the compiler.

The work to be described involved setting up an environment in which beginning programmers could be presented with a simple programming language definition and be allowed to test their understanding of it. The environment took the form of a syntax game program. The production rules of the language were first made explicit, the student then being encouraged to apply them in forming particular statements in the language. As in Miller's system, the fast and accurate computer was retained to check that the student had applied the rules correctly. Moreover, an automated system like Miller's has the advantage that it is trusted by the students to perform objectively. The work rests on an adapted form of Miller's thesis, concerning the learning of natural languages, discussed above: when people learn a programming language, they do not need to memorize all the particular programs which comprise it; rather they need to learn rules for producing and interpreting any program in the particular programming language.

In designing the program, it has been useful to draw on the ideas proposed by Jonathan D. Wexler in a report entitled "A Design for Describing (Elementary) Programming Problem Generators in an Automatic Teaching System" (1973). In this report, Wexler outlined a grammar for describing programming problems which he used in a program to teach machine-code programming. The sub-programs in the syntax game program operate in two modes; one in which expressions are generated and presented to the student for checking and one in which the student submits expressions to the appropriate sub-program for checking. In the former mode, ideas from Wexler's system have been developed; while in the latter, the work of compiler theorists in automatic syntax analysis has been drawn upon (Gries, 1971).

A generative system was chosen because of a desire to get away from the drill-practice type of computer-aided instruction which merely presents pre-stored sequences of problems. Such systems are unnecessarily inflexible in their mode of presentation. Inflexible drilling is harmful because it is not adaptive to the needs of the student and it does not provide the student with a framework in which particular examples can be related to general models. There is no reason why a computer should be used to perpetuate one of the worst possible teaching techniques. If a computer-aided instruction program emulates a programmed learning textbook, then the computer merely becomes an expensive substitute for a book.

IV. PROTOTYPE SYSTEM

The prototype system was a program which simply gave students practice in forming logical expressions and checking them. The program can be run interactively from a terminal, and the way in which it functions is described below. The rules for producing logical expressions are presented. These may be reviewed at any time during a session if the student wishes. The program can then either present randomly generated examples of expressions to the student for checking, or the student may input expressions to the program for checking, in which case the program will determine whether or not the input is well formed and will reply appropriately. The mode of operation is flexible and chosen by the student, who may alter it at any point. In both modes the program is capable of error reporting. Where the student's replies are correct this is not strictly necessary, and the program gives the student the option of having this information. Because the program allows the student to enter expressions for checking, it must be capable of doing the checking; it also checks expressions which have been program-generated as this enables errors to be pinpointed in context for the student.

The level of difficulty at which the program presents material is either determined by the sort of productions entered by the student, or in the case of program-generated examples is started arbitrarily low and increased if the student's responses suggest a readiness for more difficult examples. The level of difficulty is proportional to the complexity of the expression. The complexity is determined by the number of recursive calls of the syntax checking procedure required when checking the example. Syntax checking is accomplished using the method known as "recursive descent" (described by D. Gries in *Compiler Construction for Digital Computers*) which has been extended in the program to a functional form.

In the prototype system, example formulae are generated as follows:

(i)   Start with a proposition letter.
(ii) Add a negation sign in half the cases.
(iii) Add an operator and letter either on the left or the right in half the cases.
(iv) Put brackets around the whole in half the cases.
(v)   Repeat from (ii) until formula has the required length (where this is simply a measure of the number of symbols).

The generator starts with a branch which results in the least number of symbols. As all branches except one are recursive, obviously the non-recursive branch must be chosen first. The next branch chosen is the one which will result in the least number of symbols being added, and so on using the remaining branches in order of their generative power until a formula of the required complexity has been built up.

The generative power (g.p.) is a measure of how many symbols a branch will add to the statement under construction. In the grammar for well-formed formulae (wffs) used by the program, the generative powers of the branches are as follows:

(Branch 1) <ppn letter> has g.p. of 1;
(Branch 2) <not><wff> has g.p. of $\geqslant 2$; and
(Branch 3) <wff><connective><wff> has g.p. of $\geqslant 3$.

In this grammar, simple inspection of the grammar is enough to enable the generative power of a branch to be determined.

If the student continues to make mistakes in either checking or production mode, the program enters a remedial mode and begins to explain how it checks an example as well as indicating how it generates examples according to the rules. As mentioned above, the student may request to review the rules at any time.

The student may terminate a session at any point, and the program will give a summary of the session so far. The program then administers a brief interview which allows the student to give an evaluation of the effectiveness of the program.

All input and output which takes place during a session with the program is monitored. The information recorded includes the date of usage, the start and finish times of a session, and the student's name. These files have proved useful in determining how effectively the program functions as a teaching aid.

A short extract from a student's session with the program is recorded below (C=program, S=student).

C: THE DATE IS 02-12-78
C: THE TIME IS 17:53:48
C: I AM A LOGIC TUTOR PROGRAM. PLEASE TYPE IN YOUR NAME:
S: GEORGE
C:
C: *WELCOME TO THE FORMULA GAME*
C: . . . .
C: THIS GAME WILL ALLOW YOU TO PRACTICE PRODUCING AND
C: CHECKING OF FORMULAS. THE OBJECT OF THE GAME IS TO
C: PRODUCE ONLY WELL-FORMED FORMULAS IF I'M CHECKER
C: AND TO CHECK CORRECTLY EACH EXAMPLE I PRESENT IF YOU
C: ARE THE CHECKER.
C: I'LL KEEP SCORE ON HOW WELL YOU GET ON.
C: WOULD YOU LIKE TO KNOW THE RULES OF THE GAME?
C: JUST TYPE Y FOR YES, N FOR NO:
S: Y
C: WELL-FORMED FORMULAS (WFFS FOR SHORT) ARE PRODUCED
C: USING THE FOLLOWING RULE:
C: $\langle$WFF$\rangle$: := $\langle$PPN LETTER$\rangle$ | $\tilde{}$$\langle$WFF$\rangle$ |
C: $\langle$WFF$\rangle$$\langle$CONNECTIVE$\rangle$$\langle$WFF$\rangle$
C: $\langle$PPN LETTER$\rangle$: :=A|B|C|D|E|F|G|H...ETC
C: $\langle$CONNECTIVE$\rangle$: :=&|| AND OR
C: N.B. ANY WFF MAY BE ENCLOSED BY BRACKETS, FOR EXAMPLE:
C: A|B IS A WFF AND SO IS (A|B)
C: WOULD YOU LIKE MORE INFORMATION?
S: Y
C: THE RULES TELL YOU HOW A WFF IS PRODUCED:
C: A WFF IS EITHER A PROPOSITION LETTER WHICH IS ANY LETTER
C: OF THE ALPHABET (E.G. A) OR A WFF IS A NEGATION SIGN ($\tilde{}$)
C: FOLLOWED BY A WFF (E.G. $\tilde{}$A) OR A WFF IS A WFF FOLLOWED
C: BY A CONNECTIVE (& OR |) AND ANOTHER WFF (E.G. A&$\tilde{}$A).
C: ANYTIME WE PRODUCE A WFF, WE CAN PUT BRACKETS ROUND IT,
C: FOR EXAMPLE, (A&$\tilde{}$A) IS A WFF.

```
C:
C: IF AT ANY POINT, YOU'D LIKE TO REVIEW THE RULES,
C: JUST ENTER THE MESSAGE: RULES
C:
C: IF AT ANY POINT, YOU'D LIKE TO QUIT WHILE YOU'RE AHEAD
C: OR OTHERWISE, ENTER THE MESSAGE: QUITS
C: AND I'LL GIVE YOU A RUN DOWN OF THE GAME SO FAR BEFORE
C: QUITTING.
C:
C: EITHER I CAN ACT AS CHECKER OF WFFS OR YOU CAN. YOU CAN
C: CHANGE PLACES BY ENTERING THE MESSAGE: CHANGE
C: DO YOU WANT TO BE CHECKER?
C: JUST TYPE Y FOR YES, N FOR NO:
S: Y
C: AN INTERPRETATION OF THE FORMULA IN ENGLISH IS:
C: DOGS LIKE BANANAS AND PIGLETS HAVE TAILS
C: INTERPRETATION KEY:-
C: ˜=NOT  &=AND  |=OR
C: H=DOGS LIKE BANANAS
C: V=PIGLETS HAVE TAILS
C: IS THE FOLLOWING FORMULA WELL FORMED?
C: H&V    ?
C:
S: Y
C: THAT'S CORRECT
C: AN INTERPRETATION OF THE FORMULA IN ENGLISH IS:
C: NOT.
C: INTERPRETATION KEY:-
C: ˜=NOT  &=AND  |=OR
C: ˜ ?
C:
S: Y
C: THAT'S INCORRECT. DO YOU WISH TO KNOW WHY?
S: Y
C: ˜
C: >
C: PPN LETTER REQUIRED AT THIS POINT.
   ..............................................................
C: AN INTERPRETATION OF THE FORMULA IN ENGLISH IS:
C: PEOPLE ARE MILK AND (NOT COWS HAVE BANANAS AND (PEOPLE
C: HATE FLEAS OR PIGS LOVE PEOPLE ) ).
C: INTERPRETATION KEY:-
C: ˜=NOT  &=AND  |=OR
C: D=PEOPLE ARE MILK
```

```
C: M=COWS HAVE BANANAS
C: V=PEOPLE HATE FLEAS
C: U=PIGS LOVE PEOPLE
C: IS THE FOLLOWING FORMULA WELL FORMED?
C: D& (~M&(V|U)) ?
C:
S: Y
C: THAT'S CORRECT.
S: CHANGE
C: ENTER A WFF FOR CHECKING:
S: D& ~~~~~~~~~~~~~~~D
C: THAT'S CORRECT.
C: ENTER A WFF FOR CHECKING:
S: QUITS
C: FINAL STATE OF PLAY
C: I WAS CHECKER FOR
C:            4 WFFS
C:            3 OF THESE WERE CORRECT.
C: YOU WERE CHECKER FOR
C:            18 WFFS.
C:            11 OF THESE WERE CORRECT AND YOU CHECKED
C:            9 OF THEM OUT PROPERLY. OF THE
C:            7 DUFF WFFS, YOU LET
C:            2 OF THEM SLIP BY.
C: THAT WASN'T A BAD GAME. BETTER LUCK NEXT TIME.
C: THE TIME IS 18:16:22
C: NOW THAT THE GAME IS OVER, I HOPE YOU WON'T MIND
C: TAKING PART IN A SHORT INTERVIEW. AFTER EACH QUESTION,
C: ENTER AS MANY LINES AS YOU WISH IN REPLY AND WHEN
C: YOU HAVE COMPLETED YOUR REPLY, ENTER: #FINISH
C:
C: DO YOU THINK YOU'VE LEARNED ANYTHING BY PLAYING THIS GAME?
S: YES
S: #FINISH
C: DID YOU ENJOY PLAYING THE GAME?
S: YES THANKS
S: #FINISH
C: ANY COMMENTS, CRITICISMS, OR SUGGESTIONS?
S: MORE INCORRECT EXAMPLES PLEASE
S: #FINISH
```

The program was nicknamed the "Logictutor" and proved popular among first-year students; many of them are addicted to interactive computing in any form. An element of novelty was introduced by including an interpretation of the expression in "English" which greatly amused the students. Although Miller found that undergraduates could not learn Polish notation for logical expressions by his purely inductive method, students using the program had little difficulty mastering the notation it gave for logical expressions.

It has been difficult to abstract any recurrent themes from the scripts of student sessions. It was certainly very rare for the program to enter into its remedial mode; possibly because the student needed to make three consecutive mistakes to trigger the remedial mode of the program. Students were more likely to make mistakes in the checking mode than in the production mode, although checking was usually the mode in which the students chose to begin playing and so inexperience rather than any inherent difficulty in checking may be the reason for this difference.

The Logictutor was not developed any further because it did not provide enough complexity in either the production set or the language described by the rules to test this method of teaching. With the Logictutor, it was clear that if the students failed to understand the notation of the production rules, they could not approach the tasks set except by trial and error. Their induction was not as crude as that employed by Miller's subjects; they explained their strategy as determining exactly what the rules meant. This emphasis reinforced the view about the importance of the rules in providing a general model of the language.

V. GENERALIZED SYSTEM

In order to investigate further this method of teaching an artificial language, it was generalized so that it could be used to teach the syntax of any language which could be specified using production rules. One object of this generalization was to determine how complex a language could effectively be presented in this way, and another was to experiment with various notations for the production rules themselves. In particular, the generalized program was designed to enable some ideas from Van Wijngaarden or two-level grammars to be incorporated into the rules.

As the set of production rules becomes larger, it is more difficult to grasp easily as a whole. Two-level grammars provide a means of generalizing the production rules. In a two-level grammar there is at the top level a context-free system for defining metanotions in the language; these metanotions may be substituted for hypernotions in the hyperrules which are models of the production rules, thus the rules of the context-free grammar describing the language are derived.

Van Wijngaarden's notation for the context-free grammar may be used to present the rules to the student. This notation is more compact than BNF and has the advantage of including a rule terminator.

The following extracts from rules giving a two-level definition of SEQUEL illustrate the form of input to the sub-program generator:

Metaproductions
ALPHA:a;b;c;d;e;f;g;h;i;j;k;l;m;n;o;p;q;r;s;t;u;v;w;x;y;z.
NOTION::ALPHA;NOTION ALPHA.
EMPTY::.

General Hyperrules
NOTION list: NOTION; NOTION, comma symbol, NOTION list.
NOTION sequence: NOTION; NOTION, NOTION sequence.
NOTION option: NOTION; EMPTY.
NOTION expression: NOTION term;
        NOTION term, NOTION operator, NOTION expression;
        left par symbol, NOTION expression, right par
        symbol.
....

Hyperrules
Statement: Basic Query expression.
Basic Query term: Label option, selection list,
                where clause option.
Basic Query operator: union symbol;
                    intersection symbol;
                    difference symbol.
Label: string, colon symbol.
string: letter sequence.
letter: letter ALPHA symbol.
selection: select from option, table name,
                group by option, dupl option.

The generation of a recursive-descent syntax-checker from the rules turns out to be quite simple. A function which returns "True" or "False" according to whether or not it recognizes a notion is generated for each notion in the language. The general hyperrules are dealt with by functions of functions which utilize the simple functions and return "True" or "False" as each hypernotion is recognized. By retaining recursive descent as the checking method, the final program can still obtain a measure of complexity from the depth of recursion and can pinpoint with ease the cause of errors in a production.

The programming of the sub-program generator, to produce the sub-program which presented examples to the student, brought out the need to examine how a context-free grammar (CFG) may be used to generate statements with a specified level of difficulty. In theory, a CFG is specifically a generative grammar. A CFG generates a language in the following way:

   (i)   Start with a string (called the "string in hand") consisting only of the distinguished symbol.

   (ii) Apply productions from the grammar's set of production rules to the string in hand until it consists only of terminal symbols (i.e. members of the terminal vocabulary).

Such a string is said to be a member of the language generated by the grammar (Martin, 1972).

Depending on the replacement alternative chosen from any particular rule when it is applied, different statements are generated. A systematic method of application is required for generating statements with specific properties. For any given grammar, it may be possible to outline a strategy which enables statements with a desired property to be generated. Wexler (1973) brought up the problem in his report without attempting a solution:

> There are two important difficulties that arise with problem generators that are not dealt with in this current design. One involves the need to generate problems of a particular level or degree of difficulty. The other difficulty of problem generators is more subtle: how to generate problems that have particular kinds of features or properties.

VI. ALGORITHMS FOR GENERATING EXAMPLES

In the more general teaching system, a "top-down" approach to generation was attempted. This took two forms which might be characterized as explicitly recursive and explicitly non-recursive; the main distinction was in the way in which recursively defined notions were handled. Using these two methods, generators for the SEQUEL language were produced and an evaluation of these generators now follows.

In the SEQUEL generator (version 1), the branches are merely chosen at random. This method of generation has been recommended by Neil Rowe (1978). It is only adequate for simple grammars; in particular, if there are several recursively defined notions in the language, this method cannot be ensured to terminate in a reasonable time. Using this method of generation with the SEQUEL grammar, it was not possible to generate SEQUEL statements. More importantly it offered no control over the complexity of the statements generated. It must be concluded that if it is desired to have some mechanism whereby statements with specified levels of difficulty are generated, mere random replacement is not adequate.

In a second generator, statements are generated by a random replacement scheme only where the notion is not recursively defined. In this modified form, all explicit recursion during the generation of examples is removed; all recursive notions are dealt with by iterative generation of limited length. If an easy statement is required then all options are omitted and the minimum number of symbols are returned from functions generating any recursively defined notion. This method, while resulting in productions for most grammars, may not terminate in a reasonable time if the grammar has several indirectly recursive notions. It does not allow for the specification of a very exact measure of difficulty of the individual statements. The generation of hard and easy sentences is adequate for some teaching systems but is rather unsatisfactory for those where the teaching strategy requires a gradual progression from very easy to difficult examples.

The third generator uses a set of rules to guide generation. These take into account the generative power of each alternative and allow for a finer discrimination to be made between alternative branches.

The knowledge of how statements with the required properties are to be generated is imported into the production rules. The trade-off is that the production set loses generality. Two sets of production rules are required: one which gives a general model of the language and which is presented to the student for reference; and another which embodies a teaching strategy and is used to generate examples for the student to check.

The system outlined above would seem preferable to that of Koffman (1972), who employed a "probabilistic grammar" to generate logical expressions for use in a computer-aided instruction program. A probabilistic grammar is a formal language in which each rewrite rule is assigned a probability of being applied. The teacher must specify separately the method for initializing and updating the probabilities, and there is the overhead of recalculating the probabilities after any change in the student's level of competence.

Allowing the teaching strategy to be expressed entirely in the production rules enables the teacher in effect to program using the grammar only as an author language, and has the advantage that no other specification is necessary.

VII. CONCLUSION

A grammar only comes alive when it is used, so in further work on a more generalized system it must be recognized that the language most effectively being taught is the notation which describes the production rules, for it is that notation which the student must first come to understand. The syntax game programs described here are most effective at testing a student's understanding of the production rules notation. The ultimate productions are in a sense disembodied and do not have any honest employment in the syntax game program; it is the production rules that are actually given a sense by their use in producing statements in the language. Nevertheless, this does not detract from the merit of the programs. They provide an introduction to particular languages through their syntax, while at the same time giving the student practice at understanding the notation of the formal definition.

The advantages of defining a programming language formally are obvious (Zemanek, 1974). A formal definition of a programming language enables a student to grasp the language as a whole rather than by piecemeal induction. If the notation of the formal definition is not easily understood, these advantages cannot be realized to their full potential. While students should not be encouraged to neglect writing programs when getting to grips with a programming language, a familiarity with the syntax of the language is a helpful preliminary which will cut down the occurrence of syntactical teething troubles and will better equip the student to use the language to its full power. Where the production set is large, decomposing the rules for separate presentation is of value provided that the rules are linked together in a wider context of usage, preferably in actually writing programs.

Just as Miller distinguished between people learning to make the machine behave in a certain way and those gaining an understanding of the language, familiarity with the formal definition of a programming language gives the programmer a means of generally understanding a program as opposed to understanding the particular meaning it may exhibit when it is run. We must clearly differentiate between concrete implementations of languages and their abstract definitions; it is knowledge of the latter which enables programmers to gain an understanding of the meaning of their programs and to rise above the ability to simply make the machine do things. As programming languages move further away from their machine-code origins and become more fully abstract (Geurts and Meertens, 1978), it is imperative for programmers to acquire this understanding so that they may benefit from these conceptual advances.

Ideally the grammar of a programming language should reflect its usage, so that its application becomes transparent in the formation of the problem solution. This implies a grammar of problem-solving. In programming, analysis of the problem is often followed by two separate steps: construction of a solution and translation of the solution into a program. We should be thinking of grammars which will bring these two steps together.

REFERENCES

Chamberlin, D.D. and Boyce, R.F. (1973). SEQUEL: A structured English Language query language. Research Report, IBM Research Laboratory, San Jose, California.

Chomsky, N. (1957). *Syntactic Structures.* The Hague: Mouton.

Cleaveland, J.C. and Uzgalis, R.C. (1977). *Grammars for Programming Languages.* New York: Elsevier North-Holland.

Geurts, L. and Meertens, L.G. (1978). Remarks on Abstracto. *Algol Bull.,* **42,** 56–63.

Gries, D. (1971). *Compiler Construction for Digital Computers.* New York: Wiley.

Koffman, E.B. (1972). A.I. in C.A.I. *Proceedings of the AFIPS Spring Joint Computer Conference,* **40,** 379-389.

Lyons, J. (1970). *Chomsky.* Fontana Modern Masters Series. London: Fontana.

Martin, D.F. (1972). Formal languages and their related automata. In A.F. Cardenas (ed.) *Computer Science.* New York: Wiley-Interscience.

Miller, G.A. (1970). *The Psychology of Communication.* London: Pelican Books.

Rowe, N. (1978). Grammars as programming languages. *Creative Computing, 4,* 80–86.

Van Wijngaarden, A., Mailloux, B.J., Peck, J.E.L., Koster, C.H.A., Sintzoff, M., Lindsey, C.H., Meertens, L.G. and Fisker, R.G. (1976). *Revised Report on the Algorithmic Language Algol 68.* Berlin: Springer-Verlag.

Wexler, J.D. (1973). A design for describing (elementary) programming problem generators in an automatic teaching system. *Technical Report No. 66,* Dept. of Computer Science, State University of New York, Buffalo, New York.

Zemanek, H. (1974). Formalization: past, present, and future. In B. Shaw (ed.) *Formal Aspects of Computing Science.* Newcastle: Newcastle University Press.

Part III
The Design of the User Interface

Introduction

The authors of chapters in Part I universally asserted that the user interface of traditional application software is usually much more complex and confusing than is necessary. This theme is restated most forcibly by James (p. 337) in the first chapter of this section. James argues that if the computer industry is successfully to extend its user base it must urgently attend to developing user-friendly interfaces. Moreover, the design of good interfaces is as much a matter for behavioural scientists and ergonomists as for computer scientists, since many design problems involve accounting for such variables as user knowledge, attitudes and the quality of the user environment. The designer will, of course, also have to take account of the limitations imposed by a particular piece of hardware or of existing systems software. James therefore argues that there is a need for a new type of computer professional—the interface engineer—who will combine skills in both areas. He will be responsible for designing a system which is optimized for human efficiency rather than machine efficiency and his design effort will be focused upon upon what James terms "protective ware".

Protective ware will consist of a set of separate interface programs, possibly residing in a microprocessor, which monitor user responses to the system and translate messages from the system into forms which given groups of users will understand. It will therefore enable the system to be tuned to the needs of a defined group of users, or even to the needs of an individual. The notions that an applications design team should include an interface specialist and that a set of protective interface programs should be placed between the computer and user are proposed by several of the authors in this section.

One of the main tasks of an interface engineer would be to help establish users' requirements, these including such factors as the functions the system would be expected to perform, user characteristics and user support needs. Damodaran and Eason (p. 373) discuss means of seeking such information given varying degrees of user involvement. They argue that traditionally the process is controlled by computer experts who have little knowledge of the users' application area and are machine-oriented. This method has severe weaknesses, the resulting systems often failing to be fully integrated into the users' work situation. Various methods of user participation in the design process are proposed, including design by users with experts taking the role of advisors. We would suggest that because most commercial computer systems are very complex and because at some level the designer will be required to maximize the use of limited hardware, user-controlled design is unlikely to be adopted. A more satisfactory solution would result from a better understanding of the user by the computer professional rather than the user trying to understand and control the complexities of systems analysis and software production. An interface engineer would be expected to be able to accurately assess the user's needs—not simply to accept his stated requirements—to predict the degree of flexibility the system should possess so it may evolve with user expertise, and to be able to communicate effectively with the client, individual users and systems staff. Furthermore, he should also be responsible for education and advice during the bedding-down of the system, and for support at a later stage when the client wishes to make changes.

The final three chapters are all directly related to the implementation and evaluation of the man–computer interface. The chapters by Edmonds (p. 389) and Thomas (p. 427) offer possible methods of providing users with adaptable interfaces. Edmonds describes a system which fulfils the requirements of protective ware proposed in the chapter by James. Edmonds's interface language offers a means of specifying possible dialogues between computer and user. Moreover, the language allows for them to be easily modified, extended, or for additional dialogues to be composed. A notable strength of the language is that it allows the systems designer to incorporate possibilities for adaptation *by a user* into the interface software. For example, the interface can be set up for adaptation to take place at three levels. At the operator level, the system can be programmed to conduct a dialogue with various degrees of verbosity and even to suggest to the user the most appropriate degree to use for a given interaction. Facilities can also be provided for the interface to be modified by a local expert. He could, for example, be given the means of "opening up" pre-programmed routines as users become more experienced, or of making changes to the way the system reports errors. Finally, the interface engineer himself has available the full power of a high-level language to add major new facilities or to create new adaptive possibilities for the local expert.

Thomas (p. 427) describes a design for an adaptable terminal which gives the user considerable freedom to determine the way information is displayed on a VDU (visual display screen) and the way the man–computer dialogue is structured. Adjustments are made to the terminal by a local expert—or "Teacher"—for the terminal "User", employing a technique which Thomas calls "programming by imitation". This is achieved by giving the Teacher a set of primitive functions which enable him to:

- partition the VDU screen into an arbitrary set of windows;
- organize communication with the host computer;
- compose transactions consisting of sequences of functions which are stored for subsequent use by Teacher or User.

The Teacher thus constructs transactions appropriate for a given application which are then retained by the terminal for regular use by the user.

The Chapter by Embley and Nagy (p. 465) discusses methods for studying the human acceptability of computer editors. Many computer operations require the manipulation of files, hence editing is a very basic computational function. The chapter reports in detail a variety of objective techniques for assessing editors; these range from the use of formal notations for describing editor performance to methods which take account of empirically derived data on computer response and human usage. We would argue that studies of the type conducted by Embley and Nagy are of the greatest importance at the present time. Such work is necessary in order to form a firm descriptive basis for experimentation aimed at deriving sound principles for the design of effective interfaces to be employed in the next generation of applications software.

10. The User Interface: How We May Compute

E.B. JAMES

Computer Centre, Imperial College, University of London, London, England

---

I. THE PRESENT SITUATION

This chapter has three aims. The main aim is to express a deep concern over the inadequacies of the interface between computer and user. The present arrangement makes the effective use of the computer far more difficult than it need be, particularly for inexperienced users. The second aim is to examine interface design from the user's viewpoint and then, after analysis, to define the design objectives. The final aim is to describe two attempts to put this analysis and definition into practice.

A study of the way in which users interact with computers at present shows some strange anomalies. It is suggested that the design of existing interfaces is based largely on three assumptions about the users and their objectives which are twenty-five years out of date.

First, those who initially used computers were often the original designers of the machines and therefore had an intimate knowledge of their method of operation. They normally had a scientific or technical background and were very capable of looking after a complex machine, even relishing the effort of dealing with difficulties in use, and it is still assumed that the user is a technical expert with a similar background.

Secondly, the machines themselves are assumed to be large, centralized, very expensive, and to work in the batch mode; a sequence of monolithic programs being presented for computation with the printed results eventually returned to the user. Although this is clearly no longer the case in many of the time-sharing systems, closer examination reveals that time-sharing terminals are really only alternative input positions for what is essentially batch work. There is very little genuinely interactive use of existing computers.

Thirdly, the assumption that the hardware is strictly limited in its performance underlies the design of all software, so calling for the absolute minimum of hardware use. The user is thus burdened with a great deal of specialized preparation before approaching the computing system. This means that the documentation provided is often totally inadequate, even for the dedicated user.

These assumptions may have not been formulated explicitly by the designers of existing systems, but they are typical of the attitudes inherent in those who are primarily interested in hardware and software rather than the human situation surrounding the use of computers. The designer's background is likely to be strongly technical; it is unlikely that he will have training in ergonomics or in any aspect of educational technology which can be related to the activities of users of complex systems.

A closer analysis of the structure of existing computing systems brings other fundamental problems to light. If we look at the software in greater detail, we will discover that it is arranged in various isolated *layers* reflecting an historical development rather than operational convenience. One such layer consists of *user programs*, conceived as long, monolithic sequences of statements in a formalized language, to be performed without reference to other similar programs. This type of program is a relic of the earliest days in computing, when no other type of software existed. The user would insert such a program into the computer by hand and press a series of switches to set it into operation. If external data was required, it would be loaded into the machine as the program requested it. As users have grown more numerous and machines have become faster, professional operators have replaced amateur users at the console. Information on how to run the program has been enshrined in another layer of software, called the "operating system", which requires the user to provide information on resources needed and data files to be made available in a form totally unrelated to the original program.

The removal of the user from the computer room and the substitution of a series of operating system commands also removed the possibility of interaction with the program as it was producing results. This possibility seemed to have been retained with the advent of time-sharing systems in the 1960s. Unfortunately, the time-sharing facilities were added as another conceptual layer to the existing "system" and in many cases the terminals provided merely a range of positions from which a traditional "batch" job could be inserted.

The development of the present multi-layer systems has involved enormous expense and it is understandable that hardware and software providers are not prepared to reconstruct new, co-ordinated systems from scratch on existing machine ranges.

However, a new factor has arisen which may make such changes inevitable. The advent of the microprocessor has fundamentally altered the technical constraints under which the present systems have been built and makes nonsense of existing design methods.

Sutherland and Mead (1977) explain clearly the anarchical impact of the large-scale integrated circuit on practical and theoretical design. Existing methods presuppose that hardware is very expensive and that the minimum of circuits should be employed. Elaborate theoretical techniques have been built up to aid this minimization of active switching elements, while the cost of the people who carry out the investigation has been neglected. Now we discover that with integrated circuits the absolute number of switching elements may be much less significant than the number and complexity of their interconnections, a factor which has not been previously considered at all. The hard-won experience of the so-called "experts" may no longer be relevant.

Providing a good user interface is basically concerned with human patterns of learning, using, remembering and forgetting. People with interests in these things call themselves educationalists, psychologists or specialists in ergonomics. Why have they been unable to do anything significant in this field so far? I suggest two reasons: firstly, they have rarely been invited by users or system designers to participate in the design process, and secondly, there is a very complicated machine on the other side of the interface; even where such specialists have been involved they have not been able to appreciate how the machine itself can make things easier for the user.

We require a new breed of interface engineer, who can understand the limitations and possibilities on *both* sides of the interface. Let us consider some basic terms of reference within which this new sort of person may work.

II. HOW WE MAY COMPUTE: THE DEFINITION OF OBJECTIVES

In this section I shall attempt to define the qualities which are required of the user interface, trying as far as possible to separate these definitions from a discussion of the techniques for realizing them in a computer system. This will be covered in the following section. Many of the difficulties with current user interfaces arise from a confusion of objectives, and some of these will be considered later.

In any study of the user interface, we must first define a "user". As suggested already, the background of the typical present-day user is different from that of earlier users and even greater changes are likely in the future. In recent times there have always been professional intermediaries between large computing systems and their users. Now, to an increasing extent, the users will have no technical knowledge of computing systems and will not intend to submit to a discipline of technical training before using the computer.

In very general terms, we may define three classes of user. First, there is the systems programmer, who is a person concerned full-time with the maintenance of a computing system. Secondly, there is the applications programmer: that is the engineer, scientist or worker in another discipline who needs to make regular and intensive use of computing facilities. Finally, there is the general "member of the public", and this last group will increasingly become the dominant class of computer user. Only three points have been chosen in what is essentially a continuum; in particular, the "applications" programmer can range between someone who uses the system as intensively as the systems programmer and another one who is an infrequent and casual user of the computer system, like a member of the general public. In defining objectives attention will be focused on the general public as the dominant class of users because I am convinced that the facilities provided for such users are in reality exactly those required by all other users.

Having identified the classes of user, we have to determine what they are trying to do with the computing system; again, there is a vast range of possibilities. Miller (1976) provides an important assessment of the objectives of computer users and the way in which they may be related to the design of computing systems. He stresses the importance of looking at the task of the user as a whole and not forcing its description into a series of preconceived categories which are derived from the current capabilities of computers.

The very word "computer" is misleading in this context. While traditional applications in science and engineering may still emphasize its use in the computation of numerical solutions to precisely formulated mathematical problems, this is no longer the principal task of the computer. More and more it is concerned with the provision of essentially non-numeric information from existing data-bases and its reorganization in a form suitable for meaningful presentation to the user. With this in mind, let us move on to consider the interface between the user and a computing system.

It is notoriously difficult to define the concept of an interface. It may be identified vaguely as that area of a system where unexpected things happen quite frequently. Certainly, the present user interface is more or less a battleground of opposing models of the computing process. On the "machine" side, we have a model of the computing system as a collection of electronic and electro-mechanical devices, each with its own characteristics. The requirement of the interface, seen from this side, is to issue a sequence of instructions to control and co-ordinate these devices to provide the required results. The commands of a typical operating-system control language reflect this physical situation. On the user's side of the interface, we have a set of possibly conflicting models. For example, there is the model inherent in all the traditional programming languages. The programming tools provided imply the construction of a long sequence of commands which specify in a totally prescriptive manner a very large number of practically identical computations on serially presented data. Existing languages are clearly designed for use in the old fashioned "batch" method of processing, and by their structure bear little relation to current and future requirements for continuous interaction.

Winograd (1979) describes well the archaic situation in the design and programming of total computing systems. He points out that computers are no longer primarily used for solving well-structured mathematical problems, but instead are *components* in complex systems. The building blocks from which these complex systems are built are no longer at the level of individual program instructions. They are sub-systems in their own right, each containing an integrated collection of data structures, programs and protocols for communication with other sub-systems. Much more emphasis must be given to describing the behaviour of these sub-systems in a coherent way so that they may be understood and used effectively, rather than continuing the existing concentration on writing new "programs".

While others have searched for inspiration in the formal methods of mathematics, I believe that it is much more fruitful to consider two people collaborating on a task as a model of interface requirements. Let us consider those characteristics of a personal collaboration which may suggest desirable qualities for the user–machine interface. Essentially this involves the communication of needs from both sides.

A first consideration is the medium of communication. People rely mainly on speech for rapid instruction, usually supported by facial expressions, gestures and quite possibly by sketching when something complex is being described. On the man–machine interface we have to rely on much less effective methods. Most users are restricted to the equivalent of typing a letter, with possibly a long delay in its acknowledgement. The messages sent to the machine must be very precisely specified and written in an incredibly limited language. The typical answer received will also be printed, probably very badly, in a limited character set. The advent of microprocessors which can be dedicated to input and output functions has raised hopes that at least we may achieve a fairly crude form of speech output before long. Pictorial output has been available for many years but is again only just becoming economical for a majority of users. The input of conveniently rapid speech and hand-drawn pictures poses problems at the forefront of studies in so-called "artificial intelligence". Kriloff (1976) provides a useful summary of the human factors involved in the design of interactive graphical displays, which represent the most effective form of communication available. The majority of users are unfortunately still restricted to sending and receiving typed messages.

Another characteristic of human communication is the wide variation in the level of detail at which a solution to a task can be discussed. A problem or its solution may be described in general terms, with particular detail being added only when necessary. At the user–machine interface solutions can be specified only at the single, very detailed descriptive level of existing programming languages.

A third factor is concerned with the control of dialogue. When two persons discuss a problem, each one takes it in turn to guide the conversation. This is referred to as a "mixed initiative" dialogue. In the man–machine interface we normally have a monologue with imperatives, that is, commands, being transmitted in one direction only.

A fourth feature concerns the use of language. Two people communicate most effectively when they can both use the language which has been familiar to them since birth. Special jargon can be used to speed communication, but only when each knows the other to be familiar with it. At the current man–machine interface, the user is forced to specify requirements in a very unnatural language. In order to communicate at all, the user is required to make a study of a job-control language and at least one programming language. Even when using a "simple" program package, an intimate knowledge of particular input formats for data and parameters is usually assumed.

Finally, an obvious characteristic of human communication is its logical incompleteness and inaccuracy when considered solely in terms of what is actually stated at a particular time. Two persons bring to any effective dialogue a vast range of common remembered experience and attitudes, and communication can proceed perfectly well through a series of statements only vaguely related to an official grammar and syntax. When we turn to the man–machine interface, we find an oppressive demand for precision in syntax and no ability on the machine side to remember any previous transaction except in terms of the "results" it may have produced. Certainly there is no building of understanding through a history of discussions.

It is suggested that the qualities of human behaviour described are fundamental to effective communication of a problem on which human co-operation is required. Why should they not be essential qualities of a man–machine interface?

The foregoing considerations lead us to define a series of desirable qualities for the user–machine interface which might well be called for in the future. Newman (1978) provides a valuable general discussion and specifies a comprehensive list of qualities. We concentrate here on certain psychologically relevant attributes which the machine might be required to display.

The first and most important quality is reliability. When everything is operating smoothly, this is mainly a question of providing a consistent response to user activities. However, reliability becomes much more difficult to display when things are not working correctly. A vast range of problems will be encountered when there is a degradation in the computer system. It is essential for a continuous and consistent response to be maintained as far as possible even when parts of the system are not functioning correctly. Another range of problems arises when the user performs incorrect operations or makes incorrect requests. It is essential in this situation that the system continues to perform in a consistent manner and, most important of all, continues to communicate. Clearly this implies a great deal of tolerance of the user's behaviour on the part of a computing system.

The second quality is adaptability. We are particularly concerned here with the ability of the computer system to provide a dialogue which is consistent with the user's previous experience. This implies that the system is able to learn a "required" pattern of behaviour from a particular user and also to remember and reintroduce this pattern when the same user is in contact again.

A third quality is self-sufficiency. This is an aspect of system reliability, in that the user does *not* have to rely on some external agency in order to be able to use the computer. In the past, the serious user would require help from voluminous documentation and extensive consultation with "experts" in order to use the facilities. We propose that this assistance should be built into the existing system, so that it provides not only a range of facilities but also the ability to train the user in exploiting them in the most effective way.

A fourth quality, ease of use, is very much connected with reliability and tolerance. Clearly, ease of use is dependent on the individual background of each user. There is no particular style of use which can be correct for all users. This implies that the system must cater for a wide range of styles. In particular it must cater for and support the inexperienced user with information on how to proceed. At the same time, it must permit the experienced user to develop a personal, idiosyncratic style which represents optimum performance. Negroponte (1976) argues a successful case for personalized patterns of use. "Ease of use" implies that the system can adapt to human methods of solving problems. Weiss (1971) shows how deeply the concept of hierarchical organization is built into our ways of understanding and acting. The machine will need to provide facilities for modelling hierarchic structures even if its current architecture is uncompromisingly linear.

Ease of use also implies "efficient" use, but it cannot be stressed too strongly that this is not the efficiency in the mind of the typical systems designer, who is concerned with the efficient use of *machine* resources. Efficiency here means a minimization of the *user*'s resources deployed in obtaining the required "results" from a computing system.

I believe that the qualities just described are absolutely fundamental to a good interface design, and yet experience of many different computing systems suggests that these objectives have never been met in practice.

It appears that this is due mainly to a confusion of objectives. Because it is so difficult to specify what needs to be done to make computing convenient for the user, many workers have adopted much more limited and more easily specified objectives in the belief that achievement of these would contribute to the overall requirements. Unfortunately, much of the work towards these more limited objectives has been carried out in an academic environment where there have always been pressures to disguise computing as an academic discipline similar to mathematics. As a result many computer scientists have adopted the objectives of pure mathematics: conciseness, precision, generality and elegance, and their work has ignored such considerations as practical application by non-specialists, convenience in use and "learnability". While there is nothing inherently wrong with the adoption of well-tested principles in a new field of study, this has produced an undesirable emphasis on certain aspects of computing which are not very helpful at the user interface (Hume, 1977). For example, the mathematical objective of precision is often achieved through the ability of the mathematician to abstract a problem until it is sufficiently simple to be tackled with the very precise tools of conventional logic. Unfortunately, in the design of practical engineering systems we are not free to simplify a problem unless we wish to produce solutions which do not work in the real world.

Overall, the principal problems have arisen from a failure to consider the practical use of systems together with the user's characteristics, a failure to consider the pattern of learning which users must undergo in order to use facilities, and a failure to appreciate the changing nature of users' requirements and therefore of the resulting methods of solution. As an example of these failures, we may cite the vast amount of work which has been done on the development of an "ideal" programming language. Many workers in this field have become so fascinated by the study of the formal properties of languages abstracted and separated from their practical use that they have justified their interest by suggesting that if the user can be provided with such a "perfect" language, then all problems of using computers will disappear. Recently, there have been hopeful signs that many computer scientists realize the emphasis on such work to have been misplaced. Backus (1978) criticizes language designers for following the Von Neumann model of a computer, which was conceived thirty years ago, as a basis for new developments. Senn and Ives (1978) sketch out the much wider syllabus which will be needed by computer specialists in the future. They stress the behavioural and managerial components which will be brought in to balance the previous exaggerated emphasis on formal techniques.

Confused objectives have also arisen when the developers have taken themselvs as "typical users". Since they themselves are full-time specialists in the field, it has been assumed that the user has unlimited time to study and learn the intricacies of any system which may be devised. This has led to well-meaning but ridiculous attempts to provide "helpful" packages which are so difficult to operate that it is easier for users to learn the original language in which they were constructed, and to devise a program which does specifically and efficiently what is required. The providers of such packages are also totally unaware of the need for adequate documentation and well-organized methods of teaching the use of their packages.

Again, the desire on the part of "hard" scientists for certainty in their theories and conclusions has led to a great deal of work on "proving" programs. While every careful investigation of programs, and the way in which they work, can be helpful in promoting our ability to improve them, it seems likely that the current methods are going to work only where the objectives of the original program are simple enough to be defined and to be seen to be definable in extremely simple and rigorous mathematical terms. Unfortunately, this is just not true in the case of *any* significant program, especially one which is going to change with time.

Let us hope that before long the problems and interests of genuine users of computer systems will be no longer confused with the problems and personal interests of the providers. While in the past the less experienced users have been in the minority and unable to exert much influence on the course of development, their strength is growing continually so that in due course it is likely that the providers of the present poor user interfaces will be called from their ivory towers and asked to account for their failures. In a range of papers, Sterling (1979) investigates the sad history of the end-users who have had bad computing systems forced on them without opportunity to complain or escape from involvement.

In the next section I will propose a strategy for attacking these very real problems before a substantial part of the user population is permanently antagonized.

III. HOW WE MAY COMPUTE: A TECHNIQUE FOR REALIZATION

Our present objective is to consider how the qualities of the user interface previously discussed may be achieved in practical computing systems. It will first be necessary to define more clearly the current situation at the user interface.

When we consider the hardware and software on the system side, we must first recognize that existing interfaces are already obsolete because of the remarkable developments over the last few years. The microprocessor makes possible an entirely different approach to the design of the hardware of a computer and at the same time it forces a new appraisal of the previously well-defined line between software and hardware. The previously accepted hardware base on which software systems were constructed is now a shifting sand (Sutherland and Mead, 1977). The fact that the fundamental design of the hardware is likely to change even more rapidly in the future makes it more important that the user should not be directly concerned with the details of its structure. However, as we are still surrounded with obsolete hardware and software systems, it is necessary to build acceptable interfaces to these in the first instance. Some easily used systems have been designed and built both for the professional and amateur user but these have generally been restricted to specific machines and specific groups of users (Evans, 1971; Sandewall, 1978). The principal difficulty seems to be in bringing better designed interfaces to large numbers of users on existing large computer systems. In this field we simply cannot just design a new system from scratch, so we must accept the constraints inherent in the existing system.

Consider the constraints within which the designer of the user interface must work. First, there are many restrictions due to the primitive design of existing hardware. The design of computers at the hardware level has changed only in detail from that discussed by the designers of the original systems in the 1940s. Computers are designed to be smaller, faster and cheaper, but the larger machines are still laid out essentially to facilitate numerical calculation via a strictly serial sequence of instructions working on data supplied from a serially addressed store. The parallel and independent activities required both by the individual user in a particular application and by a group of concurrent users can only be simulated through an elaborate and hyper-complicated "soft" machine built on top of this primitive hardware.

While the basic design of all machines is similar, there is a continuous variation in detailed design associated with the introduction of new ranges of auxiliary storage and peripherals, necessary to give the buyer the impression of progress. For this reason, any part of the user interface which depends on specific underlying hardware features is unlikely to remain stable. The manufacturers would prefer to forget that every machine goes wrong at some time, and although the reliability of the hardware is remarkable compared with machines other than computers, there are so many individual components to go wrong that faults can occur rather too frequently. There are well-known techniques available which could enormously improve matters through the duplication of equipment, but the designers still retain the outworn criteria of hardware minimization. Normally it is precisely when the hardware breaks down that the user has the greatest problems.

Next, let us consider the software situation. Nowadays most programs, particularly those which are part of the operating system, are so large that they inevitably contain large numbers of un-detected errors. These are not usually of an obvious type, such as the incorrect specification of an arithmetic operation, but are much more subtle inaccuracies in the "logic" of the program, so that it performs unexpectedly only on certain occasions and under particular conditions in the pattern of data being processed.

Also, programs require to be changed rather frequently, either for correction or amendment to perform some slightly different function. A program which is not being changed is likely to be at the end of its useful life. An associated consideration is that since existing programs require a very great deal of effort to produce, we must look to their continued use and therefore continued modification over a long period. This emphasizes the importance of a stable environment for the underlying hardware and software support.

A third overall consideration is the users themselves. They are human and have human frailties; they continually make mistakes and they change their minds on the requirements of a particular program. They forget what has previously been done; they forget how to specify instructions correctly. Finally, they require constant reassurance that everything is working as expected or they will lose confidence and go elsewhere.

Now let us look at two inherent limitations on the type of system which may be provided for the user in the future. The requirement for a "human face" to the computer system may lead us to try to provide the possibility of a totally natural dialogue in the user's native language. Twenty years ago we may have been more hopeful of succeeding in such an attempt than at present. The massive effort expended, to comparatively little effect, on machine translation since that time should warn us of the difficulties. It becomes obvious that any attempt to work on language which is more significant than, for example, the automated page turning of a dictionary, requires the creation of an internal "model of the world" as a vehicle for "understanding" what individual words "mean". Such partial success as has been attained so far has been through restricting the "universe" of understanding to a tiny part of the real world, such as ordering a plane ticket from a single departure point (Bobrow *et al.*, 1977). Such sophisticated work is unlikely to find a place in the extremely reliable systems which we are trying to provide in the near future.

The other inherent limitation is concerned with the problem of *generality*. Since every user's requirement is in some sense special and individual, it is unlikely that any system we design will fit *any* user's needs exactly. We must aim at a compromise which provides a satisfactory service for a majority of users.

As the final constraint under which we must work, let us consider the "politics" of manufacturing computing systems. While all manufacturers may pay lip-service to the provision of universally usable systems, they actually base their sales policy on the provision of something "better than" and therefore *different* from their competitors. Even in the comparatively standardized area of computing languages, the talk will be of extra "goodies" in addition to those defined by the standard. Since we are not proposing to alter the structure of the computer market, it is clear that we are not likely to receive massive support from the manufacturers in our attempt to iron out all the differences in the method of use of all computing systems.

In solving any real problems we are hedged round with practical constraints. We must be aware of the limitations, but it need not prevent us from trying to improve the current quality of the user interface. I will now describe the basic idea behind my current work.

My method for improving the quality of the current man–machine interface is very simple in principle. It is to place between the user and the existing interface a layer of software which we may call "protective" ware. This operates rather like a communication channel in that it has at its front end an interface with the user and at its rear an interface with the existing operating system of the machine. All messages between the user and the original operating system are intercepted, monitored, and if necessary, interpreted. For example, an obscure, jargon-ridden message from the computer can be recognized and translated into a message meaningful to the user. In the opposite direction, a message from the user expressing rather approximately what is required may be converted by the protective ware into the sequence of control commands required by the operating system. It is possible that a single request from the user could generate a series of interactions between the protective interface and the original operating system.

In due course we would expect the protective ware to incorporate all the techniques employed in current computer-assisted learning programs. For example, a user's requirement can be determined from a succession of replies in the form of "Yes" or "No" answers, or through selection from a menu of possibilities. It may even be possible for the user to reply in no very definite fashion. Something similar to a grunt of general agreement can possibly be indicated by pressing, for example, the return key. The interface program, possessing a memory of previous users' responses, could select the answer which is most commonly given at this point.

Although the aim is to simplify the situation for the user, the design of the protective ware will require the most sophisticated processing techniques available. Providing tolerance to inaccuracy on the user's part requires subtle methods and a great deal of computing power. Details of how this can be done and how the methods can be applied to speech and handwritten input have been provided in a previous paper (James and Partride, 1973). The amount of processing power necessary would have been considered prohibitive until quite recently. Now, the ability to dedicate a microprocessor to the task makes it entirely practicable, if no simpler.

It is comparatively simple to lay down proposals for action. It is much more difficult to achieve worthwhile results with real-life users. In the next section I describe some results of applying my approach in practice.

IV. THE APPLICATION OF PRINCIPLES: A REPORT ON PROGRESS

A. The Science Museum Project

1. *The System*

Having started to apply, in a modest way, the principles discussed previously, a system was constructed which fulfils some of the requirements stated above; in fact such a system has been in use for several years. Its principal limitation is that it is only relevant to use in a very specialized environment, and this environment is the Computing Gallery of the Science Museum in London. We provided in the museum a terminal, attached to the Imperial College computing system, which enables any visitor to the Computing Gallery to initiate a dialogue with the computing system, and to have practical experience of what the computer can do, all in the space of five minutes. This has to be possible for any user who is able to read, and all that is available in the way of preliminary information must be found in a few sentences beside the computer terminal. The user presses a single button called "Start" and immediately enters the computing system. All further information as to what is to be done is provided through a visual display unit. In this particular case, the user is given only the choice of calling into operation one of three simple programs to illustrate the potential of a computer system. Technically, one has only to be able to type some words in English and to reply "Yes" or "No". There is a considerable amount of tolerance of typing mistakes. A particular feature of this system is that it is not possible for the user to interfere with the satisfactory operation of the computer terminal and operating system by any means at all. The terminal has been programmed to accept any input whatsoever, and to tolerate errors by continuing as far as possible with a reasonable dialogue. Every system message sent out from the computer is hidden from the user and never allowed to reach the screen. A great deal has been learned about the behaviour of inexperienced computer users by observing the use of the Science Museum terminal. I will therefore describe how the hardware and software has been designed in relation to the principles laid down previously, and then describe the observation of the users' behaviour.

The first concern in this project has been with the reliability of the hardware. This has been pre-eminent because the terminal operates in a public place and there is no possibility of having an engineer on call to deal with malfunctions. The terminal installed in the Computing Gallery is of a very special construction. A Control Data Corporation alphanumeric visual display unit has been encased in a purpose-built protective surrounding cabinet. The casing of the terminal reflects our first requirement concerning reliability. A great deal of attention was paid to the design of the special keyboard which fitted over the top of a commercial one. This protective keyboard and its surroundings were constructed in stainless steel, which makes it impossible for a user to damage the underlying keyboard and contacts whatever the strength of arm applied to the keys. The precision construction of the casing surrounding the keys prevents the insertion of any weapons which may be used in an attempt to stop its correct action. The outer protective keyboard also enables us to make it impossible to operate certain of the keys normally available to a user of the underlying keyboard. Our original keyboard design enabled users to provide only numerical inputs, but further consideration and experience has enabled us to make available most of the characters found on a conventional typewriter. The means of output from the computer system, in this case, a visual display, was also provided with a protective coating of armoured glass approximately a quarter of an inch thick, and this again proved able to withstand the assaults of all comers. Early experience with the terminal demonstrated that the rather small area of the display itself did not enable users to obtain a very good view of progress. Since many visitors wish to observe the activities of the one person actually using the keyboard, we duplicated the display by means of a large television screen placed eight feet above the original screen. This enables approximately 30 people to view the proceedings fairly easily. Although this display was originally selected from a range of computing systems, it has proved in practice rather difficult to maintain a steady display, and this raises serious questions on viewing by mutliple users of this type of activity. This is not a side-issue at the Science Museum, because it is clear that most visitors learn from observing the activities of other users rather than waiting to try themselves.

Our principle of maintaining contact with the user even when the computer has broken down provided many problems for the designers. It was necessary to install some indicator lights which could be controlled by the operators in the Computer Centre and which were separate from the terminal. A red light indicates that the terminal is not operating. This light can also be switched on locally by a member of the Science Museum staff if the terminal appears to be working incorrectly. By controlling the light, the Computer Centre staff carry the main responsibility for indicating to users when the terminal should be operating correctly. This has, of course, certain drawbacks. For example, if the computer is being operated unattended, as it often is over a weekend, then it is possible for the light to be set incorrectly. The red light is naturally set to "On" when the computer is being used for the maintenance and development of control programs and is not available to ordinary users. Since it is inconvenient to have random inputs from the terminal under these circumstances, it has been arranged that the presence of the red light also results in the disconnection of the keyboard from the computer. The keyboard is also disconnected at any time when output is being sent from the computer. The precise timing of this disconnection and reconnection has raised problems which are noted later. Beside the keyboard and display screen is a carefully worded, very short notice which tells a user how to start a terminal session. Above the display are short summaries of the user's choice of principal activities during the session. This extra information is not necessary for the correct operation or use of the terminal, since we apply the principle already stated that once a session is initiated the user should be instructed directly what is required next. It is placed there to help the prospective user to decide whether to *start* to use the terminal. A sample session of a typical dialogue, in this case describing the various things which the user may do, is shown in Fig. 1.

```
IMPERIAL COLLEGE COMPUTER CENTRE
SCIENCE MUSEUM TERMINAL


GOOD AFTERNOON THE TIME IS 16.28 HRS

DO YOU KNOW HOW TO USE THIS TERMINAL?
PLEASE TYPE YES OR NO AND PRESS SEND
(WAIT FOR THE ?)
? no

VERY WELL IT IS EXTREMELY SIMPLE
1. THE MOST IMPORTANT THING YOU NEED TO KNOW IS
   THAT EVERYTIME YOU TYPE SOMETHING IN TO THE
   COMPUTER YOU MUST 'SEND' IT BY PRESSING THE
   BUTTON MARKED 'SEND' OTHERWISE THE COMPUTER
   CANNOT REPLY TO YOU
   E G  IF THE COMPUTER ASKS YOU :
   WHAT IS YOUR NAME?
   YOU MUST REPLY :
   ?FRED 'SEND'
   NOW YOU TRY IT

WHAT IS YOUR NAME?
? jacqueline
THANK YOU JACQUELINE

2. IF YOU MAKE A MISTAKE YOU CAN
   CANCEL THE WHOLE LINE BY TYPING
   E G  FRED    'SEND'
3. IF YOU DON'T UNDERSTAND SOMETHING
   YOU CAN TYPE:
      HELP 'SEND'
4. IF YOU WANT TO STOP YOU CAN
   TYPE > 'SEND'
   OR TYPE END

DO YOU NOW KNOW HOW TO USE THIS TERMINAL?
? yes
GOOD
WOULD YOU LIKE TO KNOW THE DAY OF THE WEEK ON
WHICH YOUR NEXT BIRTHDAY FALLS?
? no
```

(continued)

```
O K JACQUELINE
THIS IS WHAT YOU CAN DO NOW
YOU CAN PLAY ONE OF TWO GUESSING GAMES:
              ANIMALS OR NUMBERS
OR YOU CAN FIND OUT HOW TO GET FROM SOUTH
KENSINGTON TUBE STATION TO ANY OTHER STATION
ON THE LONDON UNDERGROUND SYSTEM
DECIDE WHAT YOU WANT TO DO AND TYPE
ANIMAL OR NUMBER OR TUBE
? tube
PLEASE TYPE THE STATION YOU WANT TO GO TO
? uxbidge
DO YOU MEAN UXBRIDGE?
? yes
FROM SOUTH KENSINGTON TRAVEL ON THE UXBRIDGE BRANCH OF THE PICCADILLY LINE
WESTBOUND FOR UXBRIDGE
NOTE: UXBRIDGE STATION THROUGH ROUTE AT PEAK PERIODS ONLY AT OTHER TIMES
         CHANGE TO METROPOLITAN LINE AT RAYNERS LANE
THE SINGLE FARE FOR THE TRIP WILL BE 35 PENCE

GOODBYTE JACQUELINE

PLEASE LET SOMEONE ELSE HAVE A GO NOW

+++ WAIT 5 SECONDS +++

GOOD AFTERNOON THE TIME IS 16.32 HRS

DO YOU KNOW HOW TO USE THIS TERMINAL ?
PLEASE TYPE YES OR NO AND PRESS SEND
(WAIT FOR THE ?)
```

Fig. 1. Sample of Science Museum dialogue.

One of the terminal keys has been labelled "START", and a dialogue may be started by pressing this key alone. A combination of specially designed hardware and software then enables the user to avoid the conventional logging-in procedure associated with a typical computer time-sharing service. This implies that there is no security checking on this particular terminal, and that it is not necessary to produce a job number or other form of authorization to use it. This is arranged by ensuring that only the single control program relevant to the Science Museum terminal can actually be accessed and used from that terminal. Although this arrangement was originally difficult it is now comparatively easy to implement on a recent re-issue of the operating system.

Once the user has pressed "START", entry is made to a section of the program which instructs the user, if necessary, how to use a terminal; that is, how and when to type in instructions. The user is also introduced to two ways of correcting mistakes. The control of typing errors is made difficult because the time-sharing system can respond only to complete lines of input. An "intelligent" terminal which could respond to each character as it is typed and enable an error to be corrected immediately would be of great value. It would also save much time if single keys indicating "YES" and "NO" were available. However, having to type the individual letters of "Yes" and "No" provides practice for typing more complicated responses later on. After "Yes" and "No" have been tried, users are requested to type in their name, which is again a very familiar thing. Afterwards, users can obtain the day of the week on which their birthday falls, which is not obviously simple to produce and indicates something of the power of the program working behind the scenes. This is followed by a choice of participating in three simple "games".

In the "Number Game" the user thinks of a number between 1 and 100 and answers a series of questions which enable the computer program to determine which number has been thought of using the binary search technique. The user is then given a description of the binary search method so that the apparently mysterious rapidity with which the answer can be obtained is made clear.

In the "Animal Game" the user thinks of an animal and is asked a series of questions to determine what that animal is. The program has a short-list of the most frequently used animals, and if the user's choice is not on that list the user is eventually asked for its name. The user is then asked to type in a question which will differentiate the animal thought of from the guess which has been made by the program. The new animal, and the question which differentiates it, are then added to the data-base for the duration of the present user's session, after which they are discarded. Originally, all new animals were added to the data-base and made available to succeeding users but it was discovered that the data-base soon became unwieldy in size, and since the information provided by users was usually not serious, it became clear that this possible demonstration of a program which continues to learn could not be justified.

The final "game" is in fact a perfectly serious data retrieval application. The user can type in the name of any station on the London Transport underground system and is then told which line to take and where to change in order to get there from South Kensington.

We originally believed that the demonstrations chosen were only three out of many which were possible. On reflection, it has become clear that they represent very effectively the three major areas of computer application: numerical calculator, word processor and information source.

2. *Experience with Users*

Ireland and Shane have carried out an analysis of the performance of Science Museum terminal users and an informal survey of their reactions as users (Ireland, 1978). A program was written which monitors the terminal and stores a record of all interactions, together with the time at which each takes place. The program also computes certain summary statistics. User reactions were obtained by observing the terminal directly over several days, approaching some of the users and asking for their views on a predetermined list of topics. The original aim was to interview *all* users during certain periods selected at random, but this proved not possible due to the pattern of use. The visitors to the Science Museum are mainly groups of school children and the users of the terminal are almost invariably young people, many of whom are not prepared to wait and reply to questions. Each "user" tended to be a group of young people, one of whom acted as typist while the others suggested what should be typed in. Successive sessions might well be generated by the same group of "users" with a different typist. Individual, more mature users are much more inhibited and tend to use the system only when no-one else is looking. This pattern of use, which can be confirmed by any observer, provides useful feedback on design aspects of more "serious" terminal services for members of the public.

It is clear, for example, that older "first users" will require privacy from onlookers before they pluck up courage to approach the terminal. Also, if terminals are in a public place any measurements made without reference to the collaborative activities of user groups will be sadly in error. Groups of collaborating youngsters will provide very misleading statistics on ease of use, since they seem able to overcome almost any inadequacy in terminal provision. We now consider some more detailed points raised by an examination of the printed reports of terminal sessions.

By far the greatest number of problems in using the Science Museum terminal are raised by the "inhibit" facility on input. As explained previously, it is not permitted to type in anything while output is being produced from the computer. There is an actual mechanical interlock which means that although the keys may be pressed while output is still appearing on the screen, the actual characters corresponding to those key depressions are not retained. This inhibit period continues for a very short interval after the completion of an output line, and it is this interval which gives rise to the problem. Over half the responses from users omitted one or more letters from the beginning of an expected response. Clearly this was due to them "beating the gun" in replying. In fact the results of pressing these keys too early would not appear on the screen but it is clear that they did not look at the screen to see the results of their incorrect action. It seems likely that a good proportion of these responses were started even before the output line had been completely displayed at the terminal, and thus there was no way in which the first few letters could not have been lost except by the provision of special hardware at the terminal. This common human tendency to interrupt the other person in a dialogue must clearly be allowed for in the next generation of responsible systems.

A majority of the remaining problems occurred in connection with correcting incorrectly typed inputs. Users are able to press a backspace key in order to remove a previous single wrong character, but the backspace does not result in the displayed character on the output screen being removed; instead, an underline character is added to the apparent input. Users wishing to remove several characters frequently make the wrong number of back spaces, and so this facility must obviously be improved in future versions. Similarly the "CANCEL" key, which users can press to cancel a complete line of input text, raises difficulties in that the "CANCEL" character must be followed by pressing "SEND" to enable the central computer to remove the incorrect line of text. Clearly, this is better dealt with as a local operation at the terminal so that "CANCEL" does not need to be followed by a "SEND" to remove the previous line. Both these difficulties can be overcome by a very small amount of data-processing local to the terminal.

A frequent problem is associated with typing in the date of birth. A space is required between the month and date of the month. This was typically omitted, which is to be expected from users not familiar with the space bar in normal typing, and clearly should be corrected by a software check in future programs.

Another problem often occurs, at an entirely different level, in the Animal Game where the user is asked to type in a question which distinguishes between a new animal and the computer's last guess. Most users tend to state a fact about the animal they have in mind rather than putting in the *question* which should be asked to ascertain whether that fact was correct or not. This problem could be overcome if the control program was capable of turning a statement into the corresponding question, but this represents a sophistication outside the range of the present small-scale processing program.

Another weakness in the Animal Game was indicated by the performance of "awkward" users when the game had given up (when it had exhausted its stock of animals and requested the name of the user's animal). The difficult user may then type in one of the names already in the computer's list. This could be guarded against in future versions by arranging the user's input to be matched against the complete existing data-base. Presumably the majority of users doing this were determined to see whether the computer was clever enough to detect that their answer was already in its list. This behaviour again reflects a typical human tendency, in this case to test a colleague before placing confidence in his replies, and so a further requirement of the user interface is that it should display this ability to detect obviously "silly" input in order to build confidence in later replies.

Most of the observations of users have duplicated the findings obtained by analysing the monitor files, but some valuable supplementary information has been obtained. Some of these observations are of great interest as patterns of social behaviour and can be taken as indicators of the way in which first-time users will approach *any* computer system. We observed that the people around the computer terminal were usually in two groups. One group was close to the terminal and one member of this group was actually carrying out the typing, though sometimes other members of the group assisted. The people in this inner group sometimes looked at the output screen but more often observed the keyboard while the typing was going on, only looking at the screen after the typing had been completed. The other group stood away from the terminal, looking at the large monitor screen and showing a more peripheral interest. In fact the majority of users in the inner group were children and adults rarely dared to approach them. This reflects the usual diffidence of older people towards new learning experiences and certainly would cut them off from the learning experienced in the close group.

Observation of the users provided more information about difficulties with the keyboard. Typically, they took from one to three seconds to find each key. Often they forgot to press the "SEND" key until reminded by someone else in the group. Since they concentrate on the keyboard when typing in and do not look up at the screen to see what has actually been produced they do not notice spelling mistakes or missing first characters until it is too late. Strangely enough, the longer responses are more likely to be correctly input, since the users tend to look up in the middle of a longer response and therefore discover mistakes which they are able to correct.

The helpful notices surrounding the terminal, which were prepared with great care by the original design staff, are hardly ever read. The one which explains the initial logging-on and how to correct mistakes is not read until the user actually has difficulties. This observation reinforces the principle already laid down that information should be transmitted solely through the responses and should not presuppose a study of written material.

Nearly all new users learned from observing the previous user, since they typically watched for some time before daring to "have a go". If this observation were not taken into account the remarkable continuity of behaviour between successive sessions at the terminal, which is made evident in the monitor file, would be difficult to understand.

The situation at the time when the computer ceases operation provides interesting behavioural information. Unfortunately, it is sometimes not possible to complete a user session since the computer service is withdrawn half-way through. In this case the user may continue to type in for some time; only gradually does the crowd watching disperse. Since the previous terminal session is not cleared from the output screen, users continue to try the keyboard while the computer is not operational. This is reasonable because the screen seems to indicate that the computer is in the middle of an interesting game. Related behaviour is observed when the response time is long due to heavy loading by the other users of the terminal system. In this case Science Museum users may type in one or two complete lines before the keyboard inhibit comes on to provide a new output from the computer. Often extra messages such as "Hurry up" are typed in as well. It is possible for the response to be too slow to be acceptable, but previous experiments have demonstrated that too rapid a response can also lead to confusion about what to do next. In fact it seems best for the output to be presented at about the normal rate of reading rather than flashed rapidly on to the screen, and our system has been slowed-down somewhat to satisfy this requirement. This is clearly an interesting field for further observation.

In the event only fifteen users were questioned on their attitude to computer use. This was because the pattern of replies was stereotyped and also because the pattern of use was different from the original expectation. The system was designed assuming that single users would complete the sequence in five minutes or so and leave the terminal. In practice each "user" consisted of a group of five or more people, and each of these groups occupied fifteen minutes or more at the terminal. Only one of the fifteen "users" questioned said the computer was not *very* easy to use, and this was because of the difficulty with the interlocking arrangement at the beginning of typing each line. This presumably allows us to claim a moderate success for the design principles we have embodied. Six out of the fifteen claimed they had not learned anything from using the system, but of course they had all learned to use it successfully, which was the principle objective. Four users found the "computer" cleverer than they expected, because of the capability built into all our sequences of making reasonable guesses at mis-spelt words. One user found the system "very stubborn", and reminded us how far we have to go before approaching human flexibility. Finally, one user reminded us of the fundamental weakness of nearly all interactive systems. He wanted to ask the computer questions but found himself restricted to answering the computer's questions.

3. *Assessing the Science Museum Project*

How far does the terminal at the Science Museum display the qualities we have previously specified as desirable: reliability, adaptability, self-sufficiency and ease of use? In order to assess this we must consider how the service provided by the terminal fits into the total spectrum of computer use.

Clearly we have designed the terminal for the non-specialist. Our observations indicate that the majority of users have no previous computer experience whatsoever and that we are probably providing the first computer service to reach a significant number of users in this category. The range of "applications" is obviously very limited but nevertheless represents a kernel of possibilities in numerical calculation, word processing and data retrieval.

The software has proved itself totally reliable over several years, and the immediate surroundings of the terminal have proved rugged enough to withstand the assaults of all users. This provided a contrast with other "working" displays in the Museum, of which a certain proportion are usually unavailable because of previous misuse.

The least reliable part of the system has proved to be the time-sharing computing system which services the terminal. The time-sharing service at Imperial College is generally of high quality, but as with all very large computing systems it suffers from periods of instability arising from subtle errors in the control software. Such errors are extremely difficult to correct and are not reproducible during testing sessions because they appear only under extreme loading conditions. They require continuous monitoring of the system by senior staff over long periods of time. The clear message for designers is that ultra-reliable performance can be realized only on time-sharing systems whose working load is very strictly controlled, in itself a very difficult requirement to meet. The alternative, which is only now becoming practicable, is to abandon time-sharing and provide a dedicated microcomputer to drive *each* terminal.

The Science Museum terminal is no more or less adaptable than the vast majority of "sessions" terminals. There are no facilities built into the software or hardware to enable a different style of use to be made available to different categories of user.

On the third quality, self-sufficiency, it seems possible to claim a moderate victory. The users have been provided with no other way of learning how to use the terminal *except* by using it, apart from a minimum of printed information beside the keyboard. As we have already noted, very few users read even the initial instructions, and usually pick up the necessary experience by watching the previous user. All this is in stark contrast with the large amount of preliminary information which must be absorbed before approaching any other time-sharing terminal.

Finally, when assessing ease of use, the Science Museum system seems to break new ground. Clearly it is designed for the inexperienced user only, and does not claim to provide assistance with any user's individual computational requirement. Nevertheless the information provided on the details of the London Underground is not trivial and represents a principal service to be expected from computers in the future. This information is obtained by answering a few questions in English. There is no requirement to learn any jargon, any particular condensed representation of commands, or any rules as to the format in which requests must be typed. A similar service is *still* not available, to the best of our knowledge, from any computer system, without the mediation of a skilled operator to "get the system working" and to look after problems which arise when the user does something not quite right. Many thousands of first-time users have successfully obtained an experience of what a computer system can provide without a tedious apprenticeship.

Clearly there is a wide range of desirable improvements which could be made to the Science Museum system in the future and which will be indicated later in a proposed general plan of attack.

I will now describe progress on a second project which takes as its target audience the existing users of large-scale computing facilities.

B. Protective Ware for Program-writers

I described in Section III the technique of interposing a level of software between the user and an existing system as a shield against the unreasonable demands on expertise made by the current primitive operating systems. Such a shield is provided in the program which controls the Science Museum terminal. However, that system permits only a very limited range of requests to be made from the terminal. The second project is aimed at more experienced computer users such as those trying to obtain useful results from the installation at Imperial College. Similar requirements obtain for an army of research and development users in industry and government. While we may not believe that users of this type should be required to program in conventional programming languages, we nevertheless have accepted the current restrictions and have attempted to improve the effectiveness of program preparation. Most users find that the difficulties with programming are not normally connected with the programming language and its details. These provide problems at an early stage which can gradually be overcome through experience. The principal problem is concerned with the use of the operating system's control language or "job-control language". As noted previously, this second type of language has arisen as the original manual operation of the earliest machines has been replaced by automatic sequences, such as those connected with making available the files of input data for the program to use. While the programming languages normally used (COBOL, FORTRAN, ALGOL, etc.) are standardized over many different machines, the job-control languages are specific to each manufacturer and even to each type of computer. Typically they reflect principles of language design far less advanced than the standard programming languages, and specifically they are intolerant of any variation of the very precise "machine-code" format.

The principal aim in this second project is to place a protective coat around a particular job-control language, the NOS control language provided for a range of large Control Data Corporation computers. This has already been done to some extent in the Science Museum project, but in this second project the aim is to cover a significant proportion of the job-control language and therefore a wide range of powerful facilities. I have started with a sub-set of the most frequently used instructions and my aim is to extend this

```
(Job authorisation for local computer)
(compiler specifier)
COPYSBF(TAPE6,OUTPUT)
REWIND(TAPE6)
COPY(INPUT,FILEA)
QUEUE(FILEA=IN/I=ULCC)
REWIND(TAPE6)
END OF RECORD
(Program which produces results to be put on microfiche)
END OF RECORD
(Data for program)
END OF RECORD
(Job authorisation for computer producing microfiche)
FICHE(TAPE6,START,CMNDS=HERE,FMT=NONE)
*TSQ1,1,3,N,442
*COL,100:'P.M.K. MORRIS AND E.B. JAMES'
*COL,200:'PENTATEUCH TABLE 25'
*TFD 1(5,16,1,2,69,100)
*TFD 2(5,16,7,2,69,200)
*TFD 9(18,18,1,1,3,442)
XMIT(TAPE6)
FICHE(TAPE6,END)
END OF FILE
```

Fig. 2. Original control instructions for microfiche production.

incrementally until the requirements of most users can be satisfied.

The instruction sequence of Fig. 2 is an example of the problems which we face with a complex job-control language. This gives a list of the control instructions typically required to produce a piece of microfiche containing the output from a computer program. It will be noticed that several of the instructions are in "machine-code" levels of detail and these are used to specify the format of the microfiche heading. While the knowledge of such a detailed method of specification will enable the user to create an entirely arbitrary design for the title and heading of the microfiche, it is perfectly practical for the majority of users to have available only the ability to write one or two lines of title in a standard size. This limited facility can be provided by a simple, one-word command, replacing the full instructions. Here is an example of an interactive sequence:

Do you require the output on the line printer, on microfilm or on microfiche?

microfiche

Please give the title you require on the microfiche (here the user types in the required title).

. . . .

It should also be noted that the underlying job-control instructions for providing program results on the line printer or on microfilm are in turn entirely different from those required for microfiche production. A number of our current users produce large amounts of paper as output from the line printer merely because they find that learning the control instructions for microfilm or microfiche takes too much effort to make it worthwhile. It seems likely that the provision of a simple microfiche facility for users would have a considerable impact on the economy of the typical computer centre.

In this second project, the protective ware consisted of an interactive interpreter for the host job-control language. The first version to be constructed assumed that the user would be involved in various basic kinds of activity. These were: obtaining a file of data from storage, listing on output the data file, printing the output in some permanent form, editing the file of data, compiling a file which is actually a list of program statements, replacing an existing data file with a new one, and finally, leaving the computing system. On entering this system, the user was provided with a list of keywords concerning these operations as given above. Then the system requested "What do you want to do?" The reply expected was one of those keywords, and if this was not recognized then the list was repeated. If no parameters were provided with the command word then an interactive sequence was started and the parameters required were asked for in succession. If the user wished to edit a file for example, the next question would be: "What is the name of the file that you wish to edit?" If a particular data file was already in use, then the user could simply press the return key to indicate a "null" reply and the file currently in use would be assumed to be the object of the editing operation. If the user gave some other file name then it would be retrieved from storage automatically.

A pilot version of the software for the second project was written in the PASCAL language and designed to run on the large CDC Computer. We have since obtained a Research Machines 380Z microcomputing system and have discovered that protective ware is far more effective if it can be implemented on a dedicated processor close to the user. We therefore propose that users of all large machines should in the future make use of them through an "intelligent" terminal which will implement the protective ware. The local processor will interact with the user, determine requirements on the remote machine and automatically generate the necessary protocols to request service from the remote machine. As an example of what has already been achieved, we have made it possible for the user to obtain a named file of data from the remote machine merely by providing its name. In response to the request, the local machine initiates entry to the time-sharing system on the remote machine, obtains the required file, and stores it locally for later use. All of this can be carried out without the user requiring *any* knowledge of the remote machine or its protocol. Indeed, the user can be totally unaware that his local machine is "talking" to a remote computer. There is no technical reason why remote computations cannot be carried out in a similarly painless way.

It should be noted that in using this technique we have overcome the fundamental difficulties of defining and enforcing a standard on all operating systems. As long as a specialist is able to keep the protective ware up to date, the end-user is not concerned with the job-control language of any machine that can be accessed through the protective ware.

Proposed new developments on this second project will be included in a general plan of development specified in the final section of this chapter. Before that I aim to deal with objections raised against the overall policy.

V. OBJECTIONS TO THE NEW APPROACH:
THE LIMITS TO SYMPATHY

Since becoming involved with the production of user-friendly inter-faces I have been aware of considerable disagreement on methods and approach. Here are some of the counter-proposals which have been put up and my views in defence of my present position.

The direct criticism of the work usually arises from those who deny the findings concerning the present situation. They suggest that the current interface, since it is used by so many, is perfectly satis-factory and if not exactly right, needs only a gradual improvement of the existing situation. They look forward to an increasing expertise among users, and many genuinely believe that the existence of an improved formal language will make the problem of approaching the computer a comparatively trivial one. Behind most of these sugges-tions lies the belief that a precise, disciplined approach to the solution of problems will provide the necessary answers, and that users who do not employ this discipline should not expect to receive help. Certainly, many critics do not believe that it is either practical or sensible to try to put any significant amount of tolerance into the machine side of the interface. Again, the conventional line is to suggest that the answer to all problems lies in the improvement of external documentation and this is naturally expected to be in a written or printed form.

I believe that soon it will not be necessary to counter this type of criticism. It seems to arise mainly among those who have no appreciation of the change in the type of computer user and the acceleration of this change in the future. Our survey at the Science Museum and elsewhere has made it absolutely clear that even if effective documentation is provided it will not be read by the majority of users. They will naturally expect all the information to be in one place and that place to be the interface with the computer. We have observed that the majority of even the most sophisticated type of users regularly have problems with the present interface, and I have no belief that other, less experienced users will find it any easier. I am also certain that the newer type of user will just not tolerate the level of effort presently required to learn about computing systems in order to make use of them. We have spent a great deal of time in attempts to produce adequate documentation to support existing systems, and have found this a difficult task. We do know that if sufficient information is provided to cover all the likely points of difficulty, then it is likely to be so voluminous that it will be almost impossible to structure in such a way that a beginning user can really achieve anything for some considerable time. Even if we were able to point out all the problems in advance, I see no reason for the user to be demoralized before starting by a list of all the things that could go wrong. Surely these problems should arise as and when the user needs to know about a particular aspect of the system! I also believe that many of the difficulties could be removed entirely by minor improvements in the design of the interface, and see no reason why extra trouble should not be taken to do this. In summary, I would suggest that those critics who hold that the current interface is satisfactory have simply not had experience of the difficulties of less experienced users or do not wish to be concerned with them.

A second form of criticism is related very much to the same attitude of mind displayed by those who make the first type of criticism. They would say that making things easy for users is counter-productive. They suggest that by providing the facility for users to express themselves somewhat imprecisely and get away with it, we are encouraging a sloppy approach to programming, and to using computers in general, which will not stand the users in good stead later on.

This type of criticism has arisen very much in connection with our work on fault-tolerant systems; that is, in providing a useful answer to those who indicate their requirements imprecisely. It is clear that our critics in this area have a particular approach to problem-solving that is typical of the formal mathematician. They are psychologically inclined towards precision and have an emotional distaste for imprecision. This attitude is typical of the thorough-going theorist and, naturally, that produces an approach whereby the part of the real world which is not strictly definable is ignored in the development of a theory. While this is perfectly possible in the academic world, it is clear that people solving real probems work in the real world where imprecisions abound on all sides. I would counter the accusations of sloppiness by suggesting that the imprecision is in fact not counter-productive at all. The level of precision is one of those variables which controls the amount of effort involved in producing a solution. Often it seems likely that we aim at an arbitrarily high level of precision both in the accuracy to which the original situation is defined and, incidently, in the accuracy with which we measure and calculate the data. This arbitrary level becomes in due course fixed as acceptable and any-thing below that level is "not satisfactory". Such an arbitrary level of precision comprises the whole existing structure of programs and methods of computation. In the future I believe that it will be possible to specify requirements much less precisely than now and to obtain results which although imprecise are nevertheless good enough for a particular purpose. It should be possible to define a level of precision which lies somewhere between existing formal methods and the use of managerial hunches. I hope that a greater knowledge and appreciation of the inherent advantages of the apparently sloppy thought-processes of human beings will demon-strate their fundamental correctness in the solving of complicated problems in the real world (Partridge and James, 1972).

A third type of criticism comes from those who, while not denying the usefulness of our approach, suggest that the necessary methods which are required on the machine side of the user interface will make the computer system too inefficient.

I believe that this type of criticism stems from the level of machine efficiency which is considered to be acceptable at present. This arbitrary level is one which has been familiar in computing for the last twenty years, where the computer is employed in a calcula-ting role and any other type of operation is normally carried out by the human user either before or after the computation. I suggest that this arbitrary level of "acceptable" efficiency should be re-examined. It is clear, for example, that the increasing use of very cheap micro-processors will enable us to give the computer far more work to do in controlling the user interface than has seemed practical in the past. Many critics, when speaking against the existence of helpful interfaces, probably have in mind earlier work, which tended to produce systems where the user was asked an interminable series of questions and was unable to speed things up by using detailed instructions when these were known. Clearly we must provide in all systems for some time to come the facility to *not* make use of the helpful interface, and to create instruction sequences in the old-fashioned way.

In summary then, I believe that the criticism of work on user-helpful interfaces is in the main due to misunderstanding the aims of this work. I believe that there are no limits to what the machine can or should do in order to minimize the overall resources required of the person in charge. I see the only serious barrier to work in this area to be the psychological problem connected with the inability of the user to accept advice from an impersonal computing system. The next section summarizes what has been achieved in the user interface work so far, with a sketch plan for further development.

VI. A PLAN FOR DEVELOPMENT

In conclusion, let me summarize the objectives of my current work in terms of the "user-friendly" interface I would like to see in the future.

The immediate objective is to improve the interface with existing computer systems through the addition of protective ware. By this means we hope to produce a climate of opinion which will enable a radical revision of the organization on the machine side to take place. The extent to which this new style of interface proves acceptable to the user will provide a measure of its ability to define what the user requires. New designs of hardware and software can therefore be devised with greater confidence.

I have concentrated my early work on controlling the naive user's access to a simple package at the Science Museum. Current work is concerned with enabling the more experienced user to specify operating systems requirements in a way which does not demand knowledge of specialized formats relevant to a particular machine. In the future, I expect the work to develop in several directions. The first involves integrating earlier work on the adaptive analysis of program statements into our protective ware (James and Partridge, 1973). By enabling the program which processes user requests to learn commonly used *sequences* of operations we can later prompt less experienced users towards these expected sequences. If the system "knows" that certain patterns of use are commoner than others then it can cope with a greater inaccuracy in their specification.

Another direction for development will involve moving this computer-assisted learning style of interface down to the more detailed level of program use. For example, there are comprehensive libraries of programs already available in the area of numerical computation, which are not used widely because it seems more difficult to understand their written documentation than to recreate the program from scratch. Our new style of interface can also assist in the preparation of programs in conventional programming languages. In this area I see our work as complementary to that of Hoffman (1973) and Cunningham and Pugh (1976).

Bennett (1976) also describes an area of development very much in line with our orientation towards inexperienced users. He provides a *decision support system* in which the user can summon to a display screen, in a variety of convenient graphical formats, the collection of data on which a decision is to be made. This provides assistance in the problem definition stage rather than in the computational stage of an already well-defined problem, which is the only area supported by current prescriptive programming languages. I would propose to continue this line of development and make available a range of tools for organizing and re-organizing data through a mixed-initiative dialogue, which would enable the user to survey continuously how machine activities are progressing. Facilities would also be provided to enable users to define sequences of operations which *they* use frequently as single operational commands. The groundwork for this development is provided in a more formal programming context by Lee (1973).

A third area of work is concerned with the revolutionary changes in the method of communication with the computer made possible by microprocessor developments. While always desirable, it is now essential to break the domination of the written word as the only means of interaction. In this area, the "games" market is spearheading developments by the provision of spoken output (e.g. Texas Instruments, 1978). In due course the "professional" market may catch up. Again, the provision of cheap *moving* graphical displays in full colour should soon make our previous ideas on the production of results obsolete.

Making it possible for the user to speak to the computing system and draw pictures for it is much more difficult. It has been suggested that unless the machine has in some way learned what to expect, in other words what is commonly provided by users, then it will never be able to interpret the garbled, incomplete messages which people find to be the most effective means to use in specifying their requirements. The groundwork for setting up the necessary learning and interpreting structures in the machine has already been laid, (Partridge and James, 1974; James and Partridge, 1976). It is now necessary to implement these proposals on the high-speed, low-cost systems becoming available.

Finally, I suggest that developments in user interface techniques are related closely to their provision on practical computing systems, for testing by non-expert people with a serious task to perform. We must counteract the natural desire of researchers to retire to their ivory tower and dream of idealized systems for idealized users. Only by continually associating the end-users with new development proposals shall we progress towards truly sympathetic computing systems.

REFERENCES

Backus, J. (1978). Can programming be liberated from the Von Neumann style? ACM Turing Memorial Lecture, *Communications of the ACM,* 21, 613–641.

Bennett, J.L. (1976). User-oriented graphics systems for decision support in unstructured tasks. *Proceedings of the ACM/SIGGRAPH Symposium Workshop on User-Oriented Design of Interactive Graphics Systems,* 3–11.

Bobrow, D.G., Kaplan, R.M., Kay, M., Norman, D.A., Thompson, H. and Winograd, T. (1977).   GUS: A frame-driven dialog system. *Artificial Intelligence,* 8, 155–173.

Cunningham, R.J. and Pugh, C.G. (1976). A language-independent system to aid the development of structured programs. *Software-Practice and Experience,* 8, 487–503.

Evans, C.R. (1971). A study of on-line interrogation by a time-sharing terminal with computer/consultant comparison analysis. *Report Comsci 52,* National Physical Laboratory, London.

Hoffman, H.-J. (1973). Programming by selection. *Report PURI/73,* Research Group on Programming Languages and Compilers, Technical University of Darmstadt, West Germany.

Hume, J.N.P. (1977). Education in computing versus user needs. *Proceedings of Information Processing 77,* 47–51.

Ireland, D. (1978). The user population at the Science Museum. M.Sc. Thesis, Dept. of Computing and Control, Imperial College, London.

James, E.B. and Partridge, D.P. (1973). Adaptive·correction of program statements. *Communications of the ACM,* 16, 27–37.

James, E.B. and Partridge, D.P. (1976). Tolerance to innacuracy in computer programs. *J. Br. Computer Soc.,* 19, 207–212.

Kriloff, H.Z. (1976). Human factor considerations for interactive display systems. *Proceedings of the ACM/SIGGRAPH Symposium Workshop on User-Oriented Design of Interactive Graphics Systems,* 45–52.

Lee, I.R. (1973). A model for computer-assisted programming. Ph.D. Thesis, London University.

Miller, R.B. (1976). The human task as reference for system interface design. *Proceedings of the ACM/SIGGRAPH Symposium Workshop on User-Oriented Design of Interactive Graphics Systems,* 97–100.

Negroponte, N. (1976). An idiosyncratic systems approach to interactive graphics. *Proceedings of the ACM/SIGGRAPH Symposium Workshop on User-Oriented Design of Interactive Graphics Systems,* 53–60.

Newman, I.A. (1978). Personalised user interfaces to computer systems. *Proceedings of Eurocomp 78,* 473–486.

Partridge, D.P. and James, E.B. (1972). Machine intelligence: the best of both worlds? *Int. J. Man–Machine Stud.,* 4, 23–31.

Partridge, D.P. and James, E.B. (1974). Natural information processing. *Int. J. Man–Machine Stud.,* 6, 205–235.

Sandewall, E. (1978). Programming in an interactive environment: the LISP experience. *Computing Surveys,* 10, 35–71.

Senn, J.A. and Ives, B. (1978). Behavioural education requisites for application-oriented computer scientists. *Proceedings of the Tenth SIGCSE Technical Symposium on Computer Science Education,* 195–201.

Sterling, T.D. (1979). Consumer difficulties with computerized transactions: an empirical investigation. *Communications of the ACM,* 22, 283–289.

Sutherland, I.E. and Mead, C.A. (1977). Microelectronics and computer science. In *Scientific American* (eds) *Microelectronics,* pp. 110–123. San Francisco: W.H. Freeman.

Texas Instruments (1978). "Speak and Spell" toy. Available from many toy shops.

Weiss, P.A. (1971). *Hierarchically Organized Systems in Theory and Practice.* New York: Haffner.

Winograd, T. (1979). Beyond programming languages. *Communications of the ACM,* 22, 391–401.

11. Design Procedures for User Involvement and User Support*

L. DAMODARAN and K.D. EASON

Department of Human Sciences, University of Technology, Loughborough, England

I. INTRODUCTION

Computer systems stand or fall on the ability and willingness of users to make effective use of them. Systems designers may feel they have created a perfect system for the users but if the users are not also convinced, their efforts may have been wasted. The medium by which issues of users' ability and willingness may be tackled is the contact between users and systems staff before and after systems implementation. For convenience these phases may be defined as user involvement in systems design and user support during the operational life of the system. For the user, however, these phases form a continuum which shapes his attitudes and responses to the system.

The aim of this paper is to examine the purposes of user involvement and user support, and to evaluate critically the many procedures that now exist to meet these aims.

II. USER INVOLVEMENT IN SYSTEMS DESIGN

Few systems which are designed for a known user population (e.g. the employees of an organization) are designed without some form of user involvement. The tradition is that a team of computer systems experts take responsibility for the design and implementation of the system and invite user involvement to the degree and in the form that they deem appropriate. The reasons for which they may seek user involvement can be listed as follows.

*First published in the Infotech State of the Art Report on "Man–Computer Communication" (ed.) B. Schakel, Infotech International Limited, Maidenhead (1979).

Local Knowledge. To create an effective system it may be necessary to develop a detailed understanding of the task environment within which the system must operate. Only the potential user population may have this knowledge in detail and the systems designer may seek involvement to tap this expertise.

Resistance to Change. Many systems have been rejected or poorly used because users felt the system was being imposed upon them. There is a widely held belief that by involving users in systems design, the chances of resistance to change when the system is implemented are reduced.

User Demands. Computer systems can lead to widespread changes in vital interests of employees; jobs can be lost, cherished skills can become irrelevant, sources of power can be lost, etc. Many employees, and especially their representatives, have become aware of these possibilities and are now demanding the right to examine, and if necessary challenge, the systems design plans.

"Because it is Right." Throughout the Western world there is a move towards industrial democracy. In practice this means that employees have more say in decisions that affect them. The decisions taken in computer systems design certainly affect employees and, where industrial democracy is being pursued, it is considered right and appropriate for employees to be involved in systems design.

It will be apparent that these different routes to user involvement will lead to different forms and degrees of involvement. Underlying the different approaches is the question of power in systems design. At one extreme designers retain all decision-making powers and users simply provide information requested of them. At the other extreme the whole concept of systems "experts" taking the decisions is under challenge. The concept of control in systems design is rep-

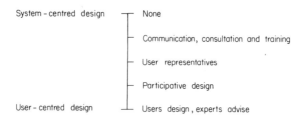

Fig. 1. Types of user involvement.

resented in Fig. 1 as a dimension upon which can be located the variety of user involvement procedures currently in use.

Each stage along the continuum will be examined with three questions in mind: what arguments are there in favour of the approach, what methods are employed within the general framework, and what is known of its success and failure?

A. No User Involvement

It is worth considering the case against user involvement because there are undoubtedly disadvantages. The arguments are either that it is unnecessary because the design team contains all the expertise it needs or that involvement is costly and impractical within the time and resource constraints of the project. The argument about necessity relates only to the need to tap the local knowledge of users and may be valid where systems designers have extensive experience as users. However, to adopt this view is to deny that users have any right to be involved in decision processes which may affect their future. This argument is becoming progressively less acceptable to employees in modern organizations.

Arguments about the cost and effectiveness of user involvement are more germane because it takes time and effort to involve users and it is a difficult process to manage effectively. There is therefore no guarantee that it will be successful. Groholt (1980), a Norwegian systems manager, reports for example, that in his considerable experience user involvement has rarely been successful because neither designers nor users have access to procedures suitable to this purpose. Far from suggesting the abandonment of user involvement however, Groholt advocates more far-reaching forms of involvement, to be discussed below. He does this because in his experience design without user involvement was far worse, with considerable time lost in systems implementation because of resistance to change. The present position is that there appears to be no alternative but to attempt user involvement although success may be limited.

B. One-way Involvement: Communication, Consultation and Training

These techniques share the common feature that they are under the complete control of the design team. There are various communication media which can be used to keep users abreast of systems developments (newsletters, meetings, notice-board announcements, etc.) but they all tend to limit the response the user can make. These techniques are useful for reducing rumour but they cannot be expected to lead to active commitment and support. "Consultation" is here taken to mean the process by which designers might seek to elicit the expert knowledge of users by conducting some form of task or job analysis. This process does enable the user to contribute and his contribution can be very valuable. However, typically, the user is constrained by the structure of the question he is asked and, if he has any fears about redundancy or loss of skill etc., it is unlikely he will be able to voice them. Finally, training is an essential part of system implementation but it is a one-way process (from trainer to trainee) and occurs when it is too late for the user to influence design decisions. These techniques therefore each have a valuable contribution to make and from the designers' viewpoint are relatively safe and straightforward to conduct. Where users have serious doubts about the wisdom of systems design solutions however, these techniques are unlikely to allow those doubts to be heard.

C. User Representatives

When the aim is to ensure that the voice of the users is heard effectively within systems design, a very popular strategy is to involve representatives of the users in the process. This can be accomplished in many ways and we may group the alternatives into two categories: involvement in the design team, and involvement in a consultative or steering committee.

1. *Representatives in the Design Team*

Employing users to supplement the technical experts in the design team has a number of advantages. It means designers have user expertise close at hand whenever they need it. If the user is trained in systems techniques, the design team effectively expands its manpower. As many organizations have discovered, user representatives can also perform very useful liaison roles between users and the system after implementation. We shall consider this possibility more fully in Section III.

Inevitably there are also disadvantages, which Hedberg (1975) has referred to as "hostage phenomena". One advantage a technical designer might see in this arrangement is that it provides safe and controllable user expertise within the design team. Hedberg considers this a disadvantage because the user will rapidly be influenced more by other designers than by his user origins and will become progressively less representative of users. Indeed, if the user has volunteered for full-time membership of the design team, he probably has aspirations for a career in systems design and is not a typical user. There are also other problems. With user representatives close at hand, the design team may not see the necessity to contact and consult other users. If they get the whole-hearted support of representatives they can be lulled into believing that they have the support of all users, which may be a serious mistake. One way of avoiding the "hostage" problems is for the representative to be a part-time member of the design team and to retain contact with the users he represents, but this too has its problems. Representatives of all kinds suffer role conflict; they find themselves caught between equally convincing but incompatible arguments by users and designers, and it needs maturity and understanding by everyone to help representatives cope with the dilemmas in which they find themselves. Finally, many user representatives who are not trained in systems techniques find it difficult to understand design drawings and flowcharts and impossible to understand the ramifications of system proposals for their colleagues. Similarly they will have difficulty expressing the needs and knowledge of users in a way that is useful to technical designers. This relates to a general problem of all methods of user involvement; we may find the right medium of involvement but we need methods by which to make effective use of the medium.

2. *Representatives in Consultative or Steering Committees*

User involvement in the design team is primarily useful in the detailed specification of the system, but there remains the question of assessments of the wider implications of proposals for users' jobs and the organization. These implications are more often examined within steering committees which manage system projects and these committees frequently include user representatives. At this level users are more able to see the strategic issues associated with system proposals and they may be in a position to challenge unacceptable consequences. Experience with this arrangement has however raised a number of issues. The first issue concerns the power of the relevant committee. Many users have now become disillusioned because they were members of consultative committees which had no executive control over the design team and whose views tended to be ignored when they were contrary to design-team objectives. Ineffective involvement of this kind is probably counter-productive and hardens user attitudes, and users are tending to seek committees with direct executive powers. A second issue is the membership of the committee. There is a need for all sections of the user population to be represented, but frequently senior members of departments are expected to represent junior staff, and departments which are not central to the design are not represented although their vital interests may well be at risk. The question of role conflict is again an issue. Representatives can find themselves explaining the systems design case to their colleagues and being accused of joining the "other" side. The whole question of representation is a problem because usually the committee member is officially given no time to consult the people he represents or to report back to them. The dangers of this are twofold. The user may represent no-one's views but his own and, whilst he may become enthusiastic about the project, uninvolved users may remain apathetic or hostile.

Finally, there is frequently a large element of negotiation in deriving an acceptable system solution. There may be questions of redundancy, retraining, loss of job skills, demarcation etc. to be settled before the system can be implemented. As a recent survey by the National Computing Centre (Farrow, 1977) has shown, most organizations have formal negotiating machinery for dealing with questions of pay and conditions, and the relationship between this machinery and a project steering committee can be a problem. Farrow further concludes that the existing machinery is usually incapable of dealing with the broader social and organizational implications of design proposals and recommends that companies and unions review the methods of consultation and negotiation they employ to assess their ability to cope with the new demands of computer technology.

D. Participative Design

The failure of one-way involvement techniques and user representative techniques is that they cannot adequately utilize the expertise nor gain the commitment of all of the user population. To counteract this, various forms of participative design are now being employed which seek to bring all users into the design process. Case studies of this approach have been reported for example by Clausen (1978), Hedberg (1980) and Mumford (1980). The general principle is not that all users should be involved in programming, technical systems design etc. but that they should be involved in selecting the form of work organization they will operate, i.e. the jobs they will do, how tasks will be allocated between them, and the task relationships that will exist between employees and the computer system. It is only after decisions are taken at this level that the technical system specification can be formulated. Thereafter, as the technical system is developed, users are consulted on detailed issues associated with the achievement of the agreed specification.

When this approach is successful, as it has been in the cases reported by Mumford, users greet the system with enthusiasm and commitment. Inevitably, however, there are problems in applying the approach. It means that technical systems designers play a minor role in the early stages of the project because it is the users who specify the requirements of the system and this can be a lengthy process. It is difficult to manage a design process of this kind when there are a large number of users, and the most successful applications have been with small groups of users (or with user populations which form clearly identifiable sub-groups which can participate in the process independently). Hedberg, however, reports a case in which all the employees of a Swedish building society were effectively involved in participative design conferences. The central problem is again technique; users need considerable help to conceive of different forms of work organization and to consider which is most appropriate to them. Participative design therefore requires skilful management by people who are able to provide information and concepts in the right form to be useful without precluding users from making their own decisions. There can also be problems with regard to user attitudes to this process. When an organization has hitherto not involved employees in participative design, they will inevitably be suspicious of the motives for soliciting this involvement and it can take a considerable time before confidence is gained. Finally, a scheme of this kind can have a very successful beginning and then can go badly awry when computer systems designers seek to implement the agreed specification. The problems of meeting user requirements within the time and resource constraints can mean designers radically change the specification. Hedberg reports a case in which design problems led to a radical change proposed by employees and accepted by management and designers being subsequently rejected in favour of a system which supported the *status quo*. In our own work (Eason, 1977; Damodaran, 1980) we have found that a continuous process of trials, consultations and pilot schemes is necessary to prevent this kind of drift occurring.

E. Users Design; Experts Advise

The frequency with which the various approaches outlined above have led to users finding their requirements ignored or rejected has led to a number of more radical proposals. These proposals have one feature in common: power and responsibility for systems design firmly resides with the users, and computer technology experts are cast in the role of advisors. This is in contrast to the normal arrangement whereby senior management give the power and responsibility for design to the technical experts who thereafter may involve users as they consider appropriate. The critics of this approach point out that it frequently leads to a re-assertion of technical control whenever problems occur, and user needs are ignored.

1. Legislation

One way in which this shift in power is being brought about is by legislation, and in those countries where industrial democracy is already enshrined in law there are rapid movements in this direction. In Norway, for example, an employee has the legal right to be involved in the design of any computer system that is going to affect his work. There are a variety of laws in Sweden which affect systems design, and Docherty (1980) has produced a useful summary together with a commentary on the effects they have had to date.

2. Union Action

The other major source of pressure for moves in this direction comes from trade unions. There is growing recognition amongst unions, particularly on the continent, that computer technology has widespread implications for their members and they are making major efforts to ensure they are able to protect the interests of their members in systems design. Within the continental unions there now appears to be a major division of opinion about how this may be accomplished. One view is that it can be done by working within the current framework, e.g. joining steering committees, etc., and participating in design in order to promote user interests. The other view is based on a conflict strategy. It takes as its fundamental premise that the requirements of management and workers are in conflict and that, by joining a structure dominated by the requirements of management, the requirements of the workers will not receive adequate attention. The demand is therefore that the users should control the design process and, if this is not acceptable, that the unions should adopt a negotation posture in which they assemble technical experts to complement the experts employed by managers. Systems design would then become a process of negotiation, with each side supported by an expert team which can put forward systems design proposals and challenge the proposals of the other side. The degree to which this confrontational strategy gains support will no doubt be inversely related to the degree to which users find they are able to participate successfully in systems design within the current framework.

F. Conclusions

In the early years of data-processing applications within commerce and industry the accent in systems design was upon solving technical problems and it is not surprising that the current power-structure for systems design has evolved. The growing awareness amongst users, and those who represent their interests, that computer technology is capable of re-structuring the way work is conducted, means that the system-centred design approach is being challenged. In particular, in this field and in many others, the role of the technical expert and especially his right to decide what is appropriate for other people, is being questioned. It is unlikely that the more limited forms of user involvement will be able to answer these demands although they may be useful in circumstances where they meet the expectations of management, users and technical designers. As Clausen (1978) has pointed out, the form of user involvement to be employed needs to be geared to the culture and political situation of the country. In some nothing short of complete user control is acceptable and there are others where such a strategy would leave users bewildered and suspicious. The trends however are quite clear: as users appreciate the powerful force for change that the computer represents, so they are progressively becoming better equipped and more organized to demand more effective forms of involvement in systems design. The problem is that there needs to be the will on the part of managers and designers to involve users, and more importantly, the development of effective methods by which users can participate successfully. If we are too slow to respond or too slow to develop effective methods, the dominant strategy for the future may be confrontational. It seems unlikely that systems designed at both the strategic and the tactical level by a process of negotation will be a very successful means of harnessing computer technology for the individual user or for the organization.

III. USER SUPPORT

User support has not received the degree of attention associated with user involvement. However, every system pays some attention to the need to support users in their interactions with computer technology. User involvement and user support are closely linked processes which both dramatically influence the effectiveness of any computer application.

The use of any technological system has generally to be supported through maintenance of the hardware and by promoting relevant skills and behaviours of the user. In the case of the computer user the technology is usually in a state of evolutionary development. The dynamic nature of the relationship has a fundamental significance for the nature of the support system it demands.

A. Minimum Compensatory User Support

In examining the purpose of user support it is clear that its primary function is to compensate for the lack of "transparency" in the human–computer interface. In other words, interaction with a computer usually requires the human user to compensate for the limitations and shortcomings of the technological system. The user has to learn how to initiate interaction, how to terminate it or how to change direction. He must learn to interpret system messages, to understand output, to cope with system malfunctions and even with system breakdown. In the design context it is important to be able to define the scale and type of user support needs. As a starting point it is useful to identify the minimum user support which is required to sustain human–computer interaction. This minimum requirement apppears to be that which ensures (i) that essential data is provided to the system by users, and (ii) that system output is received, understood and assimilated.

B. Evolutionary User Support

Beyond meeting the basic system needs, the second purpose of user support is to promote continued viability of human–computer interaction. This evolutionary user support function is complex and varied since it is concerned with an evolving computer system applied in a changing environment through the activities of a human user who is also changing as a result of his learning from experience. Successful computer applications are characterized by the number and diversity of mechanisms which have arisen to meet these needs. The importance of supporting an evolving human–computer relationship lies in the fact that unless a given system can continue to develop and to match the needs of the environment in which it functions it ceases to have value. The crucial mediator who transforms potential computing power into an actual resource is the human user. It is therefore essential that the system develops in a way which is consistent with development of the users' interests, needs and skills. It is clear that defining design criteria for evolutionary support mechanisms is far more difficult than describing minimum user support needs. Designing for growth and flexibility of both the user and the computer system becomes the guiding force.

C. Methods of User Support

Research into user support mechanisms, methods and techniques reveals a variety of ways of meeting compensatory and evolutionary user support needs.

1. *Training*

Clearly the compensatory needs are the most widely recognized support needs because systems cannot become operational until the minimum requirements are met. Consequently training needs are the most commonly acknowledged user support needs. Prior to or concurrent with system implementation prospective users can expect to receive training. The initial training needs of the new user considered earlier are first, for sufficient contextual information to understand what the computer system can do for him, his business function or work role. This kind of need is frequently met, with varying success, by presentations or appreciation seminars. Second, the user requires a working knowledge of routine operation procedures. In a batch system this can involve completing computer data request forms, while in an on-line system it will require operation of a keyboard, light-pen or other input devices. Instruction in operating procedures is always recognized as an essential activity. In some instances it is the only kind of support need which is acknowledged and for which formal mechanisms exist. In these situations training is seen as a "one-off" exercise that ceases after initial instruction has been received.

2. *Documentary Support*

Often there is also recognition of the need for documentary support (user instruction manuals and circulars) and for availability of computer personnel to assist when problems arise in operation. It will be evident that these mechanisms are all compensatory in function. From the above it will emerge that two classes of user support need are being discussed. One concerns the initial training for new users and the other involves provision of continued support once "normal" systems running is in progress.

Where continued user support is concerned, computer applications differ widely in the degree and extent of both formal and informal methods and techniques of user support. The range of support mechanisms identified in research are listed in Fig. 2. Some organizations will feature only two or three of these mechanisms while a minority will include them all in varying proportions and with differing degrees of formality.

Documentary
1. Instruction manuals
2. Within-system aids
3. Circulars

Human Support
1. Formal training instructors
2. Computer advisory personnel   }   System-centred
3. Dedicated programmer
4. Local experts
5. Human interface   }   User-centred
6. Organizational representatives

Fig. 2. Methods of user support.

Each of these support mechanisms fulfils a different kind of need and each has its limitations and problems. While a full consideration of each is beyond the scope of this chapter there are certain general points of relevance here. First, the documentary support is characterized by its standardized nature and by the one-way nature of the communication. Typically, instruction manuals will be issued when a system is first introduced and, subsequently, to new users. These documents attempt, usually, to cover the entire range of system facilities, are bulky and cumbersome and have a variety of indexing problems. This manual is then followed by the issue of circulars sent out by the computer department to update the manuals. These are rarely incorporated into the manual and are frequently discarded. Manuals and circulars share the very serious shortcoming of having standardized format and contents irrespective of the type of user for whom they are intended. Since user type and the nature of the user's task will have a crucial bearing on the kind of interactions he has with the computer system it is clear that standardized documents will rarely be appropriate for all users. Within-system aids frequently suffer similar shortcomings. However, increasingly sophisticated designs, offering choice to the user on the degree of help he requires and allowing for varying levels of skill, show great promise for making the computer interface increasingly transparent.

3. Human Support Mechanisms

With regard to the human support mechanisms, the system-centred support personnel fulfil a formalized and largely compensatory role. They are responsible for training users, resolving problems when they arise, providing assistance with hardware and software failures and developing further computer facilities. "Dedicated programmers" refers to the situation where a programmer is designated to support a user function by developing appropriate computer facilities. Close liaison between programmer and user is essential for successful development and fulfils an evolutionary support function. However, there are relatively few examples of this kind of use of system-centred personnel. Among user-centred support personnel the "local expert" can often be identified. This is an individual who, as a user, has become more skilled in use of the computer system than most other users (Eason, et al., 1974). He becomes recognized, generally informally, as a readily accessible source of expertise in the user department. Research is beginning to reveal that local experts are a valuable and important factor in determining the success of a computer application. The second category of user-centred support is the "human interface". This term refers to individuals who operate a computer system on behalf of other, indirect, users such as a senior manager or a doctor. The role of the human interface is essentially a compensatory one which is necessitated because the demands of using a computer system are seen as incompatible with the work roles of the indirect users. Finally, organizational representatives are a special category of human interface who also fulfil a compensatory role in acting on the boundary between the public and the computer system of their parent organization. Bank cashiers and airline reservation clerks are examples of organizational representatives. In concluding this brief review of user support mechanisms it is important to recognize that the potentially crucial role of supporting user system evolution is generally a function which is fulfilled informally. Organizational changes and policy decisions are long overdue to formalize and to reinforce the effectiveness of the "local expert".

Because of the limitations of each support mechanism there is in most computer applications a network of mechanisms which has developed in response to *ad hoc* user needs rather than as a designed feature. The network generally comprises a series of human intermediaries, some system-oriented and some user-based, who facilitate use of documentary support and use of the system itself. The human support mechanism forms a chain of contacts to bridge the gap in focus, language and concepts between computer users and the computer system. This kind of network operates most successfully when the user can choose the level of help he needs and when he is allowed access to relevant sources of support at his behest.

D. Designing a User Support System

To design a user support system requires an appraisal of the range of support needs. In this chapter the minimum needs have been stated briefly and the needs for an evolutionary form of support described. These needs have implications for the design of software, hardware, documentation, human support and organizational policy. Much of the current literature on user involvement and support might suggest that these activities are divorced from considerations of hardware and software choice. Yet designing operating procedures, for example, to promote "transparency" by simplification, use of user terms, careful structuring of abbreviations and codes, can only occur successfully through user involvement. Similarly, selecting hardware to meet user needs requires involvement of users in the decision process.

It is important to emphasize the close relationship between user involvement and user support. Throughout the discussion of user support systems there is tacit acknowledgement that the precise statement of relevant design criteria can only come from involvement of the user in the design process. For instance, the design of appropriate within-system aids requires the user to assist in their definition.

IV. CONCLUSION

In conclusion we have noted in studies of many systems that systems design does not, in practice, end with system implementation. If the system is in any way successful it stimulates the development of the user which in turn leads to new demands upon the system. The aspect of user support which we have termed "evolutionary" may therefore be regarded as a direct extension of user involvement in systems design since it often leads to further systems design. The simultaneous consideration of the two topics of user involvement and user support in fact leads to possibilities which may ease some of the problems which beset user involvement in systems design. For example, it might perhaps be useful to blur the point of implementation so that users become progressively more involved with an evolving system. Perhaps also the concept of user support should be developed from the beginning of system design, so that a major aim of designers is to help users to be involved so that they may first design and then use their own system.

Finally, it should be noted that all of the trends point to a change in the role of the applications system designer in the future. From being the designer, the man who determines and operates the system, he is being asked progressively and on all fronts to adopt an indirect role in which he advises, supports, liaises with and helps to develop the ability of the user population to make effective use of computing resources.

REFERENCES

Clausen, H. (1978). Concepts and experiences with participative design approaches. *Proceedings of the Conference on Design and Implementation of Computer-Based Planning Systems*, Cologne.

Damodaran, L. (1977). User involvement in system design—why? and how? In A. Parkin (ed.) *Computing and People*. London: Edward Arnold.

Damodaran, L. (forthcoming). The role of user support—actual and potential. In B. Shackel (ed.) *Man-Computer Interaction*. Amsterdam: Sijthoff and Noordhoff.

Docherty, P. (1980).* Some consequences of acts and agreements in the Scandinavian countries regulating user participation and influence on systems design. In N. Bjørn-Andersen (ed.) *The Human Side of Information Processing*. Amsterdam: North Holland.

Eason, K.D. (1977). Human relationships and user involvement in systems design. *Computer Management*, **19**, 10–12.

Eason, K.D. Damodaran, L. and Stewart, T.F.M. (1974). A survey of man-computer interaction in commercial applications. *LUTERG No. 144*. Dept. of Human Sciences, Loughborough University.

Farrow, H.F. (1977). The effects of computer-based systems on employees' attitudes and working skills in small and medium-sized companies. Research Report, National Computing Centre, Manchester.

Groholt, P. (1980).* Social development and accountability, professionalism and the future of systems designers. In N. Bjørn-Andersen (ed.) *The Human Side of Information Processing*. Amsterdam: North Holland.

Hedberg, B. (1975). Computer systems to support industrial democracy. In E. Mumford and H. Sackman (eds) *Human Choice and Computers*. Amsterdam: North Holland.

Hedberg, B. (1980).* Using computerised information systems to design better organizations and jobs. In N. Bjø rn-Andersen (ed.) *The Human Side of Information Processing.* Amsterdam: North Holland.

Mumford, E. (1980).* Participative design of clerical information systems. In N. Bjørn-Andersen (ed.) *The Human Side of Information Processing.* Amsterdam: North Holland.

* This book contains the proceedings of the Copenhagen Conference on Computer Impact, 1978. It provides good coverage of current thinking on user involvement, especially with regard to the Scandinavian countries.

12. Adaptive Man–Computer Interfaces*

E.A. EDMONDS

School of Mathematics, Computing and Statistics, Leicester Polytechnic, Leicester, England

I. INTRODUCTION

A. Man–Computer Interaction

For a computer system to be effective it is not sufficient for the equipment and programs to be efficient. If the system is to work well in practice then it must be used well. It follows that the particular ways in which people are intended to interact with it are very important. Hence the part of the system with which users interact, the man–computer interface, needs to be designed with care. Because we understand human behaviour much less well than we understand computers, the designing of man–computer interfaces is one of the hardest aspects of systems design. Psychological studies of man–machine interaction can provide information that helps the designer. However, he or she normally uses off-the-shelf hardware components and standard systems software to realize the design. Clearly, that hardware and systems software needs to be of a form that facilitates the implementation of good man-computer interfaces. A key concept in the following discussion will be that the software component of an interface should be treated as a separate module within the computer system as a whole and not simply be embedded at a range of points throughout it. One of the reasons for this is that the design of an interface is difficult to complete without letting people experience it. It follows that it needs to be easy to change. Our theme will thus be concerned with ways in which interfaces can be built and then, whilst in use, adapt or be adapted to the needs of users.

*Some of the material in this chapter was included in a paper presented at Eurocomp 78 and is reproduced with the kind permission of Online Limited.

389

B. Planning and Design Method

When attempting to design a computer graphics facility for creative designers at Leicester Polytechnic considerable difficulty was found in formulating a clear specification for the system. This was because the users in question did not find it possible to be at all precise about their requirements. The solution was seen to be to make the system design process an adaptive one, so that potential users could gradually become clearer about their needs in the light of experience and consequently the design could also evolve (Edmonds, 1971). The only feasible alternative was simulation, which in the case of interactive graphics was not attainable at a cost significantly less than that for a full implementation.

In an elaboration of these ideas (Edmonds, 1974) the central problem was seen to be the particular difficulty that arises whenever the provision of a new tool causes unpredictable change in the process under consideration. In such cases, any deduction of specifications is liable to be invalidated by the very achievement of them. A parallel problem exists where the process is regularly changing. An assumption that the process is fixed may make the development easy to manage but may completely invalidate its result, leading, if not to a rejection of the system, to a series of modifications which have not been planned and thus could cause serious difficulties.

The first concern of a system designer must be the choice of design method. Despite the impression given by many basic computing texts, a choice of method does exist. The proposal that adaptive methods might be necessary for certain computing problems is unusual in the context of computing but not in the broader field of planning and designing. For example, Hirschman and Lindblom (1962) have described how a group of social scientists, working independently, came to hold similar views concerning uncertainties in objectives and the consequent need to consider an adaptable system. The views in this paper come from work on economic development, technological research and development and general policy making. Amongst the points of convergence noted between the members of the group are that one step ought to be left to lead to another, so that it is unwise to specify objectives in much detail before the means of attaining them are known, that in rational problem-solving the goals will seriously change as a result of experience, and that consideration of what can be attained is important in determining what is required. Thus they concluded that the methods used need to allow for adaption in the light of experience. In many situations clear detailed objectives are very hard to define. One problem is that it is not always possible to specify the requirements of a given facility until users have experienced it. Another is that users' needs are constantly changing and consequently cannot be fixed.

Schon (1971) has described many examples of systems in which it is no longer possible to find a stable state so that adaptive approaches need to be used. The rate of change of many important factors has become such that to assume stability, even over a short period, is likely to lead to significant errors. Schon goes on to argue that the systems in question need to be seen as learning systems and to be organized accordingly.

Swanson (1977) has looked at methodologies for the development of information systems. He describes the traditional approach in terms of four steps. The first step consists of identifying some sort of "need" on the part of certain individuals or organizations with respect to relevant information, "users surveys" and "feasibility studies" being the most commonly used methods. The second step is the design of the information system. The third step is implementation which consists of obtaining the necessary resources, etc. In the fourth step, the system becomes operational.

Swanson goes on to describe how this approach fails in many cases and leads to the implementation of an information system which is rarely used. He says that:

When applied to planning information systems . . . the traditional approach to system development fails in part, I believe, because of its insistence on anticipating and identifying information needs in advance of the origin of the actual planning problems themselves.

Swanson then describes a particular solution to the design problem that could be used in the special case of the development of an issue-based information system.

It can thus be seen that viewing design and planning as adaptive processes has been found to be valuable in a range of disciplines. Consideration of the particular problems associated with the adaptive design of man-computer interfaces is given in the following sections.

II. THE MAN-COMPUTER INTERFACE

It is common to separate the interface between the user and the main system from the main system. Perhaps the most well-known example of such a separated unit is a compiler, which in effect interfaces the user to the machine. The role of the interface is to take from the user strings which are meaningful to him and to transform them into strings which are meaningful to the machine, or the main system. A secondary role is to vet those strings and to reject clearly erroneous ones. Thus a compiler will not necessarily generate an object program but may instead generate error reports.

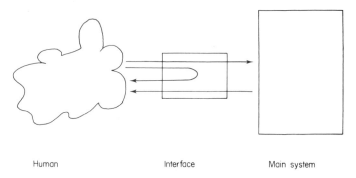

Human   Interface   Main system

Fig. 1. The functions of the man–computer interface.

Three modes of operation of the interface can be identified (Fig. 1). It may cause a transformed message to be given to the main system; it may cause what is in effect a transformed message to return to the user; it may take a message from the main system and transform it into a meaningful form to give to the user. In the second case we could consider that the transformation of the first kind fails and an error report is generated. However we will see that it is equally reasonable to view it as a transformation of the original message as in the first case, the distinction only lying in the intended recipient of the message.

The identification of the operation of an interface as a separable process leads inevitably to the idea that it might be worth devoting a separate processor to that process. In the case of the interface, the use of an "intelligent terminal" that has a processor devoted to it and which separates it from the main computer is particularly attractive because it enables the system's response times to be carefully selected and controlled.

We are concerned with providing tools that will help designers of interfaces. Two particular tools are required. The first one would help with the development of an interface to fulfil a given specification and the second would assist with the modifications of an interface needed to make desirable changes based upon experience. Clearly the right kind of development aid can also satisfy the modification, or adaption, function by simplifying the work of changing specifications.

Although the interface itself might reside in a microprocessor, it is not necessary for the development/adaption tool to reside there. The program used by the system designer to implement an interface might well reside in a main-frame computer. This tool, however, needs to be able to generate an interface which can, if required, reside in the microprocessor.

It is worth noting that an arrangement of this kind provides the opportunity to isolate the user from the main-frame operating system, so that the interface acts as "protective ware" (Partridge and James, 1976). The use of this idea to provide interfaces designed for specific groups of students in a college has been described by Edmonds (1979).

III. DESIGN METHOD FOR MAN-COMPUTER INTERFACES

A. Adaption

From the point of view of the designer of computer aids, the important characteristic of creative problem-solving is that it involves the use of informal and unpredictable methods. It is important to notice that such tasks as searching a data-base can well fall into this category because, although particular search specifications might be very formal and clear, the sequence of specifications tried by the user, leading to the one which achieves his or her aim, is quite informal. It follows that it may not be possible to predict how the user of the computer aids will operate. Trying to constrain him to a formalized method might seriously affect his performance. An example of this has been discussed by Edmonds and Lee (1974), where the problem of providing computer aids to architects was looked at in relation to their normal working methods. It was concluded that considerably more flexibility was required than computer aids normally provided. The extent to which informal methods are important is not always obvious. Even in a study of solution methods used to solve very formal problems it was found that informal methods were most important (Gurova, 1972). To quote from Stewart (1974):

> it is important that the formal computer procedures do not prevent the user from changing his representation of the problem or the task environment necessary to reach the best solution.

If such factors are to be taken into account then it is clear that a system needs to be tailored to its users after they have worked with it.

A study of managers as computer users (Eason, 1974) found significant discontent with the man–computer interfaces provided for them. In particular,

[the manager] will not adapt his own behaviour to accommodate inflexibilities in the system, and he demands a complex service because his needs are diverse and changing.

An alternative to making the design process adaptive is to provide a wide choice of facilities from which the user can select those he requires. Eason's survey found that this approach was not successful.

If, on the other hand, an adaptive method is used, the design . . . will tend to recover from mistakes; consequently, evaluation is less critical than a once-and-for-all investigation would be. The software will also be modified as the users' requirements change . . . [and] the development need never be considered complete.   (Edmonds, 1974)

Given a method that allows adaption of an interface design it would be possible to develop a variety of interfaces to the same system. This could be valuable when the needs of various users of the same system are not the same. Eason (1976) has shown that task and role factors are important in interface design and that if the tasks or roles of users of a system vary then interface requirements will also vary.

In Edmonds (1974) design methods were considered for cases where the available implementation tools were such that modifications could not be performed in a short time. This led to a number of approaches to design, all of which wasted more implementation effort than when the modifications could be easily performed. As has been argued, by providing suitable implementation tools it becomes possible to readily use adaptive design methods (Edmonds, 1978).

Two main components would seem to be needed in a method of adaptive design. First there must be some method for evaluating the performance of the interface (i.e. of the user at the interface). This evaluation could, in certain circumstances, be entirely in the hands of users. The second component is a simple and convenient method for specifying the design. Put at the most basic level,

Since feedback is necessary to user interface design and not available until the program is working, it is important to allow time in the schedule for considerable revision of the interface after the program is working.

(Sneeringer, 1978).

In an adaptive process the starting point is clearly very influential in determining the time and effort required to reach a satisfactory design. Although it will not be discussed in detail, it must be noted that any advice or methods that can be used to arrange for a good starting point for the design of a man–computer interface should be fully exploited. The standard text on this topic is Martin (1973). Particularly useful discussions can be found in Gaines and Facey (1976) and in the contribution by James to this volume, who give clear sets of recommendations to interface designers. If these are followed, then the resulting design will be a good starting point for the adaption.

B. Evaluation

If a system is to be adaptive it must contain a mechanism for providing negative feedback. In looking at the adaptive design of man–computer interfaces we need therefore to consider evaluation in order to provide the feedback. The concept of *testing* computer systems is a relevant one. One limitation of testing is that it is generally seen as a phase that is passed through before the system is allowed to "go live". A second problem is that testing leads to modifications to the system that have not been predicted. Although concentrating on building systems that have no error might cause the number of corrections needed to be small it might nevertheless allow situations to arise in which some corrections might be very expensive to make. Good system design, even using traditional methods, does not view errors as mistakes that ought to have been avoided but as inevitable events, the occurrence of which needs to be taken fully into account. This latter view must be taken in adaptive design as "corrections" are planned for. Evaluation can be seen as an extension of testing in which termination is not at the point when the system becomes acceptable, but is well after the system "goes live". It may even be undefined, so that the feedback remains available throughout the life of the system.

In a discussion of testing, Carney (1975) pays particular attention to human factors. He is concerned with what he terms "user-oriented testing". In Carney's approach, the test team are required to identify all of the direct and indirect users of the system. The concerns of each class of users are then identified and the relevant mode of testing (e.g. dry run, presentation of description for subjective evaluation) noted for each case. Particular personnel are then allocated to perform each of the tests. The method used then is primarily one of seeking opinion on the results of the tests by questionnaires, with particular note being taken of a log of user problems completed during the test period. Clearly this kind of approach can be extended to fulfil the requirements of evaluation in the case of an adaptive design method. The main change is to enlarge the range of options of modes of testing (now "modes of evaluation") to include the monitoring of live systems.

One method for monitoring man-computer interfaces, which has been considered by Rosenberg (1973), is protocol analysis. He proposes that two records be kept. The first is a log of all of the transactions between the user and the machine, together with the elapsed time at each step. This can be produced automatically. The second is a tape-recording of the user's thoughts made during the same period. This tape-recording is transcribed and the elapsed times added beside the text. By close comparison of the two records it is possible to discover something of the user's thought-processes as he or she interacts with the system. Although, Rosenberg points out, the volume of both records can be quite large, he argues that the information obtained would justify the effort of analysis.

Evaluation of design ideas at an early stage of design is often performed with the aid of simulation. A simulation tool for interface dialogues has been described by Lenorovitz and Ramsey (1977). The tool uses the idea of formal grammars to define the software interface to be tested. This notion will be considered in greater detail in Section IV, but it might be noted at this stage that, as Lenorovitz and Ramsey maintain,

> there is nothing about the . . . concept which restricts its use to the *simulation* of man–computer dialogues. Similar software could be used to control the dialogue of operational systems.

They also mention the idea, referred to above, that the interface software could reside in an intelligent terminal. Whether or not such software is used in an operational system, monitoring facilities clearly need to be built into it. Thus, even for early evaluation, the mere advocation of simulation is not adequate, because the selection of monitoring techniques for analysing the results must be considered.

Whilst research methods for man–computer interaction are not the direct concern of this discussion, it can be seen that, because of our poor knowledge of the behaviour of man–machine systems, the evaluation process is at least somewhat akin to research. Innocent (1978) has produced a particularly interesting paper concerned with experimental methods in man–computer interaction research. He concludes that it is not advisable to restrict experiments to those that fit the traditional well-controlled pattern. He advocates the use of "unplanned experiments", in order to determine which variables are controllable and observable, before adopting traditional experimental approaches. Clearly care needs to be taken when evaluating interfaces to ensure that the results obtained are meaningful. It would seem that a significant volume of work remains to be done in this area. Beyond this, the development of monitoring tools to be used with operational man–computer systems needs further work and is bound to increase as advances in evaluation methodologies are made.

C. Specification

The value of considering the man–computer interface as a separate part of an applications computer system has been discussed above. Maher and Bell (1977) have in fact proposed that the interface should be seen as a virtual machine. The dialogue specification methods below all assume some such view.

The meaning of the term "dialogue" is intended to include a broad range of types of exchange between users and computers. Whilst these exchanges might well be in terms of character strings (using a keyboard and visual display, for example), they could equally well include the depression of function buttons, the selection of graphical components from a displayed image or the generation of a diagram. For the purposes of the following exposition it will be adequate only to consider character strings as inputs or outputs. The encoding or decoding of such strings, to deal with the broad range of possible media, introduces an extra stage in the process. This is not particularly difficult to deal with in principle at the design level, although it does introduce an extra practical problem.

Parnas (1969) proposed the use of *state diagrams* in order to clarify the specification of dialogues. Figure 2 illustrates this approach. On entering a given node an associated output is generated. The following input is then matched with one of the strings referenced on the arcs leading out of that node and that arc is then followed, leading to the next node. If no match is found the output is repeated and the resulting new input considered as before. *Tasks* are functions to be performed by the computer that do not form part of the interface, e.g. the searching of a data-base or a calculation. Figure 3 shows an example of a dialogue conforming to the state graph shown in Fig. 2. It is important to notice that the convention of returning to a node when no match is found can to some extent be circumvented by introducing special arcs associated with certain input errors as in Fig. 4.

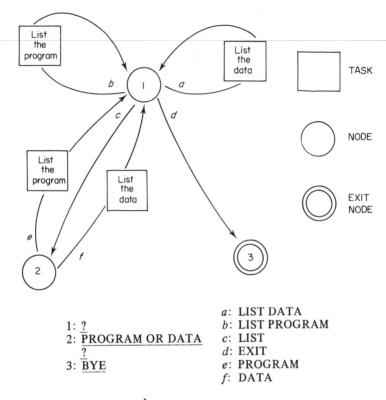

	a: LIST DATA
1: ?	b: LIST PROGRAM
2: PROGRAM OR DATA	c: LIST
?	d: EXIT
3: BYE	e: PROGRAM
	f: DATA

Fig. 2. A state diagram representing a dialogue system.

? LIST PROGRAM
    GET IT
    PRINT IT
    STOP
? LIST
PROGRAM OR DATA
? DATA
    abc
    xyz
? EXIT
BYE

Fig. 3. A dialogue generated using the specification of Fig. 2.

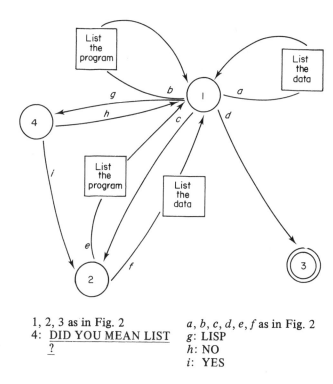

1, 2, 3 as in Fig. 2 a, b, c, d, e, f as in Fig. 2
4: <u>DID YOU MEAN LIST</u> g: LISP
   <u>?</u> h: NO
                              i: YES

Fig. 4. An elaborated version of Fig. 2.

If one considers the set of all possible dialogues that could occur whilst conforming to a given state diagram, then the set must be regular; see for example Arbib (1969). Conway (1963) has extended the idea of a state diagram in a way that enables a broader set to be represented. Similarly Denert (1977) has used an enhanced type of state diagram in a system for specifying dialogues. Using Denert's approach we introduce complex nodes which are, in effect, calls to other state diagrams.

Any of the state diagrams in a specification may contain complex nodes so that, for example, recursive calls are possible. Figure 5 shows a simple example of state diagrams containing complex nodes. The process starts with the initial state (i.e. 1) of G1. Denert points out that the use of complex nodes leads naturally to a top-down design method, and so might be valuable even when the extra power that they make available is not required.

Edmonds and Guest (1978) have devised a notation for representing translation specifically intended for use in man–computer

COMPLEX NODE e.g.

meaning = "go to the diagram starting with 4 and return along
the branch corresponding to the exit node
used, either 9 or 10"

(a)   (b)

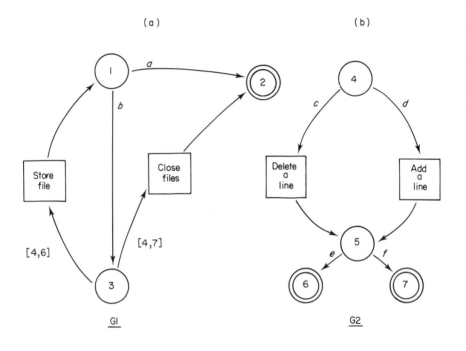

(a) 1: ?   a: EXIT
     2: BYE   b: EDIT

(b) 4: ADD OR DELETE   c: DELETE
        ?   d: ADD
     5: STORE OR CLOSE   e: STORE
        ?   f: CLOSE

Fig. 5. A state diagram representation using a complex node.

interfaces. The source language is specified in an extended BNF-like, or context-free, style (see for example Foster, 1970). The significant feature that extends the range beyond context-free languages is an "**if . . . then . . . else**" construct. The statement "**if** A **then** B **else** C" can be roughly interpreted as meaning "if the input string is of the form A **then** try to match it to form B **else** try to match it to form C". It is thus possible, whilst analysing a string, to take the context of an element partly into account. This can be termed the introduction of "following context". Figure 6 illustrates the use of the notation in its simplest form. It is possible to embed instructions relating to the generation of output in the definition. An example of the very simplest variety of output specification is given in Fig. 7. This notation will be discussed in greater detail in Section IV.

I INPUT = 'SAY PROGRAM'/'SAY DATA'/'SAY'/'EXIT'/.

Fig. 6. An example of input specification ("/" = "or").

I INPUT =   'SAY PROGRAM' ['PROGRAM'] */ –
            'SAY DATA' ['DATA']/'SAY' ['WHAT?']/ –
            'EXIT'/.

Fig. 7. An elaboration of Fig. 6 to include output specifications.
*That is, if the input is 'SAY PROGRAM' then the output is to be 'PROGRAM'.

By combining the state graph notation and the translation notation of Edmonds and Guest (1978) a powerful and flexible language can be formed. This language and its use has been discussed in detail in Edmonds and Guest (1979). In Fig. 8 the state graph is as in Fig. 2. except that the labels on the arcs now correspond to the specifications indicated, rather than to simple character strings. We will see that instead of a single string causing a given arc to be traversed, any one of a possibly infinite set of strings can now cause that action. It follows that, with the "not" construct available in the language, it becomes possible to associate a set of unrecognized strings with a given arc, e.g. any string starting with a character other than "Y" or "N", as illustrated in Fig. 9. It thus becomes possible to include an appropriate message to be output in such cases. The system allows the use of complex nodes in exactly the same way as described above.

A particular feature of this design specification method is the possibility of embedding output instructions in the definition of the source strings for a given arc. This feature can be used to incorporate actions in the definitions of source strings, the output being treated as output from the man–computer interface to the main computer

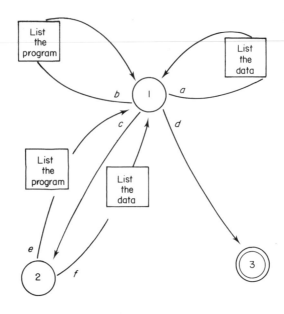

1: ?
2: <u>PROGRAM OR DATA</u>
   ?
3: <u>BYE</u>

a: I INPUT = 'LIST DATA'/'LIST THE DATA'/.
b: I INPUT = 'LIST PROGRAM'/'LIST THE
     PROGRAM'/.
c: I INPUT = 'LIST'/.
d: I INPUT = 'EXIT'/'BYE'/'GOODBYE'/.
e: I INPUT = 'PROG'/'PROGRAM'/.
f: I INPUT = 'DATA'/.

Fig. 8. A representation of a dialogue system using the method of Edmonds and Guest.

system, i.e. as a task. The specification of output directed to the user can then be generally confined to that associated with the entering of nodes. A simple example using this idea will be given in Section IV.

Hall (1977) has pointed out that it is often desirable to arrange for an interface to be attractive to users of varying levels of competence. In particular, he shows how BNF definitions of language structures can lead naturally to the definition of an equivalent sequence of menu lists. Figure 10 illustrates this equivalence. Hall gives four rules for devising menus from BNF forms and vice versa. This approach could be used with the method of Edmonds and Guest described above. Work on the clarification of the relationship between the two methods is proceeding.

Alternative formulations of somewhat similar ideas can be found in Anderson and Sibley (1972) and Losbichler and Mühlbacker (1974).

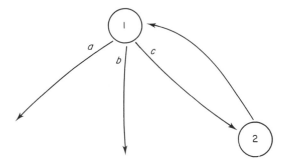

1: DO YOU WANT A CAKE? a: 'Y'/.
2: I DON'T UNDERSTAND. b: 'N'/.
   LET'S TRY AGAIN c: $\neg$ 'Y'/$\neg$ 'N'/.

N.B. a, b, c are tested in that order ("$\neg$" = "not").

Fig. 9. An example of the use of "not" in the input specification. Note that the transition from 2 to 1 is performed on a null input, i.e. it is unconditional and takes place without a request for input from the user.

BNF: <INPUT>::= ADD/DELETE/REPEAT

Displayed menu: ADD
                    DELETE
                    REPEAT

Fig. 10. An example of language and menu equivalence.

In the latter case certain editing commands to be used for modifying the interface design are incorporated into the formalization. The degree of the need for this depends on the way in which the design method is eventually used in implementation and will be discussed below.

D. Formal Remarks

As has been noted, the set of paths through a state diagram is regular. Lomet (1973) has formalized state diagrams involving complex nodes, terming that formalization a "nested deterministic pushdown acceptor". He demonstrated that the sets characterized by this enhanced state diagram were LR(k).

The following context available in the system of Edmonds and Guest (1978), SYNICS, can be seen to be equivalent to augmenting context-free grammars by allowing productions of the form "$k\alpha \rightarrow \beta\alpha$" (where k is a non-terminal and α, β are strings over the alphabet of terminals and non-terminals).

The SYNICS statement

$$k \rightarrow \text{ if } \beta\alpha \text{ then } \beta \text{ else}$$

is equivalent to the production, in such a grammar, "$k\alpha \rightarrow \beta\alpha$". The productions "$k\alpha \rightarrow \beta\alpha$" and "$k \rightarrow \gamma$" together, may be included, in effect, in a SYNICS grammar by providing the single statement $k \rightarrow$ if $\beta\alpha$ then β else γ. (The notation used in the diagrams is an extended form of that of Lomet (1973).)

IV. IMPLEMENTATION METHODS AND TOOLS FOR ADAPTABLE INTERFACES

A. Tools

For a design method to allow adaption it is, in practice, necessary for it to be supported by implementation methods that reflect the adaption possibilities. In other words, a minor design change should not lead to a major implementation change. We are thus led to consider implementation tools for man–computer interfaces that allow relatively easy adaption.

In Edmonds (1978) three main types of adaption tool are identified: those that allow
  (a)   adaption by a computer specialist,
  (b)   adaption by a trained user,
  (c)   adaption by any user.
The extent and nature of user involvement in the design process would determine which types of facility were required. Clearly there is a trade-off to be considered between the cost of the facility for providing easy adaption and the cost of specialist manpower.

It was argued above that for certain applications a tool that helps the specialist to adapt the interface design is needed. Given the correct tools it should be possible to make substantial changes without great cost. For small and easily understood changes, such as a replacement of one term by another, it might prove attractive to allow users to perform their own adaption. Some ways in which adaption by more or less untrained users might be possible are discussed later.

B. Adaption by a Specialist

1. *The Principles*

In order to make an interface adaptable by a computer specialist it is only necessary to provide a comparatively high-level implementation facility. The provision of extensions to existing computer languages that are capable of describing interface actions is an obvious method of doing this. Lafuente and Gries (1978) have proposed extensions to PASCAL for this purpose. Similar extensions to COBOL are also considered by Lafuente (1977). Gaines and Facey (1977) have implemented, and used in a range of applications, a language similar to BASIC that provides special interface specification commands, the analysis of input strings being powerful enough to handle context-free languages. Bloom *et al.* (1978) have described a less powerful facility that exists as a component of the system in the way that has been discussed above. Florentin (1977) has developed an interactive tool for implementing dialogues that is easy to use and consequently allows fairly ready adaption. Newcome (Computer Aided Design Centre, 1979) is developing a system that includes some of the features described below, with particular reference to applications in computer-aided design.

The design methods of Anderson and Sibley (1972) and Losbichler and Mühlbacher (1974) have been mentioned previously. In both cases the provision of software to which interfaces can be specified in equivalent terms to the design language is considered as an integral part of the work. This approach will be followed by describing an interface implementation tool that corresponds to the design method of Edmonds and Guest (1979) discussed in the previous section. The use of formal languages to implement interfaces has already been mentioned in relation to Lenorovitz and Ramsey (1977).

A system called SYNICS (Edmonds and Guest, 1978) has been written that enables adaption by a specialist to take place. SYNICS was devised to help with a computer-aided learning project, although its applications are in no way restricted to that field.

The heart of the system consists of a table-driven top-down recognizer and table-driven tree-traverser that uses the tree produced by the recognizer to transform the input string.

SYNICS accepts a set of syntax and semantic rules and then translates strings, providing details of the tree produced by the recognizer. Once satisfactory rules have been developed, the user may perform transformations as part of his own program by making certain sub-routine calls.

Two facilities are provided. One is an aid to writing and testing transformational rules. The other is a set of routines which may be used in the actual interface itself, together with data files generated by the first program, in order to implement the particular interface that has been designed. It may be used to implement transformations of each of the three kinds identified above.

This has been used in a system for the computer-aided learning of programming (Edmonds and Guest, 1977) in order, in particular, to provide a flexible method of producing error reports. It is possible to vary both the error messages and the error discrimination comparatively easily. The approach could be used for the design and modification of both input and output strings.

A particular concern in the computer-aided learning system was with "incorrect" input strings, and a development of the method of Burgess (1972) has been used for dealing with them. All input strings are treated as legal and are transformed. A sub-set of them generates the special class of output strings consisting of error messages. The main value of this method is that decisions concerning error detection and the discrimination between errors can readily be changed, as they are embodied in the syntax and semantic rules provided for the translator. A second advantage is that it is easy to continue to parse an input string after an error has been detected in order to improve the diagnostic. In the pilot system 45 error types were used, but as SYNICS allows the generation of them to be readily changed it proved possible to increase the number of errors and to change the conditions under which they were generated even during the running of a short programming course at secondary school level.

When input strings are processed the UNPAK facility of the latest version of SYNICS is used in Edmonds and Guest (1977) to generate three internal strings. The first contains the error codes. The second string lists all variable names used, indicating when they have been assigned a value by a "LET" or "INPUT" instruction. This information is used to look for variables that have been assigned values but are not otherwise referred to, and ones that have been used but are at no point assigned a value. This check is essentially the same as the label check. The third internal string is used to produce a skeleton. In the case of ACE (Open University, 1973) the features that are looked for when the completed skeleton is analysed by SYNICS are:

(i)   the existence of an END;
(ii)   the existence of a PRINT;
(iii)   termination by a GOTO or an END;
(iv)   the existence of a label on any instruction following a GOTO.

Both the number and nature of these strings can be readily adapted, as could the error codes mentioned above.

2. *An Implementation Tool*

Edmonds and Guest (1979) have constructed an implementation

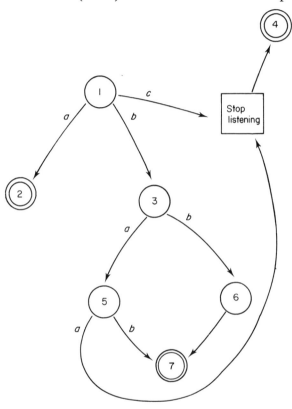

1: <u>ARE YOU WELL</u>
<u>?</u>
2: <u>GOOD. GOODBYE</u>
3: <u>IS IT SERIOUS</u>
<u>?</u>
4: <u>I MUST RUSH. GOODBYE</u>
5. <u>IS IT FATAL</u>
<u>?</u>
6. <u>GOOD</u>
7. <u>LIFE COULD BE WORSE,</u>
<u>GOODBYE</u>

a: 'Y'/.
b: 'N'/.
c: ¬'Y'/¬'N'/.

Fig. 11. The representation of a dialogue system. Note that the transition from 6 to 7 is unconditional, as illustrated in Fig. 9

AT NODE 1
    ARE YOU WELL
    ?
    TO 2 IF
       'Y'/.
    TO 3 IF
       'N'/.
    TO 4 IF
       ¬'Y' ['STOP LISTENING']/¬ 'N' ['STOP LISTENING']/.
AT NODE 2
    GOOD. GOODBYE
    EXIT

AT NODE 3
    IS IT SERIOUS
    ?
    TO 5 IF
       'Y'/.
    TO 6 IF
       'N'/.
AT NODE 4
    I MUST RUSH. GOODBYE.
    EXIT
AT NODE 5
    IS IT FATAL
    ?
    TO 4 IF
       'Y'/.
    TO 7 IF
       'N'/.
AT NODE 6
    GOOD
    TO 7
AT NODE 7
    LIFE COULD BE WORSE.
    GOODBYE.
    EXIT

Fig. 12. Figure 11 specified in a form suitable for input to the programs of Edmonds and Guest.

ARE YOU WELL
? NO
IS IT SERIOUS
? YES
IS IT FATAL
? YES
I MUST RUSH. GOODBYE.

Fig. 13. A dialogue generating the specification of Fig. 11.

tool that incorporates many of the features of SYNICS and corresponds to the design specification method described above.

Figure 11 shows the state diagram of a simple dialogue. Figure 12 shows the description of the dialogue required by the implementation program. The output to be generated on entering a node is described on the lines following the node number, given in the "AT NODE" line. This is followed by a list of the node numbers to which control may pass, in the form of "TO *n* IF", each followed by a description in a BNF-type notation on the input that would cause that branch. The square brackets contain descriptions of messages to be sent to the main system for action before the next node in the interface is entered, as described above. Figure 13 shows a sample dialogue.

Although the example only shows a very simple dialogue, the system will accept descriptions of input forms (and associated output) of a class larger than those of context-free languages.

The notation used to describe acceptable input for a given node is based upon that of BNF or context-free notation, and uses the concept of a syntax tree (see for example Foster, 1970). BNF notation specifies how to *generate* strings in a language, and if treated in certain ways can double as a way of specifying how strings in the language might be *recognized.* In a translator writing system it is only necessary to specify how to recognize the source language. It thus becomes possible to extend the notation to include commands that direct the recognition process even though they would not be readily meaningful with respect to the generation of strings. In our system, as noted above, an "if . . . then . . . else" command is included.

Semantic rules, i.e. the specification of output to be generated, may be inserted into the specification using a language similar to that of Foxley and King (1968).

An important aspect of the system is the possibility of using clearly defined errors to guide the dialogue. As before, a technique that is an extension of that of Burgess (1972) is used. James (1975) has proposed a similar approach in a more limited context.

3. Source-language Specification

BNF-like languages have two kinds of object, terminals and non-terminals, which yield *terminal nodes* ànd *non-terminal nodes* in syntax trees. In BNF the non-terminals are distinguished by being enclosed thus: "$<>$". For example, in:

$$<\text{term}> ::= <\text{variable}> * <\text{term}>$$

$<\text{term}>$ and $<\text{variable}>$ are non-terminals and the asterisk is a terminal. This rule states that the component shown in Fig. 14 may occur in a syntax tree.

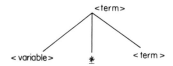

Fig. 14. A component of a syntax tree corresponding to a BNF alternative.

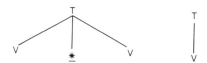

Fig. 15. Syntax tree components corresponding to rules in the notation of Edmonds and Guest.

In our notation the *terminals* are distinguished by enclosing them in single quotes. The names of *non-terminals* are restricted to a single letter or a single letter followed by up to four digits.

The BNF rule given above could then be expressed (apart from termination, see below) by

$$T = V \text{ '*' } T$$

Other examples of terminal strings are '3', '**' and of non-terminals T3, K1234. As in BNF it is possible to specify *alternatives* in one statement, e.g.

$$T = V \text{ '*' } T / V /.$$

which simply states that both the components shown in Fig. 15 are allowed. All statements must terminate with "/.", as shown.
  If we also had the rule

$$V = \text{'A'} \ / \ \text{'B'} \ / \ \text{'C'} \ /.$$

an example of a legal 'T' would be

$$A * B * C$$

In order to make the language more readable *comment* is allowed to immediately precede the equals sign, e.g.

$$T \ TERM = V \ \text{'*'} \ T \ / \ V \ /.$$

$$V \ VARIABLE = \text{'A'} \ / \ \text{'B'} \ / \ \text{'C'} \ /.$$

The "not" symbol "¬" may also be employed, but must only apply to a terminal or to a non-terminal which can only generate one terminal. Any terminal apart from the set specified is then taken to be acceptable. Thus if the rule

$$K = T\text{'+'}K \ / \ T\neg V \ /.$$

is introduced then one allowable sub-tree would be that in Fig. 16.

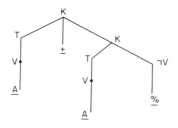

Fig. 16. A sub-tree including a "not" operator.

In the place of a simple alternative an *if then else* statement can be used. The statement may be of the form

if alternative 1 **then** alternative 2 /

else alternative 3 /.

with the meaning that, if alternative 1 is matched then alternative 2 is used for the analysis and transformation, and if not then alternative 3 is used.

Thus in, for example,

C = if 'AAB' then 'A' / else 'AA' /.

(i)   AAB would match the first 'A' and generate the sub-tree in Fig. 17 leaving AB still to be incorporated.
(ii) AA would match 'AA' and generate the sub-tree in Fig. 18.
(iii) AB would fail.

Fig. 17. The result of a parse using an *if* operator.

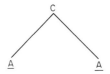

Fig. 18. A second example using the same *if* rule as used in Fig. 17.

The first rule listed at a node is taken to refer to the root, i.e. the non-terminal left of the equals sign in the first rule will be used as the root of all trees built.

Two *restrictions* are placed upon the rules that may be provided:
(i)   left recursion is not allowed (see for example Foster, 1970), e.g.

T = T '*' V /.

would be illegal, as would

T = S '*' V /.
S = V / T /.

(ii)   alternatives should be presented so that the first match is the
correct one, e.g.

$$T = V / V \text{ '*' } T /.$$

would cause, when considering A*B, the sub-tree in Fig. 19
to be built, and the second alternative (the correct one)
would never be tried.

Fig. 19. The result of a parse using a rule in which the alternatives were in an
inappropriate order.

In order to speed up the recognition process it is advisable to
place alternatives with common first parts next to one another, e.g.
in

$$T = V \text{ '*' } T / V /.$$

if, in the first alternative, the V is matched but the '*' is not found
then the second alternative will be accepted without further searching and, on the other hand, if the first alternative fails because the V
cannot be matched then the second alternative will be failed without
further consideration.

4. *Output Specification*

Corresponding to any specified alternative an output rule may be
provided. Its function is to indicate the action that must be taken
when a given alternative occurs in a syntax tree that has been
constructed. Following analysis the tree is scanned under the
direction of the output rules and the object strings are generated.

The object string is passed to the main program for its attention.
Characters are inserted in it from left to right as the rules are obeyed.
An output rule consists of a string of output commands. There are
three commands that can directly generate output:

(i)   '$n_1 n_2 \ldots n_m$' outputs the strings of literal characters
$n_1 n_2 \ldots n_m$ into the next m locations, e.g. '+', 'WORD'.

(ii)   "ddd ... d" outputs the single integer terminal dd ... d into the next location, e.g. "7", "54". Integer and character terminals may be mixed.

(iii) L (*n*) outputs the *n*th node in the syntax alternative, *counting from the right*, if it is a terminal, or the string of terminals that it generates if it is a non-terminal, e.g. L (2) applied to V*T would cause * to be output and L (1) applied to the uppermost K in Fig. 16 would cause A+A% to be output. $L(n_1,n_2 \ldots n_m)$ is equivalent to $L(n_1)L(n_2) \ldots L(n_m)$.

A fourth command directs the order in which the rules are obeyed, by specifying the way in which the syntax tree should be scanned:

(iv) C_n causes the rule to be obeyed that corresponds to the alternative used to generate the next level of the tree from the non-terminal that is the *n*th node in the syntax alternative *counting from the right,* e.g. C3 applied to the uppermost K in Fig. 16 would cause SYNICS to obey the semantic rule associated with the alternative T = V.

Output rules are enclosed thus: "[ ]" and placed directly after the syntax alternative to which they apply, e.g.

T TERM = V '*' T [C3C1'*'] / V [C1] /.

V VARIABLE = 'A' ['1'] / 'B' ['2'] / -

'C' ['3'] /.

would cause an input of A*B*C to generate 123**.

The order in which the nodes are visited to do this are shown in Fig. 20.

The output is generated at nodes 3, 6, 8, 9, 10 in that order.

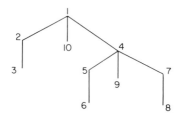

Fig. 20. The order in which the nodes of Fig. 16 are visited during the generation of output.

5. *Mode of Use*

Figure 21 shows the required description of the dialogue specified in Fig. 5. Note the use of complex nodes. An elaborated version of the dialogue is shown in both forms in Fig. 22 and Fig. 23. A sample dialogue using this system is given in Fig. 24.

The system is structured in a similar way to SYNICS. One program can be used in order to test interface specifications and to produce object versions of them. The object versions are interpreted by routines that can be called from a programmer's own main program. In one version of the system these routines run in a microprocessor dedicated to a terminal, as proposed in Section II.

```
AT NODE 1
   ?
   TO 3 IF
      'EDIT'/.
   TO 2 IF
      'EXIT'/.
AT NODE 2
   BYE
   EXIT
AT NODE 3
   CALL 4
   TO 1 IF 6
      ['STORE FILE']/.
   TO 2 IF 7
      ['CLOSE FILES']/.
AT NODE 4
      ADD OR DELETE
      ?
   TO 5 IF
      'DELETE'['DELETE A LINE']/'ADD'[ADD A LINE']/.
AT NODE 5
      STORE OR CLOSE
      ?
   TO 6 IF
      'STORE'/.
   TO 7 IF
      'CLOSE'/.
AT NODE 6
   RETURN
AT NODE 7
   RETURN
```

Fig. 21. Figure 5 specified in a form suitable for input to the programs of Edmonds and Guest.

(a)

G3

(b)

G4

(a) 1: ? a: 'EXIT7.
     2: BYE b: 'EDIT'/.
     8: EDIT OR EXIT c: /.

(b) 4: ADD OR DELETE c: 'DELETE'['DELETE']/.
        ? d: 'ADD'['ADD']/.
     5: STORE OR CLOSE e: 'STORE 'F['STORE'L(1)]/.
        GIVE FILE NUMBER   F = CF//.
     6: OK   C = '1'/'2'/'3'/'4'/−
        ?   '5'/'6'/'7'/'8'/−
     7: OK   '9'/'0'/.
        ? f: 'CLOSE 'F['CLOSE'L(1)]/.

Fig. 22. An elaboration of Fig. 5.

It is proposed that computer-aided learning techniques be used in making the tool easy to understand and use. In the spirit of the previous sections the syntax of the specification language will not be fixed until further trials with users have been completed.

C. Adaption by a Trained User

In order to allow trained users (non-computer specialists acting as "local experts") to modify a dialogue, certain extra facilities need to be provided. Such users need to be able to modify any given dialogue within certain limits. For major modifications it would still be necessary to call in a specialist. The facilities provided need to include such commands as:

change text (abbreviate input or output, expand input or output, change a term, etc.);

change formats;

abbreviate a section of dialogue (using some standard input).

More sophisticated possibilities that could be considered, but would probably be inappropriate; include such modifications as "given a newly specified condition relating to an input string, generate a given output". No direct access to information sent from dialogue program to the main system should be allowed; indeed the user would be unlikely to have any knowledge of such messages.

Newman (1978) has constructed some experimental systems in order to explore adaptable personalized interfaces, and Watson (1976) has incorporated similar features in an interesting system. Thomas and Pyle (1978) have constructed an adaptable terminal with the aid of local intelligence (see Chapter 13 by Thomas in this volume). Their system enables users to readily change screen formats. The screen is divisible into regions, each of which acts as an

```
AT NODE 1
    ?
    TO 2 IF
    'EXIT/.
    TO 3 IF
    'EDIT'/.
    TO 8 IF
    /.
AT NODE 2
    BYE
    EXIT
AT NODE 3
    CALL 4
    TO 1 IF 6
    TO 2 IF 7
AT NODE 8
    EDIT OR EXIT
    GOTO 1
AT NODE 4
    ADD OR DELETE
    ?
    TO 5 IF
    'DELETE'['DELETE']/-
    'ADD'['ADD']/.
AT NODE 5
    STORE OR CLOSE?
    GIVE FILE NUMBER
    ?
    TO 6 IF
    'STORE 'F['STORE'L(1)]/.
    F = CF/f.
    C='1'/'2'/'3'/'4'/'5'/'6'/'7'/'8'/'9'/'0'/.
    TO 7 IF
    'CLOSE 'F['CLOSE'L(1)]/.
AT NODE 6
    RETURN
AT NODE 7
    RETURN
```

Fig. 23. Figure 22 specified in a form suitable for input to the program.

isolated output device and can be specified as one which, for example, pages or rolls. Each region is termed a "window". The system is very easy to use:

Half a dozen people found they were able to understand its principles of operation within a few minutes, and adjust windows; after an hour they could make quite elaborate "adaptions".

? CHANGE
EDIT OR EXIT
? EDIT
ADD OR DELETE
? ADD
STORE OR CLOSE?
GIVE FILE NUMBER
? STORE 1234
OK
? EXIT
BYE

Fig. 24. A dialogue generated using the specification of Fig. 22.

Thus the system moves towards the position briefly covered in the next section. A somewhat similar philosophy has led to the production of the HP2645A terminal (Hewlett Packard, 1976).

D. Adaption by Any User

A further set of features is currently being investigated by Edmonds and Guest in order to both allow and encourage any user to adapt the dialogue in use to his preference. It will, in particular, be possible for the dialogue designer to specify that the system should log given events and should report to users on possible improvements. Two kinds of log could be available. The first looks at analysed input strings for common strings or sub-strings, at common output strings and at common sequences of dialogue. On the basis of this record it would be possible to identify areas where the user might find abbreviation attractive, by noting frequently used sequences of dialogue. The second type of log looks for common errors and so identifies areas where expansion (or some more extensive change) might be called for. None of these facilities will exist in a given dialogue unless specified by the designer.

When possible areas for change are identified the program will converse with the user in order to discover whether he in fact desires modification and, if he does, to define the required changes. The user need not know any special commands relating to the adaption system, although some simple edit commands will be available, and they will be supported by tutorial help built into the program.

V. SELF-ADAPTIVE INTERFACES

When a man–computer interface changes automatically in response to its experience with users, we term it a *"self-adaptive"* interface.
In a number of projects attempts have been made to use artificial intelligence methods in order to make computer-aided learning systems self-adaptive. This work arises from the realization that:

> the teacher's problem is itself a problem-solving activity, i.e. at any time the teacher's problem is to transform the student from his present state to some goal state using one or more of a set of possible teaching actions.
>
> (Self, 1977)

The method most commonly used was also described by Self:

> They maintain a vector of "measurements" intended to describe the student and on the basis of this vector attempt to classify the student into a category sufficient to determine the next teaching operation. As the lesson progresses, the vector is modified according to some model of learning, intuitive or mathematical.

Recognizing that the provision of interactive aids to programmers, whose main concern is not with computing, is essentially a tutorial provision, Jones *et al.* (1978) used descriptive vectors of users to control an adaptive program. The program is an editor for FORTRAN programs that provides tutorial support to users as they build their programs or modify them. In order to cope with users with varying knowledge of FORTRAN, possible errors are classified and a *competence rating* kept for each classification. It then becomes possible to tailor responses, not only to a particular user, but also to a particular error type. For certain purposes it seems best if the mode of response remains unchanged during a given session. For this reason two versions of the vector are maintained. One is updated at every transaction, the other only at the end of a session. Particular attention has been paid to the algorithms used for updating the vectors and for interpreting them when responding. The algorithms all contain parameters which will be set on the basis of the observed performance of the editor in an extended trial.

Clearly the precise nature of an interface ought to be determined in relation to, among other things, the particular characteristics of users, and hence the interest in adaptive interfaces. In tutorial systems some of those characteristics will be changing during the course of the interaction; the user will hopefully learn. In systems which do not have a tutorial component it is often the case that, for any given user, all of his or her relevant characteristics can be taken to be constant. This then presents a simpler problem in making the interface adaptive. The adaption is restricted to setting certain parameters once the user's characteristics have been identified. In an investigation into adaptive interfaces of this kind (Lucas *et al.*, 1976), experiments were performed in order to determine whether the intelligence of users, in the sense of a score on the Mill Hill Vocabulary Scale (Raven, 1962), could be easily estimated. The objective in estimating intelligence is to select suitable terminology and phrasing:

> It is extremely important to present medical questions to patients of lesser verbal ability using common words and simple grammar . . . However, the acceptability of computer interrogation to more intelligent patients might be increased if they were asked about their "Navels" rather than their "Belly Buttons" . . . .

It was found that a knowledge of a user's age together with the user's mean response time to questions posed by the computer were adequate to estimate intelligence.

A third category of adaptive interface is one in which the nature of the interface does not change, although its performance improves. An example of this would be a system which learns to tolerate more errors or to deal with them more quickly. James (1975) has developed methods of achieving such adaption using adaptive decision trees.

In all forms of adaptive interface, except perhaps the last, a particularly difficult problem is that the human and the computer both try to adapt to one another. Such situations require very careful handling if problems are not to arise, and it would seem that considerable work remains to be done in this area.

VI. ADAPTABLE INPUT DEVICES

We have seen that the needs of computer users vary considerably, and the consequential design of the man–machine interface also ought to vary. Clearly the input device must be considered as an adaptable machine. Even within one particular interactive program, being used by one individual, the ideal input device might vary. Typically a full keyboard is used, most of which is redundant most of the time. The alternative is to use very specific keyboards (function buttons) or an elementary dialogue that only requires a small range of responses by the human operator (Evans, 1972). Clearly these various arrangements are compromises based upon the constraint of having to use a fixed (hard) keyboard.

In computer graphics applications, a light-pen or equivalent device can be used to "pick" items from an available selection. Consequently, in such systems, menus and a pick device have become a common and attractive alternative to using a keyboard. It has become possible to use "soft" input devices because at each point in the exchange between man and machine a fresh menu can be displayed that is specifically designed for that moment and does not contain redundant keys. One rather elaborate approach to the solution of the general problem is described by Knowlton (1976). This involves the use of a projection system to label the keys dynamically. Lucas *et al.* (1976) have developed a simple adaptable input device that allows a three-button system similar to Evans (1972) to be changed to a seven-button device under program control.

A new design of terminal is proposed that would be advantageous in cases where it was not to be used for a specific application in a specific environment. In such situations what is required is a reasonably inexpensive "soft" input device that is under program control. The manipulation of the input device needs to be at a high enough level for the high-level language programmer to find it a simple and natural extension to the facilities normally available to him.

Edmonds and Guest are working on an elaboration of the work of Suret (1971); a two-screen terminal where one screen is used for output in the conventional way and the second is used for input. The input screen can be used to display menus, Yes/No/Don't Know "buttons", a conventional full keyboard or whatever. Whilst very sophisticated touch panels are constructable, e.g. the Elographics E270 (Elographics, 1979), a simple one with a resolution adequate for the case where a conventional full keyboard is being displayed is all that is needed. The terminal built at the University of Geneva, which uses light beams and photoelectric cells instead of a touch panel, would be more than adequate (Ibrahim and Levrat, 1979).

Complementary to the basic hardware construction an investigation into keyboard specification methods and the design and implementation of supporting software is being carried out. The proposal is to design and implement a soft keyboard specification language, the compiler for which would produce data tables that would be accessed by certain special FORTRAN sub-programs, calls to which would be used by a programmer in order to cause a given design to appear on the input screen and to enable inputs from the terminal to be understood in that context. Although for experimental purposes this limited implementation will be quite adequate, in practice it will be necessary to enable the terminal to be controlled from programs written in various languages.

VII. CONCLUSIONS

A considerable amount of research and development remains to be done if the ideas discussed above are to be fully exploited.

Studies are required of reactions to adapting systems. Four categories of adaption have been identified and need separate and comparative study. The categories are adaption performed by specialists, trained users and untrained users, and self-adaptive systems. The studies need to evaluate the overall performances of the man–computer systems, since studies of the performance of people and computers treated separately may not be helpful in determining systems' quality in practice.

In order to make the dialogue system described above easy for system implementors to use, the advice facilities need to be extended, so that computer-aided learning would be available to help with particularly difficult problems. Other possible refinements include the incorporation of Hall's ideas, the provision of windowing facilities similar to those of Thomas and Pyle, as discussed above and the incorporation of computer graphics.

It is necessary to develop facilities to enable systems designers to specify ways in which users, trained or otherwise, could modify the interface. A particular problem here is to ensure that the user's ability to modify the interface is suitably limited, so that he or she cannot harm the system. Ways also need to be found of specifying the information that is to be kept about the dialogues that take place, and of specifying what action should be taken (e.g. prompting a user to abbreviate an output statement).

The work on a soft keyboard specification language has yet to be completed and the proper ergonomic design of such hardware remains to be fully studied. Clearly the full investigation of the adaptive design of soft keyboard arrangements, along the lines of the dialogue work described above, has yet to be made.

REFERENCES

Anderson, R.H. and Sibley, W.L. (1972). A new approach to programming man–machine interfaces. *Report No. 876,* Advanced Research Projects Agency, Santa Monica.
Arbib, M.A. (1969). *Theories of Abstract Automata.* New Jersey: Prentice-Hall.

Bloom, S.M., White, R.J., Beckley, R.F. and Slack, W.V. (1978). Converse: a means to write, edit, administer, and summarize computer-based dialogue. *Computers and Biomedical Research,* 11, 167-175.

Burgess, C.J. (1972). Compile-time error diagnostics in syntax-directed compilers. *Computer J.,* 15, 302-307.

Carney, A.C. (1975). What to know about human factors testing of software applications and systems. *Canadian Datasystems,* 7, 60-68.

Computer Aided Design Centre. (1979). The language processor user documentation. *GILT document No. 1,* Computer Aided Design Centre, Cambridge.

Conway, M.E. (1963). Design of a separable transition-diagram compiler. *Communications of the ACM,* 6, 396-408.

Denert, E. (1977). Specification and design of dialogue systems with state diagrams. *Proceedings of the International Computing Symposium,* Liege.

Eason, K.D. (1974). The manager as a computer user. *Appl. Ergonomics,* 5, 9-14.

Eason, K.D. (1976). Understanding the naive computer user. *Computer J.,* 19, 3-7.

Edmonds, E.A. (1971). The development of software for artists and designers—a methodology. Research Note, Leicester Polytechnic.

Edmonds, E.A. (1974). A process for the development of software for non-technical users as an adaptive system. *General Systems,* 19, 215-217.

Edmonds, E.A. (1978). Adaptable man/machine interfaces for complex dialogues. *Proceedings of the European Computing Congress,* London, 639-646.

Edmonds, E.A. (1979). Protecting users from a main-frame. *Report No. 26,* Man–Computer Interaction Research Group, Leicester Polytechnic.

Edmonds, E.A. and Guest, S.P. (1977). An interactive tutorial system for teaching programming. *Proceedings of the Conference on Computer Systems and Technology,* Brighton, 263-270.

Edmonds, E.A. and Guest, S.P. (1978). SYNICS–a FORTRAN subroutine package for translation. *Report No. 6,* Man–Computer Interaction Research Group, Leicester Polytechnic.

Edmonds, E.A. and Guest, S.P. (1979). A man–computer dialogue system. *Report No. 27,* Man–Computer Interaction Research Group, Leicester Polytechnic.

Edmonds, E.A. and Lee, J. (1974). An appraisal of some problems of achieving fluid man/machine interaction. *Proceedings of the European Computing Congress,* London, 635-645.

Elographics, Inc. (1979). Transparent position sensor E270. *Report E270-1/79,* Elographics Inc., Oak Ridge, Tennessee.

Evans, C. (1972). Simplifying the user interface: the key to effective man-machine dialogue. In *Interactive Computing,* pp.151-165, London: Infotech.

Florentin, J.J. (1977). Automatic generation of interactor programs. *Proceedings of the International Conference on Displays for Man/Machine Systems,* Lancaster.

Foster, J.M. (1970). *Automatic Syntactic Analysis.* London: Macdonald.

Foxley, E. and King, P. (1968). A meta-semantic language for use with a top-down syntax analyser. *Proceedings of the IFIP Conference,* 366-372.

Gaines, B.R. and Facey, P.V. (1976). Programming interactive dialogue. *Proceedings of the Conference on Computing and People,* Leicester.

Gaines, B.R. and Facey, P.V. (1977). BASYS–a language for programming interaction. *Proceedings of the Conference on Computer Systems and Technology*, Brighton, 251–262.

Gurova, L.L. (1972). Heuristic processes in solution of descriptive-logical problems. In V.N. Pushkin (ed.) *Problems of Heuristics*, pp. 34–55. Jerusalem: Israel Program for Scientific Translations.

Hall, P.A.V. (1977). Man–computer dialogues for many levels of competence. Internal Report, Scicon, London.

Hewlett Packard. (1976). HP2645A display station. *Report No. 9/76 5952-9963 42*, Hewlett Packard, Palo Alto, California.

Hirschman, A.O. and Lindblom, C.E. (1962). Economic development, research and development, policy making: some convergent views. *Behav. Sc.* 7, 211–222.

Ibrahim, B. and Levrat, B. (1979). Improved security through on-line signature recognition. *Proceedings of the IFIP European Conference on Applied Information Technology*, London, 491–498.

Innocent, P.R. (1978). An experimental approach to man–computer interaction research. *Report No. 15*, Man–Computer Interaction Research Group, Leicester Polytechnic.

James, E.B. (1975). Adaptive analysis: a model for perception. *Report No. 74/45*, Dept. of Computing and Control, Imperial College, London.

Jones, P.F., Curry, N.A., Edmonds, E.A., Radford, A.S. and Toon, K. (1978). A tutorial FORTRAN source editor. Research Report, Leicester Polytechnic.

Knowlton, K. (1976). Virtual pushbuttons as a means of person–machine interaction. *Proceedings of the ACM Symposium of Graphic Languages*, Miami, 350–351.

Lafuente, J.M. (1977). The specification of data-directed interactive user-computer dialogues. Ph.D. Thesis, Cornell University, Ithaca, New York.

Lafuente, J.M. and Gries, D (1978). Language facilities for programming user-computer dialogues. *IBM Journal of Research and Development*, 22, 145–158.

Lenorovitz, D.R. and Ramsey, H.R. (1977). A dialogue simulation tool for use in the design of interactive computer systems. *Proceedings of the Human Factors Society*, 21, 95–99.

Lomet, D.B. (1973). A formalisation of transition diagram systems. *J. ACM*, 20, 235–257.

Losbichler, B. and Mühlbacher, J. (1974). Entwicklung eines Mensch–Maschine-Kommunikationssystems durch top-down Entwurf. *Angewandte Informatik*, 16, 453–463.

Lucas, R.W., Knill-Jones, R.P., Card, W.I. and Crean, G.P. (1976). An adaptive system for the interrogation of hospital patients. *Proceedings of the Conference on the Applications of Electronics in Medicine*, Glasgow, 161–170.

Maher, P.K.C. and Bell, H.V. (1977). The man–machine interface–a new approach. *Proceedings of the International Conference on Displays for Man/Machine Systems*, Lancaster, 122–125.

Martin, J. (1973). *Design of Man–Computer Dialogues*. New Jersey: Prentice-Hall.

Newman, I.A. (1978). Personalised user interfaces to computer systems. *Proceedings of the European Computing Congress*, London.

Open University. (1973). ACE reference manual, Open University, Milton Keynes.

Parnas, D.L. (1969). On the use of transition diagrams in the design of a user interface for an interactive computer system. *Proceedings of the National ACM Conference,* 379–385.

Partridge, D. and James, E.B. (1976). Compiling techniques to exploit the pattern of language usage. *Software-Practice and Experience,* **6**, 527–539.

Raven, J.C. (1962). *Extended Guide to Using the Mill Hill Vocabulary Scale with the Progressive Matrices Scale.* London: H.K. Lewis.

Rosenburg, V. (1973). A technique for monitoring user behaviour at the computer terminal interface. *J. Am. Soc. Information Sci.,* **24**, 71.

Schon, D.A. (1971). *Beyond the Stable State.* London: Temple Smith.

Self, J.A. (1977). Artificial intelligence techniques in computer assisted instruction. *Aust. Computer J.,* **9**, 118–127.

Sneeringer, J. (1978). User interface design for text editing: a cast study. *Software-Practice and Experience,* **8**, 543–557.

Stewart, T.F.M. (1974). Ergonomic aspects of man–computer problem solving. *Appl. Ergonomics,* **5**, 209–212.

Suret, P. (1971). Simplifying the man–machine interface with the touch terminal. *Proceedings of the I.E.E. Conference on Displays,* 307–313.

Swanson, E.B. (1977). A methodology for IBIS data gathering and development. *Design Methods and Theories,* **11**, 256–260.

Thomas, R.C. and Pyle, I.C. (1978). The adaptable terminal: a user adjustable man–computer interface. *Proceedings of the Workshop on Computing Skills and Adaptive Systems,* University of Liverpool.

Watson, R.W. (1976). User interface design issues for a large interactive system. *Proceedings of the AFIPS Conference,* **45**, 357–364.

13. The Design of an Adaptable Terminal

R.C. THOMAS

Department of Computer Studies, University of Leeds, Leeds, England

I. INTRODUCTION

How can we make the non-computer specialist feel at home with the computer? One approach is to improve the interface between the user and the computer. The interface has software and hardware components; this chapter describes some software developments aimed at tailoring terminals to suit individual user requirements.

This chapter reviews some research into the design of better user interfaces, and outlines the design and programming of an adaptable terminal that could be developed as a series of final-year projects. Possible research topics are also outlined, and it is hoped to show that research into this area need not necessarily be expensive in the initial stages.

Most of the chapter is concerned with ways of making computers easier to use. One method of achieving this is by using special-purpose terminals, such as the cash dispensers which many banks are introducing. These terminals permit a restricted dialogue designed for a particular task, which enables them to be used by the general public without any training. Terminals with special hardware often have the advantages of:
- low user training;
- simplicity of operation;
- fast keying speeds;
- flexibility in the order of a dialogue.

The design of most dialogues involves balancing trade-offs between these factors so that the demands of the anticipated user population are satisfied. It is rare to find applications which can justify the use of special-purpose hardware, because of its cost and long-term inflexibility. To reduce terminal cost we need a standard mass-produced product, which is usually the visual display unit (VDU). Because the VDU is a general-purpose device, all the user-oriented features that help to achieve a good balance between the above factors have to be incorporated into the software, thus turning the dialogue into something designed especially for the application. Traditional methods of software development mean that a central systems group usually has responsibility for the design and maintenance of the user facilities; with a little luck they will have consulted the user, but they will still do the programming.

The experimental device reported in this chapter is called simply the "adaptable terminal". It was developed in the belief that the user, not the systems designer, knows which special dialogue features are useful, and that the user should be able to adapt the dialogue for himself to suit his own needs. The techniques available for adjusting the terminal are called "programming by imitation".

The present work is concerned with software rather than with ergonomics. I will discuss, among other issues, the software needed to support special function keys, whose physical implementation on the adaptable terminal was limited by the equipment available. The best ways to provide and arrange the keys from the point of view of user convenience is a matter for ergonomic research. For a discussion of research into the ergonomic aspects of man–computer interaction see Shackel (1980).

II. IMPORTANT FACTORS AND TECHNIQUES IN INTERACTIVE COMPUTING

A great deal has been written about techniques for interactive computing, most of which concentrates on the provision of hardware, software or both. As yet there is no widely accepted method for measuring the effectiveness of a person–computer interface, although the existence of a large number of research projects suggests that existing interfaces are far from ideal. Progress has generally been made by examining systems already in operation and learning from the deficiencies found in them. This chapter follows the same pragmatic line, and seeks to address user probems by the application and extension of techniques that have shown promise.

Guidelines for designing dialogues between a person and a computer have to be based on practical experience because of the absence of a well-established method for measuring their effectiveness. Both Martin (1973) and Hebditch (1976) discuss various techniques that are available and indicate the circumstances in which each is likely to be suitable or unsuitable. Both authors have developed reference tables so that selection is made easier for the designer. The message from these authors is clear: dialogue design can be systematic even though the factors that have to be considered are fairly diverse, e.g. data volumes, "intelligence" of the operator, terminal type, and available training time.

A. People, Organizations and Computers

Palme (1975a) has identified four groups of people affected by computer systems:
- Experts (system designers, programmers, engineers, etc.);
- Managers (who hope to improve efficiency with computers);
- Employees (whose tasks are affected by computers);
- Outsiders (who work outside the place where the computer is used, but who are influenced by it in various ways).

A person's attitude to, and acceptance of, computers is likely to depend upon the group to which he or she belongs. Experts often undertake creative and varied work, constructing systems for the other groups to use. This gives them power and they usually get high job satisfaction from computers. Managers wish to reap the economic and social benefits that computers might bring, which demand that employees accept computers. Employees find this hard to do while systems are inflexible and in the sole control of experts. Palme argues that employees are more likely to accept computers if they feel ". . . they have power over the computer, that they can get the computer to do what they want, that the computer is a useful tool helping them". A well-designed interface will go some way towards making the computer into a useful tool, but additional facilities should be provided which allow the user to change his mind and alter his requirements within reasonable limits. A central systems group could make all the changes on behalf of the user, but because this is often a slow process over which the user has limited control, Palme believes the users would lose any feelings of power over the system. Accordingly, he proposes the development of an interface which is designed to be programmable by users themselves, so that they do not need to contact a central systems group to make small changes to the dialogue. Such a dialogue would consist of the normal system commands plus an additional user language, which would be recursive, so that programs written in it could use both system commands and commands previously defined in the user language. More detail is given towards the end of this section.

Eason *et al.* (1974) used the term "naive computer user" to denote "a person in paid employment who utilises the computer in some significant way as part of his job " (see Chapter 3 in this volume). In their survey of man–computer interaction in commercial applications they found that 80% of all users wished to assist in future systems design. Naive computer users required various forms of documentary support, such as manuals and help facilities, as well as human support, which was provided from three sources: formal trainers, computing advisory personnel, and local experts. A local expert will

> often arise spontaneously from being an "ordinary" user by asking questions, experimenting with the system and developing more knowledge about it than other users . . . . A source of local experts was generally required once system staff had absented themselves from the user department.

Now Palme recognized that his programmable interface ". . . requires that one person close to each user group is trained in writing programs in the user language", and Eason *et al.* seem to have demonstrated that this is a natural organizational possibility. In view of the large proportion of users wishing to assist in future systems design, it may be concluded that local experts would need to consult their colleagues closely when writing programs in Palme's user language, otherwise its point would be lost.

B. Some Perspectives on Errors

Florentin (1977) has designed a system for someone without expertise in computer programming, whom he calls the "Author", to produce a dialogue to be used by someone else, called the "Operator". A combination of string manipulation and function interpretation techniques is used to give about 20 basic functions to the Author. Coping with Operator errors has been shown to be a major problem, since it is necessary to anticipate error situations during dialogue design, and Florentin argues that it would be better to improve the error-handling routines "in actual service". This is another example of a system which allows non-computer specialists to design and write dialogues concerned with their functional job. There is also a hint that better methods of dialogue generation do not necessarily overcome the basic problem of deciding what it is one wants the system to do; this theme is pertinent to the present work.

The need to improve error handling as a result of experience has been recognized by Edmonds and Guest (1977) in the interactive Ace system, which provides computer-aided learning in computer programming. Flexible error discrimination and message generation methods have been employed, so that the system can evolve in the light of practical experience. Note the emphasis on improving the system as a result of use. Can a centralized systems group participate in this sort of evolutionary process, or is it too remote?

There are thus at least two reports of workers who have found it necessary to design a system and then let it change as and when they find design deficiencies, which are sometimes called errors but which are really new or obscure requirements. They provide evidence to support the earlier proposition that the user should be able to change his mind and alter his requirements.

Gilb (1976) sees error handling as a dynamic problem, and recommends amongst other things the "self-adjusting limit" technique. This technique would involve a normal range check on a field of numerical data, but the upper and lower bounds of the range would alter over time according to one or more predetermined rules. For instance, if the value of an entry went beyond the upper bound, the user could be asked by the system to verify that the entry was correct; the entry would then be accepted and the upper bound set to the value of the entry. Periodically, say weekly, the value of the upper bound could be reduced by 10% to adjust the limit downwards. Self-adjusting limits such as these could be set for each geographical location, thereby increasing the chances of trapping errors; local processing of input makes this particularly attractive. Gilb also points out that there is often no way to check the validity of a record without access to the related records; even if an entry includes a valid self-checking customer number, the existence of the customer can only be confirmed by access to the record. The emphasis here is on making sure that systems can adjust to changes in the operational environment, such as those brought about by a high rate of inflation or by changes in customer records, rather than on recognizing that it is difficult to design a system which is flexible in terms of its command structure (cf. Palme, 1975a), or its error discrimination (cf. Florentin, 1977, and Edmonds and Guest, 1977).

Alsberg et al. (1976) used an intelligent terminal as an agent to improve the user interface to a data-base. A feature of their system is the use of a touch-sensitive display instead of the usual keyboard, which they consider to be a psychological barrier to the casual user. The display tells the user in application-oriented terms what he can do next, so that he does not need to memorize a precise command syntax or individual command options. The result was that people could use the system without any training, but it was found that users wanted combinations of displays that the designers had never considered. It was concluded that "there are some subtle inter-actions between a user and his application that simply cannot be predicted by the computer systems designer".

C. Keyboards

Well-designed systems should guide users towards making valid input choices from a selection of alternatives and should cut down the amount of unnecessary keying. The design of the keyboard has an important bearing on these factors, and can indicate techniques that could be applied in the adaptable terminal.

Knowlton (1975) reports that Bell Laboratories have experimented with a computer console which consists of a computer-controlled display and an array of black unlabelled buttons. The operator "sees" the labels on the buttons on a semi-transparent mirror between the display and the array of buttons. Only those buttons which are "labelled" are visible, so that the keyboard can be grossly recon-figured to suit the particular task at hand. When only a sub-set of the buttons is displayed, the operator is guided towards making correct requests of the computer via the console, which could be particularly helpful in training new telephone operators, for example. This interesting idea has similarities with the system of Alsberg *et al.*, which uses touch-sensitive displays—both systems are aimed at giving the user a meaningful choice of "buttons" to press. Such special-purpose keyboards are particularly useful when the blend of factors such as speed and complexity of the task is right.

Du Boulay and Emanuel (1975) describe another system which dispenses with the usual teletype keyboard because it is difficult to use. The aim of their work was to teach children, who are not com-petent typists, to program via a device called a "button box". Most of the 16 buttons give commands to a floor-crawling vehicle (a turtle) to move forwards or backwards, turn right or left, etc. Additionally there are three buttons labelled "TEACH", "END" and "RUN". A sequence of commands can be recorded by the computer by preceding it with "TEACH" and finishing it with "END"; the "RUN" button can be pressed at any subsequent time, and causes the recorded sequence of commands to be given to the turtle. Adults have tried the system, and it was found that "using the button box rather than a teletype initially appears to put them a little more at their ease since there is very much less chance of 'making a mistake' ". I attribute this to the direct visible response by the turtle to the stimulus they provide at the button box, plus the reduced choice that the special keyboard gives the user.

D. Displays

It is becoming fairly common to divide the screen into a number of areas, each with attributes such as high intensity, blinking display, inverse video, and numeric characters only. Forms can then be designed to help the user to enter data which is complex and involves related fields. An example of a form to enter basic hotel details into an inclusive holiday reservation system is shown in Fig. 1. The disadvantage of "form-fill", as the technique is called, is the difficulty of error correction.

```
            BASIC HOTEL INFORMATION

HOTEL CODE  ......   LOCATION  ....    GATEWAY ...
HOTEL NAME  .......................................

FACILITIES    BAR . LOUNGE . POOL . PARKING . GOLF


              ROOM ALLOCATION

ROOM TYPE    .... .... .... .... .... .... .... ....
NUMBER       ...  ...  ...  ...  ...  ...  ...  ...

SELLING DEADLINE ...
```

Fig. 1. Example of the form-fill technique.

An example of a user interface being improved with home-developed software is the Viscom system at Portsmouth Polytechnic described by Coleman *et al.* (1976). This enables VDU screens to be split into two areas, and users have several commands available to call up display editing facilities as required. Donzeau-Gorve *et al.* (1975) also found a split screen to be useful for a program editor, but in this case the screen was divided into three areas called "windows", with

21 lines at the top for displayed program, then a line of diagnostics and finally two lines for entering commands. The use of such windows is an important element in the adaptable terminal.

E. Programming by the User

This section reviews some of the range of possibilities for giving the user programmable facilities.

According to Anderson and Gillogly (1976) the Rand Intelligent Terminal Agent (RITA) was designed to enable non-computer specialists to tailor available computer services to their specific needs, and especially to "free them from routine interactions and protocols which are not directly relevant to the context of their task". The designers considered it would be necessary for RITA to explain its behaviour to the user, who should then be able to modify it (cf. Palme, 1975a). RITA is based on a DEC PDP11/45 and is a very advanced user agent: not only does it have text-editing facilities (using the window concept), communications capability and local storage, but it can also be programmed by naive users. The designers of RITA considered that traditional, high-level, algorithmic programming languages were unsuitable for their purposes, because naive users are not programmers and do not tend to think in algorithms, and because nested control was considered "unnatural" and error-prone. It was decided, therefore, that the programming should be accomplished through production systems (developed in artificial intelligence work—see Davis and King, 1975, for an overview). A major benefit of this approach is that it enables the user to ask the question "Why?", and all in all it is a bold step towards giving people their personal programmable machine.

Palme (1975b) has called for an "intermediate program" to give the naive user more control over his work:

Here are some examples of what such an intermediate program might do:

- log a user onto the system, initialize system parameters to suit him, start up an application package, give the application package a number of default parameters and then let the user use the application package.
- take short simple one-letter commands from the user, expand these to longer commands or series of commands to the application package.
- save the answers which a user gave when processing one record with an application package. The user can then with a special command to the intermediate program ask it to process another record with the same parameters, saving the user the effort of repeating these para-

meters. (The user may for example make the same editing operation on a number of records).
- ask the system to load some data from a tape onto a disk, then signal the user with the bell inside the user terminal when the data has been loaded.
- sum the value of one output parameter from the application package over a number of interactive uses of the package.
- check the things typed in by the user for errors which he·easily makes.

On the DEC-10 computer the TECO editor (1972) has the facility to define one-letter commands: for example "*nxq*" inserts *n* lines of text in register *q*, "*gq*" inserts the contents of *q* into the editing buffer, and "*mq*" will execute the commands stored in *q*. TECO has some of the facilities which Palme thinks the intermediate program should provide.

The MIC (1978) files facility (Macro Interpreted Commands), developed at Hatfield Polytechnic, can store in a file a series of commands which can subsequently be executed by typing "/filename". This makes it very easy for inexperienced people to use certain parts of the system, as well as giving experienced users the facilities to tailor the operating system command structure to meet their own needs.

F. Programming by Imitation

Some of the ways in which the user interface can be improved have been discussed; the experimental adaptable terminal blends many of these techniques together, and the present work builds on the following major themes:
- naive users adjusting the local programmable interface;
- recognition of the local expert concept by allowing modes of operation which are similar to Author and Operator;
- the creation of user-defined functions by use of keys such as "TEACH", "END" and "RUN";
- the capacity to tailor the screen to the user's requirements by the creation of windows.

Instead of having an Author and Operator, the terms "Teacher" and "User" describe the population of naive computer users with its local experts who may adjust the terminal to suit particular applications. In a business organization a Teacher might be a User's supervisor, but is unlikely to be a professional programmer. This means that a conventional programming language is unlikely to be suitable for adapting the terminal.

The use of high-level languages removes many artificial coding encumbrances such as machine architecture details, but does not solve the real problem, which is concerned with thinking and problem-solving. People can solve problems without necessarily following a formal method, and very often without being able to state explicity how they solve them. What is needed is a system which can react directly to actions made by the Teacher through the keyboard, so that he can see that the terminal has "understood" what he is trying to do. Ideally, in the words of Shackel (1980), a system should "do what I mean, not what I say". The scheme of "programming by imitation" for the adaptable terminal goes some way towards addressing these problems in that it "does what I do" to a large extent.

Programming by imitation is achieved via a set of "Primitive Functions" which give the Teacher facilities to:

− partition the VDU screen into an arbitrary set of windows;
− organize communication with the host computer;
− compose transactions consisting of sequences of functions which are stored for subsequent use by Teacher or User.

The Teacher constructs transactions appropriate for a particular application; they are retained in the terminal, available for regular use by the User. These "Composed Transactions", as they are called, consist of strings of Primitive Functions.

III. THE ADAPTABLE TERMINAL

A. Overview

In order to gain a better understanding of programming by imitation, the DEC GT40 graphics terminal at the University of York was programmed as an alphanumeric adaptable terminal. Details of the program for the GT40 are given in Section IIIC; for further details see Thomas (1979). The programmed terminal has the following features:

− communication with certain host computers;
− programming by imitation through the keyboard;
− an alphanumeric display of 71 columns by 32 rows;
− about 10K bytes of working storage;
− about 8K bytes of program;
− 25 Primitive Functions and storage for up to 52 Composed Transactions.

The GT40 graphics terminal has a display processor which drives a refresh cathode-ray tube. The display processor is connected via a Unibus to 32K words of 16-bit store. Also connected to the Unibus is a PDP11/05 processor, a keyboard, and a DL11E interface which provides external communication at 4800 baud.

One feature which the GT40 lacks is a suitable pad of special-function keys. Therefore the sequence "home key, alphanumeric key" has been taken to designate a special function call.

The next part of this chapter is a description for Teachers of the adaptable terminal. It is deliberately written in a style that could be suitable for naive users, in order to demonstrate that it is possible to discuss programming the device without resorting to an "algorithmic" approach. It would be useful to develop a grammar for programming by imitation to facilitate communication amongst computer specialists. In this description and the remainder of the chapter, Primitive Functions are referred to as "PFs", and Composed Trans-actions as "CTs".

B. A Description for Teachers of the Adaptable Terminal

1. *Introduction*

The adaptable terminal is like an ordinary VDU except that it has facilities which enable it to be programmed by non-computer specialists. These facilities control the way the screen is used, and they can also combine together commonly used sequences of key-strokes into just one or two keystrokes. The result is that people can adapt the terminal to suit their own requirements and save themselves unnecessary repetition in keying.

The various facilities (PFs) provided for the Teacher are usually invoked by pressing "home key" followed by the "function identifier". Figure 2 shows the keyboard layout of the terminal, together with the positions of the special-function keys.

The Teacher may adapt the terminal using the PFs so that it is easier for the User to make the host computer perform his applica-tion via the terminal. Two of the PFs enable the Teacher to move from what is called "text mode" to "frame mode" and vice versa; initially the terminal is in text mode. Figure 3 lists the PFs that are available in each mode. PFs may be combined together by the Teacher to form CTs. Once the Teacher has finished adapting the terminal he can "lock" it so that only CTs and certain PFs are available to the User.

The notation to be used in the rest of this description for referring

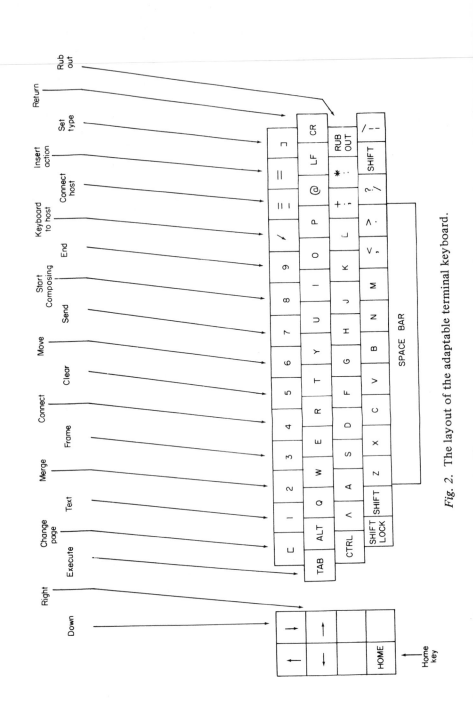

Fig. 2. The layout of the adaptable terminal keyboard.

(a) *Frame-mode Primitive Functions:*
   <u>clear</u>
   <u>down</u>
   <u>divide</u>
   <u>merge</u>
   <u>rename</u>
   <u>right</u>
   <u>select</u>
   <u>text</u>

(b) *Text-mode Primitive Functions:*

<u>clear</u>	<u>change page</u>
<u>frame</u>	connect
<u>inject</u>	connect host
<u>move</u>	keyboard to host
<u>return</u>	
<u>rubout</u>	
<u>send</u>	
	dump
start composing	execute
<u>end</u>	insert action
<u>run</u>	<u>set type</u>

Fig. 3. Functions available to the Teacher in frame and text modes.

to the special functions–PFs and CTs–is to underline the name. Thus "home key, x" would be written as "$\underline{x}$" and "home key, clear" as "<u>clear</u>".

2. *Frame-mode Primitive Functions*

When the displayable area of the screen is divided into a number of arbitrarily sized rectangular windows, each window is uniquely identified by an upper- or lower-case letter, giving a maximum of 52 windows. The terminal contains four "pages" of windows in rather the same way that the display area contains several windows, except that only one page can be displayed at any time. The rest of this section deals with creating windows on any one page by specifying actions through the keyboard. All characters entered through the keyboard will operate on at least one window, which is called the keyboard's "destination": this will change during the course of a session in frame mode.

PF: <u>frame mode</u>   ENTRY: home key, frame-mode key

Windows can only be created or changed when the page is in frame mode. In order to put the page into frame mode from text mode, PF <u>frame mode</u> is used. It results in a display of the windows, each one being filled with its identifier so that their shapes are easily visible (see Fig. 4). Additionally, the cursor is positioned in the "prime position" of one of the windows, i.e. the top left-hand corner.

```
AAAAAAAAAAAAAAAAAAAAAAAAAAAAAAAAAAAAAAAAAAAAAAAAAAAAAAAAAAAAAAAAAAAAAAAAAAA
AAAAAAAAAAAAAAAAAAAAAAAAAAAAAAAAAAAAAAAAAAAAAAAAAAAAAAAAAAAAAAAAAAAAAAAAAAA
AAAAAAAAAAAAAAAAAAAAAAAAAAAAAAAAAAAAAAAAAAAAAAAAAAAAAAAAAAAAAAAAAAAAAAAAAAA
AAAAAAAAAAAAAAAAAAAAAAAAAAAAAAAAAAAAAAAAAAAAAAAAAAAAAAAAAAAAAAAAAAAAAAAAAAA
AAAAAAAAAAAAAAAAAAAAAAAAAAAAAAAAAAAAAAAAAAAAAAAAAAAAAAAAAAAAAAAAAAAAAAAAAAA
AAAAAAAAAAAAAAAAAAAAAAAAAAAAAAAAAAAAAAAAAAAAAAAAAAAAAAAAAAAAAAAAAAAAAAAAAAA
AAAAAAAAAAAAAAAAAAAAAAAAAAAAAAAAAAAAAAAAAAAAAAAAAAAAAAAAAAAAAAAAAAAAAAAAAAA
AAAAAAAAAAAAAAAAAAAAAAAAAAAAAAAAAAAAAAAAAAAAAAAAAAAAAAAAAAAAAAAAAAAAAAAAAAA
AAAAAAAAAAAAAAAAAAAAAAAAAAAAAAAAAAAAAAAAAAAAAAAAAAAAAAAAAAAAAAAAAAAAAAAAAAA
AAAAAAAAAAAAAAAAAAAAAAAAAAAAAAAAAAAAAAAAAAAAAAAAAAAAAAAAAAAAAAAAAAAAAAAAAAA
BBBBBBBBBBBBBBBBBBBBBBBBBBBBBBBBBBBBBBBBBBBBBBBBBBBBBBBBBBBBBBBBBBBBBBBBBBB
ccccccccccccccccccccccc■dddddddddddddddddddddddddddddddddddddddddddddddddd
cccccccccccccccccccccccgdddddddddddddddddddddddddddddddddddddddddddddddddd
cccccccccccccccccccccccgdddddddddddddddddddddddddddddddddddddddddddddddddd
cccccccccccccccccccccccgdddddddddddddddddddddddddddddddddddddddddddddddddd
cccccccccccccccccccccccgdddddddddddddddddddddddddddddddddddddddddddddddddd
cccccccccccccccccccccccgdddddddddddddddddddddddddddddddddddddddddddddddddd
cccccccccccccccccccccccgdddddddddddddddddddddddddddddddddddddddddddddddddd
cccccccccccccccccccccccgdddddddddddddddddddddddddddddddddddddddddddddddddd
cccccccccccccccccccccccgdddddddddddddddddddddddddddddddddddddddddddddddddd
cccccccccccccccccccccccgdddddddddddddddddddddddddddddddddddddddddddddddddd
bbbbbbbbbbbbbbbbbbbbbbbbbbbbbbbbbbbbbbbbbbbbbbbbbbbbbbbbbbbbbbbbbbbbbbbbbbb
nnnnnnnnnnnnnnnnnnnnnnnnnnnnnnnnnnnnnnnnnyuuuuuuuuuuuuuuuuuuuuuuuuuuuuuuuu
nnnnnnnnnnnnnnnnnnnnnnnnnnnnnnnnnnnnnnnnnyuuuuuuuuuuuuuuuuuuuuuuuuuuuuuuuu
nnnnnnnnnnnnnnnnnnnnnnnnnnnnnnnnnnnnnnnnnnyPPPPPPPPPPPPPPPPPPPPPPPPPPPPPPP
nnnnnnnnnnnnnnnnnnnnnnnnnnnnnnnnnnnnnnnnnnyPPPPPPPPPPPPPPPPPPPPPPPPPPPPPPP
nnnnnnnnnnnnnnnnnnnnnnnnnnnnnnnnnnnnnnnnnnyPPPPPPPPPPPPPPPPPPPPPPPPPPPPPPP
nnnnnnnnnnnnnnnnnnnnnnnnnnnnnnnnnnnnnnnnnnyPPPPPPPPPPPPPPPPPPPPPPPPPPPPPPP
nnnnnnnnnnnnnnnnnnnnnnnnnnnnnnnnnnnnnnnnnnyPPPPPPPPPPPPPPPPPPPPPPPPPPPPPPP
nnnnnnnnnnnnnnnnnnnnnnnnnnnnnnnnnnnnnnnnnnytttttttttttttttttttttttttttttt
```

Fig. 4. Example of a frame-mode display. (Eleven windows are shown: A, B, C, b, n, g, d, y, u, P, t. The cursor is in the prime position of window g.)

PF: <u>down</u>   ENTRY: down key

<u>down</u> moves the cursor along the left-hand column of the window one position each time the down key is pressed; it is described in more detail with <u>right</u>.

PF: <u>right</u>   ENTRY: right key

<u>right</u> moves the cursor along the top row of the window and is controlled by the right key; <u>right</u> and <u>down</u> must not be used in combination as this would move the cursor into the middle of a window. Any attempt to do this is signalled as an error by ringing the bell.

PF: <u>select</u>   ENTRY: window identifier

At all times the keyboard is connected to one window, called the keyboard's "destination". This may be changed by using <u>select</u> a new window.

PF: <u>rename</u>   ENTRY: window identifier

<u>rename</u> is similar to <u>select</u>, except that if the desired window does not exist and the cursor is in the prime position of a window, then that window's identifier becomes the letter that was entered through the keyboard.

PF: <u>divide</u>   ENTRY: window identifier

<u>divide</u> window is used when the cursor is not in the prime position, i.e. after one or more consecutive <u>down</u> or <u>right</u> moves. The window containing the cursor is divided into two rectangles. The cursor's current position becomes the prime position of a new window whose identifier was entered through the keyboard; this new window becomes the keyboard's destination. The old window is divided horizontally or vertically depending upon whether <u>down</u> or <u>right</u> was used.

PF: <u>merge</u>   ENTRY: home key, merge key

<u>merge</u> attempts to combine the keyboard's destination with the window to its left if their heights are the same, or else with the one above it if their widths are the same.

PF: <u>clear</u>   ENTRY: home key, clear key

<u>clear</u> merges all the windows in a page into one covering the whole screen, which is called "A" on page 1, "B" on page 2, etc. In other words, the prime window is restored.

PF: <u>text</u>   ENTRY: home key, text key

Once all the desired windows have been set up, the page must be set into text mode; <u>text</u> does this and causes the page to be filled with spaces and the cursor to appear in the prime position of the keyboard's destination.

3. *Some Text-mode Primitive Functions*

PF: inject   ENTRY: alphanumeric character

When a page is in text mode, characters may be injected into the keyboard's destination window by entering them through the keyboard. When the end of a line is reached, the cursor moves to the first position of the next line down. When the end of a window is reached, the cursor wraps around to the window's prime position. The wrap-around facility is a default action which may be changed (see insert action in part 6). Any alphanumeric character may be injected unless a specific set of characters has been designated as valid for a particular window (see set type in part 6).

PF: rubout   ENTRY: rubout key

The rubout key moves the cursor back one position and puts a space there.

PF: return   ENTRY: return key

The return function moves the cursor to the first position on the next line filling all positions between the old and new points with spaces. If the end of the window is reached, appropriate action is taken, the default being wrap-around.

PF: clear   ENTRY: home key, clear key

The keyboard's destination can be filled with spaces and the cursor returned to the prime position by using clear.

PF: move   ENTRY: home key, move key, optional
                                     page digit, window identifier

The contents of another window can be injected into the keyboard's destination using the move function. If a page number is not included, the same page is assumed. There are two restrictions: first, a window cannot be moved to itself, and second, a window is regarded as a string of characters and no carriage returns are moved (subject to exceptions of CTs—see part 4). Hence all trailing spaces after the text on each line are included in the move. The string of characters to be moved starts at the prime position of the source window and ends at the cursor position.

PF: <u>frame</u>   ENTRY: home key, frame key

The page can be put in frame mode using <u>frame</u>; all text on the page is lost.

PF: <u>send</u>   ENTRY: home key, send key, optional page digit, window identifier

The contents of a window can be transmitted to the host computer using the <u>send</u> primitive; the comments about trailing spaces for <u>move</u> apply here also.

4. *Introduction to Composed Transactions*

Composed Transactions give the adaptable terminal its main programmability features. This section gives an introduction to what they are and how to use them from the keyboard. Each CT has an identifier which is an upper- or lower-case letter, and is in fact the identifier of the window which stores the transaction. These windows are located on pages 3 and 4 of the terminal.

A transaction can be composed only if the following conditions are satisfied:

(i)   the keyboard is used to make the entry;

(ii) a window exists in pages 3 and 4 which has the same identifier as the proposed transaction;

(iii) pages 3 and 4 are in text mode;

(iv) no other transaction is being composed at the same time.

Creating windows on pages 3 and 4 is the same as for any other page, except that window identifiers must be unique over both pages, not just over the displayed page. Because of restriction (iii), a CT cannot record the setting-up of windows on these pages.

PF: <u>start composing</u>   ENTRY: home key, transaction identifier, string of PFs

The string of PFs is recorded, including invocations of other CTs, keystroke by keystroke, in the window whose identifier is the same as the transaction identifier. As each keystroke is made, it is actioned in the normal way as if no recoding were taking place, so that it should be possible to see if the transaction does what is wanted. The recording process takes into account all characters whether they are displayable or not; thus carriage return would be recorded as a carriage return, but actioned as return; "CONTROL C" would be recorded as itself but would not be displayed.

PF: end   ENTRY: home key, end key

Once the Teacher has made all the keystrokes that he wants in a CT, he ends the recording process by using end.

PF: run   ENTRY: home key, transaction identifier

This PF invokes a previously defined CT: run can be called while a transaction is being composed, so long as it does not invoke the one being composed or one which is already running. These restrictions are necessary to avoid infinite loops around transactions which call each other. If a transaction cannot be run, a bell rings to indicate an error.

5. Changing Destinations

The expression "keyboard's destination" should now be familiar: it has been used simply to describe the window to which characters entered through the keyboard are sent. The destination concept now needs to be explained further: the keyboard can also have the host computer as a destination, and the host computer always has a window as its destination.

PF: keyboard to host   ENTRY: home key, keyboard to host key

keyboard to host is used to send all characters entered through the keyboard (except "home key") directly to the host without being entered into any window.

PF: connect host   ENTRY: home key, window identifier

When the terminal is initialized the prime window of page 1 is the host's destination. This means that all input to the terminal from the host is displayed in this window, provided the characters are displayable; connect host changes the host's destination to a window on the displayed page. It can be used to transfer the host's destination from a hidden page to the currently displayed page, but not vice versa.

PF: changepage   ENTRY: home key, changepage key, page
                                   digit

<u>changepage</u> alters the keyboard's destination to the current position of the prime window of another page. The text or frame on the previous page is not lost.

PF: <u>connect</u>   ENTRY: home key, connect key, window
                                            identifier

The keyboard's destination may be changed to another window on the same page using <u>connect,</u> which may be invoked from either the host or the keyboard. If, however, the host invokes <u>connect</u>, then the destinations of both the host and the keyboard are changed.

6. *Advanced Use of Text Mode*

PF: <u>set type</u>   ENTRY: home key, set type key, type
                                            identifier

This function enables the Teacher to state the permitted character set for the window which is the current keyboard's destination. The valid type identifiers are:
"0" for any displayable character;
"1" for letters and spaces only;
"2" for numbers and spaces only;
"3" for spaces only;
"transaction identifier" for any defined character set.
The transaction identifier refers to a CT, and all input into the window is checked to see if the character exists in the CT.

PF: <u>insert action</u>   ENTRY: home key, insert action key,
                                            action identifier

By default when the end of a window is reached, wrap-around occurs and text starts appearing in the prime position of the window. This default can be changed using <u>insert action</u>; the possible action identifiers are:
"0" for wrap-around;
"1" for scroll;.
"2" for progress;
"3" for progress and clear;
"transaction identifier" for CT.
If "progress" is used, then the destination will change to the next window on the same page whose identifier is next in the alphabet, so that if we are in window "K" we would progress to "L" if it exists.

"Progress and clear" does the same thing, but the next window ("L" above) is cleared as well. These two options can be used for form-fill. If a transaction identifier is used, then the CT it refers to is invoked.

PF: <u>execute</u>   ENTRY: home key, execute key

<u>execute</u> performs the end of window action without the need to fill the whole window with characters.

PF: <u>dump</u>   ENTRY: home key, send key, "="

This PF sends all the CTs down the line to the host, where they may be stored for future use.

7. Example of Use in Word Processing

This example shows how the adaptable terminal can be used to help solve a word-processing problem. Suppose that a list of names and addresses is stored in a word processor, and that only some of them are required for a particular task. The selection criteria are known to the operator, but are not codified in the word processor, so it is necessary for the operator to scan through the names and addresses to select the relevant ones for further processing.

The adaptable terminal can assist the operator by being adapted to: display the next name and address on the screen; allow the operator to use <u>y</u> (for "Yes") if the data are to be retained for further processing, or <u>n</u> (for "No") if the data are not required; save the data if needed, and then display the next name and address from the file in the host computer.

The names and addresses stored in the host computer could be retrieved using the following commands (plus a carriage return) from an ordinary VDU:

open the file	OPEN NAMES
display next name and address	NEXT
close file	CLOSE

The adaptable terminal can be used as follows:

Step 1: Rename window <u>v</u> on page 4 to become <u>y</u> for "Yes" by keying:
<u>changepage</u> 4
<u>frame</u>

v

y

text

changepage 1

Step 2: Compose transaction b̲ to begin by opening the file:

start composing b

keyboard to host

OPEN NAMES

return

clear

end

When the file is open and ready on the host, an asterisk will appear near the top left-hand corner of the blank screen.

Step 3: Compose transaction n̲ to display the next name and address on the screen:

start composing n

clear

keyboard to host

NEXT

return

end

Step 4: Compose transaction y̲ to store the currently displayed name and address and then display the next record:

start composing y

rubout

changepage 2

move 1A

changepage 1

n

end

Step 5: Compose transaction s̲ to stop reading records from the host and close the file:

start composing s

keyboard to host

CLOSE

return

end

Thus the terminal has been adapted using 78 keystrokes. Four transactions have been composed, and there are only two keystrokes required to process each record. The selected names and addresses are stored on page 2.

C. The Program for the GT40

The adaptable terminal program is written in Wirth's (1977a) language MODULA, which is "intended primarily for programming dedicated computer systems, including process control systems on smaller machines". An outline of the program is given in Fig. 5, which uses Wirth's (1977b) notation for MODULA programs.

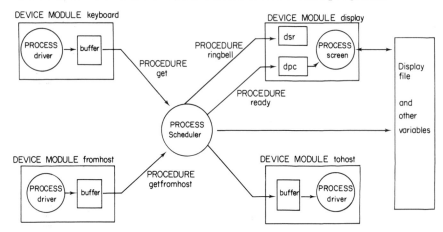

Fig. 5. Outline of the adaptable terminal program.

There are two input modules, to handle the keyboard and the host, which together feed a process called "scheduler", which has outputs to the display processing unit (DPU) and to the line to the host. The various processes shown in Fig. 5 can run in parallel, which is how the terminal's multiprogramming features are achieved.

1. *Main Process*

Process "scheduler" polls the host and keyboard buffers for input on a character-by-character basis. If the input is from the keyboard and a transaction is being composed, then the character is stored in the CT window using procedure "remember". An outline of the process is as follows:

```
LOOP
  IF hostbuf > 0 THEN
                  getfromhost (ch) ;
                  useinput (ch,hostconnect,source[2]) ;
                  END;
  IF keybuf > 0 THEN
                  get(ch) ;
```

IF composing THEN remember (ch) END;
useinput (ch,kbdconnect,source[1]) ;
END;
END { polling loop } ;

2. *Pages*

The "np" pages in the system are declared as an array called "page" whose element structure is given by "disp":

```
TYPE disp= RECORD
              posn :     integer;    { DPU set point command}
              px :       integer;    { DPU x coordinate data }
              py :       integer;    { DPU y coordinate data }
              cmode :    integer;    { DPU character mode command}
              c :        ARRAY 1:sw*sh OF char; { display file }
              dstop :    integer;    {DPU display stop command}
              mode       (frame,text) {mode of page }
              END;

VAR        page:      ARRAY 1:np OF disp;
                      { array of pages for display }
```

The structure consists of DPU commands plus a file of characters which is interpreted by the DPU sequentially so that the entire screen is scanned. The screen width is "sw"-2 characters and the height is "sh" rows; the extra spaces on each line are for the carriage return line feed characters needed by the DPU.

3. *Window Control Blocks*

Every window in the system is associated with a window control block (wcb); there is an array of "nw" wcbs called "window" of type "wcb", declared as follows:

```
TYPE wcb= RECORD
              pid:       integer;    { page number of this window }
              wid:       char;       { window identifier }
              chtype:    char;       { type identifier }
              eow:       char;       { action identifier }
              home:      integer;    { index in page[pid] .c of
                                       prime position of window }
              ca:        integer;    { index in page[pid] .c of
                                       cursor position in window}
```

ymax:	integer;	{ height of window in rows }
xmax:	integer;	{ width of window in columns }
x,y:	integer;	{ current column and row of cursor in window }
status:	(called, free)	{ "called" when window's contents are running a composed transaction }

END;

VAR   window: ARRAY 1:nw OF wcb;
           { array of window control blocks }

4. *Sources*

The terminal has two external sources of input: the keyboard and the host computer. Procedure "useinput" needs to know which source is being used as well as what state it is in; we therefore define array "source" with element type "sourcestatus":

TYPE sourcestatus=RECORD
        sourcetype: (gt40,host) ; { type of source }
        wp:integer;   { temp working page number }
        nextch: { s t a t u s   t a b l e }

(any,	{ any char expected }
fid,	{ function id expected }
p1,	{ changepage parameter }
c1,	{ composed transaction id }
m1,	{ move parameter }
c2,	{ connect parameter }
i1,	{ insert action id }
k1,	{ kbd to host operation }
s1,	{ chtype identifier }
r1,	{ receiving boot }
c3,	{ connect host parameter }
s2)	{ send to host parameter }

END;

VAR source: ARRAY 1:2 OF sourcestatus;
                         { [1]=kbd, [2]=host }

The value of "nextch" for each source tells the analysis procedure ("useinput") what to expect, for example: in text mode when characters are being injected into a window, "nextch" is equal to "any"; if the home key were pressed it would change to "fid"; then perhaps "ml" for move while the window identifier and optional page number are awaited; after the move has been actioned it would go back to "any". The finite state transition diagram for "nextch"

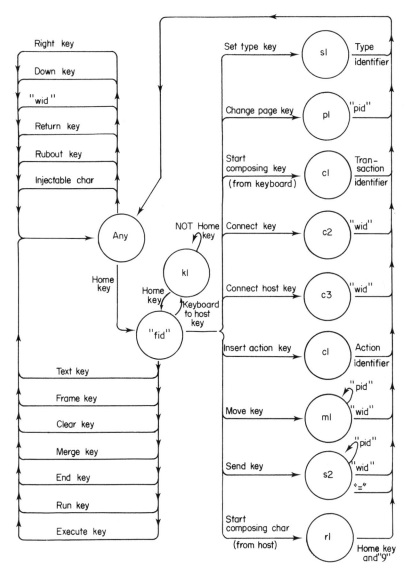

Fig. 6. Finite state transition diagram for "nextch" ("wid" = window identifier; "pid" = page identifier).

when the terminal is not locked is given in Fig. 6. The treatment of errors has been excluded for clarity, but the usual method is to ring the bell and return the status to "any".

5. *Procedure useinput*

All input is analysed by procedure "useinput"; an outline of its structure, together with some detail about composing and running transactions is given below. In many respects the grammar of programming by imitation can be gleaned from this code.

```
PROCEDURE useinput
    (ch: char; VAR dest: integer; VAR ss: sourcestatus);

    { ch is usually a char from kbd or host, but can be from a transaction;
      dest is the current destination window of the source; ss is the status of
      calling source.}

VAR gx, gy:        integer;      { counting variables }
    transaction:   integer;      { CT this call refers to }
    character:     char;         { workspace }
    lastch:        boolean;      { true if window read }

BEGIN
    WITH ss, page[window[dest].pid] DO
    CASE nextch OF

    any: { single char functions expected }
    BEGIN
    IF ch = homekey THEN
        nextch := fid
    ELSIF mode = text THEN
        { look for text mode functions without home key}
        IF ch = ruboutkey THEN rubout
        ELSIF ch = returnkey THEN return
        ELSE { inject character }
            . . .
            . . .
    END
    ELSE
        { look for single char frame mode functions }
        IF ch = rightkey THEN
            { code for this and other functions }
```

```
          . . .
          . . .
    END
END
END; { case value any }
fid: { after home key expect special function id }
BEGIN
nextch := any;
IF transactionidentifierinput THEN
    { try to run from window[transaction] }
    IF transaction = ct THEN
        { abandon − recursion }
        ringbell
    ELSIF window[transaction].status = free THEN
        { run composed transaction }
        window[transaction].status := called;
        mov(transaction,dest);
        window[transaction].status := free
    ELSE
        { transaction already running }
        ringbell
    END
ELSIF (locked) AND (NOT invoked) THEN
    { only CTs allowed from kbd and host when locked }
    ringbell
ELSIF (ch = ' { ') OR (ch = '[') THEN
    { changepage function: expect page number }
    nextch := p1;
        . . .
        . . .
END
END; { case value fid }

p1: { page digit is expected }
BEGIN
    { perform change to new page }
    nextch := any;
    changepage
END; { case value p1 }

{ further case values }
        . . .
        . . .
```

(continued)

END { case nextch statement }
END { with scopes }
END useinput;

CTs are run using procedure "mov" which calls "useinput" recursively. When "mov" is called characters are taken from the source window and are analysed as though they came from a keyboard or host source; initially they will be injected into "dest" which is the destination that the invoking source had at the call of the transaction. If the CT contains PFs, these will be actioned by the terminal in the normal way so that characters from the transaction window may not be injected into the destination window, but treated as other PFs. When the CT contains no PFs, it is identical to a move primitive, providing "nextch" was set to "m1".

D. Discussion and Assessment

1. *Display Files*

The preceding section shows that the display file is very simple. The system was effective and efficient in store and programming terms, but did not use many of the graphics features of the GT40. It was hoped that a design would be created with the potential for use by intelligent terminals without vector graphics features, but towards the end of the experiment it became clear that a more elaborate display file structure would be desirable. The major problem was the lack of storage of control characters, such as "carriage return" or "CONTROL C"; in the ordinary windows on the first two pages. Without this facility true programming by imitation is difficult because control characters have to be stored in CTs. Single unique graphic characters do not exist for control characters, so storing them in windows means that a suitable display convention has to be adopted, such as displaying " CONTROL C" as "%C", thus requiring two display positions for one character in the window. Underscoring control characters might avoid these mapping problems, but this would then preclude their use in text. A common technique is to allow the user to specify which graphic symbols shall be used to display the control characters, but this would mean losing the layout of the text in a window (see Primitive Function <u>move</u> in the description for Teachers). This problem could be overcome by a system of pointers, but this was not implemented because it was not central to the objectives of the research.

It is recommended that if any other adaptable terminal is built then the file structure should include a display buffer, so that whenever characters are written to the currently displayed page the buffer will be updated as well. This would require more processing, but would be a valuable improvement. It could be implemented within an intelligent terminal, in an adaptable interface box, or as part of a main-frame intermediate program: all that is required in the last two cases is a full duplex VDU plus an addressable cursor.

It has been found that scrolling is somewhat processor-bound when a window covers the whole page, but could be hastened if individual windows had pointers to each line, so that there would be no need to move large quantities of data about. If the full graphics capability of the GT40 were used, scrolling would not cause any problems.

2. *Window Management*

The methods used in frame mode for creating windows have been successful: people can learn to use a terminal within minutes if an experienced Teacher is present. Part of this success seems due to the direct visual feedback given in programming by imitation: nothing is hidden in frame mode.

The possibility of having one long file of lines, with only several contiguous lines actually displayed at any time, was considered. This system would oblige the Teacher to take into account what he could not see. He would be presented with partially visible windows, and the window naming system would need to be more complex to cater for more than 52 windows. The page approach, on the other hand, is simpler and helps the Teacher by dealing only with what is on the screen.

Although the page approach is good for managing displays, it is not so good for handling CTs. The teacher has to be conscious of storage for CTs, and it would be preferable for the adaptable terminal to handle this storage automatically.

3. *Destinations*

The control of the destinations of the keyboard and host could be improved. First, keyboard to host would not be necessary if a display buffer were used, as control characters would be handled by:

(i) setting up a one-character window and connecting the keyboard to it;

(ii) giving the window an action identifier of a CT, which would send the contents of the window to the host and then clear it.

Secondly, a single PF change destination could replace changepage, connect and connect host. Its arguments would state the page to be displayed and the new keyboard and host destinations.

4. Composed Transactions

If the changes suggested above were implemented, CTs would be even easier to create than they are now. A general guideline seems to be that the CTs should be as explicit as possible, so reducing the need for abstract thought about irrelevant possibilities.

The safeguards used to avoid looping transactions are:
- nested composition is not allowed; only one transaction can be composed at a time;
- a transaction cannot be called recursively during composition;
- a transaction can only be invoked if it has not already been invoked.

It is easier to build these safeguards into the program than to have an "abandon" button which the Teacher could press if he realized he had created a loop.

It would be useful to have a facility for single-stepping through a CT, with options to delete or insert PFs as required.

5. Number of Primitive Functions

It has already been suggested that the destination PFs could be rationalized, but there are trade-offs between the number of PFs and their complexity. For instance, it would be possible to have a single PF dispose, made up of send and clear.

Another trade-off lies in the use of operands: if clear had a window parameter, then we might say clear B instead of connect B, clear, connect A. It was decided to minimize operands so that the user could obtain as much feedback as possible from each keystroke. Thus the longest keying sequence is four characters, for example home key, send key, page number, window identifier.

Future versions of the adaptable terminal ideally ought to contain window-editing functions such as "insert into a string of text" and "delete a character inside a string". These were not programmed as they are fairly standard and do not really involve programming by imitation.

6. Teacher Feedback

When an error is made a bell rings, which is adequate for error detection and correction, but it has become clear that more feedback would be desirable. Therefore it might be advantageous to have a display showing the current destinations, the transaction being composed, and the action identifier and type identifier of the keyboard's destination. This would enable the Teacher to concentrate fully on creating the facilities he wants. As far as possible the Teacher should be able to see everything that is relevant to him at a given time.

7. Overall Assessment

The experiment has provided firm evidence that the adaptable terminal is a viable proposition, and has shown that this sort of software could be generated by students as one or more projects. I also feel that working in this area makes one more aware of the possibilities for improving the man–computer interface using relatively simple techniques, although it is difficult to assess their usefulness without systematic observation of their use in a working system.

Programming by imitation has been particularly effective for frame-mode work. In order to improve it for text-mode, PFs must be designed to be as explicit as possible, so that the Teacher has to state exactly what he wants the terminal to do.

IV. GENERAL DISCUSSION AND FURTHER POSSIBILITIES

A. Relationship between Terminal and Host

The method of dividing an application between the host computer and the terminals is extremely important. This sub-section considers the likely effects of connecting adaptable terminals to a major airline reservation system, and shows that tangible advantages can be gained from their use.

Most users of reservations systems are clerks handling telephone calls, who create a high volume of transactions. The design of transaction formats reflects this. All input to the system from a terminal is handled by software called the "Agent's Assembly Area" (AAA), which stores information about the context of the current dialogue with the computer from a particular terminal.

1. Reduced Keying

In the Helsinki office of a London-based airline, most flight enquiries are for flights on the Helsinki–London route. The entry to book a flight is:

0 SF832 Y 16AUG HELLHR NN2

where: 0 is the transaction code for the flight segment; SF832 is the flight number; Y is the class; 16AUG is the date of the flight; HELLHR is the origin-destination city pair; NN2 means "try to book 2 seats". The adaptable terminal in Helsinki could be set up with keys for: BOOK, WAITLIST, etc; each month of the year; each flight to and from Helsinki. This could reduce the above booking entry of 21 characters to 7 keystrokes, including: book key; 2; flight key; class key; 16; month key. The chances of a booking error would be lessened by this reduced keying. The clerk selects a series of items from several fixed menus, the adaptable terminal being used as a sub-set of menu-selection in that menus are fixed for flights, but also as a super-set of menu selection in that several menus are combined to form a complicated transaction. Advanced display techniques such as those reported by Knowlton (1975) would improve the presentation of several menus simultaneously. The menu technique would help the clerk to key data as the passenger provides it, rather than in the order required by the lengthy flight segment entry.

The adaptable terminal can only reduce keying for flights if most requests are for a few routes. In a major city in the route, network clerks can be asked for any one of a large number of routes, and so this application of the adaptable terminal is only suitable for certain offices.

2. *Transactions within a Context*

Consider now a request to display the available flights from London to Paris:

A12SEPLONPAR

The response is a list of up to six flights which have at least one seat available. To book one of these the entry might be "N1F2" which books one first-class seat on the flight shown in line 2 of the display. If a satisfactory flight is not shown, a further search for flights can be requested by entering "A*". It is reasonable to analyse and process these last two commands within the host as they use a data-base access involving previously displayed flights. This information belongs in the AAA unless the applications software is distributed in a fundamentally different way.

It can be seen that the whole reservations project relies on the AAA acting as an efficient switch and temporary store, so it is important that changes to the AAA are kept to a minimum to maintain efficiency and reliability.

3. *Low-volume Transactions*

Some applications have fewer transactions but need to have complicated transaction formats to keep down the complexity of the AAA. Consider a transaction to load hotels into the system:

KXSXT8132/H/DELFIN PLAYA/O/PMI . . .

The adaptable terminal can be used to make this input sequence more attractive to users, as has been described in the Teacher's description.

If all the terminals in a system are adaptable, then the application can be split into several parts. For low-volume transactions, such as hotel work, a strongly machine-oriented transaction format could be designed to suit the host computer, with the adaptable terminal being used to make this format especially suitable for the users. Whatever is done to the terminal it will not affect the main application, as a barrier exists between the terminal and the host which is designed to protect the host and give the user flexibility.

The adaptable terminal also allows for flexible responses to changing circumstances. For example, in the oil crisis of 1973 airlines were faced with an enormous cancellation and rebooking problem, which meant abnormally repetitive use of a few transactions. An adaptable terminal could have been reprogrammed to ease this burden.

B. Branching

Although no conditional statements were built into the experimental system, it seems that programming by imitation could cope with branching given the appropriate view of programming. Conventional programming requires that all possibilities, however unlikely, be allowed for in the program. By contrast, programming by imitation is concerned with doing what needs to be done now; with stating the valid conditions for action and ignoring all other cases. There is already a hint of this in the adaptable terminal: type identifiers indicate which characters in a window are valid, while any invalid ones are rejected and force the Teacher to consider if his conditions are too strict or whether he has incorrect data. This leads to the important principle that: *a transaction should be composed when the need for it arises, not before.*

We need to introduce branching primitives which will lie dormant in the system. When one is encountered, a logical expression will be evaluated; if it is true the system will continue to execute the CT which contains it; if false, then another CT will be invoked where possible. If none exists, the terminal "sends for the Teacher", and learns the logic of the branch by normal programming by imitation methods. I call the "sending for Teacher" idea "branching by imitation". The result would be that the logic which comprises a program in the conventional sense is accumulated gradually over time. The only demand is that the Teacher should create CTs to deal with one specific case at a time which will be defined by the branching primitives. Thus the Teacher does not have to consider abstract possibilities because he knows the terminal will "send for him" when conditions arise whose actions are undefined. It is possible, therefore, for naive computer users to be able to create and maintain quite complicated program structures, so reducing the need for conventional applications programming specialists.

This gradual accumulation of program logic bears some similarity to the production systems used in RITA. Nevertheless the execution (interpretation) of "adaptations" produced by programming by imitation is quite different from the evaluation of the rules of the production system.

To illustrate the gradual accumulation of logic, suppose we had a range-check primitive; at the end of a window the action might be to perform a range check, and if satisfactory to send the contents to the host and clear the window. Sooner or later the check would fail, and a fail message would be sent to the Teacher, who might decide, for instance, that extra data needed to be entered using a new set of CTs. The Teacher would create the new transactions to deal with the data he had, and would finally get back to the original cleared window for another set of data.

Jumping into streams of CTs is almost as difficult as branching out of them. A possibility would be to give up naming transactions explicitly; instead when a transaction was composed the Teacher would start by giving a description of its function, with the filing of CTs being handled automatically by the software. When a branch was evaluated as false, the software would present the Teacher with a description of all the following transactions which would have been invoked if their branch conditions had been evaluated as true. The Teacher would form the extra CTs to deal with this new condition; he would then jump back into the existing logic by invoking the transaction he selected from a display. This approach has potential because one usually starts a problem by dealing with normal cases and then adding exception clauses. Special software would need to be developed to handle this scheme, but it turns the branching problem on its head from branching out to jumping into a transaction. The addition of branching to programming by imitation could turn it into a powerful user-oriented tool: perhaps the application of some of the techniques mentioned elsewhere in this book would be fruitful.

One particularly powerful branch primitive would be "equals", which would test for equality strings. Then, for example, the host's responses could be analysed for a particular reply such as carriage return, linefeed, dot, which would indicate the end of the logon sequence. In other words the terminal would become a response analyser (see Rosenthal and Watkins, 1974).

There are two points which arise from the principle of composing a transaction when the need for it arises. First, it makes the distinction between teaching and using the terminal less sharp since it will usually be doing a little learning. Second, it is not valid when time is critical, perhaps during process control for instance. Nevertheless, composing a transaction when the need arises is worth further study, and it could provide a method of dealing with branches, which in turn would widen the scope for programming by imitation.

C. Potential

This chapter has provided ample evidence to show that user interface techniques can be developed cheaply in teaching and research establishments. Projects can be devised for undergraduates and postgraduates, and one hopes that the systems designers of tomorrow will become aware of the importance and the possibilities of the user interface by participating in such projects. The opportunities are there waiting to be exploited.

ACKNOWLEDGEMENTS

I would like to thank: the SRC for supporting this work with a studentship; Professor I.C. Pyle for introducing me to the idea of adaptable terminals and his supervision of my research; Professor J.J. Florentin for suggesting the word-processing example; and Adrian and Gill Smith for their help in the preparation of this manuscript.

REFERENCES

Alsberg, P.A., Bailey, J.F., Brown, D.S. and Mullen, J.R. (1976). Intelligent terminals as user agents. *Proceedings of the IEEE Symposium on Trends and Applications: Micro and Mini Systems,* 129–135.

Anderson, R.H. and Gillogly, J.J. (1976). RAND intelligent terminal agent (RITA): design philosophy. *Report R-1809-ARPA,* RAND Corporation, California.

Coleman, M.J., Godliman, G.S. and Leonard, G.L. (1976). The viscom—a system of soft video-terminals. *Software-Practice and Experience,* 6, 569–575.

Davis, R. and King, J. (1975). An overview of production systems. *Report STAN-CS-75-524,* Artificial Intelligence Laboratory, Stanford University.

Donzeau-Gorge, V., Huet, G., Kahn, G., Lang, B. and Levy, J.J. (1975). A structure oriented program editor: a first step towards computer assisted programming. *IRIA Report No. 114,* Rocquencourt, France.

Du Boulay, B. and Emanuel, R. (1975). LOGO without tears. *D.A.I. Working Paper No. 11,* Dept. of Artificial Intelligence, University of Edinburgh.

Eason, K.D., Damodaran, L. and Stewart, T.F.M. (1974). A survey of man—computer interaction in commercial applications. *LUTERG No. 144,* Dept. of Human Sciences, Loughborough University.

Edmonds, E. and Guest, S. (1977). An interactive tutorial system for teaching programming. *Proceedings of the Conference on Computer Systems and Technology,* Sussex University.

Florentin, J.J. (1977). Automatic generation of interactor programs. *Proceedings of the International Conference on Displays for Man–Machine Systems,* University of Lancaster.

Gilb, T. (1976). *Data Engineering.* Stockholm: Studentlitteratuer.

Hebditch, D.L. (1976). Design of user/terminal dialogues. In *Practical Tele-processing.* Uxbridge: Online Conferences Ltd.

Knowlton, K. (1975). Virtual pushbuttons as a means of person–machine interaction. *Proceedings of the IEEE Conference on Computer Graphics, Pattern Recognition and Data Structures,* Los Angeles.

Martin, J. (1973). *Design of Man-Computer Dialogues.* New York: Prentice Hall.

MIC (Macro Interpreted Commands) (1978). Computer Centre, Hatfield Polytechnic.

Palme, J. (1975a). Interactive software for humans. *FOAI Report C10029-M3 (E5),* Swedish National Defence Research Institute, Stockholm.

Palme, J. (1975b). Real time—easing the user task. *Software World,* 5, 8–11.

Rosenthal, R. and Watkins, S.W. (1974). Automated access to network resources, a network access machine. *Proceedings of the IEEE Symposium on Computer Networks: Trends and Applications,* 47–50.

Shackel, B. (ed.) (forthcoming). *Man–Computer Interaction.* Amsterdam: Sijthoff and Noordhoff.

TECO (Text Editor and Corrector) (1972). DEC-10-ETEE-D, Digital Equipment Corporation, Maynard.

Thomas, R.C. (1979). An adaptable terminal: a locally adjustable man–computer interface. M.Phil. Thesis, University of York.

Wirth, N. (1977a). Modula: a language for modular multiprogramming. *Software-Practice and Experience,* 7, 3–35.

Wirth, N. (1977b). The use of modula. *Software-Practice and Experience,* 7, 37–65.

14. Empirical and Formal Methods for the Study of Computer Editors

D.W. EMBLEY and G. NAGY

Department of Computer Science, University of Nebraska-Lincoln, Lincoln, Nebraska, USA

I. INTRODUCTION

This paper presents an account of our sustained attempts to gain an understanding of computer editors important to various classes of user. Our objective is to give an account of methods for studying the behavioural aspects of text editors. We give a brief description of the various functions of computer editors, discuss diverse means of studying them, and provide pointers to applicable areas of psychology and human factors research.

We take the point of view that the goal of the design and evaluation of text editors is to minimize the cost incurred by a user performing a number of editing tasks over a period of time. Ultimately, this cost is a function of the time taken by the user and the computer to complete each individual task. One may conjecture that task time depends on the nature of the task, the expertise of the user, the responsiveness of the machine, and the time spent learning and relearning methods and procedures. Many factors, including the user's alertness and motivation, the availability of documentation and help, the editor's command structure, the ease of committing and correcting errors, and whether or not a hard-copy device runs out of paper, may also influence task time. Some of these time factors are beyond the control of the designer, but others can be evaluated and improved.

II. CHARACTERIZATION OF EDITORS

The two primary functions of the class of computer programs generally known as "text editors" are to facilitate (i) the creation, modification and execution of computer programs, and (ii) the preparation of documents for human use. Since one or both of these activities are of overwhelming importance to many computer users, editors frequently dominate a person's entire interaction with the machine, and therefore tend to subsume all kinds of secondary functions as well.

During the editing process, the text being edited must be accessible to the editor in machine-readable form. Editing therefore consists of operations on a set of files stored in the host machine. In a narrow sense, one may consider the editing process strictly as a transformation from an existing string of symbols, known as the "source file" (which, in the case of initial text entry, may be null) to a new string of symbols, known as the "target file" (Oren, 1974; Heckel, 1978; Anandan, 1979). A broader interpretation, however, would also include access to other files on the system, utility programs, message systems, status information such as the number of current users or the time of day, and the outputs of compilers, interpreters and of other programs submitted for execution (including, of course, the one being edited).

Since many types of editors are now available, and new developments have been following one another too rapidly for the emergence of a stable vocabulary, the following taxonomy is proposed to help sort out the functions of the various types of editors.

General-purpose interactive text editors allow the transformation of the contents of any stored file in any manner compatible with the restrictions imposed by the organization of the host computer system. The specifications necessary to perform the transformations or to invoke auxiliary functions are entered in the form of *editing commands* on an interactive terminal. The transformations are generally carried out piecemeal; an editing session consists of dozens or even thousands of commands interspersed with the responses of the system. In this chapter, we use the phrase "text editor" to mean general-purpose interactive text editor; other types of editors are appropriately qualified.

Text editors are available for both multi-user time-sharing systems and single-user dedicated computers. Time-sharing editors often include facilities for communication among the users. Some text editors may be available on several hardware and software configurations offered by the same manufacturer; a few are portable even between systems offered by different manufacturers. Editors vary widely in the range of terminal devices supported by them; most systems, however, are compatible with at least standard low-speed ASCII terminals. Some manufacturers deliberately restrict their own terminal products.

Text editors are often characterized as "line-oriented" or "screen-oriented". The distinction between a line-oriented editor designed for display-terminal use and a screen-oriented editor is, however, rather questionable.

Program editors are text editors specifically designed for program preparation. A thorough survey of program editors appears in VanDam and Rice (1971), with more recent contributions referenced in Riddle (1976) and Reimhen (1978). Widely known examples of general-purpose interactive editors are QED (1967), TECO (1969), WYLBUR (1975), WIDJET (1978), and CMS (1979).

Manuscript editors are text editors primarily intended for manuscript preparation. Program editors can be, and often are, used on natural language documents, but manuscript editors usually include features such as hyphenation, right-justification, pagination and spelling correction, which are not necessary for working with computer programs. While manuscript editors are often available on general-purpose computers, many systems, known as " *word processors*", are marketed exclusively for increasing the efficiency of office typing operations. These systems often include rudimentary file-handling facilities, graphics and page-formatting features, and interfaces to high-quality multi-font hard-copy output devices such as photocomposition machines. Carls (1978) provides a good introduction to word processing.

Batch program editors perform transformations on source files according to a set of instructions or commands submitted in batch mode. Because batch editors can easily provide a log of all changes and economically preserve all back-up versions, they are sometimes used for maintaining large software systems. Batch editors are also suitable for modifying magnetic tape or card files. PANVALET is a popular example of a batch program editor (Pansophic, 1977). Other examples of batch editors are the programs used for final copy preparation for photocomposers and high-quality printers. These programs usually include embedded commands for functions not available on the source medium, such as proportional spacing, justification, subscripts, or esoteric type styles.

Language-dependent editors are restricted to program modifications in a single programming language and can, therefore, incorporate syntax validation, diagnostic messages and error-correcting functions normally reserved for compilers and interpreters (Hansen, 1971; Teitelbaum, 1979). Conversational programming languages such as APL, BASIC and LISP include an *embedded editor* considered to be part of the language environment (Iverson, 1962; Kemeny and Kurtz, 1971; Bingham, 1976; Sandewall, 1978).

Data editors facilitate the entry and correction of data files. Personnel engaged in data entry constitute one of the largest segments of the data-processing industry. Data-entry systems range from the standard keypunch, through on-line and off-line key-to-disc and key-to-tape systems, to the entire data-creation and updating facilities of complex data-base systems. Gilb and Weinberg (1977) provide an enjoyable introduction to common shortcomings of such systems.

III. PSYCHOLOGICAL FINDINGS RELATED TO EDITORS

The publication of Gerald Weinberg's influential book, *The Psychology of Computer Programming* (1971), may be considered as marking the coming of age of the behavioural approach to computer science. As the continuing increase in the cost-effectiveness of computer equipment exposes more and more people without specialized training (and without the tolerance that reflects such training) to computers, concepts and methods that are second-nature to psychologists will find increasing application to the study of human factors in computing (Miller and Thomas, 1977). A review of applicable results from cognitive psychology reveals, however, relatively sparse results so far (Embley and Nagy, 1981).

Temporal models, where editing session time is analysed in terms of elementary user activities, are capable of predicting session time for routine editing tasks with an accuracy comparable to individual variations between subjects. This accuracy is achieved, however, under the simplifying assumption that users perform editing tasks perfectly—without error—and thus represents an upper bound on how well an expert user might perform (Treu, 1975; Card *et al.,* 1976, 1979; Card, 1978; Embley *et al.,* 1978).

Observation of subjects performing editing tasks in a controlled experimental environment revealed that error detection and correction, and unpredicted mental activities, account for a sizeable portion of session time (about 25% is suggested by fragmentary data available) (Roberts, 1979).

Experiments in interactive environments suggest that response-time variability may be even more detrimental than prolonged uniform delay (Miller, 1977; Shneiderman, 1979). Response-time tolerance in an editing environment, however, has not been tested.

Analysis of editor structure and command languages in terms of cognitive psychological models takes into account the limitations imposed by short-term memory. Recent work shows some promise that formal grammars may play a role in assessing the load on short-term memory and in predicting learnability and ease-of-use characteristics (Ledgard and Singer, 1978; Moran, 1978; Anandan, 1979; Reisner, 1979).

Controlled experiments to measure learnability are difficult to design and expensive to perform. Lengthy training periods are involved, and the results depend heavily on subject background and ability and on the quality of instruction (which depends on both instructors and passive and interactive training materials) (Walther and O'Neil, 1974; Roberts, 1979).

It is reasonably certain that key-entry rates cannot be greatly improved without excessive operator training. It is unlikely, however, that even keying rates comparable to stenotyping (the fastest data entry mode known), would dramatically reduce session time (Fox and Stansfield, 1964; Hershman and Hillix, 1965; Shaffer and Hardwick, 1968; Alden *et al.*, 1972; Seibel, 1972; Schoonard and Boies, 1975; Baddeley, 1978).

Studies of pointing skills for menu and text-item selection show that direct (light-pen) and indirect (mouse, tracker-ball) pointing devices are superior to control of the cursor through the keyboard. It appears, however, that for certain types of "short range" commands, stepping and text keys are useful and should therefore be retained (English *et al.*, 1967; Goodwin, 1975; Ritchie and Turner, 1975; Card *et al.*, 1977; Fields *et al.*, 1978).

Only modest steps have been taken to study the nature of error feedback and the effect of automatic error-detection and error-correction features (Klemmer and Lockhead, 1962; Shaffer and Hardwick, 1968; Alden *et al.*, 1972; Seibel, 1972; Segal, 1975; Baddeley, 1978; Fosdick, 1978).

IV. FORMAL NOTATIONS FOR THE DESCRIPTION OF EDITORS

Formal descriptions of editors serve as design and evaluation tools. They provide insights that help crystallize observations and lend support to design decisions. Trivial details and special cases are brought to light, design flaws and ambiguities are uncovered, and consistency is more easily maintained. Once formal specifications exist, implementation can proceed more rapidly and with a minimum of misunderstanding, and portability and standardization are enhanced. After extensive experience using formal definitions as a practical aid in the design of computer systems, and editors in particular, Ledgard and Singer (1978) report:

> Because of our experience with the editing system, we now believe that the major benefit of formal definitions is as *a basis for the detailed design of computer systems.* It is our contention that writing a formal definition serves system designers and implementors much as the development of an *architectural blueprint serves the design and construction of a building.* If precise definitions are developed during the design process, a much deeper understanding of the entire system results. Furthermore, the definition readily points out the difficulties and special cases that must be resolved before implementation. Finally, the definition allows one to develop a view of the entire system, including special cases, into a coherent whole.

We agree with this view and in this section report on our efforts to apply formal definition to the design, development and evaluation of an editor called SIMPLE (Embley and Nagy, 1979).

A. An Example of a Formal Specification for an Editor: SIMPLE

SIMPLE is a line-oriented text editor for beginners and for computer users with minimal system requirements. It is intended primarily to provide a friendly programming environment for introductory programming classes. It may be accessed through either typewriter or screen-display terminals (or both) under either a multi-programmed operating system or a single-user system such as a dedicated microcomputer.

It has a simple command structure, with few commands, and a simple file structure, with one and only one file per user open at any time. There are provisions for program creation, modification, translation and execution. Facilities are also provided for two-way inter-user communications through the terminal. A state diagram of SIMPLE showing its entire command set is presented in Fig. 1.

SIMPLE files may be WRITE (for program development), READ (for supervisor-to-user communication), or ADD (for inter-user communication). One or more *account supervisors* may further simplify and tailor the use of SIMPLE for arbitrary groups of users under the overall control of a single *system manager*. The design

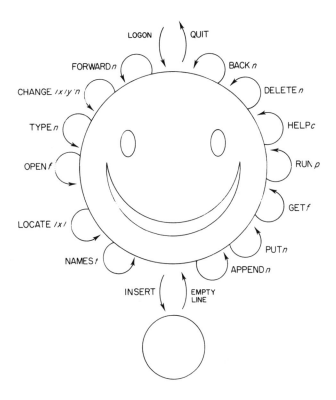

Fig. 1. State diagram of SIMPLE.

specifications of SIMPLE are system-independent and include a formal definition to assure portability and standardization.

In the design and implementation specifications, each SIMPLE command is described by:
 — a phrase giving the function of the command;
 — a detailed informal English description of the command;
 — default value specifications;
 — a formal syntactic definition in a BNF-like notation;
 — conditions for command validation and suggested responses;
 — a formal behavioural definition of the semantics.
The last three of these need further explanation.

1. *Formal Syntactic Definition*

The usual BNF metalanguage syntax is extended to include a construct to facilitate a definition of the initial sub-string idea that occurs frequently in SIMPLE. (Since each command is uniquely identified by its first letter, SIMPLE allows users to specify command keywords by the first letter or any other initial sub-string.) A terminal string with its initial character underlined stands for the terminal string or any of its initial sub-strings. Thus, for example, SIMPLE means "S", "SI", "SIM", "SIMP", "SIMPL" or "SIMPLE".

The following non-terminals appear in the definitions of the commands and have the meanings given:

$<n>$ ::= "sequence of digits (not all zero) - - an unsigned positive integer"

$<b>$ ::= "zero or more consecutive blanks"

$<string>$, $<string1>$, and $<string2>$ ::= "sequence of characters"

$<filename>$, $<user id>$ and $<processor>$ ::= "meaningful sequence of characters defined by the SIMPLE system manager"

A SIMPLE editing session consists of logon followed by a sequence of SIMPLE commands, the last of which is "QUIT". When the "INSERT" command is issued it is followed by zero or more lines of text, the last of which is empty.

$<$sequence of commands$>$ ::= $<Q>$ | $<$command$>$ $<$sequence of commands$>$

$<$command$>$ ::= $<A>$ | $<B>$ | $<C>$ | $<D>$ | $<F>$ | $<G>$ | $<H>$ | $<$insert$>$ | $<L>$ | $<N>$ | $<O>$ | $<P>$ | $<R>$ | $<T>$

$<$insert$>$ ::= $<I>$ $<$sequence of lines$>$

$<$sequence of lines$>$ ::= $<$empty line$>$ | $<$line$>$ $<$sequence of lines$>$

$<$line$>$ ::= "non-empty sequence of characters on a line"

$<$empty line$>$ ::=

2. Validation Conditions and Responses

Validation conditions are given in terms of nested **if..then...else** statements whose predicates make use of the state constants and variables (explained below) and the variable that represents the command argument. These validation conditions determine whether a command is "valid" or "invalid". Only valid commands are executed.

Each command issued elicits an appropriate response. Suggested messages appear in upper case with generic names appearing in lower case. When the command keyword itself is non-determinable the standard response "ILLEGAL COMMAND" is displayed. Commands that expect numeric arguments require unsigned positive integers. If the argument of one of these commands is recognized as numeric but is less than or equal to zero, or is unrecognizable, the response "THE ARGUMENT MUST BE AN UNSIGNED NONZERO INTEGER" is given.

Since some conditions will have to be determined by the SIMPLE system manager, it is not possible to specify all conditions that may arise. All implementation-independent conditions are addressed, however, as well as conditions that will be typical in most installations. System managers must provide meaningful messages for all other implementation-dependent conditions.

3. Formal Semantic Definition

When a SIMPLE command is executed, it may or may not change a user's *state*. A user's state is shown pictorially in Fig. 2 and is

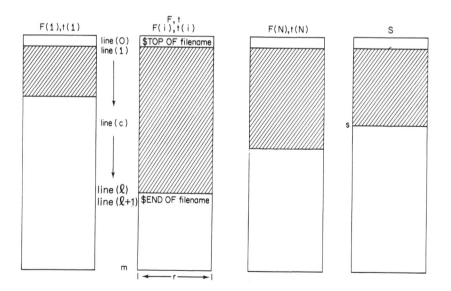

Fig. 2. A SIMPLE user's state.

defined by the state vector

$$(F, \ell, c, S, s)$$

where:

F = the current file of type t one of F (i) ($1 \leqslant i \leqslant N$), the files available to the user (each file consists of at most m lines of length $\leqslant r$ of text);

ℓ = the actual length ($0 \leqslant \ell \leqslant m$) of the current file, one of ℓ (i), the respective lengths of the files, F (i);

c = the index ($0 \leqslant c \leqslant \ell + 1$) of the current line in the current file, one of c (i), the line indexes of the files F (i) (when c=0, c references the "line" ($TOP OF filename) immediately preceding the first actual line of the file and when c=ℓ+1, c references the "line" ($END OF filename) immediately following the last actual line of the file);

S = the save area (also of at most m lines of length $\leqslant r$);

s = the actual length ($0 \leqslant s \leqslant m$) of the save area.

These state constants and variables appear in the validation and state change sections of the command description along with temporary and command argument variables. The state change section also uses the functions "min", "max", "index", "substr", and "length", borrowed from PL/1, and a block transfer function defined as follows:

<filename1> (<start index1>) ← <filename2> (<start index2>, <length>)

meaning transfer "length" lines in "filename2" starting at "start index2" to "filename1" starting at "start index1".

FORWARD n

Function: To move forward through the file.

Description: Moves forward n lines. This line becomes the new current line. If an attempt is made to move forward beyond the end of the file, $END OF filename becomes the new current line.

Default: n = 1

Syntax: <F> ::= FORWARD <b> [<n>]

Response:

types new current line

State change:

c ← min(c+n, ℓ+1)

Fig. 3. Definition of the "FORWARD" command.

INSERT

Function: To allow for text insertion.

Description: Permits text insertion beginning after the current line. Insertion terminates when an empty line is entered or when the file is full. When the current line is $END OF filename, insertion is initiated before this line. The current line remains unchanged.

Default: none.

Syntax: <I> ::= INSERT

Validity check and response:
if t = Read (* filetype of current file is Read *) then
    invalid: YOU MAY NOT ALTER THIS FILE
else if t = Add (*filetype is Add *) then
    invalid: YOU MAY ONLY ADD TO THIS FILE WITH 'GET'
else if ℓ = m (* file is full *) then
    invalid: filename IS FULL
else
    valid: START TYPING
    while typing
      if length (line_typed_in) > r (* line too long *) then
        LINE TOO LONG; ONLY THE FOLLOWING ACCEPTED:
        Types the first r characters of the line
      if ℓ = m (* file is full *) then
        INSERTION TERMINATED, filename IS FULL
        insertion terminates

State change when valid:
if c = (ℓ+1) then c ← ℓ (* adjust when c is $END OF filename *)
i ← 0
loop
exit when ℓ = m (* exit if file is full *)
    accept(line_typed_in)
exit when length(line_typed_in) = 0
    i ← i +1
    F(c+i+1) ← F(c+i, ℓ+1-(c+i)+1) (* make room for line to be inserted *)
    line(c+i) ← substr (line_typed_in, 1, r)
    (* insert first r characters of line typed in *)
    ℓ ← ℓ +1
end loop

Fig. 4. Definition of the "INSERT" command.

A state change may take place only when a SIMPLE command is judged "valid" as defined in the command validation section of the description.

Definitions for two of the fifteen commands are shown in Figs 3 and 4.

From our experience with the formal definition of SIMPLE, we learned that such formalization can indeed expose special cases and trivial details that may otherwise be overlooked and can speed implementation and enhance quality. While designing the details of the "DELETE" command, for example, we discovered several special cases not previously considered. The formalism provided a means to write down exactly what was desired in every instance, assuring that the behaviour of the editor as implemented would match the design expectations. The formalism also proved to be a superior means of communication between designer and implementor, and enabled a single programmer to implement the SIMPLE system completely in an amazingly short period of time.

B. Quality Measures Derived from Formal Descriptions

Formal descriptions may also be subjected to analysis and evaluation. For example, Reisner (1979) described user actions at a terminal for two command languages by means of a BNF-like grammar, and compared the number of different terminal symbols, the lengths of terminal strings, and the number of rules necessary to describe the structure of some set of terminal strings for a given task. An examination of these aspects of the formalism led to predictions about user behaviour, and observations showed that subjects' performance was consistent with the predictions. In a similar vein, we have investigated the usefulness of using state-transition-diagram descriptions to compare editors and to gain insight into the effects on ease of use of grammatical aspects of the interface language (Anandan, 1979).

Typical editing tasks consist of a sequence of commands interspersed with text insertions, and can be considered as a sequence of keystrokes executed by the user. Valid sequences of keystrokes can be represented by BNF grammars or transition graphs. Transition graphs for a sub-set of two editors, Nebraska University Remote Operating System (NUROS, 1979) and SIMPLE (Embley and Nagy, 1979), are shown in Figs 5 and 6 respectively. These diagrams consist of states and transitions with one arc-labelled LOGON representing the start position. The arcs represent keystrokes; however, in order to reduce the number of states in the graphs, states with a single inward transition and a single outward transition have been collapsed. This results in transition arcs being sequences of keystrokes that represent commands. The sub-sets of the two editing languages illustrated include only those commands necessary for editing and job submission. Commands useful for searching and reading files are not included.

Tables 1 and 2 summarize pertinent information about the two

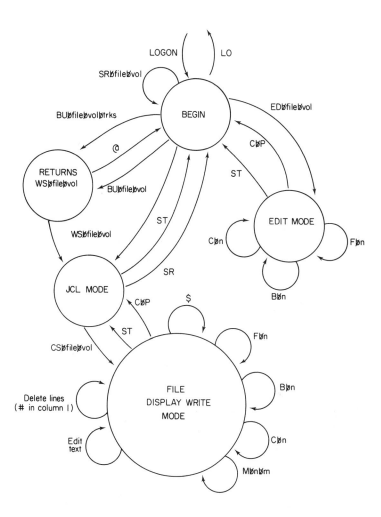

Fig. 5. Transition graph for NUROS sub-set. @ = Press shift and start keys together; $ = press shift and enter keys together; ⌀ = obligatory single space.

transition graphs, including the number of states, their out degrees, the number of commands, the total number of context dependencies and the minimum, maximum, and average number of keystrokes used for a command. The different states are the different contexts or modes of operation encountered while using the command language, and represent the different frames of reference that must be

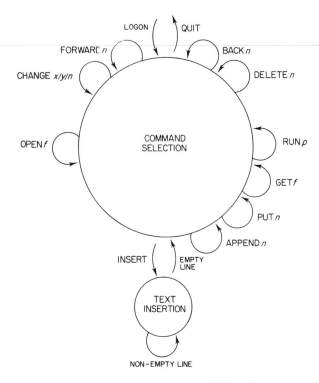

Fig. 6. Transition graph for SIMPLE sub-set.

learned. The out degrees of the state give the number of choices a user in a given state has. Any lack of modularity is reflected by the difference between in and out degrees; modularity is a likely indicator of how easy/difficult it is for a user to shift from one reference frame to another. Context dependencies arise when the use of a command from different states causes different effects. The typing effort required in using the editing language is proportional to the number of keystrokes required per command.

From the two graphs for NUROS and SIMPLE, it can be seen that SIMPLE has fewer states, commands and context dependencies; its typing requirements are less, and its modularity is more easily definable. This suggests that it may be easier to learn and use SIMPLE. These results are confirmed by informal observations of students.

Quantitative measures of the graphs or other formalisms, however, provide only an indication of the user effort required to learn and use a command language. Given these and similar measures, the real

TABLE 1

Information for NUROS

Number of states		5
Number of different commands		19
Total number of context dependencies		7
Number of keystrokes necessary per command	Min	1
	Max	14
	Av.	5.28

State name	Out degree	Difference between in and out degree
BEGIN	6	1
RETURNS WS file vol	2	0
JCL MODE	3	1
File DISPLAY WRITE MODE	9	1
EDIT MODE	5	1

challenge is to produce a model that accurately predicts user performance. The achievement of this goal would give designers a tool to predict the user-perceived quality of an editing system from its formal specification.

V. TRACE-DRIVEN MODELS OF EDITORS

As mentioned above, the most important general goal in editor design is to minimize the amount of time it takes for a user to complete an editing task. Indeed, the relative quality of two editors can be ascertained by comparing the times it takes users of similar ability to complete the same editing task on the two systems. Direct measurements of elapsed editing-session time, however, are difficult

TABLE 2
Information for SIMPLE

Number of states		2
Number of different commands		13
Total number of context dependencies		0
Number of keystrokes necessary per command	Min	1
	Max	9
	Av.	3.25

State name	Out degree	Difference between in and out degree
COMMAND SEL. MODE	11	0
TEXT INSERTION	2	0

to interpret because several not-so-easily controlled factors are introduced: the choice of editing commands, user alertness and motivation, and errors both minor and disastrous. Moreover, since these measures are only obtained after implementation, they provide little assistance during the design phase.

Predictive models avoid these difficulties and further have the advantage of being useful at design time (Card *et al.*, 1976, 1979; Card, 1978; Embley *et al.*, 1978). These models are based on quantities such as keystroke count, typing rate, computer response time, and mental preparation time. The predictive power of these models depends on how accurately the constituent quantities can be estimated and the validity of any simplifying assumptions.

Our proposed model predicts session time by accumulating the time required to perform the individual request–response pairs that comprise the editing session:

$$T_{session} = \sum_{i=1}^{m} T_e(i) + T_r(i)$$

where:
 m = the total number of request–response pairs in the session;
 $T_e(i)$ = the duration of the ith request; and

$T_r(i)$ = the duration of the ith response.

The duration of the ith request may be further decomposed into the time necessary for the user to decide what to do next and the time necessary to actually type the entry. While both of these intervals may depend on the particular command entered, we assume as a first approximation that the "think" time is constant for any command and that the typing time depends on the total number of keystrokes. Thus:

$$T_e(i) = T_t + n(i) \times T_k$$

where:

T_t = the average time necessary to formulate a request;

$n(i)$ = the number of keystrokes associated with the ith request; and

T_k = the reciprocal (in seconds per keystroke) of the typing rate.

The response time of the machine may also depend on the request, but here again we assume that it is a constant,

$$T_r(i) = T_r$$

where T_r is the average response time of the computer and includes time required for the output of the response.

The time required to perform a particular program-editing task may now be expressed as:

$$T_{\text{session}} = m \times T_c + n \times T_k$$

where:

$n = \sum_{i=1}^{m} n(i);$

$T_c = T_t + T_r$ is the delay per command, and

T_k is the delay per keystroke.

The quantities m and n, i.e. the total number of commands and the total number of keystrokes associated with a terminal session, depend only on the editing task to be performed and on the available command language. Thus, if m and n can be measured with reasonable accuracy, then the duration of a terminal session for a selected editor and task can be predicted for various values of (i) T_t, the user's "think" time, (ii) T_r, the computer response time, and (iii) T_k, the user's typing rate. Statistical information on these three parameters is routinely collected on many interactive systems.

The procedure for predicting program editor performance with this model is summarized as follows:

1. Select the editing tasks to be accomplished.
2. Select the editor command sets of interest.
3. With each command set, perform the specified editing tasks and determine the number of commands and keystrokes associated with each task.
4. Calculate terminal session times for the various command sets using appropriate values for computer and user response times.

This procedure can be carried out even when an editor is only in a design stage by writing out the command sequence necessary to accomplish a given task.

In a case study, we investigated the applicability of this model to the evaluation of two editing systems—NUROS (1979) and CMS (1979)—widely used by students at the University of Nebraska (Lan, 1977). Evaluations were performed at both novice and intermediate levels of user competence using the program editors.

Selection of Editing Tasks. Twelve tasks were selected for NUROS and for CMS. Four of these tasks consisted of initial creation of a program and data. The other eight were modifications of existing programs and data. Four arbitrarily selected students from beginning courses in computer science turned in their work at all stages of a programming project. One student programmed in PL/1, and the other three programmed in FORTRAN. An initial version, an intermediate version, and a final version of each student's project were selected. The final versions of three of the programs were between 30 and 50 lines long and the fourth program was about 120 lines long.

Selection of Command Sets. The command sets of interest were those used by novice and intermediate users. Novices find it difficult to remember many commands and are, therefore, willing to suffer somewhat tedious editing sequences in exchange for having less to learn and remember about the system. A minimum set of capabilities considered necessary for a novice is the following:

1. Add lines.
2. Delete lines.
3. Release a program for execution.
4. Recover immediately from typing mistakes.
5. Display a portion of a program.

6. Create and preserve a program.

7. Delete a program.

An intermediate user is willing and able to remember more commands and techniques in order to be more productive than the novice. Typical additional capabilities for intermediate users are:

1. Quickly locate a line of interest.

2. Modify a line without necessarily retyping the entire line.

3. Move a group of lines.

4. Monitor program execution.

Corresponding to these novice and intermediate user requirements, actual command sets were chosen.

Data Collection. CMS maintains a good record of a terminal session on its typewriter terminal. NUROS does not, but the terminal hardware does provide the capability of copying the current screen on to an IBM 1053 printer. A copy of the screen was taken just before and just after each command was entered to record the request made and the state of the screen before the next activity. Notations were necessary to show the activity of the experimenter.

The data collected for the session-time model was the total number of commands including cursor movements and the total number of keystrokes required in the terminal session. The twelve tasks, two editing systems, and two levels of competence generated a total of 48 cases.

Results. We obtained raw counts from the tasks and applied the model with parameters T_c = 5 seconds and T_k = ½ second to obtain the normalized differences in terminal session times using NUROS as the standard. To interpret this data, we applied Student's *t*-test to the four cases of initial program entry, to the eight cases of novice-level modifications, and to the eight cases of intermediate-level modifications. The statistical analysis showed that CMS is significantly better than NUROS except at the novice level (Embley *et al.,* 1978). The largest factor in NUROS's superiority at the novice level is that it is so natural on a screen to simply type correct information over incorrect information, and this is allowed at the novice level in NUROS. CMS, on a typewriter terminal, needs string replacement commands to accomplish the same thing and that is not allowed until the intermediate level.

A more elaborate and perhaps more accurate form of the model could be developed by considering the number of occurrences of each type of command and keystroke. Additional parameters would then have to be introduced, with specific assumptions about the "think" time, system response, and typing speed associated with each category of user request. In our experiment, for example, we did keep track of the number of cursor movements, which are generally entered more rapidly than program text, but counted all of the keystrokes together to simplify the model.

This technique can also be applied to selected sub-sets of commands within the same editor. For instance, one could determine the effect on user performance of excluding a particularly expensive command (in terms of machine time or space).

VI. FUNCTION-DRIVEN MODELS OF EDITORS

In this section we turn our attention to the nature of the editing task itself. One approach is to develop a theory that explains how a user accomplishes an editing task, for example as some researchers have suggested, in terms of goals, operators, methods for achieving the goals, and selection rules for choosing among competing methods (Card *et al.*, 1976; Card, 1978). Another approach is to consider the text being altered and how it is transformed into the desired form.

Considering an editing task as a string transformation problem, we have developed a file-comparison model of text editing (Anandan *et al.*, 1979). Given an imperfect version of a program text and an improved version incorporating desired modifications, this model allows us to isolate the necessary changes in a manner suitable for further analysis.

The file-comparison model formalizes the transformation of a *source file* F_s into a *target file* F_t by means of editing operations. To provide a concrete illustration, the following program fragment is used to illustrate an editing task:

F_s	F_t
READ;A	READ,A,B
C=A+B	C=A+B
PRNITT,C	PRINT,C

Both F_s and F_t are defined recursively in terms of sub-files. A sub-file at level n is identified by an n-component label $i^{(n)}$, where the components of $i^{(n)}$ correspond to the indices of the sub-files, at levels 1 to n, that contain the sub-file in question. The K sub-files of $i^{(n)}$ at the next lower level $(n+1)$ are denoted as $i^{(n)}.1$,

$i(n).2, \ldots , i(n).K$. In the above example, the files have three levels: statement, "word", and symbol (Fig. 7). The model is hierarchical to allow consideration of editing operations at any level.

F_s	i(n)					j(n)	F_t
R	1.1.1				1.1	1.1.1	R
E	1.1.2	1.1		1.1		1.1.2	E
A	1.1.3		1			1.1.3	A
D	1.1.4			1		1.1.4	D
;	1.2.1	} 1.2			1.2	1.2.1	,
A	1.3.1	} 1.3			1.3	1.3.1	A
C	2.1.1	} 2.1			1.4	1.4.1	,
=	2.2.1	} 2.2			1.5	1.5.1	B
A	2.3.1	} 2.3	2		2.1	2.1.1	C
+	2.4.1	} 2.4			2.2	2.2.1	=
B	2.5.1	} 2.5		2	2.3	2.3.1	A
P	3.1.1				2.4	2.4.1	+
R	3.1.2				2.5	2.5.1	B
N	3.1.3	3.1				3.1.1	P
I	3.1.4		3			3.1.2	R
T	3.1.5				3.1	3.1.3	I
T	3.1.6		3			3.1.4	
,	3.2.1	} 3.2				3.1.5	T
C	3.3.1	} 3.3			3.2	3.2.1	,
					3.3	3.3.1	C

Fig. 7. Sample files with labels.

A transformation at the nth level between F_s and F_t can be represented by a *bipartite graph* $G(n)$ (Liu, 1968). The nodes of $G(n)$ are the sub-files $i(n)$ in F_s and the sub-files $j(n)$ in F_t. All edges $e(i(n), j(n))$ of $G(n)$ connect a node in F_s with a node in F_t, and each node in F_t has at most one edge incident upon it. Each edge represents a *match* between two sub-files. Such a match may be either a perfect match or an imperfect match.

A *perfect match* is defined recursively as follows. Two sub-files at the nth level, $i(n)$ and $j(n)$, each containing the same number of sub-files K, are *perfectly matched* or *identical* ($i(n) \equiv j(n)$) if and only if

$$i(n).k \equiv j(n).k \quad k = 1,2,\ldots,K.$$

If $i(n)$ and $j(n)$ are atoms, then $i(n) \equiv j(n)$ if they represent the same symbol.

Sub-files $i^{(n)}$ and $j^{(n)}$ are *imperfectly matched (similar)* at level n if some of their sub-files differ at a lower level. The differentiation between pairs of imperfectly matched and unmatched sub-files depends on a criterion of similarity built into the file-matching algorithm.

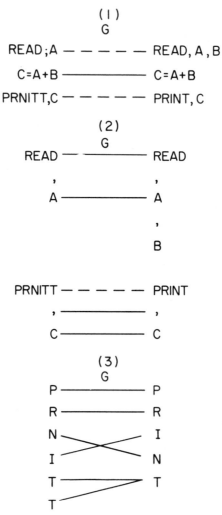

Fig. 8. Graphs showing the comparison between the two sample files. (Solid lines represent "identical" matches, and dashed lines represent "similar" matches. Absence of a line incident to a file element means there is no match.)

If any nodes in F_s or in F_t have no edges incident upon them, they are *unmatched*. The difference between files F_s and F_t, which represents the editing task, consists of the set of all unmatched and imperfectly matched sub-files.

At the lowest (atomic) level of analysis, all sub-files are either unmatched or perfectly matched. For our example, the family of graphs $G(n)$ is shown in Fig. 8; the nodes corresponding to sub-files perfectly matched at a higher level are not expanded at the lower levels.

In terms of this model, the function of the file-comparison algorithm is to obtain the graphs $G^{(n)}$, given two original files F_s and F_t and the manner in which they are partitioned into sub-files at various levels. The information provided by the graphs can then be used to derive the editing operations, such as "MOVE", "INSERT", "DELETE", and "CHANGE", necessary to accomplish the task. For instance, nodes in the source file that have no edges incident upon them correspond to deletions. Nodes in the target file without edges correspond to insertions. Nodes in the source file with multiple edges represent move or copy operations. Edges connecting perfectly matched entities may have to be moved, but are never altered. Edges connecting imperfectly matched entities require additional changes at a lower level.

Although several algorithms to detect file difference have been published, Heckel's (1978) algorithm for isolating file differences seemed most easily adaptable. His algorithm makes use of a central table of strings into which lines are hashed. Corresponding lines over the entire range of the files are then trivially matched and movements of blocks of adjacent lines are easily detected. The algorithm, however, detects block movement only if one of the lines in a block is unique in both versions of the file, and thus possible some block equivalences may remain undetected.

Three types of enhancements are required to adapt Heckel's algorithm to the file-comparison model described above. First, it is necessary to detect differences at several levels corresponding to the implementation of typical program editors. Such editors, for instance, normally provide "DELETE" options at the character, line, and block (multiple lines) level.

Second, Heckel's algorithm fails to detect some matches corresponding to many-to-one and one-to-many mappings. In a many-to-one mapping, it is desirable to select the match among the alternatives that allows the largest grouping of adjacent sub-files or, in the case of a lone sub-file, is the closest in terms of relative position. With a one-to-many mapping, there is an option of selecting the best single match on the basis of relative position or preserving all of the matches for subsequent analysis.

Third, and most important, it is necessary to modify the algorithm to detect similar items as well as identical ones. In editing a program, there are instances where an entire block of lines may be moved even though a single character in one of those lines may also have to be corrected. In this case it is appropriate to recognize the two blocks as imperfectly matched (similar), make the block move, and take care of the single-character correction at a lower level. In order to recognize similarity, it is clearly necessary to examine the structure of the item at a level lower than the correspondence being considered. The criterion for similarity does pose a difficult problem and requires further research.

A program incorporating these modifications to Heckel's algorithm has been written by Anandan (1979). It accepts two files, the source file and the target file, and produces a comparison between the files in terms of sub-files that are *identical, similar,* or *unmatched.* Figure 8 shows in schematic form the output for our particular example.

Having produced the file-comparison specifications by executing the algorithm for a source and target file, it is natural to think of generating a sequence of editor commands to transform the source into the target file. A question arises, however, as to whether or not an editing sequence produced automatically from the file-comparison model would be a reasonable approximation to one followed by an actual user. In order to partially answer this question, a program was written to generate a SIMPLE command sequence given two files and the comparison between them.

Of the fifteen SIMPLE commands, only seven are needed to perform any editing task: "FORWARD" and "BACK" to move from place to place within the file, "INSERT" to add lines of text, "DELETE" to remove lines of text, "PUT" and "GET" to copy a group of adjacent lines to another position in the file by putting them into a save area and getting them out at the desired position, and "CHANGE" to alter lines of text by replacing one string of characters by another.

The program that automatically generates SIMPLE commands to transform the source into the target file produces a sequence of these seven commands with appropriate arguments. It makes two passes over the new file to generate the required editing commands, one for each logical level (lines and characters) in the original file. In the first pass, lines in the old file are moved around, deleted, or kept, and new lines are inserted as necessary. In the second pass, appropriate "CHANGE" commands are generated to alter those lines marked as similar. A heuristic in the second pass prevents excessive changes to a single line, making use of a deletion followed by an insertion of the altered line instead.

This program generated a SIMPLE command sequence to perform an editing task consisting of successive versions of the same program written by a student for an introductory PASCAL programming course. For comparison purposes, several subjects were asked to

TABLE 3

Summary data for editing sequences for an editing task [a]

	Length of editing task		
Source	Number of lines	Number of keystrokes	Time (min)
User A: Expert SIMPLE user	28	239	7
User B: Familiar with computers but not with SIMPLE	33	308	38
User C: Somewhat familiar with computers but not with SIMPLE	30	283	28
User D: Unfamiliar with computers and SIMPLE	28	236	39
User E: Unfamiliar with computers and SIMPLE	36	283	55
Command generation program	24	220	—
Optimum (minimum number of keystrokes)	21	168	—

[a] Users unfamiliar with SIMPLE were given approximately 30 minutes of individual instruction before beginning the editing task.

perform the same editing task. Table 3 shows the number of lines and keystrokes and the time taken by each subject. It also shows the number of lines and keystrokes for the generated editing sequence and for the optimal editing sequence (the one with the least number of keystrokes). In order to normalize the keystroke count, extra keystrokes in unabbreviated command keywords and unnecessary blanks were ignored.

The program performed better than any of the subjects, but it did not perform optimally. One reason the program performed so well is that the file-comparison algorithm consistently recognizes identical and similar lines, which led to a more frequent use of line movement and line modification commands as opposed to deletion and insertion of complete lines. Too frequent use of line modification is avoided by the heuristic mentioned above.

The program can be tuned to behave as a typical user by varying the criterion for identifying similar lines in the file comparison algorithm. Additional heuristics such as recognition of global changes could also be useful for improving the program.

One possible application of the file-comparison model is to generate the sequence of editing commands for a given task using the command sets from two different editors. These editors could then be compared with respect to the total number of commands used, the number of keystrokes, and so on (Embley *et al.*, 1978; Card *et al.*, 1979).

Given a corpus of editing tasks, the editors can be compared automatically without the bias introduced by the skill, experience and preference of experimental subjects.

The file-comparison model can also be used to detect frequently occurring patterns of transformations. Given a large enough database of editing tasks, the statistical characterization of the sequences of elementary editing operations may be useful in the evaluation of alternative forms of certain commands and even in the design of the entire command set of new program editors.

VII. STATISTICAL ANALYSIS OF EDITOR USAGE

This section outlines our current efforts to determine how much time users spend performing various portions of their editing tasks. Since no results are available to date, we must confine ourselves to describing the proposed experimental protocols and outlining the type of conclusions we expect to draw from our experiments.

Our objectives are:

1. To produce concise yet realistic descriptions ("models") of various types of editing activities. The models should incorporate aspects neglected in previous studies, such as file manipulation and error correction.

2. To learn to predict task duration (in terms of time, number of commands, or deviation from "standard" performance) according to subject, task, and system characteristics, and to differentiate significant components of editing tasks (with regard to time) from insignificant components.

3. To validate the new models experimentally and to compare them with previous models proposed by others.

4. To characterize editing errors in terms of deviations from the performance of "best" or of "average" subjects.

5. To derive quantitative measures of editor quality for given subjects, tasks and systems, and thereby obtain improved guidelines for editor design.

Four types of experiments will be conducted. The first type is essentially a field observation, while the three others represent controlled experiments designed to remove certain sources of variability from the first type. The four types of experiment are described below:

(a) A task is performed on an editing system by subject A, who has no awareness (except as required by ethical considerations) of the data collection process. To begin with, we may observe students performing routine homework assignments or preparing term papers using the text-editing facilities provided by the computing centre.

(b) A print-out of subject A's source file (which may be null) and target file is given to subject B, who is asked to accomplish the necessary transformation. Subject B thus knows exactly what is to be accomplished, but has no help with the editing process.

(c) The print-out of subject A's source file is marked, using standard proof-reading symbols, with the corrections necessary to bring it to the target state, and subject C is asked to accomplish the necessary transformation. Subject C thus knows exactly what and where the the necessary changes are, but has no help with the editing process.

(d) Subject D (or a committee equivalent to a knowledgeable subject D) is asked to study the editing task performed by subject A, and is requested to find the best possible means of accomplishing the transformation. Subject D is then asked to perform the optimal transformation as rapidly as possible using the editing system.

Except for the first experiment, which defines the task, each experiment may be performed by several subjects. The data, consisting of transcripts of terminal sessions with *time stamps* inserted, is to be collected in the same way for each of the four or more experiments. Measurements of interest include counts or sums of selected items and times in a session. The items may be commands, arguments, characters, or computer responses.

The distribution of the measurements will be statistically analysed as follows to accomplish the objectives listed at the beginning of this section.

(i)   Comparisons between individuals.
(ii) Comparisons between editing tasks.
(iii) Comparisons between editing systems.
(iv) Comparisons between actual performance and types of "accelerated" performance described above.
(v)   Estimation of model parameters.
(vi) Profiles of editor users, clustering by characteristics.
(vii) Correlations between primary variables for a given subject, task, or system.
(viii) Detection of changes in individual characteristics over time (learning and forgetting).
It is clear that we have a good deal of work ahead of us.

VIII. CONCLUSIONS

In discussing editors, firm opinions abound: everyone, from greenhorn to old hand, knows exactly what the best and worst features of given editors are and just how new editors ought to be designed. The only problem is the striking lack of consensus. Nor are there universally acceptable means of determining who is right: the distinction between conventional dogma and scientific fact is often blurred. There are, nevertheless, some established means of studying editors and the editing process.

We have reviewed briefly the use of formal techniques, such as syntactic analysis and finite-state machine models, for the characterization of editors. These techniques are found wanting in that they provide no tool for investigating the actual use of editors.

The trace-driven models provide some information as to how the user's time is spent, but the level of analysis is too microscopic to allow insights into the higher-level processes that occur during editing.

The function-driven models, such as the file-difference model, may eventually be developed to a level sufficient to provide useful characterizations of editing tasks. Such refinement may also allow determination of the optimal means of performing a given task with a particular editor, and thus provide guidelines for the development of frequently occurring "macro" commands.

While cognitive psychology abounds in elegant and sophisticated studies of mental processes, and many important facts have been established, its tools have been applied to the study of text editors only in rudimentary fashion. Among areas where expanded research appears to be particularly timely, we note the following: additional experimentation is needed on split screens and multiple screens for editing operations, since a change of screen may disorient the user. An important variable that does not appear to have been investigated is the screen size and the amount of material exposed to the user. Experiments dealing with the use of colour, audio input, and audio feedback in text editing are lacking, yet the technology has progressed sufficiently to permit serious consideration of their use. Aspects of text editors related to the use of files—including message systems—have not yet been investigated with regard to human factors, yet these aspects may well be more important and more time-consuming for most users than mere symbol manipulation. More detailed experimentation is necessary to compare the individual features of particular editors; most of the work reported to date compares complete editors against one another.

Other interesting areas of research are at the boundary between editors and interactive system interfaces such as query–answer systems, data-base and knowledge-base systems, non-procedural programming languages, author languages for computer-aided instruction, and word processing. In these applications one would expect that an editor that provides structural information, rather than just windows on the actual text or data, would prove convenient. The question is whether the convenience would be offset, for most users, by the additional level of complexity.

Among the avenues open to us, we have decided to concentrate on finding out what are the most significant components of the enormous amounts of time spent collectively on editing. We hope that the results of our experiments will indicate where effort to improve editing systems (and perhaps editor users) may be best invested. We will also try to find out whether there is indeed a need for the immense number of editors currently available, or whether there is still hope for editor standardization (we are a little tired of learning new ones). We look forward to hearing from others with similar interests.

REFERENCES

Alden, D.G., Daniels, R.W. and Kanarick, A.R. (1972). Keyboard design and operation: a review of the major issues. *Human Factors,* **14**, 275–293.

Anandan, P. (1979). Formal analysis of program editing. Master's Thesis, Dept. of Computer Science, University of Nebraska-Lincoln.

Anandan, P., Embley, D.W. and Nagy, G. (1980). An application of file-comparison algorithms to the study of program editors. *Int. J. Man-Machine Stud.*,**13**, 201–212.

Baddeley, A.D. (1978). The influence of length and frequency of training sessions on the rate of learning to type. *Ergonomics,* **21**, 627–635.

Bingham, H.W. (1976). Text-editing using APL/700. *Proceedings of the APL 76 Conference,* Ottawa, 78–82.

Card, S.K. (1978). Studies in the psychology of computer text editing. *Xerox Research Report SSL-78-1,* Palo Alto Research Center, Palo Alto, California.

Card, S.K., English, W.K. and Burr, B. (1977). Evaluation of mouse, rate-controlled isometric joystick, step keys and text keys for text selection on a CRT. *Xerox Research Report SSl-77-1,* Palo Alto Research Center, Palo Alto, California.

Card, S.K., Moran, T.P. and Newell, A. (1976). The manuscript editing task: a routine cognitive skill. *Xerox Research Report SSL-76-8,* Palo Alto Research Center, Palo Alto, California.

Card, S.K., Moran, T.P. and Newell, A. (1979). The keystroke-level model for user performance time with interactive systems. *Xerox Research Report SSL-79-1,* Palo Alto Research Center, Palo Alto, California.

Carls, C.B. (1978). Getting ready for word processing's second generation. *Datamation,* **24**, 139–144.

CMS (1979). A conversational context-directed editor. *Report No. 320-2041,* IBM Scientific Center, Cambridge, Massachusetts.

Embley, D.W., Lan, M.T., Leinbaugh, D.W. and Nagy, G. (1978). A procedure for predicting program editor performance from the user's point of view. *Int. J. Man–Machine Stud.*, **10**, 639–650.

Embley, D.W. and Nagy, G. (1979). SIMPLE—A friendly programming environment for beginning and casual users. Internal Report, Dept. of Computer Science, University of Nebraska-Lincoln.

Embley, D.W. and Nagy, G. (1981). Behavioural aspects of text editors. *ACM Computing Surveys*, March, 1981.

English, W.K., Engelbart, D.C. and Berman, M.L. (1967). Display-selection techniques for text manipulation. *Transactions on Human Factors in Electronics*, **8**, 5–15.

Fields, A.F., Maisano, R.E. and Marshall, C.F. (1978). A comparative analysis of methods for tactical data inputting. *Report AD-A060562/6*, U.S. Army Research Institute for Behavioural and Social Sciences.

Fosdick, L.D. (1978). Detecting errors in programs. *Proceedings of the IFIP Working Conference on Performance Evaluation of Numerical Software*, Baden, Austria.

Fox, J.G. and Stansfield, R.G. (1964). Diagram keying times for typists. *Ergonomics*, **7**, 317–320.

Gilb, T. and Weinberg, G.M. (1977). *Humanized Input: Techniques for Reliable Keyed Input*. Cambridge, Massachusetts: Winthrop.

Goodwin, N.C. (1975). Cursor positioning on an electronic display using lightpen, lightgun, or keyboard for three basic tasks. *Human Factors*, **17**, 289–295.

Hansen, W.J. (1971). Creation of hierarchic text with a computer display. Ph.D. Dissertation, Dept. of Computer Science, Stanford University.

Heckel, P. (1978). A technique for isolating differences between files. *Communications of the ACM*, **21**, 264–269.

Hershman, R.L. and Hillix, W.A. (1965). Data processing in typing: typing rate as a function of kind of material and amount exposed. *Human Factors*, **7**, 483–492.

Iverson, K.E. (1962). *A Programming Language*. New York: Wiley.

Kemeny, J.G. and Kurtz, T.E. (1971). *BASIC Programming*. New York: Wiley.

Klemmer, E.T. and Lockhead, G.K. (1962). Productivity and errors in two keying tasks: a field study. *J. Appl. Psychol.*, **46**, 401–408.

Lan, M.T. (1977). A procedure to measure the complexity of program editor command languages. Master's Thesis, University of Nebraska-Lincoln.

Ledgard, H.F. and Singer, A. (1978). Formal definition and design. *Technical Report No. 78-01*, Dept. of Computer and Information Science, University of Massachusetts-Amherst.

Liu, C.L. (1968). *Introduction to Combinatorial Mathematics*. New York: McGraw-Hill.

Miller, L.A. and Thomas, J.C. (1977). Behavioral issues in the use of interactive systems. *Int. J. Man–Machine Stud.*, **9**, 509–536.

Miller, L.H. (1977). A study in man–machine interaction. *Proceedings of the National Computer Conference*, 409–421.

Moran, T.P. (1978). Introduction to the command language grammar. *Xerox Research Report SSL-78-3*, Palo Alto Research Center, Palo Alto, California.

NUROS (Nebraska University Remote Operating System) (1979). A guide to NUROS. University of Nebraska Computer Network.

Oren, S.S. (1974). A mathematical theory of man–machine text editing. *IEEE Transactions on Systems, Man, and Cybernetics,* **4**, 258–267.

Pansophic Systems, Inc. (1977). Panvalet User Reference Manual OSUP 10–7712. Pansophic Systems Inc., Oakbrook, Illinois.

QED (1967). Reference Manual No. 9004-4, Com-Share, Ann Arbor, Michigan.

Reimhen, G.W. (1978). Automated text-editing (a bibliography with abstracts). Reference NTIS/PS-78/0391/9, National Technical Information Service.

Reisner, P. (1979). Using a formal grammar in human factors design of an interactive graphics system. *IBM Research Report RJ2505,* IBM Research Laboratory, San Jose, California.

Riddle, E.A. (1976). Comparative study of various text editors and formatting systems. *Report AD-A029 050,* Air Force Data Services Center, The Pentagon, Washington, D.C.

Ritchie, G.J. and Turner, J.A. (1975). Input devices for interactive graphics. *Int. J. Man–Machine Stud.,* **7**, 639–660.

Roberts, T.L. (1979). Evaluation of computer text editors. Ph.D. Dissertation, Dept. of Computer Science, Stanford University.

Sandewall, E. (1978). Programming in an interactive environment: the LISP experience. *Computing Surveys,* **10**, 35–71.

Schoonard, J.W. and Boies, S.J. (1975). Short-type: a behavioral analysis of typing and text entry. *Human Factors,* **17**, 203–214.

Segal, B.Z. (1975). Effects of error interruption on student performance at interactive terminals. *Technical Report UIUCDCS-R-75-727,* Dept. of Computer Science, University of Illinois, Urbana-Champaign.

Seibel, R. (1972). Data entry devices and procedures. In H.P. VanCott and R.G. Kinkade (eds) *Human Engineering Guide to Equipment Design.* Washington: Government Printing Office.

Shaffter, L.H. and Hardwick, J. (1968). Typing performance as a function of text. *Q.J. Exp. Psychol.,* **20**, 360–369.

Schneiderman, B. (1979). Human Factors experiments on designing interactive systems. *IEEE Computer,* **12**, 9–19.

TECO (1969). Text Editor and Corrector Reference Manual, Interactive Sciences Corp., Braintree, Massachusetts.

Teitelbaum, T. (1979). The Cornell program synthesizer: a syntax-directed programming environment. *SIGPLAN Notices,* **14**, 75.

Treu, S. (1975). Interactive command language design based on required mental work. *Int. J. Man–Machine Stud.,* **7**, 135–149.

VanDam, A. and Rice, D.E. (1971). On-line text editing: a survey. *Computing Surveys,* **3**, 93–114.

Walther, G.H. and O'Neil, H.F. (1974). On-line user-computer interface: the effect of interface flexibility, terminal type, and experience on performance. *Proceedings of the AFIPS National Computer Conference,* **43**, 379–384.

Weinberg, G.M. (1971). *The Psychology of Computer Programming.* New York: Van Nostrand Reinholt.

WIDJET (Waterloo Interactive Direct Job Entry Terminal) (1978). *Report SB30-1140-1,* IBM, White Plains, New York.

WYLBUR (1975). The Stanford Timesharing System Reference Manual (3rd Edn.) Center for Information Processing, Stanford University.

Index